Placental Politics

CRITICAL INDIGENEITIES

J. Kēhaulani Kauanui and Jean M. O'Brien, *series editors*

Series Advisory Board
Chris Andersen, University of Alberta
Irene Watson, University of South Australia
Emil' Keme, University of North Carolina at Chapel Hill
Kim TallBear, University of Alberta

Critical Indigeneities publishes pathbreaking scholarly books that center Indigeneity as a category of critical analysis, understand Indigenous sovereignty as ongoing and historically grounded, and attend to diverse forms of Indigenous cultural and political agency and expression. The series builds on the conceptual rigor, methodological innovation, and deep relevance that characterize the best work in the growing field of critical Indigenous studies.

CHRISTINE TAITANO DELISLE

Placental Politics
CHamoru Women, White Womanhood, and Indigeneity under U.S. Colonialism in Guam

The University of North Carolina Press *Chapel Hill*

This book was published with the assistance of the Authors Fund of the University of North Carolina Press.

© 2021 The University of North Carolina Press
All rights reserved
Set in Arno by Westchester Publishing Services
Manufactured in the United States of America

The University of North Carolina Press has been a member of the Green Press Initiative since 2003.

Library of Congress Cataloging-in-Publication Data
Names: DeLisle, Christine Taitano, author.
Title: Placental politics : CHamoru women, white womanhood, and indigeneity under U.S. colonialism in Guam / Christine Taitano DeLisle.
Other titles: CHamoru women, white womanhood, and indigeneity under U.S. colonialism in Guam | Critical indigeneities.
Description: Chapel Hill : University of North Carolina Press, 2021. | Series: Critical indigeneities | Includes bibliographical references and index.
Identifiers: LCCN 2020016823 | ISBN 9781469652696 (cloth : alk. paper) | ISBN 9781469652702 (paperback : alk. paper) | ISBN 9781469652719 (ebook)
Subjects: LCSH: Women, CHamoru—Guam—American influences. | Indigenous peoples—Guam—Social life and customs—19th century. | Indigenous peoples—Guam—Social life and customs—20th century. | Women, White—Guam—History. | Midwifery—Guam.
Classification: LCC DU647 .D45 2020 | DDC 305.48/89952—dc23 LC record available at https://lccn.loc.gov/2020016823

Cover illustrations: Photo of Tan Ana Rios Zamora, pattera and suruhåna, by Manny Crisostomo, used by permission of the artist; detail of kottot by Tan Elena Cruz Benavente from photo by author.

For the circle of women in my family gi iya mo'nana,
starting with my mother,
Maria San Nicolas Taitano DeLisle
From Guåhan, the Marianas, and Micronesia, across
the mattingan ... for all the strong women of Oceania and their
kin enacting and protecting the Indigenous sacred each and every day

In memory of Teresia Teaiwa

Contents

List of Illustrations ix

Preface: Decolonial Habits of History xi

Acknowledgments xvii

Introduction: Following the Historical Footnotes of
CHamoru Women's Embodied Land Work 1

CHAPTER ONE
I CHe'cho' i Pattera: Gendering Inafa'maolek in a CHamoru
Lay of the Land 38

CHAPTER TWO
White Woman, Small Matters: Susan Dyer's Tour-of-Duty Feminism
in Guåhan 79

CHAPTER THREE
Flagging the Desire to Photograph: Helen Paul's "Eye/Land/People" 114

CHAPTER FOUR
Giniha yan Pinilan Guåhan: Agueda Johnston and
New CHamoru Womanhood 151

Conclusion: Following the Historical and Cultural Kinship
"Where America's Day Begins" 198

Glossary of CHamoru Words 205

Notes 213

Bibliography 249

Index 285

Figures

0.1 Ad from *The Guam Recorder*, 1928   11
0.2 Health float, Guam Industrial Fair, c. 1933   15
1.1 Pattera, 1902   44
1.2 Susana Hospital staff, c. 1917   44
1.3 Nurses of the Susana Hospital, c. 1930   46
1.4 Joaquina San Nicolas Babauta Herrera (Tan Kina')   53
1.5 Rosalia Aquiningoc Ulloa Mesa (Tan Liang)   59
1.6 Ana Mendiola Rosario (Tan Ånan Siboyas)   61
1.7 Red Cross nurses, 1938   67
2.1 Susan Dyer and Governor George Dyer, between 1904 and 1905   83
2.2 Susan Dyer, Governor's Palace, between 1904 and 1905   92
2.3 "One of the Baile Crowds . . . taken in [Governor Luke] McNamee's yard," c. 1908   102
2.4 Susana Hospital Association, Guam Industrial Fair, between 1917 and 1918   109
2.5 Nurses and matrons, Susana Hospital, 1905   111
3.1 Hagåtña Bay, site of the Guåhan seal, between 1917 and 1919   125
3.2 *The Ancient "Capilla" of Anigua*   127
3.3 *Jesus and Dolores at School*   130
3.4 *A Young Chamorro Dandy*   132
3.5 *Mestiza Beauties of Guam*   135
3.6 Blueprint of the Guåhan flag, 1917   140
3.7 *Guam Fair Queen*   142
3.8 Guåhan flag, Guam Industrial Fair, 1918   144
3.9 *Fashion Show in Umatac Village*   145
4.1 Agueda Johnston and George Washington High School students, 1945   160
4.2 Department of Education, 1916   171
4.3 Agueda Johnston and Governor Ford Elvidge, 1956   182

Preface
Decolonial Habits of History

CHamoru women's histories are rooted in the land. Land is routed through the histories of CHamoru women's work. Literally, figuratively, genealogically, and cosmologically, the seeds of CHamoru women's labor are planted in and along the hålom tåsi (shore), the hålom tåno' (jungle), the hålom åcho' (rocks), the sabåna (savanna), the sesonyan (swamp), the fina'okso' (hilly place), the låncho (ranch), the latte (stone pillars), and the påpa' såtge (underfloor space) of homes throughout the villages of Guåhan. For generations, in the fañomnåkan (place of sunshine) and the fanuchånan (place of rain), from the fañinahi'an (time of new moon) to the fanggualåfonan (time of full moon), the ná'fafañågu (midwives) would bury the ga'chong i patgon or "child's companion" (placenta) and tålen apuya' (umbilical cord) gi tano' (in the land) because they believed that by doing so they steered newborns (into adulthood) out of harm's way and onto the right path, and kept them close to home, no matter where they went or where they travelled. The social and cultural meaning making and reciprocal relations of these embodied practices and rituals that ensured a child's safe passage in the world and that one never forgets one's home and roots are multiple and varied and run deep and wide in CHamoru conceptions of time and space and sense of place. This cordage and linkage between the Indigenous people of the Marianas, the CHamorus, and the land—captured in the vernacular taotao tåno' (people of the land)—becomes especially palpable and sentient in the generative "storied sites" and "land narratives" of the island's ná'fafañågu, "one who helps one deliver."[1]

The CHamoru Capuchin priest and historian Eric Forbes shared one such story of cordage with the land pertaining to the work of the ná'fafañågu, more commonly known as the pattera. He recalled a conversation with a CHamoru man who spoke of his intense loyalty to the place he lived in as a child over the village he resided in most of his life. When Påle' (Father) Eric asked why this had been the case, the man replied: "Siempre nai, sa' guihi nai ma håfot i tu'ayå-hu!" (Certainly, because that's where they buried my towel!).[2] It was in this context that Påle' Eric learned of the pattera knowledge and practice involving the proper care and burial of the ga'chong. At one level, as Påle' Eric discerns, there is a profound connection between CHamorus and the land such that land becomes visceral and multisensory so as to speak to CHamorus in ways that literally and figuratively root them in the soil and tie them to the land. These Indigenous placental plantings are also significant because of the way this embodied work signals a history of CHamoru women's persistence and resistance—in this case, the pattera's laboring and belaboring to ensure individual, family, clan, and community well-being in spite or precisely because of early twentieth-century U.S. naval colonial regulations that sought to stamp out Indigenous practices and specifically instructed the pattera to burn or discard what the navy deemed as dangerous human waste.

My desire to tell of these Indigenous placental plantings and politics of resistance, to historicize and theorize the work of famalao'an CHamoru (CHamoru women) under U.S. colonialism in a different light—and what eventually became an interest in the intersections of their labor with that of white American navy wives—germinated out of a public history project in my Native homeland of Guåhan. From the early to mid-1990s, I worked as a researcher and writer for the Political Status Education Coordinating Commission (PSECC) of the government of Guam ("GovGuam")—what later became the Chamorro Heritage Institute and what eventually merged into what is now the Department of Chamorro Affairs. The project entailed oral history work with manåmko' (elders) and World War II survivors as part of a broader GovGuam mandate to research, write, and publish textbooks from a CHamoru perspective for the island's public school system. To be sure, Hale'-ta (or Håle'-ta), which means "our roots" and which the textbook series came to be called, was not a project of neoliberal multiculturalism or cultural diversity but a distinct political and intellectual Native agenda of reclaiming and rewriting histories after decades and centuries of taotao sanhiyong (outsiders) writing our histories.[3]

The Hale'-ta public history project—architected, legislated, and implemented for the most part by CHamoru educators and political leaders—set out to educate the island's manhoben (youth) amid ongoing CHamoru sovereignty and self-determination struggles and political debates and contestations over Guåhan's political status with the United States. Thus, it represents a decolonizing moment and movement in the island's history. It is an example of the imperative that the CHamoru educator, historian, and former statesman Robert Underwood calls a "habit of history." Underwood describes the stakes when CHamorus choose not to acquire this habit of history—that is, when we "fail to be actors in our own history"—as one of handing down the "lesson that we cannot be actors in our future."[4] He writes: "History becomes painful not because there was pain and loss but because our agency as a people has been denied.... The failure to understand history, or to assume that only one rendering of its dimensions is possible, is tantamount to oppression. Without the knowledge of the past or access to its riches, we can be victimized by those who claim to know it and by those who wish to manipulate its lessons."[5] This habit of history, which demands that CHamorus collectively engage in the historical project as a society, gestures toward Indigenous futurities and imaginings of true liberation. Hale'-ta as decolonial habit of history can also be understood as an assertion of "intellectual sovereignty" and what Robert Allen Warrior describes as the ideological struggle for liberation not from "anything outside ourselves" but as a "process of asserting the power we possess as communities and individuals to make decisions that affect our lives."[6] Because the PSECC was also focused on planning for a specific K–12 curriculum of grounded histories, the Hale'-ta project can also be understood as a practice in "sovereign pedagogies"—as Noelani Goodyear-Ka'ōpua describes the land-based literacies of aloha 'āina and Indigenous nation building in Hawai'i.[7]

Hale'-ta led me down the path of the ná'fafañågu and fafa'na'gue (teachers), among the women who figure prominently in the oral histories of prewar Guåhan but whose stories have been erased and marginalized in conventional historiography. Since writing their (and other women's) stories back into the island's history in *I Manfåyi* (The wise ones), a middle school text that featured mini-biographies of CHamoru political, civic, and cultural leaders, I have reflected on the fraught processes of recouping and remembering and forgetting and silencing and, hence, recapitulating to the problems of history. One problem has been the way pattera narratives (among other prewar CHamoru histories) have been conveyed mostly in romanticized and nostalgic terms.[8] In her surveying of textbooks for their representation of women and Indigenous CHamorus, Anne Perez Hattori writes that Guåhan historiography, including the Hale'-ta series, has for the most part "perpetuated the Western model of history as a patriarchal, nation-state story of progress and development."[9] The crux of this is that despite its islander-centered writing, Hale'-ta falls short of accomplishing what it set out to do: decolonize Guåhan history. Tasked with finding women of the early CHamoru period for a section in volume 1 of *I Manfåyi* titled "Women of Pre-History," I experienced firsthand the extent to which the project perpetuated a Western model. The notion of "prehistory" is problematic for how it privileges written sources over other forms of historical evidence, how it legitimizes the archive (understood mostly as colonial) over Indigenous epistemologies and ontologies. This prehistory approach has inevitably framed and privileged the political accomplishments of men (CHamoru or otherwise) and in the process has marginalized the histories of CHamoru women. However, I also recognize the decolonial seeds and anticolonial plantings of the Hale'-ta project, particularly for how it would begin to lay the groundwork for future liberatory projects and especially since the project's concerted attempt to decolonize history literally and directly came out of the political drive for CHamoru self-determination. For me, rewriting nameless women back into the historical record as "The Woman from Tomhom," "Matå'pang's Wife," or "Women of the Guma' Uritao" was the beginning of following CHamoru women's multiple and divergent footpaths. Indeed, as Linda Tuhiwai Smith reminds us, reclaiming history is a critical and essential process of decolonization, and the acts of recovering, reformulating, and reconstituting require the mounting of an ambitious research agenda that is "strategic in its purpose" and "relentless in its pursuit of social justice."[10]

The ambitious research project and decolonial habit of history that grew out of Hale'-ta has for me now become the continued or stubborn pursuit of CHamoru women's histories of embodied land work through a more critical framework and framing that interrogates, along with indigeneity, the terms of CHamoru gender and sexuality through an Indigenous feminist theory and practice.[11] This process of interrogating Indigenous subjectivities, as the work of Teresia Teaiwa reminds us, means that at times new forms of indigeneity emerge, which render Native peoples unrecognizable or unintelligible but nonetheless always there.[12] A good example of this was when, during one of my interviews, I asked the pattera Joaquina Babauta Herrera (Tan Kina') which of the patteras delivered her babies, and she responded, "No way! I delivered in the hospital!" This admission on the part of Tan Kina' threw me for a loop, initially. It went against the story I wanted to tell at the time of U.S. colonial violence and its imposition on CHamoru culture. Did such an admission suggest the possibility of pattera complicity in the eventual demise of pattera labor or, perhaps worse, their lack of faith in the pattera institution? Though I never had the chance to follow up with Tan Kina' on her answer, I can only surmise that perhaps she personally felt more comfortable in the hospital under the watchful eye of navy doctors and nurses, or perhaps she held the painful memory as a youth watching her sister-in-law while under the care of another pattera lose a lot of blood during her delivery. I also wondered, given her spunk and what I sensed was a competitive and proud spirit (especially around what many now call birth work), if even though she respected other pattera, perhaps she did not trust just any other pattera to deliver *her* children. To be sure, the story that Tan Kina' relates and those of other pattera in this book exemplify the "messy entanglement" between indigeneity and colonialism.[13] *Placental Politics* builds on this entanglement by following the gendered travel—the cogent but also muddied and divergent footpaths of famalao'an CHamoru whose histories and movements in history continue to be recovered and reclaimed through decolonial habits and metanarratives of the historical footnote.

Acknowledgments

This book is the finañågu of the collective strength, wisdom, and kåhna of many. In good hagan Guåhan form, I wish to fa'taotao those who helped bring this book to life and acknowledge the relations that have sustained me between Oceania and Turtle Island and through what seemed like a marathon to the finish line. I apologize in advance if I have forgotten to mention anyone.

I must first convey my gratitude to the elders for their gineftao and gift of story. Many of them have passed on since transmitting their oral histories. Of these now manmofo'na, I wish to acknowledge the pattera—especially Joaquina Herrera, Rosalia Mesa, and Ana Rosario—and others for sharing their knowledge: Francisco Aguero, Antonio Babauta, Elena Benavente, Jose Blas, Monsignor Oscar Calvo ("Påle' Skåt"), Fred Diego, Catalina Duenas, Cristobal Duenas, Emeteria Duenas, Peter Jon Duenas, Olivia Guerrero, Felix Perez, Reverend Joaquin Sablan, Richard "Dick" Taitano, and Soledad Tenorio.

My three-year stint with Guåhan's PSECC shaped how I think and write about estorian taotao tåno' and sparked a labor of love in oral history and the archives. Dångkolu na si yu'os ma'åse to director Katherine "Doc" Aguon and the board, under the leadership of Tony Palomo, for the tremendous opportunity. Si yu'os ma'åse to my coworkers Catherine Gault and Jay Diaz, and Frani Lujan, who helped recruit me. Inagradesi and respetu go to Hope Cristobal, Laura Souder, and Robert Underwood, whom I met through the project and whose activism, scholarship, and writings on history, culture, and language, and CHamoru decolonization and self-determination continue to inspire me.

I owe a debt of gratitude to University of Guam administration, faculty, staff, and students for their support over the past three decades—from my PSECC days sifting through the ephemera and treasures of the RFT Micronesian Area Research Center vertical files, to my graduate school days perusing the Spanish collections. I begin by thanking key people in Micronesian studies and Guåhan history: Ulla-Katrina Craig, Anne Hattori, and my adviser, Don Rubinstein. Saina ma'åse to Rosa Palomo for her guidance on a fino' håya oral history project under a Foreign Language and Area Studies fellowship and Peter Onedera for help with translations. Si yu'os ma'åse to David Atienza, the late Dirk Ballendorf, Omaira Brunal-Perry, the late Bernadita "Benit" Camacho-Dungca, the late Joyce Camacho, Michael Clement,

Arlene Cohen, Karen Cruz, Mary Therese Cruz, Larry Cunningham, Vivian Dames, Arlene Diaz, the late Marjorie Driver, Anita Borja Enriquez, Evelyn Flores, Moses Francisco, Nick Goetzfridt, LaVonne Guerrero-Meno, Rose Hatfield, Dorathina Herrero, the late Emelie Johnston, Kenneth Gofigan Kuper, Hiro Kurashina, Carlos Madrid, Troy McVey, Lou Nededog, Perry Pangelinan, Lilli Perez, Carmen Quintanilla, the late John Sablan, Marilyn Salas, Cecilia Salvatore, Sharleen Santos-Bamba, Gerhard Schwab, James Sellmann, the late Don Shuster, Seyda Turk Smith, Mary Spencer, Rebecca Stephenson, Monique Carriveau Storie, the late Magdalena Taitano, Jeannine Talley, Faye Untalan, James Viernes, Rudy Villaverde, and Bill Weurch. Many thanks to fellow graduate students in Micronesian studies, Vince Diego, Betsy Kalau, Ward Krantz, Kayoko Kushima, Kelly Marsh-Taitano, Nicole Santos, Tom Taisipic, David Tibbetts, and Sophia Underwood for stimulating seminars and Friday morning gatherings in Hagåtña cafes to share work and give feedback.

I am indebted to others from the Marianas, both in the islands and from across the diaspora, for their support and creative and inspiring work. Saina ma'åse to Pulitzer Prize–winning photojournalist Manny Crisostomo for allowing me to use his beautiful photographs of the pattera, and Ann Marie Arceo and Selina Onedera-Salas for help with fino' håya spellings and meanings. Juanita Calvo Duenas engaged the colonial photographs with rich stories. I am thankful to many others: Baltazar Aguon, Julian Aguon, Ojeya Cruz Banks, the late Ed Benavente, Jill Benavente, John C. Benavente, Jesi Lujan Bennett, Leland Bettis, Michael Bevacqua, Roland Blas, the late Magdalena L. Calvo, Dakota Camacho, Santino Camacho, Jeremy Cepeda, Arlene Crisostomo, Randizia Crisostomo, Manny Cruz, Cheryl Cunningham, Micki Davis, Sheryl Day, Marisa Del Rosario, Cara Flores-Mays, Judy Flores, Påle' Eric Forbes, Jan Furukawa, Gary Guerrero, William Hernandez, Leonard Iriarte, Norma Iriarte, Cinta Kaipat, Kimberlee Kihleng, Jillette Leon-Guerrero, Rob Limtiaco, Al Lizama, Victor Lujan, Elliot Marques, Vince Munoz, Shannon Murphy, Tiara Na'puti, Rita Nauta, Suzette Nelson, Kristin Oberiano, Josephine Ong, Cecilia "Lee" Perez, Craig Santos Perez, Michael P. Perez, Rick Perez, Vivian Perez, Libby Johnston Pier, Bernard Punzalan, Debbie Quinata, Joe Quinata, Noel Quitugua, Toni "Malia" Ramirez, the late Tony Ramirez, Linda Taitano Reyes, Annie Rivera, the late Ron Rivera, David Sablan, Fermina Sablan, Jaye Sablan, the late Angel "Anghet" Santos, Anicia Balajadia Taisipic, Taling Taitano, Tyrone Taitano, and Maria Yatar. I feel blessed to be a part of the multigenerational communities that comprise I Hagan Famalao'an Guåhan and the CHamoru women writers' guåfak, among those not already mentioned: Simone Bollinger, Kisha Borja-

Quichocho-Calvo, Fanai Castro, Karen Charfauros, Monaeka Flores, Maria Hernandez, Ursula Herrera, Victoria-Lola Leon Guerrero, Alicia Munoz, Julia Faye Munoz, Leiana Naholowaʻa, Jessica Nangauta, Francine Naputi, Lisa Natividad, Elyssa Santos, Desiree Taimanglo Ventura, and Therese Terlaje.

Si yuʻos maʻåse to mentors, colleagues, and friends during my time at the University of Michigan, Ann Arbor: Phil Deloria, Damon Salesa, Carroll Smith-Rosenberg, and my adviser, Penny Von Eschen; Maria Cotera, Anne Herrmann, Carol Karlsen, Mary Kelley, Scott Kurashige, Emily Lawsin, Peggy McCracken, the late Dick Meisler, Victor Mendoza, Michele Mitchell, Regina Morantz-Sanchez, Nadine Naber, Susan Najita, Atef Said, Sarita See, Ray Silverman, Andrea Smith, Domna Stanton, Amy Stillman, and Brad Taylor. Thanks to fellow graduate students for the thriving intellectual spaces: Juanita Cabello, Kealani Cook, Veronica Pasfield, Heijin Lee, John Low, Cynthia Marasigan, Jinny Prais, Nick Reo, Kiri Sailiata, Dean Saranillio, Herbert Sosa, and Lani Teves. Despite the geographic distance, the Pacific was always *close* thanks to the kinship and warm hospitality of Damon and Jenny Salesa, Kaafi and Sharon Tuinukuafe, Sela Panapasa and Jim McNally, and their families.

Si yuʻos maʻåse to mentors, colleagues, and friends while at the University of Illinois Urbana-Champaign, especially Robert Warrior, Chantal Nadeau, and Stephanie Foote for their leadership. Thanks to Antoinette Burton, who gave feedback on draft chapters, and other colleagues: Teresa Barnes, Ruth Nicole Brown, Jenny Davis, Jane Desmond, Virginia Dominguez, Brenda Farnell, Karen Flynn, Matt Gilbert, Kristin Hoganson, LeAnne Howe, Korinta Maldonado, Paul McKenzie-Jones, Fiona Ngô, Mimi Thi Nguyen, Gilberto Rosas, and Siobhan Somerville. Many thanks to AIS's John McKinn, Dulce Talavera, and Yvonne Tiger. I am grateful to graduate students for invigorating conversations: Theresa Beardall, Rico Chenyek, Beth Eby, Raquel Escobar, Eman Ghanayem, Noelia Irizarry-Roman, Jessica Landau, Josh Levy, Christine Peralta, and Estibalitz Ezkerra Vegas. Special thanks to friends and family—Rick and Susie Aeilts, Luis Lopez, Camarin Meno, and Marvin Nogoy—whose help during the transition from Urbana-Champaign to Minneapolis made it possible for me to continue working on the manuscript.

At the University of Minnesota, I have been fortunate to have the support of a growing number of scholars doing exciting work in comparative and global Indigenous studies. My deepest gratitude to Jeani O'Brien for being there from the get-go. Si yuʻos maʻåse also to American Indian studies colleagues Brenda Child and David Wilkins for their guidance. Chairs Kat Hayes and later David Chang were especially supportive during the tenure process. I am grateful to other AIS colleagues: Sisokaduta Joe Bendickson, Zoe Brown,

Bianet Castellanos, Mike Dockry, Alex Ghebregzi, Eli Sumida Huaman, Brendan Kishketon, Cantemaza Neil McKay, Carter Meland, Juliana Hu Pegues, Chris Pexa, and Gabby Spears-Rico. Colleagues in other units I want to acknowledge include Tracey Deutsch (who, along with David Chang and family, graciously opened their home to me the first semester), Kale Fajardo, Jennifer Gunn, Karen Ho, Dan Keefe, Martin Manalansan, Monica McKay, Phyllis Messenger, Kevin Murphy, Yuichiro Onishi, Jennifer Pierce, Verajita Singh, Teresa Swartz, Ann Waltner, and Josef Woldense. Thanks to the amazing AIS staff: Wesley Ballinger, Charissa Blue, Angela Boutch, Amarin Chanthorn, Christina Martinez, Lauren Sietsema, and Rodrigo Sanchez-Chavarria. I am grateful to AIS undergraduate An Garagiola-Bernier, and graduate students: Jacob Bernier, Jonny Borja, Pierre-Elliot Caswell, Charles Golding, Rose Miron, Kai Pyle, Rosy Simas, Demiliza Saramosing, Catherine Ulep, and Jonnelle Walker. Si yu'os ma'åse to a special circle of Mni Sota Makoce Dakota and Anishinaabe scholars for their friendship and decolonial work: Roxanne Gould, Katie Johnston-Goodstar, Jim Rock, and Waziyatawin. Thanks also to my friend Shelly Wilkins, who, along with David Wilkins, made Scott Hall weekends working on the manuscript all the more rewarding.

Many individuals were helpful in navigating collections at various archives and libraries. I am grateful to Cally Gurley, Maine Women Writers Collection; Evelyn Cherpak and Stacie Parillo, Naval Historical Collection Archives; Daisy Njoku and Caitlin Hayes, National Anthropological Archives; Dale Sauter, East Carolina Manuscript Collection; Carol Radovich, Rockefeller Archive Center; and Teresita Kennimer and Florence Taitague, Guam Public Library System. Thanks to Wayne Arny for facilitating the return of the Helen Paul Collection to UOG, and to Rod Levesque, who directed me to Guåhan sources.

The book benefitted from manuscript workshops at the University of Illinois (2015) and University of California Los Angeles (2016). Si yu'os ma'åse to Aroha Harris for visiting Champaign and for her generous, inciteful read, and to a second set of enthusiastic readers at UCLA led by Mishuana Goeman and Keith Camacho that included Juliann Anesi, Victor Bascara, Alicia Cox, Michelle Erai, Alfred Flores, Sherene Razack, and Shannon Speed. I am grateful to David Hanlon, J. Kēhaulani Kauanui, Tsianina Lomawaima, Noenoe Silva, Katerina Teaiwa, and two anonymous readers for their helpful comments. I want to acknowledge the Ford Foundation for their continued commitment; a postdoctoral fellowship (2015–16) made it possible to focus on the manuscript and have Mishuana Goeman serve as my mentor.

Working with a good press and editor has been key to the life of this book. Si yu'os ma'åse to Mark Simpson-Vos of the University of North Carolina Press for the encouragement and for suggesting ways to improve the book. Thanks to Jessica Newman, Cate Hodorowicz, and Iris Levesque for guidance, and series editors J. Kēhaulani Kauanui and Jean M. O'Brien for the invitation to submit. My heartfelt thanks to Erin Davis and the team at Westchester Publishing Services for their patience, kindness, and help during the editing stage, and to David Martinez for care and attention with the page proofs and index.

This book has grown out of many good conversations (and good meals) across Oceania and Turtle Island over the last two decades. Many of these have taken place at the annual Native American and Indigenous Studies Association (NAISA) conferences. Saina ma'åse to Hokulani Aikau, Chad Allen, Holly Barker, Miranda Belarde-Lewis, Myla Vicenti Carpio, Elena Creef, Brian Dawson, Elizabeth DeLoughrey, Jean Dennison, Marisa Duarte, Kali Fermantez, the late Rochelle Fonoti, Ayano Ginoza, Noelani Goodyear-Ka'ōpua, Hineitimoana Greensill, Lisa Hall, Debra Harry, Krista Henare, April Henderson, Robert "Bobby" Hill, Susan Hill, Brendan Hokowhitu, Ku'ualoha Ho'omanawanui, Kathy Jetñil-Kijiner, Tevita Ka'ili, Anne Keala Kelly, Judy Kertesz, Karen Leong, Arini Loader, Tony Lucero, Nēpia Mahuika, Rangimarie Mahuika, Sean Mallon, Mary Jane McCallum, Davianna McGregor, Aileen Moreton-Robinson, Ēnoka Murphy, Jamaica Osorio, Jon Osorio, Danica Medak-Saltzman, Dian Million, Tina Ngata, Leonie Pihama, Vince Rafael, Kate Shanley, Setsu Shigematsu, Audra Simpson, Linda Tuhiwai Smith, Scott Stevens, Troy Storfjell, Alice Te Punga Somerville, Ty Kāwika Tengan, the late Haunani-Kay Trask, Haki Tuaupiki, Lisa Uperesa, Renae Watchman, Nuhisifa Williams, and Nalani Wilson-Hokowhitu.

There are inner circles of friends-colleagues I turn to regularly. I include Mishuana Goeman, Aroha Harris, and especially Juliann Anesi and Keith Camacho in these. The late Teresia Teaiwa, "the ancestor I always choose," was there for me from the start and was one my most important interlocutors and confidantes. Guinaiya and saina ma'åse to Tere ("Aunty Tere" to my girls), trusted che'lu and ga'chong with whom (even now, in spirit and memory) I share a deep commitment to Micronesian women's histories and Indigenous feminisms.

I close my acknowledgments returning to manmofo'na (and other spirits and higher beings) who, like saina and familia, are the pillars and foundations without which this book would not have been possible. I am eternally grateful to my grandparents, the late Juan Guerrero Taitano (Familian Liberåtu/Kabesa) and the late Maria Castro San Nicolas Taitano (Familian Nungi-Assan), for their love and support and for encouraging me by way of their own storytelling to relearn and retell our histories. My parents, Arthur "Duke" and Maria DeLisle, believe in me always and have cheered me on from the starting line, and I am thankful to them for their wisdom, love, and guidance. I must acknowledge my extended family in Guåhan and the diaspora—in particular, aunts and uncles (and kin) of a special branch of the Taitano clan along Chålan Gayinero that has been a major source of inspiration. Thanks to my siblings Yvette (and Derick Jackson) and Art and their familia for showing the love—making dinner and scanning photos. Thanks also to cousin-målle' Melissa Taitano, and Randi Sgambelluri for help specific to the book. Saina ma'åse to other branches and roots of the familia tree, the family of the late Judge Ramon Diaz and Josefina Diaz, Todos los Diazes, for their love and support. To my partner and best friend, Vince, who has been my most cherished and trusted sounding board since the start of this and many other journeys, and to our daughters Nicole (and Joseph Hernandez), Gabriela, and Eva, and granddaughter Maria-Sol whose fierce guinaiyan tåno' keeps me grounded, I offer my tåddong guinaiya and inagradesi. They have been my mighty åcho' through it all and remind me of the promise the habit of history holds for anticolonial and just futures.

Placental Politics

Introduction
Following the Historical Footnotes of CHamoru Women's Embodied Land Work

Tåya' pinekkat sin fegge. (There is no walk without footprints)
—CHamoru proverb

The first women in Oceania to confront the violence of colonization, famalao'an CHamoru of Låguas yan Gåni have for centuries labored and led the wave of struggles through a sea and sky of islands to steward Indigenous lands, waters, and peoplehood; and yet in many of the historical accounts of the archipelago, they appear as nameless objects of Spanish conflict, conversion, and conquest or, in the case of Guåhan, assimilated subjects under American colonial modernity.[1] Even local and contemporary historiographies have, for the most part, marginalized the dynamic and complex historical experiences of CHamoru women. In the epic encounters, entanglements, and political clashes and collusions between colonial and CHamoru men, CHamoru women often are like footnotes in a historical monograph, information germane to a story and needed for important backdrop or minute details but not the principal characters or main agents of the narrative. Yet footnotes—which have never simply been ancillary, tangential, obscure, incidental, or inconsequential—provide an apt beginning to a history of CHamoru women, not just to call critical attention to how women have been relegated to the margins of history but also because of what footnotes connote. Footnotes do more than provide backdrop or explanatory information; they comprise the heart of a historical narrative, ostensibly the content and form of the past, and highlight productive tensions between history and historiography. Footnotes also call attention to distinctions between colonial teleologies and Indigenous conceptions of time and space—the latter referred to in the CHamoru vernacular as mo'na.[2] Gesturing toward Indigenous notions of time and space, we might also say footnotes furnish insight into what Native Pacific cultural studies scholars have theorized as the historical, political, genealogical, and intellectual roots and routes of Indigenous mobilities.[3] Indeed, this book about the stories and narratives of CHamoru women confronting U.S. colonialism in Guåhan, originates from my own early sets of notes, especially footnotes, as I had begun to read and write in purposeful, disciplined, and interdisciplinary ways about Guåhan's history. Along a path that took me from being involved in a government-sponsored history writing project to joining academe, my engagement with footnotes as a form of understanding history has morphed into a project of recovering and articulating a new and more potent way of being in history. Thus, footnotes *in* history can also be understood as footnotes *as* history, especially when the matter involves movement *in* history and movement *as* history, and most especially when the historical subjects of that ongoing history have been so obscured or cordoned off as to have their own kinalamten (movement, mobility) arrested in its path.[4]

The absent presence of CHamoru women's social and political power in the footnotes of Guåhan's colonial historiography is akin to the discursive effects of how certain "things fall away" in the writing of larger narratives. This falling away of certain things is Neferti Tadiar's way of describing the devaluation and delegitimization of the political and historical experiences of Philippine subaltern classes, including women, in conventional accounts of global capitalism. I am reminded of how the intricacies and nuances of CHamoru women's stories can fall away in narratives and events that, ironically, were specifically dedicated to honoring them, and why "the task of creating empowered historical subjects through the representation of submerged historical experiences ... continues to be of the utmost necessity."[5]

At a 1997 public history forum highlighting the legacy of the island's pre–World War II pattera, a community of surviving pattera, their families, and those who had been delivered by pattera came together and revived sinangan famalao'an CHamoru siha (CHamoru women's stories). One by one, individuals shared heartfelt memories of grandmothers, mothers, aunts, sisters, and godmothers. The mood suddenly and unexpectedly shifted when an enraged Francisco Taitano Aguero ("Tun Frank") stood up and spoke:

> I remember growing up that my mother was a midnight wife, or pattera, and also a nurse. Somebody told me a few years ago that my mother wasn't a nurse and I said that's a bunch of malarkey! Now let me tell you something about my mom. My mom wore a cap, a nurse's cap, and she works [sic] at the dressing station between [the] post office and Leary School. I remember it so well. She went village to village from Umatac up to Machananao feeding people who were sick. Believe me you when I tell you that I'm very moved of a situation like this, because my mom is the greatest nurse and midnight wife I can ever honor. Why? Let me tell you why. When all the midnight wife [sic] left Agaña and fled to the hills during

the Japanese time, who remains in Agaña? My mom! My mother! She ate a few barley and a little gådao fish from time to time and survived. But she made sure she treated all the CHamorus who needed help. All of those years I remember so well because I used to walk from Machananao all the way to Agaña to give 'em a few fish, lemmai [seedless breadfruit] and a few dokdok [seeded breadfruit], called "hutu" [the nut or seed of the breadfruit], to her. I remember my mom. I'm not degrading some of the midnight wives that are here and I'm telling you right now that they deserve a lot of credit too. But my mom, everybody knows my mom. And looking around I don't think none of the people that she had delivered [are] still alive at this time. She is better known as Tan Marian Dogi', that Marian Dogi' from the Taitano family. That's all ladies and gentleman. I just want you to know that she is a great person.[6]

In pointing out that his mother, Maria Taitano Aguero (Tan Marian Dogi'), wore a "nurse's cap" and worked at the "dressing station between the post office and Leary School," Tun Frank was refuting claims that the legendary pattera from the village of Barigåda "wasn't a nurse." His need to make the case and to situate socially and culturally what being a pattera entailed is reminiscent of how the differences between nurse-midwives and nurses are footnote-like matters through which important details are erased. Especially troubling is that through such footnote-like matters, the navy's insidious processes of eradicating Indigenous ideas and systems of health and well-being are rendered benign and unmarked.

More than a bid to honor his mother's legacy twenty years after her death, or to set the historical record straight, Tun Frank Aguero's story and impassioned plea was about ensuring Tan Marian Dogi''s legacy did not fall away. His demur called attention to the critical tensions and complexities in the lived experiences of the island's pattera and their achafñak (family) and evoked the contested grounds of CHamoru history and historiography. In his protest, Tun Frank was referring to tensions that tend to get glossed over in the highly romanticized and nostalgic prewar CHamoru narratives of the beloved pattera. These tensions may have surfaced because of misconceptions about the different cohorts and classes of CHamoru women laborers under the navy's public health system and the presumed spaces they occupied. These misconceptions, as I argue elsewhere, may have stemmed from distinctions made between the pattera and the enfetmera (nurses).[7] The enfetmera were registered and licensed under the navy and worked in (more visible) public spaces like clinics, dressing stations, and the naval hospital in Hagåtña; the pattera were also trained, licensed, and registered by the same standards under the navy (and in addition, underwent three months of midwifery instruction) and also worked in the aforementioned public spaces, but mostly they operated independently and predominantly in the villages, in the (less visible) private spaces of CHamoru homes. In recalling Aguero's refutation, I am reminded of what happens when we follow the historical footnotes and "foot notes" on CHamoru women—and, by extension, their footprints, footpaths, and pathways, which might entail stories of feet, shoes, and walks—as themselves a way to move past colonial narratives, past erasures, and into deeper Indigenous historical and cultural realities and their political possibilities.

Read at another, deeper level, Tun Frank's political act of remembering and remembering it "so well" begins to map CHamoru women's negotiations of gendered and racialized landscapes in Guåhan and their determinations to maintain a distinctly CHamoru sociality and lay of the land, a gendered inafa'maolek. A system of values, ideas, and feelings that CHamorus collectively and as a people consider good and essential, inafa'maolek denotes balance and is based on mutual assistance, cooperation, reciprocity, interdependence, obligation, respect, peace, and reconciliation, which has direct implications for how one behaves in relation to achafñak, community, and land.[8] In her bid to fa'maolek (make good), Tan Marian Dogi' "made sure she treated all the CHamorus who needed help," especially when, according to her son, other midwives during the war "fled to the hills," and even if it meant delegating family members to walk ten miles from Machananao to Hagåtña (Agaña) to ayuda (help), to bring lemmai, dokdok, and hutu.

At another level of meaning, Tun Frank's story of Tan Marian Dogi' traversing "village to village," over twenty miles from Humåtak (Umatac) in the south to Machananao in the north, reveals some women's mobility at a time when others might not have had access to certain modes of travel and transportation. Despite the fact that the pattera's mobility and work were in service to the sick or to expecting mothers before, during, and after delivery and ultimately about stewarding families and communities, their travels also kindled deep suspicion and castigation among certain CHamorus, especially when this movement challenged specific ideas about women's proper place. Especially poignant and powerful was Aguero's reference to his mother as a "midnight wife." Intentional or not—or perhaps a reflection of "English the CHamoru way" for first-language fino' CHamoru (or fino' håya) speakers like Aguero—the reference to Tan Marian Dogi' as a midnight wife also ironically and aptly conveys the pattera's round-the-clock schedule but also some troubling connotations of CHamoru women's work, as will be discussed later in this chapter.

Placental Politics examines the complexities of this rooted and routed embodied labor through the work of famalao'an CHamoru who were among the first to confront and negotiate U.S. colonialism. Hailed and interpellated into the colonial projects of public health and public education by way of the navy's recruitment, training, and employment of them, nurse-midwives and teachers were also the descendants of an even longer line and circle (in keeping with circular conceptions of mo'na) of women who had confronted and resisted European colonization.[9] The book focuses on the pattera, drawing predominantly from the lived experiences of Joaquina Babauta Herrera, Rosalia Ulloa Mesa, Ana Mendiola Rosario, and the fafa'na'gue (teacher) and educator Agueda Iglesias Johnston. These women figure prominently in CHamoru oral histories and family narratives of prewar communities and their political, cultural, and social leaders, but their stories remain eclipsed by (if not assimilated into) conventional Guåhan historiography.[10] Following CHamoru women's footpaths down the "long road to rehabilitation"—what the U.S. navy called its modernizing and civilizing mission in Guåhan—eventually led me to cross historical footpaths with white women, most notably American navy wives and nurses.

Placental Politics expands and complicates the histories of famalao'an CHamoru by examining their labor as enmeshed and entangled in the early twentieth-century philanthropy and feminism of American navy wives and nurses. This book contributes empirical evidence to the historical study of gendered tensions between colonial formations and shifting Indigenous subjectivities. To be sure, *Placental Politics*, as decolonial history, is my bid to advance the critical Indigenous feminist project of decolonization and anticolonialism, especially as articulated by Dian Million when she writes that "to 'decolonize' means to understand as fully as possible the forms colonialism takes in our own times."[11] To do so means also necessarily contending with the complexities of indigeneity, and the "claims and conditions of aboriginal belonging to ancestral places, the demands that come with them, and their analytical implications and possibilities as articulated by those communities."[12] I trace the interactions and intersections between CHamoru women and American navy wives from the early to mid-1900s, from the start of the U.S. Navy's occupation of Guåhan following the Spanish-American War of 1898 to postwar and around the time of the 1950 signing of the Guam Organic Act, which, among other things, ended formal naval colonial rule. While my attention is on relations from the periods åntes di i gera (before the war) to despues di i gera (after the war)—the epochal bookends of a nostalgic prewar life under the United States and a postwar disruption of that life that forever changed the course of Guåhan and the CHamorus—the book also labors to resist this historical and geopolitical periodization.[13] As this history demonstrates, the legacy and power of CHamoru women and their work in stewarding lands and bodies and negotiating U.S. (and Spanish and Japanese) colonialisms travel far, wide, and deep and continue to animate CHamoru epistemologies, ontologies, and time and space. Just what is this historical and cultural legacy of CHamoru women confronting the legacy and work of white navy women and navy wives in Guåhan? What do the historical dimensions, causes, and consequences of the intersections between them reveal about CHamoru women's work? What does a prior history of CHamoru women's work in relation to the work of white American navy women in Guåhan reveal about new ways of being, enacting, and performing what it means to be CHamoru? Furthermore, what might Indigenous feminist historicizing and theorizing of colonialism offer CHamoru decolonization and sovereignty and the "repatriation of Indigenous land and life," especially in the historical present and in the presence of the increasing U.S. militarization and destruction of CHamoru homelands in the Marianas, in which white, military, and colonial women continue to assert their place and role in the gendered violence of empire, settler colonialism, and cultural genocide of Native peoples?[14]

I foreground CHamoru archives (e.g., women's oral histories, oral traditions, unpublished writings, and biographies) with naval sources (e.g., navy wives' and nurses' letters, photographs, and other writings) to argue that in the gendered landscape of twentieth-century U.S. colonialism in Guåhan and American navy wives' efforts to transplant elite white womanhood, CHamoru women experienced new mobilities and freedoms from Indigenous patriarchal proscriptions around gender and place while rearticulating new forms of womanhood and inafa'maolek. These new modes comprised an emergent modernity—that is, different ways of enacting and performing indigeneity in relation to American practices without necessarily abandoning Indigenous knowledge and belief systems, particularly those underscoring the importance of land. In tracing the historical development of CHamoru women's embodied land work and what I call an Indigenous feminist "placental politics"—women enacting and employing ancient knowledge and sacred practices, like the burying of the ga'chong i patgon—I am specifically marking the idea of distinctly Native and gendered forms of being modern. Thus, my work challenges assimilationist assumptions about Native women as simply rooted and static, and racialist discourses of modernity and indigeneity as mutually exclusive categories.[15] This book traces the productions and social formations, as well as the conditions and materiality, of these new CHamoru modernities and new forms of kinalamten famalao'an.

Placental Politics contributes to historical scholarship on Native Pacific Islander women and gender and Indigenous feminist theorizing of history and culture—an intervention in Pacific studies and the broader field of critical Indigenous studies and global indigeneities, in which feminist critiques of colonialism remain scant. It builds on the work of Indigenous Oceanic feminist scholars and activists, including mana wahine writings, deconstructing the still seemingly unmarked, stable, and neutral category of white women (feminists) and their complicity in empire and settler colonialism.[16] *Placental Politics* also builds on scholarship in disparate fields of history: the new Pacific histories, which have examined Native peoples as active historical agents rather than passive victims of colonialism and globalization, and the new imperial histories, which have emphasized white women as both products of and participants in European and American colonialism.[17] Indigenous women's historiographies have been especially crucial for understanding the gendered negotiations of empire and modernity. Mary Jane McCallum examines a history of Aboriginal women's wage labor that has been shaped and confined by a politics of modernity while levying a critique of Canadian history for its culpability in the broader absence and displacement of Indigenous women, a history that has rendered Indigenous women static by disavowing its own colonial past and privileging of white men. Despite these legacies of violence—from colonialism and the discipline of history to Native women's complicity in colonial nation building (in, for example, their participation in Indian pageants that reinforced stereotypical images of the Indian princess)—Aboriginal women, McCallum argues, utilized labor as a "strategy of cultural persistence and a means to gain recognition and control within modernity."[18]

While scholars in the field of women's history continue to advance women agents front and center, few have critically examined the mutually constitutive relations between Indigenous women and white colonial women and how these subjectivities were simultaneously constructed through the centrality of colonialism and empire. Even fewer have examined how colonialism, empire, and militarism furnished the materiality for Native womanhood and white womanhood and feminism in the American Pacific.[19] Jane Haggis has argued that even the well-intentioned project of centering women in colonial contexts entails a problematic salvaging of their experiences in response to earlier historiographical claims that empire was no place for women or was inclusive of women but only as racist memsahibs scapegoated for the fall of empire. For

8 Introduction

Haggis, these recuperative histories ignore colonialism altogether and fail to historicize and analyze white women's complicity or how white colonial womanhood and gender were forged in relation to colonialism.[20] My work focuses on how CHamoru women confronted the labor and leisure of white women and, more specifically, the historical formation feminist scholars have called the "new woman"—but as inflected and manifested by the "navy wife" (and nurse and teacher) on two-year tours of duty in Guåhan.[21] In this sense, I follow Antoinette Burton's call to examine the "unfinished business" of colonial modernity and the "new analytical possibilities for understanding how power operates and is reconsolidated in new historical forms"; I also heed Lata Mani's caution that "even as colonial modernity opened up a structure of opportunities, it simultaneously inaugurated its own logic of discrimination and submission."[22] In what follows, I lay out the colonial and Indigenous landscapes that CHamoru women traversed, followed, and crossed over; I then articulate what I call an Indigenous feminist theory and practice of placental politics inspired by this earlier history of Indigenous women's embodied land work in health, education, and community well-being.

The Gendered Landscapes of the U.S. Navy's Benevolent Long Road

Following the Spanish-American War and the signing of the Treaty of Paris, Spain relinquished its colonies in the Marianas, ceding Guåhan to the United States and selling the Northern Mariana Islands to Germany. On December 23, 1898, U.S. president William McKinley issued Executive Order 108-A, which placed Guåhan under the control of the U.S. Navy. In his orders to the island's first naval governor, Captain Richard Leary, McKinley described the terms for establishing the United States' authority over Guåhan as one of "benevolent assimilation." This new mission and "mild sway of justice" over the old "arbitrary rule"—what Vicente Rafael calls the "sentimental reworking" of the colonial frontier and divine "gift bestowed to a putatively pioneering race" under manifest destiny to the return of that gift overseas—was predicated on winning the "confidence, respect, and affection" of CHamorus by securing for them the "full measure of individual rights and liberty which is the inheritance of all free peoples," while also making sure to "repress disturbance and to overcome all obstacles to the bestowal of the blessings of government."[23]

A *U.S. Navy Report on Guam* (1951) retrospectively described the imperial project as a benevolent long road of gift giving that came in the form of public health, public works, public education, and the instruction of English.[24] This long road entailed a "transformation in the bodies and minds" of CHamorus, delivering them from a "disease-ridden medieval peonage to the dignity and demeanor of a healthy, self-reliant citizenry in the modern world."[25] For the navy, this peonage was the result of three hundred years of Spanish "misrule," which left the island "listless" and "decimated" and the CHamorus a "spiritless and mongrelized population" that only the United States, with the navy as the vehicle, could resuscitate.[26]

The first in a litany of white, male naval colonial governors to rule the island from 1899 to 1941, Leary (1899–1900) interpreted the benevolent long road in a number of different ways. During his ten months as governor, several of which were spent on the USS *Yosemite* for fear of contagion, Leary promulgated nearly two dozen edicts.[27] One of his general orders was the prohibition of peonage (General Order No. 18). Just as American colonial officials in the Philippines legitimized a form of colonial paternalism and "extension of democracy" as progressive through similar abolitionist rhetoric against the last vestiges of the Spanish-Filipino legacy, so too did Leary's administration.[28] Leary's second in command, Lieutenant William Safford, reported that the peonage system had not only forced CHamorus into debt but forced them to barter for worthless materials in exchange for farm produce, which prevented them from acquiring thrifty habits and prudent provision in case of famine, and thus the navy did what it could to "correct this evil and to encourage the natives to be provident."[29] The debt, exchange, and bartering of so-called worthless materials that Leary and his administration had encountered and clashed with is centuries old and part of what is known as kostumbren CHamoru (CHamoru custom and culture), a mix of CHamoru and Spanish-Catholic values and practices. Included in kostumbren CHamoru are the even deeper, pre-Spanish Indigenous CHamoru values and practices of inafa'maolek, with their own connotations of substance and wisdom. These tåddong (deep, profound) practices include gai respetu (having respect), gai mamahlao (having shame), mannginge' (sniffing and smelling a saina's hand to take in their essence as a show of respetu to the parent or elder relative), and, most pertinent here, chenchule', which includes debt, but of a different kind, one tied to obligation. This CHamoru debt-obligation nexus entails a gift or payment to somebody in need as a way of creating and maintaining a form of reciprocal exchange and ongoing indebtedness. CHenchule' is not based on capitalist economic notions of wealth and accumulation nor the gift giving of benevolent assimilation but debt reflecting interdependence and stewardship obligations that come with, for example, childbearing and child-rearing, which encompass nonbiological modes of reproductive labor.[30] After centuries of Spanish colonization but far from simple "Hispanicization," these tåddong values and practices have also necessarily become "contained" in CHamoru Catholic rituals, such as the fiesta (religious feast), nubena (nine-day prayer vigil), lisåyu (rosary), and the kompaire (godparenthood) system.

Leary's ban on CHamoru cohabitation (General Order No. 5), what he referred to as concubinage, and the rearing of illegitimate children (an offense of which was punishable by fine and imprisonment) reflected a broader mission to control CHamoru sociality and sexuality regarded as antithetical to decency, moral advancement, and civilized society. Leary's directives also reflected a paternal and patriarchal naval brand of the benevolent long road, which saw itself as having the "well-earned reputation" of championing the needs of the distressed and "protecting the honor and virtue of women."[31] The U.S. Navy's efforts to regulate the terms of CHamoru gender and sexuality were also fundamentally steeped in what Gail Bederman describes as a late nineteenth- and early twentieth-century crisis in U.S. masculinity. This crisis, Bederman argues, emerged because of white middle-class men's anxieties about the presence of nonwhite working-class immigrant men, African American men, and white middle-class new women in the labor force and white men's subsequent efforts to reconstruct manhood based on rugged masculinity.[32] This effort to protect the virtue and honor of women coupled with a specific civilizing mission of rehabilitating Guåhan, as we shall glean shortly, would help set the specifically gendered terms of the long road.

The navy's long road entailed the emptying (and later confiscation) of CHamoru lands. This emptying, according to Aileen Moreton-Robinson, is the process by which the "possessive logics of patriarchal white sovereignty" disavow and dispossess the Indigenous subject both confined and conscripted within modernity and yet always outside the white logic of capitalism (and progress and development).[33] In this emptied and depopulated landscape in Guåhan, according to Anne Hattori, the navy rendered CHamoru men absent on account of widespread epidemics and CHamoru-Spanish warfare and asserted power and fecundity over CHamoru women as bearers of the race. The island, Hattori argues, was "feminized not only as a terrain from which men were literally absent" but as a "space available for the colonial penetration of a masculinized naval establishment" in which it saw its mission as one of rehabilitating the CHamoru race.[34] A 1928 advertisement (figure 0.1) in the navy-run publication *The Guam Recorder* exemplifies well this feminized emptying and expropriation of CHamoru lands. Upon closer read of the ad—a call to "reputable and experienced farmers who wish to settle on this

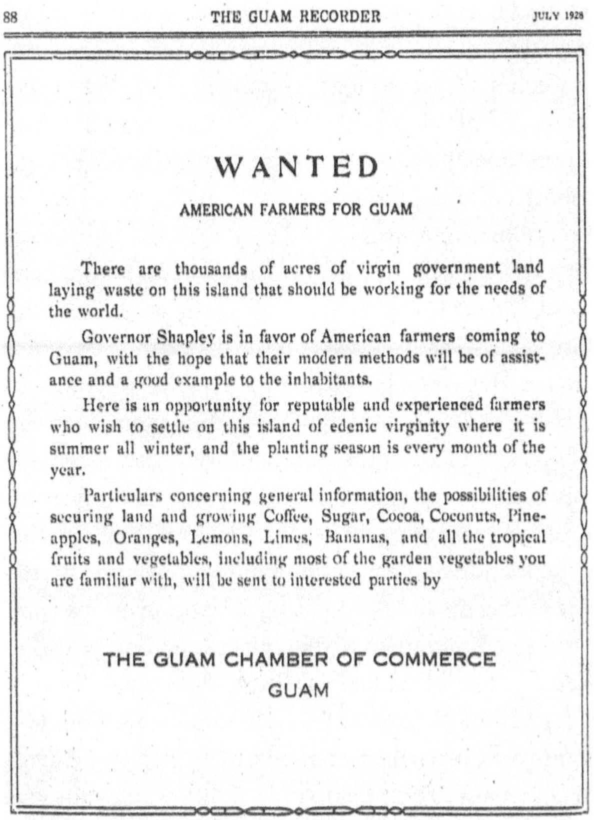

FIGURE 0.1 Ad from *The Guam Recorder*, 1928. Courtesy of the Richard Flores Taitano Micronesian Area Research Center, University of Guam.

> **WANTED**
>
> AMERICAN FARMERS FOR GUAM
>
> There are thousands of acres of virgin government land laying waste on this island that should be working for the needs of the world.
>
> Governor Shapley is in favor of American farmers coming to Guam, with the hope that their modern methods will be of assistance and a good example to the inhabitants.
>
> Here is an opportunity for reputable and experienced farmers who wish to settle on this island of edenic virginity where it is summer all winter, and the planting season is every month of the year.
>
> Particulars concerning general information, the possibilities of securing land and growing Coffee, Sugar, Cocoa, Coconuts, Pineapples, Oranges, Lemons, Limes, Bananas, and all the tropical fruits and vegetables, including most of the garden vegetables you are familiar with, will be sent to interested parties by
>
> **THE GUAM CHAMBER OF COMMERCE**
> GUAM

island of edenic virginity"—we might begin to ascertain the beginnings of what Patrick Wolfe called settler colonialism's "logic of (Native) elimination."[35] This settler colonial logic, as Maile Arvin, Eve Tuck, and Angie Morrill argue, is a gendered project of disappearing Indigenous structures of governance and kinship, gender roles, and sexuality—all "key to making Indigenous peoples into settler state citizens."[36]

The process of emptying, securing, and domesticating the female land was the colonial vehicle through which the navy subjected CHamoru families to American agriculture and sought to replace CHamoru conceptions of land use and chenchule' relations with the land with American notions of developing the land and extractive economy. In its references to "edenic virginity," the navy-run Guam Chamber of Commerce, composed predominantly of white American men (and restricted to men at the time), engendered Guåhan female in need of seasoned white American male propagation for the good of the inhabitants and the "needs of the world." The navy's perception of "thousands of acres ... laying waste" gives us an indication of the clash between Native and foreign (military colonial) desires for the land.[37]

In its vision of progress and development, the navy also deemed certain women as the path or means for helping to deliver order out of chaos. The navy would find this in a cohort of young CHamoru women like the would-be nurses and teachers who exhibited enthusiasm and eagerness and supposedly pliability and malleability. Given a lack of resources (financial and otherwise) in administering the island, the navy would also come to rely on the auspices of American women, early on especially wives (accompanying their governor and officer husbands), in mostly private but later certain public spheres.

As this book demonstrates, despite white naval patriarchy's attempts to regulate the spheres, navy wives (like CHamoru women) were also redefining the spatial politics of empire on their own terms. This may explain the impetus behind a column in an August 1928 issue of *The Guam Recorder* that revealed how white women on the island were conscripted but in a manner strictly contained in the spheres of charity and fund-raising. The anonymous (presumably male) writer, as if to remind them of their place (and only place) in charitable work, beseeched "ladies of station" (as the military would refer to wives and dependents) for a "little civic pride please": "Local conditions lack so much that could be improved upon if the Americans, particularly the American ladies, who come to Guam would only help a little. If they would only give up one afternoon a week or one a month, and meet for the purpose of discussing and recommending some little improvement that might be accomplished if presented to the authorities by a body of interested wellwishers."[38] Like the American wife-companions who accompanied their Protestant missionary husbands, navy wives were often limited to working with Native women and children and were expected to be faithful to their husbands' vocations.[39] In Guåhan, navy women were often inextricably linked to their naval husband's agendas and motivations or particularly through their identification as civic-minded, charitable workers involved in pet projects, such as building hospitals.

Other white women in the colonies distinguished themselves from the ladies of the station. The American anthropologist Margaret Mead (who conducted fieldwork in Samoa) noted that the American nurses were either "very ordinary" or "genteel" and that she did not know which was worse. She found that the wives—in particular, the ones she met at a tea party given in her honor by one Miss Hodgson (the head of the navy's nursing school)—were all the same.[40] She described the wife of one naval governor as "highly bred but apparently without any ideas." For Meade, most of the American women stationed in Samoa were "pretentious"; they knew well "enough to put rose petals in their finger bowls and complain that their nurses are not respectful." Mead concluded that if they lacked personality and brains, at least they were "well bred." Similarly, Laura Thompson wrote in a letter to her family that navy wives in Guåhan wore "long dresses and floppy hats... quite dressy but not very smart" and "took time" there to "have babies."[41]

As discussed in chapter 2, though they were of the elite classes, Maria Schroeder and Susan Dyer were two women who accompanied their naval officer husbands to Guåhan and who did not exactly fit the mold of white women the likes of which someone like Margaret Mead and Laura Thompson might encounter abroad and whom they found to be lacking in intellect. Maria Schroeder might be described as the mother, so to speak, of U.S. Navy women philanthropists, whose work helped pave the long road in Guåhan. She diligently raised funds for a hospital for Native men, but her effort was also in service to her husband's agenda and preoccupations, as well as those of a larger male colonial order of benevolent assimilation in the tropics. Governor Seaton Schroeder (1900–3) was especially concerned about sanitary conditions on the island. In the first year of his command, he passed a general order allowing civilians to receive free treatment at the naval hospital.[42] Despite such efforts, the naval hospital was still used predominantly by navy personnel. Arguing for the need for a hospital designated for CHamoru men, Maria Schroeder solicited donations from prominent CHamorus and the military to establish a separate ward within the naval hospital. The hospital, opened in 1902, was named in her honor. As if to launch in Guåhan a specific trajectory—indeed, a military tradition of civic obligation and duty for American women—Susan Dyer followed Maria Schroeder, in terms of chronology and labor, by raising funds to establish a hospital (open in 1905) for CHamoru women and children.[43]

The tradition of civic-minded and duty-bound wives of U.S. naval officers bequeathed a gendered and classed view of CHamoru motherhood that is writ across the published and unpublished historical record, as well as upon the lands, waters, bodies, minds, and heartscapes of Guåhan and modern CHamoru society, and can be traced in a July 1924 special column of *The Guam Recorder* entitled the Woman's Section. The column, whose author was unidentified, provided CHamoru women and mothers with beauty and fashion tips and instructions on how to care for babies before, during, and after birth. In the first of a two-part series, Native mothers, who are referred to interestingly in the third-person singular, are taught that "when she learns she is to have a baby, she should go to a doctor, who will tell her how to care for herself, what foods to eat, what exercises to do," and that these steps would ensure the development of a healthy baby and strong race and ensure "it is everyone's duty to better their race."[44] A month later, the subsequent Woman's Section reiterated prior governors' sentiments that unsanitary habits and improper feeding (rather than colonial violence, the introduction of disease, and the disruption of the CHamoru social fabric) were the reasons for high infant mortality and a decimated CHamoru population.

Purporting to bestow a gift of knowledge on matters pertaining to childbearing and child-rearing, the column "mom-shames" and reminds mothers that the "ultimate responsibility for the prevention of death rests with the mother" and that what was vital and critical to the "welfare of the (CHamoru) race" was that "mother love be supplemented by an intelligent comprehension of what constitutes a normal childhood."[45] More than likely, the intent behind this column was to prompt CHamoru mothers to avail themselves to navy doctors. In this objective, the Woman's Section, like other colonial apparatuses, relied on agents of the navy to act as surrogate parents and model families to transform CHamoru conceptions of achafñak—extended family, including godparents, adoptions, other forms of kin relations, and the broader village community responsible for attending to the life, well-being, and afterlife of children—into the American ideal and structure of the nuclear family.[46]

A form of surveillance, columns like this and a so-called "Better Babies" campaign imposed throughout U.S. colonies helped shape the gendered contours of U.S. colonialism in Guåhan. The Better Babies campaign, part of a larger eugenics movement in the United States, stressed the idea that properly delivered babies (starting with properly cared for expecting mothers) made for healthier and superior babies and eventually healthier and superior adults. In Guåhan (as shown in figure 0.2), "more, bigger and better" (and healthier and superior) meant modern, which meant white American.[47] After Susan Dyer came a parade of wives and activities dedicated to fund-raising for the hospital: like a Mrs. C. F. Kraber, who in 1910 organized a Christmas concert that raised thirty dollars for the Susana Hospital; the "ladies of the naval colony," who in 1914 organized an annual charity fair whose proceeds went to a modern diet kitchen at the Susana; and a Red Cross fund-raiser by the ladies of the station for the 1917 Guam Industrial Fair.[48] In the mid-1930s, the Red Cross was still raising funds for the Susana.[49]

As white women followed their military husbands aboard ships bearing and planting the U.S. flag and redefined themselves on exotic tours of duty amid the tropical landscape and Indigenous people of Guåhan, CHamorus were also following these and other divergent paths. The intersections between

Following the Historical Footnotes 15

FIGURE 0.2 Health float, Guam Industrial Fair, c. 1933. Courtesy of the Collections of the Guam Museum, a division of the Department of Chamorro Affairs.

CHamorus, especially women, and navy wives are perhaps best captured in the metaphors and historical experiences articulated in two closely interrelated phrases: "following the ship" and "following the flag." These phrases were the titles of an essay by an American naval wife, Evelyn Nelson, and a poem by a CHamoru man, Jose C. Torres.

By all accounts a new woman, Evelyn Nelson was a former economics professor at Vassar who earned her doctorate at Radcliffe. With her husband, Rear Admiral Frederick Nelson, she was stationed in Guåhan from 1932 to 1934 and credited with having written one of the first histories of the island. She published several articles on Guåhan but of particular interest are her unpublished writings, which reveal more intimate, personal matters about her role in juggling "desirable qualities" with "hobby interests."[50] In the unpublished essay "Following the Ship," Nelson elaborated on such ideals and the qualities and hobby interests as personified by historical and cultural figures of womanhood across time and space: the "beauty of Cleopatra, the faithfulness of Penelope, the domesticity of Fanny Farmer, the financial genius of Hetty Green, and the executive ability of Eleanor Roosevelt" with the "skill of a professional packer thrown in."[51] Later in the essay, Nelson would also throw into the margins of the manuscript the handwritten note "the pen of Elouisa." Actually, Nelson was not the first naval wife to pen her adventures through the circuits of military empire in ways that foregrounded the specificities of women's interests, especially their mobilities, including how these interests and mobilities were historically and historiographically subordinated to those of the men/husbands/officers. Two examples are the French aristocrat Rose de Freycinet (née Pinon) in the nineteenth century and, in the early twentieth century, the American Jane Grey Potter. Disguised as a man while accompanying her husband, the French naval captain Louis de Freycinet, Rose traveled on the *Uranie* during its scientific explorations around the world from 1817 to 1820. Both Freycinets would furnish important accounts of their travels, which included observations of Guåhan and the CHamorus. Freycinet may very well have been the first in a long line of military (navy) wives to visit the island.[52]

For her part, Jane Potter described herself as a "lass who loved a sailor." It was how this American wife of Rear Admiral David Potter chose to capture her love for travel, especially travel aboard ships to exotic locales like Guåhan, even if they were modern army transports. Referring metaphorically to the modest accommodations of army transport ships, Potter described the ideal characteristics of the traveler who was somewhat tested by the conditions of transitory or temporary dwellings. She wrote, "Frivolity ... is a person's tissue, not his garment. A stable residence encourages and engenders a sense of responsibility and obligation, so the theory goes an unstable residence promotes shallowness and flippancy of character. This ought to be true, perhaps, but is it? A roving life did not prevent one navy woman from becoming deeply engaged in hospital work, another in settlement work, another in organization connected with infant hygiene ... still another in shorter hours legislation for working women."[53] In this quote, Potter initially engendered the traveler male but then switched to the female sojourner—to herself (the roving life of "one navy woman")—after having questioned the gendered norm of travel (and frivolity) when she referred to her "roving life," which did not preclude "deeply engaged" work that a "lass who loves a sailor" might come upon while with him at sea. For Potter, as for other traveling navy wives, being away from home and its domesticity did not preclude doing the work of stability that one found at home. This work was anything but frivolous and inconsequential. In Potter's writings, we get a glimpse of the niche that navy wives like Susan Dyer (chapter 2) and Helen Paul (chapter 3) envisioned for themselves. Still, as Virginia Scharff writes, we "should not mistake female mobility for emancipation," but nor "should we assume that women's movements, if constrained, are insignificant."[54]

Just as wives followed their husbands, who followed the navy to Guåhan, CHamorus too were negotiating—were *following*, as it were—the "movements" and the terms of U.S. colonialism in the island. Consider a 1925 poem by the aforementioned Jose Torres, "Following the Flag." Torres dedicated the poem "as a memory of my friend and *partnership*, Antonia."

> They taught the Guamanian the right
> way to work
> And they thought the teaching was
> fun.
>
> They taught them to spell and to build
> themselves a road
> And the best way to handle a gun.
>
> Were their salaries so big that the task
> was worth while?
> Did they save a cent of pay;
>
> Have the average men an account with
> the Bank?
> Never a cent, not they.
>
> So we haven't a job and we haven't
> a cent;
> And nobody cares a damn,
>
> But we did our work and we have done
> it well
> To the glory of Uncle Sam
> And we've seen a lot and we've lived a lot
> In this island over the sea
>
> Would we change with our brothers
> grown rich at home
> Praise be to God, not we.

In his analysis of the poem "Following the Flag," Vicente M. Diaz suggests that the verse registers ambiguity and ambivalence concerning failure—either failure by the Americans to sufficiently modernize the CHamorus or failure by the CHamorus to properly Americanize or modernize—*and* whether the author is lamenting the failure or celebrating it, as when the author ends the poem by "prais(ing) God" (that American-style modernization did not completely or so effectively transform or acculturate CHamoru society). Adding to this ambiguity, for Diaz, is the title, which, like the body of the poem, can *fly* in either direction: in spite of America's teachings, CHamorus have not followed the flag properly, or, choosing "Praise be to God," not to follow the flag, CHamorus yearn for a day following the flag or post-flag—that is, a day when the American flag no longer flies over Guåhan.[55] For my purposes, I wish to call attention to two other levels of meaning, including yet another layer of ambiguity, offered in this poem. First, regardless of how one reads the poem, there is a clear and unambiguous history of inequality in the colonial relationship between Americans and CHamorus, such that the latter are being subordinated to the former. Second, this history is rendered all the more complicated by the additional ambiguity in the poem's usage of the third-person plural forms "they" and "theirs" in the first part of the poem (versus the second part, which uses "we") as these terms refer variously to the agents of transformation and to the forms of work and labor that comprised the efforts put forth to modernize and Americanize CHamorus. In keeping with this book's central focus and argument—indeed, exemplary of my argument—the "they" (and "we") in this poem can refer to white American colonial officials, to CHamoru men and women, to men and women in either case (in "partnership"), and to the kinds of work and intersections of that work that are at stake.

What then connects Jose Torres's poem and memorial to his partnership (with Antonia), "Following the Flag," to Evelyn Nelson's unpublished essay, "Following the Ship," are the mutual but unequal, subordinate positions that come with "following" the United States under the helm of the navy. Here we have Native and colonial subjectivities differentially trying to make sense of their space and place in empire and the collusion and clash between the gendered landscapes of colonialism and the equally (and mutually exclusive) gendered roots and routes of kostumbren CHamoru. CHamoru women's mobilities in these spaces as charted or mapped in the term *chålan* (paths and roads) were especially fraught, as will be discussed in the final section of this chapter.

The Gendered Landscapes of Kostumbren CHamoru

In June 1939, on the eve of the Feast of Corpus Christi in the island's capital city of Hagåtña, the American anthropologist Laura Thompson awaited eagerly the next day's elaborate religious procession in order to witness firsthand an example of kostumbren CHamoru, the term for what by then had become consciously understood as the set of local customs produced by a historical amalgamation of Indigenous CHamoru and Spanish Catholic values and practices after centuries of Spanish colonialism and Catholic presence in the archipelago. While waiting, Thompson chanced upon another instance of cultural fusion but in a different register. In the Native nurses' quarters in the nearby Susana Hospital, a group of nursing students huddled around a Victrola borrowed from American navy nurses, playing the same record repeatedly for an hour. Thompson had arrived eight months earlier in October 1938 aboard the USS *Chaumont*.[56] The U.S. Navy had contracted her to study why its educational system had not taken root among more CHamorus. Her answer, which was based on fieldwork and analyses culminating in the first modern ethnography of the CHamorus and which pointed to discrepancies between colonial educational practices and Indigenous cultural traits, upset naval officials enough to ban her from returning to conduct future research.

Thompson hypothesized that despite nearly two hundred fifty years of Spanish Catholic colonization, important traces of Indigenous culture remained that differentiated CHamoru children from American children. In effect, she argued that these distinctions warranted a more culturally appropriate sensitivity from the naval administration. For Thompson, the scene at the Susana Hospital was a tableau. In her field notes, she observed that Native nurses listened to the same song "over and over again" because such repetition recalled a signature pattern found in the kåntan CHamorita, a traditional CHamoru musical genre in which for her "the same tune" was used "for all songs." For the anthropologist trained to find and account for cultural difference through the synchronic workings of deep cultural structures as manifest in recurring surface patterns of personal and collective behavior and values, Thompson understood the CHamoru persistence (of listening "over and over" to the same song) in that instance to have "something to do with the constant repetition of [the] same tune one continually hears."[57]

Thompson was correct in discerning CHamoru cultural perseverance and determination across Spanish colonialism; however, her explanation and synchronic bias of the hospital scene around the Victrola—in hearing and discerning these Native nurses as an ethnographic record upon which a deeper and essential CHamoru cultural attribute continued to play itself out (and stagnate)—is patronizing at best. Following George Marcus and Michael Fischer in their discussion of synchronic bias, it is not that ethnography's "timeless present" is ahistorical and does not account for "continual social change," but rather, it is a "tradeoff for the advantages that bracketing the flow of time and the influence of events offers in facilitating the structural analysis of systems of symbols and social relations."[58] What motivated that "tradeoff" for Thompson was perhaps a search for the essential outward patterns in contemporary CHamoru cultural practices, like the kåntan CHamorita, that might contain and illustrate the persistence of deep CHamoru cultural continuity. This is what she thought she happened upon in the scene of the CHamoru women playing and replaying the record: a modern song being subjected to a cultural behavior and style from a genre in the CHamoru cultural repertoire that had settled into place after centuries of mixing with Spanish Catholic culture, the kåntan CHamorita (with *kånta* deriving from the Spanish term *canta*, "to sing" or "a song"), but retaining the Indigenous pre-Spanish term for peoplehood and language (*CHamoru*). A popular pastime performed even to this day while people engaged in such collective social activities as farming, fishing, harvesting, thatching, lashing, or just socializing, kåntan CHamorita is also an affectionate form of bonding through friendly banter as structured by whatever theme, metaphor, and verse were first sung by the caller. The listener, especially one who was specifically targeted or addressed in the call, is challenged to respond to or redirect the call in similar kind (and form) but with new content. But like CHamoru culture, society, tradition, and identity, kåntan CHamorita is also about spontaneous improvisation, a process of creativity that does not so easily lend itself to pat certainties and clear-cut definitive interpretations.[59] In other words, clearly there were many contributing factors other than a structured Indigenous *trait* for why the nurses were doing what they were doing at the time the ethnographer observed them, beginning with the ethnographic encounter itself under the behest of colonial administration and the professional imperatives to apply anthropology serving as important variables. The nurses may have simply been fascinated with the technology and enjoyed the song. Or perhaps they sought out a much-needed break or reprieve from the drudgeries of their work. Perhaps it was only because of this and a catchy tune that the Victrola—like other forms of recreation introduced by Americans that provided new forms of leisure and diversion along with new forms of labor—had this particular group of CHamorus listening to the recording again and again.

The cultural "constant repetition" that Thompson observed—of Native nurses at the Susana playing the same song repeatedly—may instead have been assertions of new and emboldened forms of CHamoru womanhood, particularly in the face of a staunch CHamoru-Spanish Catholic tradition that scorned young women for participating in American recreational activities, like dances and movies. Indeed, as CHamoru Catholics around the island prepared for a solemn celebration of the body and blood of Christ, the telling scene of CHamoru women engaged in an evening of fun and frivolity listening to the same tune on the Victrola defied religious tradition and suggests other cultural formations in the making. These novel forms exemplify what

Stephanie Nohelani Teves calls a "defiant indigeneity" but of a different set of politics and performance of culture elsewhere in the Pacific.[60] To be sure, these new modes of CHamoru women's leisure and labor cannot simply be parsed out from kostumbren CHamoru; even as they broke with tradition, they were also practiced in ways that continued other dimensions of CHamoru culture as such new forms furnished the materiality to work and rework persisting forms of CHamoru indigeneity.

In her study of contemporary CHamoru women organizers, CHamoru scholar and culture advocate Laura Torres Souder traces the historical role, status, and contribution of famalao'an CHamoru through centuries of colonization and modernization. Of CHamoru women's negotiations of kostumbren CHamoru, Souder writes that before the war, young women rarely left the home except to attend church activities, though even such sanctioned activities were conditioned on women being chaperoned. For Souder, kostumbren CHamoru proscriptions were a product of Spanish Catholicism's emphasis on female chastity and submission, coupled with CHamoru women's further "retreat into the home" and their "proper place," as taught and engendered by U.S. naval policies and educational influence.[61] Though the navy's presence began to offer a few women opportunities to enter public spaces as domestic workers, barmaids, teachers, and nurses, and thus break with tradition, physical and discursive mobility was still confined by a CHamoru Catholic social order of domestication and domesticity. This social order was premised on CHamoru women being assigned (by God) to be keepers of the home and to ensure that the souls of their familia or achafñak would be "readied for heaven."[62] To this end, CHamoru women were responsible for making sure their children attended eskuelan påle' (priest schools or catechism), said their prayers regularly, and attended Sunday mass.

Noteworthy is Souder's discussion of restricted mobility under kostumbren CHamoru, although she argues that despite the restriction of woman's freedom and their confinement in domestic spheres under U.S. colonialism, women's economic power did not lessen, at least not in terms of controlling the family/clan resources (as was the case under the terms of early CHamoru matrilineal society). Recognizing the complexity of CHamoru women's lived experience of i maloffan na tiempo (the past), Souder also describes CHamoru women as socially structured between two contradictory or diametrically opposed subject positions: between, on the one hand, the "madonna-like lady on the pedestal" and, on the other hand, the "dåma de noche" (woman of the night).[63] Similar virgin/whore dichotomies obtain in histories of the ná'fafañågu and fafa'na'gue and other modern women. Interestingly enough,

Tun Frank Aguero's reference to his mother as a "midnight wife" captures presumptions about kostumbren CHamoru gender and sexuality. A sense of this *amalgamation* of Indigenous and Spanish Catholic presumption and proscription is found in a story told by Joaquina Herrera (Tan Kina'), a pattera whose oral histories are featured prominently in this book. In an interview, Tan Kina' talked about a slight change in her facial mobility that had been caused by a stroke she suffered on account of overworking but which some CHamorus attributed to being out late at night (despite the legitimate reason of serving other families in need) and equated to a kind of wrath of ancient CHamoru spirits and ancestors, the taotaomo'na (literally, the "people of before" or the "front people").

In her ethnography of CHamorus on the eve of World War II, Laura Thompson observed that many young, unwed women were expected to join the Daughters of Mary Society, which promulgated a strict code of chastity and rules prohibiting unaccompanied women from leaving the home. The American introduction of new social practices like attending movies and dances, in particular, led the CHamoru påle' to double up on efforts to shield CHamoru Catholic society from liberal and modern behavior, especially as displayed by women. In this milieu, the only legitimate reason a young woman might leave home, especially at night, would be to attend Daughters of Mary Society functions and never without a chaperone, as Souder pointed out earlier. In her ethnography, Thompson brings home the social equations and formulations that inform the limited or restricted mobilities under kostumbren CHamoru at a time of modernization. She observed, "Except for a few prostitutes and bar girls, only the most modern girls of Agana, including some nurses, school teachers and house girls," defied such conventions.[64] For Thompson, being a modern woman in Guåhan was in effect to be associated with "prostitutes" and "bar girls" in a shared defiance of kostumbren CHamoru. In specific terms told by Tan Kina', to defy kostumbren CHamoru was to be called worse names or invite the wrath not just of the påle' but also the ancient spirits. Such was the gendered and sexualized terms of kostumbren CHamoru for the modern CHamoru "women of the times" in Guåhan—teachers, nurses, bartenders, sex workers, and other laborers.[65] The allusion to landscapes, in the subheading of this section of the chapter, can be spied in how these women's itineraries through local space—the villages, the hålom tåno', the låncho—were also gendered and sexualized in the entanglement of the supposed stable binary between tradition (kostumbren CHamoru) and modernity (under American hegemony). To understand this, we can return to Thompson's observation of the modernization of CHamorus on the eve of World War II in the Pacific. If the most modern women of Hagåtña, the teachers and the nurses, are like the prostitutes and the bar girls in terms of their defiance of kostumbren CHamoru, it is noteworthy that she singles out "the most modern" of them as coming from Hagåtña in particular.

For Thompson, the island's capital, Hagåtña, is differentiated from the rest of the island, especially from the southern villages, which were understood to be more "traditional." But as I demonstrate in chapter 1, this easy division is not upheld in the work of the pattera—as some hailed from Hagåtña but continued to engage old, tåddong cultural practices and others, such as Tan Kina', hailed from the southern villages but tended to embrace new, "modern" practices more readily and at times dismissed older practices as superstitious, while still respecting certain tåddong practices like åmot CHamoru (CHamoru medicine) and lasa (massage) or the desire of families to bury the ga'chong i patgon and apuya'. Thompson's slighting of the deep cultural resilience in modern places and "Native hubs" like Hagåtña and stereotypical siting of tradition in the rural outskirts or in the southern villages have something of an analog in her erasure of CHamoru women who worked as "prostitutes" and "bar girls" by refusing to count them in her appendix of women laborers.[66] By not doing so, Thompson also conveyed similar judgments about this class of women as any leveled at them by the Spanish padres or by the most critical of these women's men and kinfolk.

In her history of Sånta Marian Kåmalen, the CHamoru adaptation of the Virgin Mary in Guåhan, Marilyn Jorgensen likewise traces kostumbren CHamoru restrictions on women's mobilities and sexualities as engendered by Marian devotions such as the Sodality of the Children of Mary (Sodality of Mary) and the Little Miss December 8th. In the postwar December 8 processions, which honored CHamoru women's "sexual purity, devotion, self-sacrifice," devout Catholics were invited to "walk with Mary."[67] Given the gendered proscriptions, one of the implications of young CHamoru women not joining the Marian sodality is that they may have been regarded as not only having chosen *not* to walk with Mary but perhaps even to be walking *away* from her.

Indeed, in its mission to convert CHamorus of the Marianas, the Spanish implemented a system that had a profound impact on women's mobilities and embodied practices. Through a policy of reducciones ("reduction"), the Spanish forced CHamorus from villages around the island to live in centralized barrios and barangays in Hagåtña, where they were physically and temporally closer to churches and shrines. Spanish colonizers established marriage laws and prohibited Native sexual practices that the missionaries decried as evil. Nowhere is the colonization of famalao'an CHamoru mobilities and sexualities more profound than in the Spanish imposition of marriage and the effort to rid the island of the guma' uritao or guma' ulitao (bachelor homes). An important dimension of early CHamoru culture and society, the guma' ulitao was where young CHamoru men were sent to learn skills: fishing, hunting, canoe building, navigation, tool construction (such as adzes and slingstones), and warfare. According to James Viernes, the skills cultivated at the guma' ulitao had broader implications beyond training young men to be self-sustaining. He argues that they were "part of a larger means of constituting Chamorro masculinity, educating men to be active participants in the highly important and deeply embedded practice" of chenchule', which included the gifting of betel nuts or turtle shells or the rendering of labor during important clan events such as the birth of a child, a marriage, or the death of a loved one.[68] In these key educational and socializing spaces, located usually on maternal clan lands, young men (manulitao) were initiated into manhood through CHamoru male bonding and sexual practices, often with unmarried women who, much to the abhorrence of the Spanish, would move freely and frequently in and out of these spaces. Spanish missionaries found this early CHamoru practice of sexual relations outside of marriage and the idea of young women (mutually, if not equally, embedded in chenchule') exchanging sex for other services and items like iron hoops and tortoise shell so detestable and deplorable that they designated one day a week (Thursdays) to burning down these "houses of debauchery" and removing individual women (ma ulitao) from them.[69] In the Spanish missionary accounts, there is evidence that CHamorus would resist the Spanish effort to abolish the guma' ulitao institution. Just as bad, if not worse, than the forced removal of these women and their forced submission into marriage was the sequestering of CHamoru women in convents in Hagåtña under the tutelage and patronage of a priest. One such priest was the Jesuit Francisco Javier Reittemberger, who founded the congregation of Our Lady of Light of Saint Ignatius in Guåhan in 1758. Our Lady of Light congregants were CHamoru women of Hagåtña, many of whom the priest sexually abused. According to Alexandre Coello de la Rosa, these violent acts can be likened to a case of priests "playing native." He writes that, in "playing native," Reittemberger had refashioned himself into a "vestige" of the ancient manulitao who "did not marry native women but rather took them freely" in return for goods or services.[70]

CHamoru women experienced new forms of gendered spatial violence under U.S. colonialism and the navy's reconfiguration of kostumbren CHamoru spaces—particularly through local forms of empire's "deterritorialization and subsequent reterritorialization of all manner of public and private spaces."[71]

The best example of this imperial and violent reworking of Indigenous territory, besides the most obvious case of possessing it as U.S. property, was a notorious post–World War II Cold War policy requiring all travelers going in and out of Guåhan to undergo naval security clearance, which amounted to the military surveillance of civilian residents. In 1941, President Franklin Roosevelt issued Executive Order 8683, which established the Guam Island Naval Defensive Sea Area and the Guam Island Naval Airspace Reservation. This executive order authorized the Secretary of the Navy to permit entry into the island at his discretion and, by extension, authorized the Commander, U.S. Naval Forces Marianas, to "govern the conduct and movement of all persons on the island of Guam regardless of whether or not they had violated the order."[72] The navy would eventually lift the security clearance in 1962, ending its twenty-one years of monitoring civilian entry to and from Guåhan, but not before causing some resentment among CHamoru travelers. Much to his chagrin, statesman Richard "Dick" Flores Taitano, the first CHamoru to be appointed director of the Office of Territories in the U.S. Department of the Interior (what is now the department's assistant secretary of insular affairs), was detained and questioned on his return home to Guåhan in 1950 after finishing studies at Wharton. Even the American civilian governor of Guåhan Ford Elvidge (1953–56) was vexed at how long it took him to clear security in Hawai'i on route to Guåhan, all while watching American taxi dancers breeze through clearance.[73] A similar level of monitoring travel along gendered lines occurred on Guåhan years earlier. A June 1946 memo from the island's civil administrator to the island's command provost marshal (the military police) reveals that of the one hundred registered vehicles listed on Guåhan, only one of these, a jeep, was registered to a woman, who, it should not surprise us, was a pattera, the then forty-two-year-old Maria Taitano Aguero (Tan Marian Dogi')—the same woman whose son, earlier in this chapter, called her the greatest "midnight wife" who went "village to village" and who was one of the few women literally "on the road."[74] If the navy added a new level of monitoring movement to and from Guåhan and within Guåhan as a form of domesticating CHamorus—especially women who were still confined to the realm of domesticity under kostumbren CHamoru—some women, like Tan Marian Dogi', would not be kept in their place.

The CHamoru term for a woman "on the road" is *palao'an chålan* (the plural form of which is *famalao'an chålan*). It is an especially fraught and loaded term that has even greater connotations when considered in the context of naval colonial projects of health and sanitation, which in turn trafficked on other projects, like roads and transportation, and the introduction of other modern forms of recreation, like bars, nightclubs, movies, and dances.[75] These new spaces seemingly drew Native women even farther away from domestic and domesticated spheres of CHamoru hearth and home and the interiority of customary CHamoru culture, particularly as understood in kostumbren CHamoru. The paths and the modes of transportation themselves index Guåhan's cultural and social transformation, and their meanings, too, unsuccessfully attempt to confine CHamoru women. The footpaths and bull-cart trails were at this time associated with a more traditional way of life, in stark contrast to the ever increasing network of modern paved roads made of kaskåhu (crushed limestone) bound crudely by tar, over which puttered military jeeps and buses. To find a pattera like Tan Marian Dogi' (or Dominga "Tan Inga"' Ogo Blas, another jeep-driving pattera) puttering along the paved roads was to render them even more suspect CHamoru women because roads and jeeps were often associated primarily with naval officials and men.[76]

Literally on the road for significant periods, the pattera—especially younger, unmarried ones—ran the risk of being labeled a palao'an chålan. The palao'an chålan, in its most negative connotation, was the figure of impurity, cultural abandonment (if not traitor or puta even), and, in other contexts, collaborator. Cherríe Moraga, among other Chicana and women-of-color feminists who have examined the virgin/whore dichotomy, has vindicated the figure of La Malinche and reclaimed the terms *la chingada* and *la vendida* (sellout) as a way to subvert Mexican patriarchy.[77] Following Moraga, I suggest that the figure of the palao'an chålan can also mark a defiant and liberating moment in CHamoru history when metgot (powerful, strong, tenacious) and mesngon (enduring, resisting) women—in this case, pattera—dared to burst through rigid boundaries, borders, and prescribed roles that confined them even as they themselves continued to serve the needs and well-being of the familia. The figure of the palao'an chålan becomes especially significant for thinking through colonial histories of keeping women on track down the via sacra, or "sacred path" of Spanish empire, or holding women back on their trek down the long road of U.S. naval colonialism.[78]

Building with critical work in Native Pacific cultural studies, which has theorized the roots and routes of indigeneity through Stuart Hall's customization of hegemony through a theory of articulation, I argue that women like the pattera rearticulated the terms of both American and CHamoru gendered spaces and practices into new pathways that did not automatically come at the expense of inafa'maolek duties of pinilan (safekeeping), pineksai (nurturing), and inadahi (caregiving), and stewarding taotao and tåno'.[79] My focus on gendered mobilities stems from the way Native women in Guåhan (and throughout Oceania for that matter) have continuously and systematically been conceptualized and idealized as bearers of culture as a product of being stable and rooted bodies tied to land, family, and tradition in ways that fix them in heteronormative and heteropatriarchal time and space and render them static, unchanging, and outside of modernity. Theorizing and historicizing the roots and routes of Oceanic indigeneity, scholars, writers, and poets have begun to question such (tradition) bounded and gendered temporalities, including the idea that men belong to the sea and women belong to the land.[80] Aroha Harris, for example, has rerouted the history of Māori women from the marae to urban spaces of 1950s Auckland and Wellington to interrogate the tradition/modernity divide as well as unsettle the presumed spaces of women's labor and leisure, in the work of Te Rōpū Wāhine Māori Toko i te Ora (the Māori Women's Welfare League).[81]

In Guåhan, the confinement of women's work and place is in large part owing to the traditional terms of matrilineage and women's obligations as håga (daughters) and cultural caretakers.[82] Under the traditional terms of matrilineality, CHamoru women controlled titles, rights, and claims to resources, especially land, and hence have historically wielded an enormous amount of minetgot (power) and authority. Presumed deviations from their obligations were often associated with cultural or social negligence, betrayal even, but, as this book argues, it was precisely in their mobilities that CHamoru women like the pattera and such early women educators as Agueda Johnston would continue to be rooted and routed in their embodied land work to poksai (paddle forward, as well as raise and nurture), pulan (watch, guard over), and giha (steer and guide) people and Indigenous place. An example of this inafa'maolek labor of stewarding people and land is evidenced in a postwar story the grandson of one pattera recalled about a pattera from another village who, long retired by then, was asked by residents to intervene in an instance of domestic violence. In the larger-than-life narrative he told—a sign of the prominence and respetu granted to the pattera even today—the small-framed pattera stopped a man from assaulting his partner and admonished him for his actions.[83] These assertions of stewardship hold promise for Indigenous feminism and CHamoru feminist practice in a new era of militarization and destruction and as part of a broader anticolonial struggle in Guåhan, an unincorporated territory of the United States, one-fourth of which is controlled by the military and which today remains on the United Nations' list of non-self-governing territories, where a robust Indigenous sovereignty and independence movement is currently underway.

Placental Politics: The Roots and Routes of CHamoru Feminism

> They say that a woman gave birth to the land, and to the sea, and to all that is visible.[84]
>
> —Fray Antonio de los Angeles, 1596

The inspiration for articulating a theory of Indigenous placental politics comes directly from how the pattera—in defiance of U.S. naval orders to burn or discard the afterbirth, regarded as toxic medical waste—continued to bury the child's ga'chong and apuya' or allow family members to do so because they believed this practice kept children safe from harm and rooted them in home and place. Their commitment to the practice also arose out of respect for the deep symbolic, cultural meanings that connect notions of self to land and community in a system of reciprocal kinship relations and stewardship obligations.[85] Feminist and Native studies scholarship has historicized and theorized Indigenous women's negotiations of colonialism with respect to pregnancy and childbearing (and with similar references to the burial of the placenta) as deeply symbolic, place-based acts of resistance, decolonization, and sovereignty. My mode of departure is that the political, social, and cultural practice of burying the placenta, and other dimensions of this embodied work of connecting and caring for lands and peoples, can be regarded as a specifically gendered form of cultural self-determination and Indigenous resistance—one that has important implications for Indigenous feminisms, resurgence, and land struggles against colonialism, militarism, heteropatriarchy, and the destruction of ancestral and contemporary homelands.[86]

To be sure, the potential in placental politics is an Indigenous feminist-inspired theory and anticolonial practice of being and action informed by tåddong and takhilo' (high, important) ideas of self in relation to tåno' and the primacy of stewardship of tåno' amid enduring colonial transformations.[87] I am aware of a propensity in the image of placental politics to idealize a return to nature or maternal, biological, reproductive, or even heteronormative utopia. This is not my intention. Rather, I am interested in how the social and cultural histories of Indigenous women's embodied labor as it relates to land can inform ongoing struggles in new colonial landscapes in Guåhan, elsewhere in Oceania, and beyond. That the pattera and other modern CHamoru women in roles like the matlina (godmother) or maga'håga (highest-ranking daughter) saw the need to continue effectuating old practices involving the land underscores the lingering importance of land, the "singular issue" that can "radicalize even the most mild-mannered Chamorro from the loyal military retiree and the police officer to the teacher and the nurse."[88] This history of asserting Native stewardship over the land and deep connections between taotao and tåno', is especially timely given the latest military build up in Guåhan, in which the United States plans to transfer thousands of marines and their dependents from Okinawa to Guåhan over the next several years.

CHamoru women's rootedness and embodied land work are exemplified well in one of the earliest oral histories among CHamorus, the story of Fo'na and Pontan (also known as Fu'una and Puntan). There are variations of this origin story of the sibling gods of creation. According to a popular version, Fo'na utilized her powers to separate her brother's body parts; she created the sun with one of his eyes and the moon with the other. With Pontan's eyebrows Fo'na made the rainbows, and with his back (sometimes his chest), the earth. Then Fo'na threw herself onto the land, and her body became Laso' Fuha (Fouha Rock) in Humåtak in southern Guåhan, from which the first CHamorus originated, a site that CHamorus continue to pay homage to today.[89] In this old and deep CHamoru story of gendered lands and land as ancestor and kin—one that differs from the gendered landscapes of U.S. colonialism (and before that Spanish colonialism)—is the embodied land work of rooted women on the road and also the centrality of che'lu (sibling, the plural form of which is mañelu) and dual siblingship relations, most notably that which inheres between the maga'håga and maga'låhi, the "highest (ranking) son," of early CHamoru society (and perhaps the kinship that the poet Jose Torres alluded to when he spoke of Antonia and their partnership).[90]

Guåhan scholars have historicized and theorized contemporary women's activism, comparing it to another important oral tradition: the women who saved Guåhan.[91] In this story of women's embodied land work—this time rerouted to central Guåhan in the sesonyan Hagåtña and matan hånom (Hågatña springs)—a giant guihan (fish) wreaks havoc as it eats away at the island. After unsuccessful attempts by the men to capture the guihan, the women gather to sacrifice their hair and weave a net, eventually capturing it and thus saving the island from further destruction. Like the earlier story of Fo'na and Pontan, this oral history highlights the special mañelu relationship. Indeed, pattera stories too are filled with similar accounts of brother-sister, aunt-uncle, and other extended kinships' cooperative and reciprocal power relations: for example, Tan Kina' relies on her brother to help her become employed by a navy wife. Of particular interest, and what I want to insist undergirds the important anticolonial potential in the notion of a CHamoru placental politics, is the sacredness of this embodied work. In this, the creation and protection of the lands and seas entail the care and use of specific body parts: eyes, eyebrows, backs, chests, women's bodies, and women's hair. Alexandre Coello de la Rosa furnishes an example of this methodical, sacred, and embodied work of famalao'an CHamoru in times of grief. He writes that, historically, CHamoru women in mourning after losing a child would cut their child's hair; they would "save it carefully" and would sometimes wear it around their neck, knotting it each day after their child's passing.[92]

Placental politics is grounded in these and other forms of CHamoru orality and the archive of famalao'an CHamoru-tåno' (and tåsi, "ocean," and långet, "sky") relations, notably in what I suggest is the sacred practice involving not simply the burial but more poignantly the *planting* of the revered ga'chong and apuya' to ensure proper directionality, connection, and cordage. In her poem "åpuya," CHamoru poet and writer Jaye Sablan further illustrates the power and sacredness of the embodied work of sibling, kinship, and more-than-human relations. Commencing with the opening stanza, from the moment after brother (Pontan) "gives birth" to långet, tåno', and tåsi, Sablan queers the CHamoru origin story and thus subverts how we might understand the tåddong meanings, terms, and footings of inafa'maolek. From the poem's second stanza on, in what follows, Sablan herself animates the possibilities of a more expansive and generative inafa'maolek and radical relationality.[93]

   sister releases
   the breath of life
   as first pattera[94]
   and animates the world

   ya humuyong na taiguini gui[95]

   from above
   totot yan fanihi[96]
   flap their wings

   ya humuyong na taiguini gui

   from center
   åtes yan niyok[97]
   wait for mouths

   ya humuyong na taiguini gui

from below
guihan yan haggan[98]
ride the currents

these, our first relations
forever sacred
born-free

then sister
with skin bone and heart
nearly spent
made one last sacrifice

her naval-flesh
fell from the heavens
onto the shoreline

and just before hardening
into rock
from salt winds
and sun strokes

the people sprang forth
to work and love the land
and one another

An example of the kind of Indigenous feminist placental politics I envision, Sablan's queer articulation harks back to an older and deeper relationality that centers nonbiological and non-natalist kinship between all forms of lina'la' (life, living beings). Reminiscent of other Indigenous feminist articulations of decolonial love, Sablan's poetry invokes the image of the first pattera, Fo'na, her life-giving force, and the value of sacrifice and giving, and imagines and narrates a cordage, accountability, and caretaking with sacred, sentient, and sovereign beings gi hilo', talo', yan påpa' (from above, center, and below).[99]

This cordage and connection in the embodied land work of placental politics appears in other forms and dimensions of the pattera's work. In her history of the pattera, the retired Guåhan nurse Karen Cruz likens the commonalities in the individual pattera stories to the fibers of the tåli (rope). Not discounting their unique stories, Cruz instead focuses on the mutual stories that go beyond training, licensing, and protocols. Like the tåli, these shared stories—pattera reliance on the support of family and extended kin, their abiding faith in God, their strong desire to help others—when woven together "give substance form, function, and value."[100] The tåli is a useful metaphor in the context of inafa'maolek values and relations—family kinship, religion, and desire to help others—especially if we consider the tåli as a kind of cordage or, more specifically, the metgot apuya' of woven and interconnected relations. The apuya', together with the ga'chong, work together to nourish and sustain the child while in the womb and later, in their proper burial and placement gi tano', continue to safeguard and sustain the child in the future. I wish to work in the idea of the process of weaving, or tinifok, in particular, to suggest yet another CHamoru metaphor for understanding the intricacies and ingenuity in the practice and labor of the pattera: that of the kottot (basket) made of woven akgak or kaffo' (pandanus), which the pattera carried their modern implements in, and whose utilitarian form and functional artistic style are trademarks of a particular weaver.[101] In their weaving in and out of Native and colonial spaces, and skilled and meticulous negotiations of CHamoru and American cultural practices in health and childbearing, pattera were able to center CHamoru women's well-being and remain committed to helping women.

Indeed, what makes pattera ideas of progress and propriety specifically Indigenous feminist is that pattera labor was first and foremost in service to/with women while simultaneously challenging other CHamoru gendered ideas of inafa'maolek, especially as it was invoked by husbands, partners, sons, fathers, uncles, and brothers or female saina. Tan Kina' described these instances when she had to accompany her patients in the ambulance and would stay with them for days even after the delivery; quite often, she would forget to call her husband. Sometimes these actions would incur a reproach from Tan Kina''s husband concerning not so much her absence as her frequent pursuit of "what you want." This always doing "what you want" was of course linked to the vocation of helping pregnant CHamoru women in general and, in this instance, of helping them overcome fears and feeling mamåhlao (ashamed, embarrassed) about going to the clinics, especially in the face of apparent complications resulting from conditions like high blood pressure. This type of assistance to recalcitrant CHamoru women to concede (temporarily) their bodies to certain modern American delivery procedures that the pattera regarded nonetheless to be maolek (good) involved pressuring, almost guilt-tripping, hesitant mothers even as that pressure (or guilt-trip) is firmly contained within a tradition of guinaiya (love), pineksai, and pinilan aimed at achieving inafa'maolek, wellness, and balance. In other words, the terms of CHamoru women assisting other women through the regulatory colonial apparatus of the U.S. Navy's hospital and modern codes of individual responsibility and accountability are still ones of Indigenous stewardship and custodianship legible under the code of inafa'maolek. Inafa'maolek conceptions of stewardship and custodianship would also continue to invoke traditional birthing practices, like the burying of the ga'chong or apuya', considered at best primitive superstitious folly and, at worst, unsanitary and dangerous by the navy. The persistence of Indigenous practices in these women's determinations to ensure the well-being of Native mothers and children at the prenatal, birthing, and postnatal stages provides insight into an indefatigable Indigenous subjectivity whose energies and time spent away from their families and fathers, husbands, and brothers could also earn them their family's wrath for how their work would cut into what Indigenous patriarchy demanded of women's labor. What I construe to be an incipient Indigenous feminism latent in the history of the pattera can furnish early materiality and opportunity to develop a placental politics for contemporary CHamoru women's political and cultural work in stewarding the lands, waters, and communities of Guåhan.

While prenatal care was something the pattera insisted was maolek and urged CHamoru women to adhere to, there were other navy practices the pattera believed militated against kostumbren CHamoru beliefs and rituals and the deeper Indigenous knowledge and conceptions of progress, propriety, and inafa'maolek. One example is the pattera's abiding faith in God (as Cruz correctly observed), which at times challenged the navy's belief in the superiority of American men as "eminent surgeons" over life. In addition, there were, as will be discussed in chapter 1, rituals around the expecting mother's position while lying down. Though perhaps these would have been considered silly folk practices or even harmless or innocuous, their significance lies in how these beliefs could very well have been tied to earlier beliefs about proper CHamoru directionalities. When linked to other, new and old practices—American, Spanish, and CHamoru—these thoughts and actions perhaps represent a newer, holistic view of CHamoru well-being and health, or possibly even CHamoru perspectives on birth and birthing, death and dying, and other elements of Indigenous ontology. In their study of early CHamoru death rituals, David Atienza and Alexandre Coello de la Rosa observe that the majority of graves are located close to the shoreline and burials are usually oriented such that feet are "directed toward the ocean," revealing perhaps differences in the way feet are positioned at times of birth and times of death.[102]

From the knowledge and traditions passed down by an earlier generation of pattera to the new generation trained under the U.S. Navy (and as also described in ethnographic and even earlier colonial accounts of Guåhan and the

CHamorus), we learn that there is an obligation and proper way to deliver the CHamoru body from harm. Eighteenth-century Spanish missionary accounts likewise speak, albeit sparingly and condemningly, of CHamoru women's resistance to the missionaries in this regard. On a closer reading of these hagiographic narratives, one surmises the prominence and strength of these famalao'an CHamoru of early CHamoru matrilineal society in Guåhan and the Mariana Islands. The French Jesuit priest Charles Le Gobien wrote of one such woman during the seventieth-century CHamoru-Spanish wars. Referred to simply as the mother-in-law of Masongsong, a Filipino commander and among the many Filipino soldiers recruited by the Spanish to protect the Catholic mission in the Marianas, this CHamoru woman devised a plan to save the CHamorus by killing the Spanish governor Damian de Espalña. Under the pretense of bringing food to her daughter at the presidio, Masongsong's mother-in-law tried to sway her son-in-law to carry out her plan. She told Masongsong that it was a disgrace for Filipinos to be treated as colonial subjects by the Spanish and that they should join the CHamoru rebellion.[103]

Other historical accounts tell of CHamoru women who employed other methods for dealing with Spanish colonization and oppression. The Jesuit historian Joannis Joseph Delgado described such practices as a possible reason for CHamoru population decline in the early 1700s: "They cannot abide the yoke of the Spaniards because of their great pride and haughtiness, and that they would like to live as they did in the past, in freedom and [following their] barbarous customs. Because of this, many hang themselves and others kill themselves.... The women ... purposely sterilize themselves; or if they conceive, they find ways to abort, and some kill their children after birth in order to save them from the subjugation of the Spaniards."[104] The Jesuit priest and historian Juan de la Concepcion recorded that for CHamorus subjugation was the "ultimate and most deplorable calamity" and that the women "purposely sterilized themselves" and "threw their newborn children into the sea, convinced that an early death would free them of travails and a painful life," and thus, "they would be fortunate and happy."[105]

Centuries later, Laura Thompson recorded several techniques CHamoru women used to abort their pregnancies and how women afterward would bury their unborn under the house. These techniques were not as well known or publicized and to some extent were only known in specific inner circles of certain traditional CHamoru healers, like the suruhåna or pattera.[106] Stories like these of CHamorus taking their own lives and, more specifically, of women ending the lives of their newborns so they might avert subjecting their children to a future of tyranny, violence, and genocide present an even earlier CHamoru history of a placental politics. These decolonial imaginings take place elsewhere in the realm of the novel based on real-life stories.[107] That CHamoru women buried the remains of their dead babies in the påpa' såtge might suggest that these women afforded them the same rituals of deference and worship for the living and the dead and that, in a sense, they were delivering their unborn babies out of harm's way and further ensuring, even in death, their protection and well-being. According to Atienza and Coello de la Rosa, there is some evidence to suggest that CHamorus buried their miscarried babies under the haligi, or pillars, of early CHamoru homes, under the måktan (gutter or downspout) or gua'ot (steps or ladder) "since they were not baptized."[108] What is not evident is whether these were pre-Spanish Catholic Indigenous CHamoru practices, rituals transplanted through Indigenous Mexican curandera-parteras, or CHamoru practices heavily influenced by Catholicism.[109]

Across the Indigenous Pacific, there is a proper way to care for the placenta and cord. According to Vicki Lukere, these customs have "served to identify the newborn with kin, ensure the mother's or child's wellbeing, and renew a visceral connection between people and place."[110] For the Māori, the fate of the placenta, the whenua (which also means "land") marks Māori belonging to and distinctive identity within new lands, or claims to lands lost. As Naomi Simmonds writes, returning the whenua to the earth, under a special tree or stone, establishes a "homeplace" for the newborn.[111] In averring his ties to his home island upon his return to Niue, while living in Pacific diaspora communities in Māori homelands of Aotearoa, the poet John Pule wrote, "I was born here, my whenua buried on this land."[112] In Samoa and the Marshall Islands, some believe if a boy's placenta is thrown in the sea, he will become a skilled fisherman.[113] Kānaka Maoli believe the iewe (placenta) connects a child to their birthplace and, if planted next to a tree, ensures the child's growth resembles that of the tree. According to Lilikalā Kameʻeleihiwa, Kānaka Maoli believe the proper burial of the sacred iewe is a safety measure that guarantees the child's well-being.[114] In 2006, Hawai'i became the first state to pass legislation that allows hospitals to release placentas to families. For Tahitians, as Miriam Kahn argues, sense of place as rooted in the land comes together "most poignantly" in the burial of the child's placenta, the pu fenua (core, heart, and essence of the earth), and the cord, or pito (navel), in the ground, especially when these rituals are performed as everyday symbolic acts of resistance against French nuclear testing in Polynesia.[115] This sense of place and the genealogical lines of connections are embodied and symbolized by Polynesian concepts of cordage. As Ty Kāwika Tengan, Tevita Kaʻili, and Rochelle Fonoti argue, the cord literally and figuratively grounds Native Pacific

Islanders in historical, cultural, and intellectual projects. Examples of cordage in the political projects to reclaim knowledge and contest imperialism in Oceania include the braided sennit cords used in lalava (the ancient Tongan art of lashing), the pohaku piko (the place where umbilical cords were buried), and the cord and fishhook referenced in the Hawaiian Kumulipo.[116]

The conscious decision by pattera to defy naval orders and to bury and plant the ga'chong i patgon and apuya' (or allow family members to do so) in order to maintain and ensure the value of inafa'maolek, of balance and righteousness, and to guide one's growth and development properly also helps explain why and how the pattera handled compensation the way they did. Sometimes they were paid in cash and were grateful when this was possible. Mostly, the pattera accepted as a form of compensation produce from the låncho or a family's catch from the sea. The navy's efforts to regulate farming in Guåhan through a "back-to-the-farm" campaign also sought to domesticate, to tame, and to make industrious CHamoru male bodies that were viewed as rowdy and deviant. The campaign, part of a broader mission to establish a cash-based economy on the island, also included a "training-for-life" curriculum in schools, which emphasized industry and agriculture, and the establishment of an annual Guam Industrial Fair, which put added pressure on the lancheru (farmer) to be productive for the sake of being able to showcase their agricultural produce and livestock and being able to sell Native arts and crafts.

Chapter 1 examines these and other dimensions of the work of the pattera. Centering CHamoru oral histories, I show how the pattera worked Native and naval spaces, hybridizing CHamoru and American practices and beliefs around health, hygiene, and childbirth according to CHamoru women's notions of progress, propriety, and inafa'maolek. Mindful of the power dynamics entailed in historiographies of Indigenous women and the politics of knowledge production, including "giving voice" to women, I try to follow (sometimes at great length) CHamoru women in their own voices to tell this story of their labor to pulan and poksai taotao tåno'.[117] Chapter 2 examines the labor and leisure of Susan Dyer, more specifically, her new-womanhood small matters and tour-of-duty feminism. Dyer's establishment of the first hospital for CHamoru women and children in Guåhan created new opportunities for women like the pattera to rework the terms of indigeneity. Dyer's palace mixers, theatricals, and dramas—among the first American socials on the island— opened new spaces for elite and nonelite CHamorus alike. Following the dialogical relationship and the possibilities in CHamoru productions and self-imaginings to transform and subvert colonial workings, chapter 3 turns to focus on another American navy wife, Helen Paul. As a teacher at the Guam

Normal School from 1917 to 1919, Paul taught and influenced some of the island's prominent CHamoru educators and political leaders. She is also noted for her role in designing the Guåhan flag. Less appreciated is that she was an avid photographer who employed her earlier training as an architect at the Massachusetts Institute of Technology and her later experience as a photographer under the auspices of her landlooker-photographer father to comb the island's landscape for the picturesque. I argue that it was the specificities of the island's physical and social landscape—its history, culture, and people—that shaped Paul's visual optic and "desire to photograph." In chapter 4, I focus on the CHamoru educator Agueda Johnston. Johnston was a student of the navy wives Eva Peck and, later, Helen Paul. In conventional historiography, Johnston is portrayed as a product of American colonial education and as the symbol of American patriotism in Guåhan. Through an analysis of Johnston's published and unpublished writings, I argue that Johnston was a key figure in the construction of an early twentieth-century CHamoru womanhood, whose investments in American modernity reveal a complex set of negotiations around a Native woman's sense of progress, civic duty, and citizenship and what can be regarded as a latent and proto-CHamoru feminism. The desires of CHamoru women to steer and steward Indigenous lands and peoples, to giha, pulan, and poksai taotao and tåno' while negotiating the U.S. navy's public health and education systems can, I suggest, furnish a theoretical, historical, and political framework for CHamoru activism, embodied land work, and kinalamten famalao'an in a new era of militarization and development in Guåhan. In the conclusion, I glean from the historical experiences of CHamoru women laborers, in their role as matlina and maga'håga, and in their duty of inadahi and inayuda, as a way of articulating an Indigenous CHamoru feminist theory and practice in contemporary Indigenous and ally struggles and movements to protect CHamoru land, life, and sovereignty.

CHAPTER ONE

I CHe'cho' i Pattera
Gendering Inafa'maolek in a CHamoru Lay of the Land

This chapter tracks the new paths of consciousness and practice in the work (i che'cho') of Guåhan's pattera. The new modes of CHamoru women's labor (and sometimes leisure), even when they broke with tradition, were also practiced in ways that continued other dimensions of CHamoru culture—to the extent that these new forms furnished the materiality to work indigeneity and persisting forms of it. As this chapter demonstrates, the pattera were mobile yet grounded cultural and historical agents; they were constantly negotiating the terms of modern American colonial public health alongside CHamoru pregnancy, childbirth, and mothering practices that were rooted in inafa'maolek and other sociocultural registers that likewise express the specificities of CHamoru conceptions of progress, propriety, and well-being.[1] I examine the way pattera confronted and negotiated the spaces into which they were recruited, especially under the helm of American navy wives and nurses, who sought to carve out a specific niche for themselves in U.S. empire, the navy, tropical medicine, philanthropy, and public health.[2]

I foreground pattera oral histories, especially personal interviews with surviving practitioners from the naval era, and juxtapose these and other CHamoru archives (e.g., kåntan CHamorita and biographies) with naval sources (e.g., navy nurses' writings and oral histories) to argue that the pattera simultaneously continued and transgressed CHamoru-Catholic gender lines in ways that forged new social and cultural work spaces from which the pattera experienced newfound freedoms and mobilities. Again, drawing on Native Pacific cultural studies scholarship that builds off Stuart Hall's reworking of hegemony, I argue further that the pattera rearticulated the terms of both American and CHamoru gendered spaces and practices into new pathways that did not automatically come at the expense of their traditional duties to pulan and poksai Indigenous bodies and lands.[3] As we shall learn, because they both chose and were chosen to work between American and CHamoru birthing and nursing practices in ways that had them traveling the geographic footpaths and bull cart trails between hospitals and dispensaries in urban (read: modern) towns and rural (read: traditional) villages and the låncho, the pattera were a particularly mobile group that at times were also suspect within their families and communities over their potential to violate respective norms and codes of behavior. Individual pattera were sometimes derisively included in a category of scorn typically reserved for women who appeared to desire modern things and ideas that had them spending more time outside the village or home and on the road than inside at their dutiful tasks with the family. Like the American white new woman they encountered and confronted down the long road, the pattera negotiated the terms of imperial domesticity in Guåhan.

To the extent that the pattera did not abandon crucial elements of inafa'maolek—that is, to the degree that they continued to conduct themselves in ways that maintained good relations and prioritized the health and well-being of mother and child, clan and achafñak—the pattera would also affirm their roles and responsibilities as dutiful CHamoru women. Measures of this success entailed their continued employment of practices and beliefs associated with CHamoru values, such as the obligation of planting the ga'chong i patgon in order to bind children to their proper places of belonging and kinship and protect them from harm. It is in this way that the literal, embodied, visceral, and discursive work of caring for expecting mothers and delivering and caring for babies—massaging, washing, cleaning, advising, feeding, scolding, embracing—also serve as appropriate metaphors for understanding the work the pattera did and value they had for stewarding Indigenous worlds in moments of cultural, social, political, and economic change. In how they were able to massage, so to speak, the key pressure points between Native and naval prescriptive practices, the pattera enabled the imagination of alternative, or third, spaces beyond the structuring binary between traditional CHamoru and modern American colonial health and childbearing practices, all while remaining in service to CHamoru communities.[4] Interested in these dynamics and tensions of indigeneity's roots and routes, I follow the pattera as they traversed and transcended boundaries by foot, bull cart, or jeep yet also managed to remain grounded in CHamoru place. This dynamic furnishes historical, cultural, and political material that can help us begin to imagine what an Indigenous feminist placental politics might proffer against an ongoing history of assaults on Indigenous lands and bodies, whether they stem from external (military and colonial) or internal (Indigenous religious, cultural) sources and motivations.

Colonial Discourses of Old and New:
The Midwifery Problem in Guåhan

> The present midwives are a most incompetent lot, age and ignorance being apparently the requirements.
>
> —Naval Government of Guam, *Annual Report of the Surgeon General*, 1910

> The present class is composed of intelligent young women, and the medical officers have given them careful training in certain subjects. They attend [to] the confinement cases of their own people, establishing a vast improvement over the former methods of dirty old women who were native Sairy [*sic*] Gamps. The medical officers want us to instruct and supervise this important work, and the next class will come directly under our teaching.
>
> —Elisabeth Leonhardt, Chief Navy Nurse, 1914

Pacific history and CHamoru studies scholars have challenged and debunked the narrative of U.S. colonialism in Guåhan as one of "benevolence" and the image of Native peoples as passive recipients of the civilizing and benign gifts of public health, public works, publication education, and the instruction of English.[5] With regard to public health, U.S. naval policies were not simply about imparting habits of hygiene to safeguard CHamorus but about wielding power and control over presumably infantilized and primitivized bodies. These measures exemplified the naval administrators' anxieties about living in Guåhan, their desires to protect personnel from tropical diseases, and their perceived need to convince CHamorus of the good in adopting American sanitary and sanitizing measures.[6]

Shortly after its arrival in Guåhan in 1899, the U.S. Navy commenced an aggressive campaign of cleanliness, yet challenged by a lack of federal government resources (money, labor), colonial administrators actively recruited CHamoru women to train as nurse-midwives. In colonial and naval accounts, as well as in the conventional and local historiography of Guåhan, the U.S. Navy's public health system has been lauded as one of the island's biggest triumphs.[7] In this narrative, the (civil) conscription of CHamoru women is engendered teleologically as the outcome of progress through modernization, which in Guåhan, as in other colonies under the United States, is synonymous with "Americanization," which in turn is understood and carried out in terms of Indigenous acculturation and assimilation into American values, ideas, and practices. Under the terms of this historical narrativity of delivering babies properly, the certified nurse-trained midwives—who continued to be called pattera in the vernacular—were regarded as delivering

CHamorus unequivocally into American worlds. The colonial mission and colonial discourse that justified the relentless (to the point of becoming normalized and banal) Americanization and acculturation required that these women themselves be properly "delivered" from the clutches of traditional or lay midwifery.[8] These nurse-trained midwives, the naval governor Lloyd Shapley (1926–29) insisted, "filled a very important mission among the natives, especially the women and children, not only in actual treatment but in imparting hygiene as well."[9]

The paternal and patriarchal rhetoric of bringing CHamoru women into the political and social folds of the United States under the dominance of white American men included downplaying if not disavowing the critical role (the big shoes, so to speak) that women filled in colonial efforts to assimilate CHamorus. In analogous processes elsewhere in the American empire, in the context of Indian tribal–U.S. federal relations, Beth Piatote situates the resulting violence as the "workings of domesticity and all of its attendant relations, labors, and affects."[10] In these workings in Guåhan, CHamorus were infantilized as "wards of nation" under the protection of the United States, although in the case of the CHamorus, who had been under Spanish rule for the previous three centuries, the colonial work of domestication would differ from other areas on account of timing, geography, and local conditions. To present just one example, the United States' acquisition of overseas territories like Guåhan following the Spanish-American War coincided with, and even catalyzed, the development of a relatively new subfield of medicine known then as "tropical medicine."[11] In brief, tropical medicine became one arena through which the United States, through the navy's own medical arm, could stake a more superior claim to European powers, and in the context of competing colonialisms and imperialisms, CHamorus would be infantilized in categorically more modern, more civilized ways under the U.S. Navy than under Spanish rule.

Moreover, through an attendant discourse of depopulation, the U.S. Navy redefined by diminishment CHamoru cultural norms and ideas of gender, sexuality, and health, and famalao'an CHamoru—the pattera, suruhåna, and nåna (mother)—came under different levels of surveillance, regulation, and violence. If there was a single class of CHamoru women who received the brunt of the navy's regulatory attention, it was the pattera.[12] At the outset, the first naval governors, doctors, and nurses examined the possibility of training the older lay pattera, but they were quickly discouraged. Governor Templin Potts (1906–7) judged them "incapacitated by age," in stark contrast to the new cohort of young and unmarried women the navy had begun to recruit and train to become the island's (and the Micronesian region's) first group of registered and licensed nurse-midwives.[13] In view of the colonial and military logic of the (engendered) elimination of Natives in order to secure land, one might even be tempted to say that the younger CHamoru nurses were being trained precisely to incapacitate and render obsolete their predecessors. The process of differentiating the "old" from the "new" in the history of health and the nursing profession, as Alison Bashford has argued, entailed more than a mere shift in the demographic composition of nurses: modernization and the bureaucratic differentiation between the figure of the "old nurse" and the "new nurse" also involved engendered ideas about purity and contamination associated with women, around which women practitioners labored to negotiate.[14] In Guåhan, the tensions were compounded by the island's own unique cultural and political history. Many of the women, both old and new, who were targeted so by the navy were also (and continued to be) practicing suruhåna, whose routine and specialized work (which continues to be passed on to this day) included the training in and use of åmot CHamoru, åmot palai (ointments), lasa, and other age-old CHamoru regimens and practices, including spiritual beliefs both mixed with and cordoned off from Catholic teachings, to treat women at different life stages. This social, cultural, and even technological complexity is what comprised the kostumbren CHamoru subject position of being a pattera and was what constituted the literal, figurative, and discursive job of delivering CHamoru bodies.

The U.S. Navy's historic bid to transplant white American patriarchy through its customized system of modern childbearing that sought to usurp the power and efficacy of female healers and midwives would have had profound consequences and created new tensions for the young and old in the context of Guåhan's social structure and achafñak system. Even if the younger pattera may have begun to question the efficacy of the old ways and the "old-fashioned"—and especially given the characteristic respect and value that CHamorus place on their manåmko'—it is unlikely that they would have imagined themselves as replacing or eliminating "ignorant" and "dirty" "native Sairy [sic] Gamps," as their elders (and teachers) were once described by the chief navy nurse Elisabeth Leonhardt (in the second of two opening epigraphs of this chapter). In my interviews with them and in other oral histories, pattera spoke of their elder and wiser female predecessors in ways that always demonstrated gai respetu. In proper CHamoru cultural context and societal scale, these manåmko', if they were not the pattera's mañaina (parents, elderly relations), might well have been extended kin, a neighbor's or an associate's own nåna, nånan biha (grandmother), tiha (aunt), and/or matlina. For example, in an interview with Joaquina Babauta Herrera (Tan Kina') of Hågat (b. 1914), I asked if she knew the older pattera Tan Marian Dogi' (b. 1903). Tan Kina' immediately perked up, exclaiming: "She's an old midwife.... She became a nurse way back.... She's so special, so special. She got out when I joined the nurse. She's a smart one."[15] Tellingly, despite the naval colonizing attempt to differentiate between the old (whom naval officials referred to as "lay midwives" or simply "midwives") and the new and young (referred to as "nurse-midwives" or simply "nurses"), CHamorus continued to refer to the latter (younger) cohort with the same term used for the older cohort: *pattera*. This form of ethnographic refusal demonstrates an Indigenous bid to control the terms of modernization/Americanization through health professionalization, to keep the pattera firmly embedded in familiar and recognizable kostumbren CHamoru discourse, and to remain in an Indigenous place.[16]

Akin to the gendered (militarized) logic of elimination captured in the advertisement for American farmers described in the introduction, the naval colonial discourses of old and new also recall what Jean O'Brien describes as the white settler "firsting" and "lasting" narratives of writing American Indians out of modernity and ultimately out of existence.[17] In Guåhan's case at the time, this bid to erase a certain lot of CHamoru women as a condition to secure American interests, in its self-fashioning through Americanized ideas of modernization, deployed American assumptions about racial purity and authenticity. As demonstrated in its regard for the pattera, the navy's views and practices racialized CHamoru women (the lay midwives) as the last of a primitive society relegated outside American modernity (figure 1.1). Meanwhile, the nurses (figure 1.2)—although also racialized as inauthentic by virtue of their mixing with other races—were the first and beginnings in Guåhan of a Native civilized kind by virtue of modernization, a twist on O'Brien's observation about colonial historiography and the memorialization of American Indians. Though the social construction of old and new had profound and material consequences for CHamoru women healers, this binary also did not fully capture (and control) the heterogeneity, including the blurring and blending of women's health, caregiving, and childbearing practices that flowed between the work of suruhåna and pattera despite naval regulations and precisely as a way to evade the naval colonial radar.

Naval surveillance and the campaign to eliminate CHamoru lay midwives began on November 1, 1900, when Governor Seaton Schroeder ordered the midwives' licensing upon completion of a course in elementary gynecology and antisepsis at what then served as the island's first navy hospital and dispensary

FIGURE 1.1 Photograph of lay pattera taken two years after a naval order requiring their training, examination, and licensing under the U.S. Navy. Courtesy of the Richard Flores Taitano Micronesian Area Research Center, University of Guam.

FIGURE 1.2 Susana Hospital, c. 1917. Standing left is Guåhan's first chief Native nurse, Maria Roberto. Seated right is the American chief navy nurse Josephine Beatrice Bowman. Courtesy of the Guam Public Library System.

in Hagåtña. Schroeder's General Order No. 28, one of the first of two dozen policies he established during his tenure as naval governor of Guåhan, masked the violence of a seemingly innocuous paternalistic project of a particular white masculinity engendered under the U.S. Navy's public health regime in the first half of the 1900s. The navy gave lay midwives one month to become certified and licensed, after which time they were banned from practicing and faced penalties for noncompliance. If that alone were not enough, CHamoru midwives were instructed to obey the law in "prompt and cheerful obedience" and to accept the superiority of American men as "eminent surgeons" over midwives, who lacked the "benefit of a careful study and training" of a "worldwide profession" and the skills, capabilities, and "responsible work" necessary to reduce the "deplorable rate of mortality among mothers and infants."[18] Although this discourse was rooted in a specific kind of racialized and gendered discourse about the tropics, and Native women in particular, which can also be construed in the context of the "midwifery problem" in Europe and the United States during the late nineteenth and early twentieth century, it was also not simply a matter of gender or the universal oppression of traditional women healers and midwives.[19] Nor was it merely a matter of racism, ageism, and classism of the kind black granny midwives of the U.S. South encountered. To be sure, the U.S. Navy's civilizing project in Guåhan that was fixated on eliminating the old CHamoru lay midwives (through the technical training of younger women as nurses, like those pictured in figure 1.3) was also structured through an empire that viewed Natives (at least CHamorus at this time) as a particularly "mongrel(ized)" lot in dire need of resuscitation and rehabilitation after three centuries of *bad colonialism* under Spain.

In 1902, through the philanthropy and fund-raising efforts of Governor Schroeder's wife, Maria, the first permanent civilian hospital (for nonactive military and dependents) opened. The building was named in her honor.[20] The year before, only a year after implementing the licensing requirement, Governor Schroeder reported that already, "among children, unclean methods at birth still cause many deaths, although the system of elementary instruction of midwives has corrected much of the old time difficulty."[21] While the annual governor's reports of 1901 and 1902 alleged many infant deaths due to unclean methods at birth, naval archival documents provide scant evidence of midwife malfeasance. Instead, these egregious claims justified the naval government's aggressive actions against the pattera, which escalated dramatically with the opening of the Susana Hospital in 1905.[22] Despite any act or gesture of recalcitrance on the part of the pattera, the subsequent written and spoken record also shows their (eventual) capitulation. That is to say, the pattera

46 Chapter One

FIGURE 1.3 Nurses of the Susana Hospital, c. 1930. Chief Native nurse at the time was Amanda Guzman Shelton (Tan Amånda), second woman seated, from left. Courtesy of the Guam Public Library System.

learned well, accepted, and valued the navy's emphatic lessons of systematic cleanliness, especially of the hands. The interviews are replete with references to "washing," "scrubbing," "soaking," "cleaning," and "sterilizing" with hot water, soap, alcohol, and sometimes aguayente (a distilled liquor made from fermented fruit).[23] Indicative of the hybridized practices, one pattera recalled: "[I would] wash my hand with the hot water ... and then I scrubbed it," and "after that, I'd put the coconut oil [on]."[24] I am not suggesting that CHamorus *only* became conscious of keeping clean and washing their hands when the navy arrived. Even in one of the first accounts of the CHamorus written in the late sixteenth century, for example, the Catholic (Franciscan) missionary Antonio de los Angeles observed that cleanliness was one of the most esteemed values in CHamoru society and that visitors were given hot water with which to wash.[25] But there are also CHamoru notions of cleanliness that differ from American (and European) ideas of cleanliness. Some CHamorus, for example, believe that the suruhåna and suruhånu are maolek kånnai-ñiha ("good with their hands") because, by virtue of having been born in a breech position, their hands are considered clean and "gifted for massage and propagation of plants."[26]

In the chronology of the navy's anxious campaign to teach "Guam to wash her face," especially following the establishment of the Susana Hospital for Native women and children, one encounters the navy's attempt at systematic and methodical work, no doubt prompted in response to challenges and resistance, as noted earlier.[27] Following a suite of pronouncements by Governor Schroeder beginning in 1900, the naval governor William Sewell (1903–4) in 1903 required lay midwives to renew their licenses annually.[28] This requirement was literally facilitated by training and examination at the new Susana facility to which I'll return shortly. In the same year (1903), the navy also began soliciting the help of CHamoru "lay matrons" to serve as translators and chaperones and to help recruit other CHamoru women into nursing. One such lay matron was Rosa Torres (née Perez). "Señora Perez," as Susan Dyer affectionately called her, helped recruit six CHamoru women whose ages ranged from eighteen to twenty-five.[29] These young women, or "girls," as the navy nurse B. C. Bennett called them, were "chosen carefully," and, when possible, such factors as their schooling, their home environment, and their degrees of "adaptability" for nursing were considered.[30] While the navy's idea of adaptability is vague and merits further analysis, there appeared to be certain prerequisites, like a penchant for English. These traits, among others—like the ability of CHamoru nurses to imitate or mimic (but never become equal to) American nurses, whether in dress or in being able to systematically replicate routine sanitation procedures—were taken as signs of Native "racial progress" in the tropics.[31] The navy's use of the word *adaptability* also problematically presumed a smoothness to the assimilative process, which negated and marginalized the complexities of CHamoru women's experiences, as I alluded to earlier. This was the case for both the younger pattera whose crossings over to the other (naval) side (and back) caused tensions between them and their families and, I would imagine, with the older lay pattera in instances when their authority was being usurped, overridden, or even ignored.

The writings of U.S. Navy nurses furnish an important measure of the navy's desires and dilemmas (at least for the navy nurses) around the recruitment and training of a particular race and class of women in Guåhan. The chief navy nurses Della Knight and Josephine Beatrice Bowman, who arrived in Guåhan aboard the USS *Thomas* in 1914 and 1916, respectively, described the challenges of recruiting "carefully selected young women" of the "highest type" and daughters of the "better-class natives."[32] In self-congratulatory remarks of the work performed by navy nurses, Bowman reported that "information imparted" and "knowledge gained" at the naval-run Native hospitals and training schools were "inestimable."[33] Noting the stark contrast between certain races and classes of recruits, Bowman described navy nurses' training of Native nurses in Samoa as favorable because, so she claimed, "girls" there were "full-blooded" daughters of Samoan chiefs and because, collectively, they belonged to the "Polynesian race," which was educated under the London Missionary Society.³⁴ On both counts—their status as Polynesians and their earlier conversion to and education under Anglo Protestantism (versus retrograde Spanish Catholicism)—other islanders, like Samoans, were regarded by American officials as not having been as "racially corrupted" as CHamorus. In the Virgin Islands, on the other hand, the navy ran into "problems" training the "better-class" of "native (colored) girls" because their families refused to allow their daughters to perform manual labor.³⁵ There are a number of different intersecting (desirable and undesirable) markers to unpack here: notions of purity and authenticity ("full blooded"), a particular hierarchy (chiefly status), a preferred religion (London Missionary Society), relatively kindred empire (Anglo), and the ennobled race of "savages" ("Polynesian"). But Bowman's reporting of racial progress (or lack thereof in the case of the Virgin Islands) also begs the question of whether the domain of manual labor was reserved predominantly for "colored girls" (even those of the "better class") or whether it was also expected of the Native women of Polynesia, who were singled out in the history of Western colonialism as sharing biological origins with Europeans.³⁶

In Guåhan, as the chief navy nurse Elisabeth Leonhardt wrote, there was "no pure strain left," and instead they were left with a mongrelized Native race that, absent their own men, could only survive by "mingl[ing]" and therefore "deteriorate[ion]" through intermarriage with the wrong kind of men—Spanish Filipino, Japanese, Chinese, and other non-Native, including some classes of American men.³⁷ In conflicting and conflicted negotiations of appropriate femininity (and mixing), the navy nurse Wilma Leona Jackson bemoaned that these young women in Guåhan had "laid aside the beautiful native costume of their mothers for modern American dress." Jackson of course neglected the fact that the beautiful Native costume she was referring to, the mestiza, was also an Indigenous CHamoru appropriation and product of CHamoru "mingling" and mixing with Spanish Filipino–style clothing under Spanish colonialism in Guåhan.³⁸ No matter the degrees of race and class, the Native nurses could never be good enough nor compare to their American counterparts—whether it be the occasional "pure Chamorro girl" of a "sweet nature" who "works hard with her hands, imitates to a great degree her teachers," but still is a "difficult pupil to make see the light of reason" or the full-blooded Samoan nurses, who, though good imitators and doing "practical work well," could not "always understand why, except that it is right."[39] In addition to being subjected to such racialized discourses of the benevolent long road, young CHamoru women were also subjected to heteropatriarchal and heteronormative spaces in the Native nursing schools. The nursing schools promoted the idea that after training and graduation, Native women would receive the highest social status a Native woman could receive, and by virtue of this training and new status as a nurse, the Native women might be "well prepared for marriage," a status that could in turn further "elevate" civic life.[40] Indeed, even while the U.S. navy's civilizing mission depended on CHamoru women—whether it be the "mongrelized" or occasional "pure" CHamoru girl—American navy nurses and doctors continued to derride famalao'an CHamoru based on their (nurses' and doctors') own racial fears, anxieties, and desires. Even the lay matrons (who were vital to the recruitment of women) were not always exempt from the U.S. Navy's racist and ageist discourse. Still, it was the lay midwives who were the bane of the navy's modernizing mission. Described as premodern, primitive menaces by the navy, lay midwives were figurative roadblocks down the long road to resuscitating and rehabilitating CHamorus through technologies like nurse licensure or, as discussed in the introduction, through efforts like the Better Babies campaign. Expressing a viewpoint in a way that CHamorus would characterize as disatenta (disrespectful) or tai respetu (having no respect) toward manåmko' and mañaina, the American naval physician Captain Lucius Johnson decried the harm in old practices employed by the "older, self-made midwives."[41] Some examples that he cited included "putting heavy weights on the mother's abdomen to aid delivery" or "dressing the stump of the baby's cord with fresh cow dung." Though the pattera I interviewed completed their training a decade or two after Johnson was stationed in Guåhan (in 1917), none of them had ever heard of these practices from their saina or older pattera relations. On the contrary, Tan Kina' exclaimed that the pattera consciously and deliberately "took care of the cord."[42] Such care was taken precisely because for CHamorus, as for many Indigenous peoples, the cord as physical connective tissue between a child and mother also represented the cosmological linkage between humans and their homeland, or at least the physical place to which they belonged, which would also bind humans to proper behavior and protect them. For this reason, care was taken to bury the cord and afterbirth in the appropriate land in order to "ground" a person in that place and prevent that person from getting lost in life or getting harmed. These perspectives stand in sharp contrast to what the physician observed and to the disparaging remarks (in this chapter's epigraph) by Leonhardt that maligned manåmko' and mañaina as native Sairey Gamps.[43]

Elisabeth Leonardt and two other American nurses, the aforementioned Josephine Beatrice Bowman and Della Knight, were stationed in Guåhan and covered, between them, the years from 1911 to 1918. Their arrival and presence marked a key moment in this story, one that signaled an uptick in the regimen that CHamoru women endured and that clearly affected how they experienced and understood their training. Leonhardt, Bowman, and Knight were part of an elite team of nurses known as the Sacred Twenty, which was part of the Navy Nurse Corps established by President Theodore Roosevelt in 1908. Until they arrived and put into place the most regimented program of training, certification, and licensure—a moment that surely heralded key transformations, attitudes, and behaviors—the manner by which CHamoru women were trained up to this point depended for the most part on the volunteer services, skills, and talents of American women accompanying their naval officer husbands in overseas tours of duty and the facilities with which they had to work. In fact, the Sacred Twenty, the first women to serve in the U.S. Navy, under the Navy Nurse Corps, were restricted from being married. It is important that the labor of the "sacred three" in Guåhan and their respective handoffs (Leonhardt was replaced in 1914 by Knight, who then was replaced by Bowman in 1916) not be undervalued or overlooked, especially in the establishment of training programs and schools at hospitals, which were founded and maintained through the philanthropy and fund-raising of naval officers' wives. Bowman, who also taught physiology and hygiene to Native nurses in the island's normal school, attributed the progress of the training schools to the "discipline" of the Native nurses, which she claimed would not have been possible "without the moral support of white women."[44]

Though there had been a handful of nurses who cycled through in this first decade, much of the training relied on volunteer labor. One volunteer who stood out in this period was Bertha Cheney McLean, who accompanied her surgeon officer husband. Under Dr. Norman T. McLean's supervision and guidance, she carried out many of the tasks of recruiting and training CHamoru women at the Susana.[45] The hospital's existence and name are owed to the work of Susan Dyer, who accompanied her husband, Governor George Dyer, to Guåhan (1904–5). Dyer expanded on the philanthropy and fundraising work begun by her predecessor, Maria Campbell Bache Wainright Schroeder, wife of Governor Schroeder and great-great-granddaughter of Benjamin Franklin.[46] The Maria Schroeder Hospital for civilian and Native men eventually became known as Ward 1 of the naval hospital, and adjacent to it was the Susana Hospital for Native women and children, Ward 3.[47] The Susana Pharmacy's modern amenities also included the island's first ice cream soda fountain. The Dyers maintained correspondence with the Schroeders after the Schroeders departed Guåhan. Susan Dyer convinced Bertha McLean to volunteer, given her already close proximity to her surgeon husband.[48] McLean's work launched a series of milestones in the social spaces that opened up between the pattera and the American navy nurses: training that was the most systematic to that point and care and attention that developed and instilled social relations and bonding between American nurses and CHamoru nurse trainees.

An important milestone came in 1907 when CHamoru women began training as nurses and nurse-midwives at the new School for Instruction and Licensing of Midwives established by U.S. naval medical officers. Another turning point was in 1910, when the Naval Hospital Bureau of Medicine and Surgery recruited three navy nurses, the aforementioned Elisabeth Leonhardt, Julia Coonan, and Anna Turner, who arrived a year later to help organize the newly established Training School for Native Nurses.[49] It was primarily under Leonhardt (who supervised Coonan and Turner) that Native nurses, who Leonhardt infantilized as "child-women," began their systematic training under American chief navy nurses.[50] A more formal and more rigorous curriculum would be established in the 1930s, wherein pattera underwent three years of instruction in theoretical nursing, hygiene and sanitation, anatomy, physiology, materia medica, drugs and solutions, ethics, etiquette, dietetics, and bandaging, with an additional three months of midwifery training.[51]

In 1916, the *Guam News Letter*, the newspaper of the naval government of Guam, hailed yet another milestone when Native nurse-midwives were "put in uniform."[52] Literally and figuratively, the image of "dark-skinned white-capped nurses," who were often paraded along the island's capital, illustrated the colonial desire to civilize and modernize CHamoru women by bringing them to uniformed conformity with the United States and to standardize and establish an order based on marks of "simplicity," "correctness," "cleanliness," and "neatness."[53] And where earlier Leona Jackson lamented the fact that CHamoru women no longer wore the traditional mestiza, Lenah Higbee, another Sacred Twenty nurse, wrote that, though the "native costume" of the earlier cohort of nurses and midwives was "very picturesque," it was not "well adapted" to the work of "caring" and that the discriminating new uniforms had precipitated a noticeable increase in efficiency and "dignity."[54] As it turned out, "rigging" the pattera in uniform did not divest them of CHamoru tradition and culture, and sometimes the navy's effort at signifying unity and compliance was not always successful. Indeed, sometimes the pattera were out of step with the United States. According to Rosalia Aquiningoc Ulloa Mesa (Tan Liang) of Tamuning (b. 1916), for example, some pattera chose to speak CHamoru while in training, even if they had a good command of English. This seemingly small act of speaking in the fino' håya in the Susana was not insignificant; it was in defiance of the navy's English-only, no-CHamoru policy that began in 1917 under Governor Roy Campbell Smith (1916–18) and continued until after World War II.

Within the larger naval agenda, CHamoru women, as well as navy wives and nurses, would labor at creating a niche of their own. Tan Kina' (figure 1.4) revealed the CHamoru terms of this niche when she recounted a dialogue with the chief Native nurse, Amanda Guzman Shelton (Tan Amånda). In the exchange below, the student trainee articulated her motives for wanting to become a pattera in such a mature way as to impress the elder nurse, prompting the latter to inquire about Tan Kina''s age:

> TAN AMÅNDA: Joaquina, did you doing your duty?
> KINA': Yes, Miss Amanda Guzman.
> TAN AMÅNDA: And how you like your duty?
> KINA': That's number one . . . 'cause [that's] the reason why I join this nurse job to learn all this to serve the patients. And to deliver babies is the most important thing in my idea.
> TAN AMÅNDA: Oh my God, how old are you Joaquina?
> KINA': Did you forgot my age? I'm twenty-nine.

Importantly, the dialogue also showcases what seems to be "broken English" but instead might be better understood as the speaking of English the CHamoru way, which signals Indigenous ways of taking up non-Indigenous discourse. As demonstrated in the progression of Tan Kina''s recollection about how and why she became a pattera, her relative or limited command of English would be trumped by her demeanor and personality as one who would not let such a detail stop her from going after what she desired. That demeanor, like the maturity found in the answer she gave to Tan Amånda, would turn out to reveal even more about the complex experiences that some pattera underwent as part of becoming trained and fulfilling their duties than the fact that they were not the young, malleable women that the navy sought.

In recalling the circumstances that first exposed her to the possibilities of becoming a pattera, Tan Kina', who would join her che'lu (brother) Felix as domestic helpers to the Plains, an American naval officer and his wife, added toughness to the mix: "I was so tough already working for an officer's woman you know." In what was a lead-up to moving onward, past taking care of the Plains' baby, and prefiguring how she was able to succeed as a pattera, Tan Kina'

FIGURE 1.4 Joaquina San Nicolas Babauta Herrera (Tan Kina').
Used with the permission of Manny Crisostomo.

explained that it was in fact her limited command of English that caused Felix to balk at the possibility of her even being hired to work for the couple. According to Tan Kina', Felix came home one day and explained that the couple was seeking additional help for the baby:

> Joaquina did you know anybody who'll go with me to work at Mrs. Plain.... I said, why not let me do it. He said, oh no, you cannot do that. I said why? Of course, you don't know much fino' [language] ... you don't know how to speak English very much. I said to him, Oh boy Felix, didn't you know that when people going to be perfect, they have to be practice. So he said, oh, you so smart huh? So you want to go with me tomorrow? [I] said, okay, I'll ask my mom. So I talked to my mom. [I] said,

mom do you want me to go with Felix to work down there together at the house where he's working. She said what you gonna do there? I said, he was telling me that he want to look for some girl that can do the work in the house, cleaning house, and to watch the baby. . . . And she said to me, but did you want to go with him? I said, oh yes mom, we are poor and that is the only place I can make money even though not high money but a little. So she said well, if you want to it's okay. I won't stop you. So okay you go ahead. So I go with my brother and that's the starting when I'm speaking English little bit, little by little until I learn later, little bit.[55]

At this point in the story, it is sufficient to note Tan Kina''s demeanor as fiercely determined, open to learning, and even more willing to help earn "small" money for the familia. That she dared to challenge her older che'lu and seek the approval of her revered nåna showed a combination of gai respetu and gai minetgot (having strength), and a willingness to push the envelope, so to speak. In this way she also demonstrated an ability to negotiate opportunities and risks. Later, we will return to Tan Kina' and how she negotiated tensions with expecting mothers and with her husband around the amount of time she spent away from home, on the road. But even armed with such toughness and grit, women like Tan Kina' in the late 1930s were to experience an even greater challenge: World War II, the United States' surrender to an invading Japanese force, and the subsequent two and a half years of Japanese occupation in Guåhan.

Tan Kina' enrolled in the nursing school in the late 1930s, a time when diplomatic relations had been deteriorating between the United States and Japan. It was in this context, in anticipation that military dependents overseas, including women nurses, would be evacuated back to the United States, that Tan Kina''s employer, Mrs. Plain, encouraged her to enroll in the nursing school. In this case, it was toughness and eagerness and also the contingencies of wartime—inflected by a gendered sense of exigency, regardless of the class or "adaptability" of a would-be nurse—that gave Tan Kina' the real occasion to become a pattera. Tan Kina' also recalled having also begun very early on to question the efficacy of the old ways: "There's one of my brothers having a wife, and this midwife wasn't really, you know, [knowledgeable] about [how] to deliver at that time. She [the midwife] doesn't know whether it's placenta coming out. So I told my mother, 'Hey Nåna, faisen fan i pattera kao maolek ha' para mañågu'-ña si Chong, ya i taotao, håga' ha', Nåna, numa'lå'la'la' åmbre'" (Hey, Mom, ask the midwife if everything is going OK with Chong's delivery because Chong has already discharged a lot of blood and she's not looking healthy). Tan Kina' pinpointed this moment of questioning the abilities and competence of the older midwife as the impetus to her dream of helping other women.[56]

CHamoru Women's Hopes and (a Geography of) Fears

To become a pattera meant the opportunity to leave home and make money, but for most women it was the chance to help other women, as Tan Kina' indicated. In their own words, Tan Liang emphasized that it was the chance to ayuda nai ("help, you know"), while Ana Mendiola Rosario (Tan Ånan Siboyas) of Barigåda (b. 1919), who was also a suruhåna, put the motive as wanting to help women "give birth in the jungle" or at the låncho and to help women who could not or would not deliver in the hospital.[57] Tan Liang elaborated that it was not just the pleasure and rewards of delivering babies but the challenge of women's health. She was especially proud of delivering twins, and helping Eugenia Aflague Leon Guerrero give birth to her daughter, Lourdes "Lou" Leon Guerrero, a retired nurse and former senator, who has since become the island's first maga'håga, female governor.[58] As supervisor of the midwifery program in the 1930s, she trained other women to become pattera, two of whom she singled out: Guillerma Chargualaf Flores of Malesso and Antonia Blas Eustaquio of Yo'ña. "All of those [midwives], I am so pleased, you know, that we get together [and were] so friendly. [The midwives] liked to give a hand to whatever the people [need]."[59] For two enfetmera, Tan Emeteria Quichocho Duenas and Tan Soledad Pablo Tenorio, the profession allowed them to spend time with other CHamoru women and help families with little means. Tan Emeteria said it was also a way of helping her nåna.[60]

Despite the potential rewards, CHamoru women faced scorn and admonition for even expressing a desire to become a pattera. According to the retired CHamoru nurse Olivia Siguenza Guerrero, the would-be pattera's desires to leave the home, pursue a course of study in a foreign language, and work in strange surroundings under the supervision of foreigners were "something akin to horror," and to follow through demanded "strength of purpose."[61] More powerful than the dread of the would-be pattera leaving the familiarity and safety of the home was the fear of them working closely with American men in spaces that—although increasingly occupied by CHamorus (albeit mostly members of the manakhilo', or elite, class)—were still predominantly American military men's domain. One particular anxiety for CHamoru families was the nurse trainee's living arrangements, which required her to reside away from home in quarters next to American corpsmen and which reduced the number of visits she could make back home to once a week. Tan Kina' described this dilemma as such: "You know the parents before, they don't want their girls to join the nurse because some of them they said if you became a nurse, you [are a] puta [whore], because the corpsman and the nurse [are] working together. And this old-fashion woman thinks that the corpsman and the nurse are going to be together. But we are not gonna be together; we [are] working together."[62] Despite attempts like Tan Kina''s to assure families that "working together" with American white men did not mean they were "gonna be together," this close proximity was often regarded as a foolish invitation to imbroglio and even harm, for which the woman could only blame herself.

The CHamoru folklorist Carmen Iglesias Santos transcribed and translated the following prewar kåntan CHamorita, "Humalom Enfetmera," which captures the nurse trainee's predicament:

Humalom enfetmera	She enrolled as a nurse
Para utungo' nai manamti	To learn to dress wounds
Lao fina'baba ni setbesio	But the service fooled her
Sa' kineni pattrikanti	Because the corpsman took her
Ma'atkila i De Sott	They rented a taxi
Para guato gi ya Tohmon	To go to Tumon
Annai dinanchi oran-ñiha	Just at the right time
Sa' propio pa'go hommom	Because it was at dusk
Sineyo' ni' pattrikanti	The corpsman coaxed her
Para luchan gi ya Dadi (Sumay)	To go down South to Dadi (Sumay)
Tinetiling, minantieteni	Stumbling and holding
Tinehtituni nina'kate	Until she ended crying
Annai dangkolo tiyan-ña	When her stomach was big
Masaiponi ba binila	They suspected she had gas
Lao lache i sumangan	But the diagnosis was wrong
Sa patgon sinini-ña	Because a baby was inside her
Ai na ni na'ma'se' i palao'an	What a pity it was for the girl
Sa' manlalaksi panales	Because she was sewing diapers
Kada a'atan i tiyan-ña	Every time she looked at her stomach
Tumekon pa'pa ya tumånges	She bent her head down and cried

In her analysis of the song, Santos describes how the trainee's living arrangements ran directly against CHamoru proscriptions against nonchaperoned get-togethers away from home between single CHamoru women and men, particularly American men.[63] These arrangements accounted for why the nurse trainees' newfound freedoms provoked criticism and evoked feelings of embarrassment and shame for the pattera and their familia. Santos's reading, however, is an understatement, perhaps intentional out of sensitivity to the woman (and her family) about whom this song might have been written. Thinly veiled in the song is the narrative of what appeared to be the rape of a foolish CHamoru woman by a cunning and aggressive American corpsman.[64] Noteworthy is the reference in the song to the time of day, homhom (dusk), when "proper" CHamoru women did not roam (or perhaps no longer roamed) quiet, secluded beaches like Dadi (Sumay or Sumai), which the U.S. Navy confiscated after the war for its naval base, or Tohmon also known as Tomhom (Tumon), which the army used (and tried to confiscate permanently) for recreational purposes.[65] This time and place—dusk at the beach—were constructed in playful but biting banter as a kind of "geography of fear" for CHamoru women, especially young, unmarried, and unaccompanied women.[66] Hence, this narrative places the ultimate blame on the woman herself, captured in the CHamoru phrase *isao-ña ha'* ("it's her own fault"). It was she, after all, who, as the song's title captures, "enrolled as a nurse."

The determination to become a pattera, let alone enroll, was fraught precisely because doing so was tantamount to abandoning one's obligations and responsibilities at home. At stake was the sanctity of the familia, the foundation of kostumbren CHamoru, and preconceived notions of women's sexuality and their roles and responsibilities as "culture-bearer."[67] It is for this reason that young CHamoru women before the war rarely left the home except to attend church activities. As discussed previously, women's participation in even these sanctioned activities was on the condition they were chaperoned. Though the navy's presence offered a few CHamoru women opportunities to enter public spaces as teachers and nurses, and thus break with CHamoru Spanish-Catholic strictures, physical and discursive mobility was still confined by a social order of domestication or domesticity.

The unpredictability of labor and delivery (and other emergencies) often made it impossible for the pattera to keep a regular schedule at home and often prevented them from checking in periodically with their families while on duty. Tan Ånan Siboyas recalled the distance and duration of her travels:

> I asaguå-hu siña-ha' tres dihas pues guaha na ha tilifon yu' ya ha faisen yu' kao lålala' ha' yu', sa' put i ti hu ågang gui' guata gi gima' gi i tilifon kao håfa i famagu'on yan guiya yan si nåna-hu. Lao, hu kokonne' si nana-hu yanggen sumåga yu' guini gi i sagan i malångu i gimå-ña, hu kokonne' para u pulan in famagu'on-hu.

Sometimes after three days my husband calls me and asks me if I am still living because I have not had a chance to call him at home to inquire about my children and that he and my mother have not heard from me. But my mother takes care of my children if I end up staying at my patient's home.[68]

Tan Liang, Tan Kina', and Tan Ana Salas Rios Zamora (Tan Ånan Rios) echoed these tensions and prevailed on immediate and extended families to help with obligations at home. Tan Ånan Rios (b. 1905) of Piti recalled being gone for three days at a time. Tan Ånan Rios's son, Jose, explained: "My aunt used to stay here; she's single, so she [watched] us while my Mom is gone. Also a goddaughter and my grandmother, we were living together. My grandmother understands that [my mother] has to go [to deliver babies]."[69]

Keeping the pattera in their place, for the sake of family, home, and religion, could more specifically have signified a desire to control CHamoru women's sexuality along gendered and generational lines. While pattera oral histories often described the support of their kin (in helping to cook, clean, babysit, and drive), there were also times when fathers, brothers, husbands, uncles, and female saina exerted political and social dominance over daughters, sisters, wives, and nieces, based on notions of heteronormative sexuality and promiscuity.[70] The younger, single nurse-midwife trainees might have been regarded as more sexually potent and dangerous if given their freedom, as in the case of the woman who "enrolled as a nurse" and whose demise was attributed to being fooled and becoming pregnant. Senior nurse-midwives, or lay matrons, on the contrary, could be trusted and respected because they were either married and seemingly settled or unmarried and supposedly less potent. This was the case for the chief Native nurses, often older and regarded as wiser and trusted. These women served as surrogate nåna, nånan biha, and matlina, or målle' (a term used to describe the special relation between the godmother and parent of a child). In these pattera stories of pattera beginnings, the role and influence of the tiha, often a pattera, enfetmera, and suruhåna herself, also figured prominently, which seems to suggest a genealogical dimension of the pattera tradition.[71] Indeed, as many of the oral histories reveal, older female relatives were an integral part of the pattera support system, caring for the families and children of pattera so that pattera could continue doing their job. In this scenario, then, the older aunts were not simply recruitment officers but—as with partners, husbands, brothers, and uncles who also looked after pattera families—were part of the inafa'maolek system. Tan Liang (figure 1.5) insisted that even though she had enrolled of her

FIGURE 1.5 Rosalia Aquiningoc Ulloa Mesa (Tan Liang).
Used with the permission of Manny Crisostomo.

own accord, she had two aunts nudging her constantly. One of them was Tan Amånda, who was recruited by the well-known pattera Tan Marian Dogi'.[72] Tan Amånda graduated from nursing school in 1924 with only thirty-four nurses before her, as indicated by her pin number 35, and was chief Native nurse from 1934 to 1948. As chief Native nurse, she was responsible for the recruitment and discipline of nurses. Some even remembered her by the kuåtta (belt) she carried.[73] Tan Ånan Rios remembered one of her aunts taking her to work at Ward 3, the Susana.[74] Tan Emeteria attributed her enrollment to two aunts (her mom's sisters), the enfetmera Joaquina Taitingfong Siguenza of Hagåtña and the pattera Ana Siguenza Hannah of Yigu.[75] It was precisely because senior CHamoru women had the reputation of being strict that CHamoru families allowed their daughters to enroll in nursing school.

The chief navy nurse Della Knight knew this when, in 1914, she handpicked the thirty-four-year-old Maria Anderson Roberto (fluent in CHamoru and English) as an official recruiter and chaperone. Knight recalled one evening when Roberto found two nurses talking and flirting with two men outside the hospital (a "sidestepping" of strict Catholic upbringing, on which Knight blamed the "tropical beauty" of the "veritable fairyland").[76] After Roberto reported the CHamoru men to the naval authorities, they spent the night in prison for trespassing. Roberto was such an asset to the navy (and to women who dreamed of being pattera but could not convince their saina to permit them to enroll in nursing school) that the navy would promote her from lay matron to the island's first chief Native nurse (1916–1924).[77]

In the colonial landscape of Native hopes, fears, dreams, and perhaps even sexual desires and encounters, CHamoru women continued to work in service to families and communities and became highly revered mediators and authorities on new and old, and tried and tested, matters pertaining to health and well-being. Even when they themselves served as agents or instruments of surveillance—as when they acted as extensions of the navy's hand and traveled the island's villages to nå'i påtte (share and impart) knowledge, or when they adhered to certain naval regulations—the pattera continued to act for the betterment of CHamoru society, assessing a given situation and taking matters into their own hands. For example, Tan Ånan Siboyas (figure 1.6) made sure to fa'maolek (work together to make good) or fa'danche (correct) matters that needed straightening out. These included mundane but important routines like making sure to check in with the family before allowing too much time to lapse. When necessary, Tan Ånan Siboyas would na'påranñaihon (suspend) a required bureaucratic task, such as registering a birth. She elaborated:

> Humånao yu' på'go gi i gimå-hu, hu check todu i familiå-ku. Pues an monhåyan, humånao yu' ya hu chule' i pesadot ya hu pesa i patgon. Hu chule' todu emfotmasion gi i håfa gi i patgon yan i nana. Pues anggen maolek ha' todu, pues every other day måfatto yu yan hu rikononosi kao håfa manatatmanu kontra i patgon pues astaki måtgan i apuya' i patgon ma didingu i gima'.

> I return to my house first to check on my family. Then when I'm done, I take my weight scale and return back to the woman's house to weigh the newborn. Then every other day I go back to check if they are OK. Then afterwards, when the newborn's clipped umbilical cord falls off, I leave them alone.[78]

FIGURE 1.6 Ana Mendiola Rosario (Tan Ånan Siboyas).
Used with the permission of Manny Crisostomo.

Delivering the Body and Massaging Points of Tension

In how they were able to successfully tackle the challenges and effects of coming and going that came with their work, the pattera eventually were trusted to physically and emotionally enter CHamoru homes. Tan Kina' seemed to manage fidelity to her job delivering babies with modern techniques and her obligations and responsibilities to her family, though it too required additional work. She recalled: "My husband was kind of jealous one time when I was with Commander Minama and the corpsman. My husband said: Oh my God, you like those people? I said: Of course, we [have] been wanting the American people to come, and why you don't want me to talk to them? I said, [is it] okay for me to talk to them? [He] said: Okay, well you watch it. I said: It looks like you're jealous, but don't put that in your mind."[79] In this situation, Tan Kina' tried to quell her husband's anxieties by reminding him that Americans were welcome in Guåhan at the time. He relents but cautions her: "You watch it." She had the final reassuring words: "It looks like you're jealous, but don't put that in your mind."

Social and cultural differences between CHamoru methods and American techniques further complicated attempts to negotiate duties of the home and field while under the supervision of U.S. Navy health officials. There is a flurry of discourses that intersected the pattera's struggle to do her job. In the following, we find Tan Kina' laboring to perform her duty in the most responsible way possible:

> Most of the time you know when I go out delivering babies and it's not going to be a normal deliver or [if it's] high blood pressure, I won't allow them [the women to deliver at home]. I told them, "It's not my responsibility if you don't do what I said and if you die with your kid, it's your fault. So make you feel happy for me to take you [to the hospital] because I want you to live and your kid." But the lady said, "But are you going with me Tan Kina' because I'm scared of the doctor?" I said, "sure, I'm taking care of you now." So we go together in the ambulance. I didn't even call my husband to tell him that I am in there. I didn't tell him that I am leaving. That's my job and I have to have good responsibility for the patient. Most of the time my husband used to say, "Oh my goodness, you always do what you want." I say, "It's my job." I travel day and night. That's why I had a light stroke in '55, over-exercise [si] Tan Kina'. But I [am] still doing it, because it's my favorite job to deliver babies. You know how many babies I delivered? Over two hundred! They're all normal because the only thing I used to do once I see it's not going to be normal, we go there [to] the place that they can help. [I would say to the women,] "I can't give you blood transfusion, but there [at the hospital], they can help you right away."[80]

In situations like these, Tan Kina' had her hands full. It was not unusual to have abnormal deliveries, complications caused by high blood pressure, or a sudden need for a blood transfusion. Emergencies like these required transporting mothers from the security of home to a foreign hospital. Tan Kina' recalled assuring one of them: "I want you to live and your kid.... I'm taking care of you now." But in being responsible to her patient, she also risked being irresponsible to her family ("I didn't even call my husband.... I didn't tell him that I am leaving"). This, of course, incurred her husband's reprimand and charge of being individualistic if not selfish ("Oh my goodness, you always do what you want"), of placing someone else, her patient, before her family. When Tan Kina' experienced an attack on her sense of duty, she responded, "It's my job." Her job, she proudly proclaimed, was to safely deliver over two hundred babies, which also meant employing available techniques and technologies so that nobody died. In doing her job well, the pattera needed to cross over such fraught spaces. The payout was earning the deep and everlasting intergenerational guinaiya, respetu, and inangokko (trust, dependence) of many. These thoughts, feelings, and values are evidenced in the stories Tan Liang shared of families who were willing to travel far and wide to seek the services of *their* pattera or to just visit with them.

The pattera's careful and skilled negotiations of the fraught spaces between home and field in service to CHamoru families is evidenced in the fact that often those who traveled far and wide to their pattera bypassed a hospital or clinic that was much closer. Hoping to avert a fatality in one such case, Tan Ånan Siboyas labored to quell the anxieties of an expecting mother who refused to go to the hospital or clinic:

> Annai hu li' i na taiguihi yan håfa chetnot-ña pot nu lachi i patgon para hiniyong-ña, hu ågang i ambulance. Ilek-hu na' metgot hao ya ta hånao para i espitåt sa' bula guihi åmot yan bula ramenta ni' para håfa macho'gue. Åhe', ti para un mapuno', na para un na'maolek i hiniyong-ña i patgon-mu. Pues, hu konne' i malångu para i espitåt astaki monhåyan mañågu.
>
> When I detect that the woman is experiencing problems or the child is having difficulty coming out, I call for an ambulance and I usually say, "please be strong and we'll go to the hospital. There are lots of medicines and appropriate birthing tools there that will help you, not to kill you but to make things better for you and the baby." Then I escort her to the hospital and I stay there until she delivers.[81]

Tan Ånan Siboyas pleaded with her patient to be metgot, reassuring her that the hospital would have the necessary medicine and equipment to help, not to kill her, to make things maolek for her and her baby. She allayed the woman's fears of the hospital and offered to ga'chungi (accompany) her there.[82]

The staunch and calming presence of pattera in CHamoru family narratives is owed to a dialectic and dialogic between the patteras' successful labor crossing back and forth between public and private domains, as well as their ability to dutifully serve familia without abandoning their own familia.

Although the familia at times put pressure and constraints on their travel, the pattera's travel also did maolek by the familia. Indeed, these gendered negotiations exemplify the articulated sites of indigeneity made possible by the ability to secure cultural roots by successful routing, by being able to move laterally in time and geographic and discursive space precisely by being accountable to one's roots. In such ways, then, roots and routes are mutually dependent, coconstituted, and productive rather than being mutually exclusive.[83] This is demonstrated in the nature of pattera labor, in how they employed new, ostensibly intrusive techniques to assist CHamoru women in giving birth at home but when needed, to assist them in the necessary trek to foreign and seemingly hostile environments, such as hospitals and clinics. But we also discern this when tension between one's duties to the home as wife and mother and one's duties to other people's homes as pattera came to a head. For Tan Kina', that point came when, as a good wife and mother, she deferred to her husband (Tun Jesus "CHu'" Santos Herrera) and family when presented with a challenging and exciting opportunity to work in Hagåtña: "I didn't move to Agaña after the war because my husband didn't want me [to]. And Commander Minama offered us a tent, [saying] that if I want to be transferred there, they're gonna offer me a tent for my family, to keep [me] working. But my husband didn't want [this]. I wish, but that's for my husband.... [I] cannot."[84] In her recollection, however, one sees a defiant spirit in deference: "That's why I'm saying, 'Lanña' [damn, shit], if you people gonna get married, you enjoy yourself first, 'cause if you get married, lanña', they tie you like karabao [carabao]."[85] Mostly tongue-in-cheek, Tan Kina''s comment nonetheless conveyed a point of contention for the married pattera who might desire to work and be on the go. Guåhan's first Protestant minister, Reverend Joaquin Flores Sablan, echoed similar run-ins with a staunch CHamoru patriarchy and similar sentiments about married women. A product of stateside American education and non-Catholic religious training, Sablan recalled the day his father admonished him for being too liberal with his wife, Beatrice: "He said that women were like cows, who, if given too long a rope, would tangle the rope and break it in order to set themselves free. I said, Father, there is no need to be upset. In the first place, my wife is not a cow. I am sure that she has more intelligence than any of them."[86] In Sablan's story—a CHamoru example of the rich genre of Indigenous (auto)biographies centered squarely and candidly on Indigenous lives—we find both the stifling effects of patriarchal views of women's proper place and the dry humor that sometimes circumvented or at least challenged them.[87] More to the point of the pattera story is that, given an opportunity to serve the island in new yet constricting ways, some CHamoru women were able to take not "too long a rope" but only the proverbial inch and go new distances to ensure the health and well-being of other CHamoru women, babies, and communities.

Assisted by older CHamoru women, like chief Native nurses and lay matrons who learned the ropes of the navy's health care system, pattera demonstrated an ability (or adaptability) to traverse naval and Native gendered and racialized geographies. One governor wrote that Native women had "immeasurable advantages" over imported trained nurses because they knew better the "prejudices and popularities of their own people."[88] The pattera did have advantages, but even as cultural insiders, they had to constantly work and rework the spaces in between, eventually becoming, as Lenore Manderson notes of Malay midwives, "gatekeepers, whose support or resistance to Western health services would determine community acceptance and compliance."[89] Traveling between Native and naval spaces of unequal investments in modernity, pattera could also become gatekeepers regulating and directing the flow between them. This Indigenous gatekeeping, I contend, can be regarded as an Indigenous form of modernity and a manifestation of new ways to discern and assess what would be good for CHamorus. The pattera were able to persuade CHamorus, especially pregnant women, to visit the navy doctors, but this, as Governor Dyer reported, was a "matter of very slow growth" because CHamorus had "their own methods," and women, especially, were "shy about consulting with medical officers."[90] As illustrated in Tan Kina''s and Tan Liang's recollections, this "problem" of recalcitrance persisted well into the 1930s and 1940s, even as subsequent generations of licensed nurse-midwives underwent more rigorous training by regimented American nurses and the CHamoru women trained by them to take over.

In pattera narratives of getting mothers to adhere to new practices and policies, we also get a glimpse of what I prefer to call CHamoru reinscribed notions of progress and propriety, as opposed to (or alongside) American motivations. For instance, Tan Kina' and Tan Liang knew that only through the constant monitoring of pregnancies—for incidences and effects of high blood pressure, the position of the baby, or the possibility of developing eclampsia—would they be allowed to safely and confidently deliver babies in homes the way most CHamoru women preferred.[91] Building on their records of success and inangokko and confidence that families placed in them, the pattera's self-rearticulations in, through, and of health and progress also provided the groundwork for CHamoru women and their families to begin to build inangokko in American doctors. Tan Kina' urged her patients to have that trust and faith because, as she put it, the doctor "cares for you."

I used to tell them, "Why did you afraid to [see] the doctor?" And then the patient said, "Oh no, I'm scared to see the doctor on account of seeing my ... you know, seeing her ... they [were] mentioning that. But I told [them], "the doctor doesn't care your bebe' [vagina], he cares for you, inside your stomach to see how the baby is, whether it's a normal presentation. That's why we want you to see the doctor once a month. Whether you're gonna have high blood pressure. Everything, we have to follow that rules." So some of them believing [that] and they [are] convinced to go see the doctor. And I told them that I am always with the doctor, because they're scared. They're ashamed. I don't blame them. I don't blame these women, but I'm giving them advice to do that because that is for their own sake.[92]

According to Tan Kina', CHamoru women were mamåhlao to be seen by the American doctors. Some were also mamåhlao because they did not have a lot of money and a change of clothes for themselves and their babies if they were to have their babies delivered in the hospital. Tan Liang added that many women did not want to leave their other children at home during their hospital stays. She also said that some unmarried mothers were mamåhlao because of the stigma attached to having *illegitimate* children.[93] The way the pattera massaged these women's sense of honor and virtue, how they sought to help save face in the face of stigmatizing remarks, reveals how off base and discrepant (from CHamoru realities) the terms of the navy's hubris and self-congratulatory project of benevolence were.

In their work of symbolic and discursive massaging, the pattera could be counted on to assist unwed women during their pregnancies, to advise them and their partners on matters pertaining to sexuality, and to support them even in their decisions not to marry. Laura Thompson, who was privy to such private matters and "gossip" during her fieldwork in Guåhan in the 1930s, noted that because Tan Marian Dogi' (figure 1.7) was a Red Cross nurse making the rounds, she was often confided in. Thompson also noted that Tan Marian Dogi' herself, practiced birth control, and that many CHamorus criticized her because it was "against the will of God." Perhaps it was less that she was a Red Cross nurse making the rounds than her abilities and determinations to make the rounds back and forth in the new spaces that permitted Tan Marian Dogi' to "teach about sex and birth control" under the radar of CHamoru Catholicism (another watchdog of female virtue) and nå'i påtte knowledge about åmot CHamoru and prubleman famalao'an (women's problem) as a form of reproductive health.[94] As evidenced in oral histories and

FIGURE 1.7 Some pattera, like Tan Marian Dogi' (left), were also Red Cross nurses who conducted home visits and advised women on matters pertaining to health, diet, sex, and birth control. Photograph from *The Guam Recorder*, 1938. Courtesy of the Richard Flores Taitano Micronesian Area Research Center, University of Guam.

Thompson's fieldnotes, the pattera qualities of gai mamahlao and being manungo' (knowledgeable), menhalom (wise, sharp), and maggem (quiet and cautious, discrete), explain how and why pattera like Tan Marian Dogi' might be trusted when it came to matters pertaining to broader issues of reproductive health. There were even times during the interviews when the pattera would stop in their tracks for fear of divulging too much, indicating: "It's not for me to say" or "That's not my business." These qualities certainly contrast with those of the pesky, unloveable utak, the CHamoru mythological bird who could not be counted on to keep a secret. According to CHamoru legend—a legend that even today exists in some CHamoru households—the utak cries loudly in the night to announce to the saina in the house that a woman (usually one who is unmarried) is pregnant.

There were yet other ways the pattera-suruhåna assisted women in having traditional forms of sovereignty over their bodies—through åmot palai and lasa, to induce miscarriage with the aid of oral medicines, such as tea. The preparation and application of åmot palai could also help women who experienced difficulty achieving sexual orgasm. Privy to the kind of information that was skillfully withheld from the American doctors or the nosy gatekeeping agents of CHamoru Catholic families, pattera were able to work at the comfort level of CHamoru women without sacrificing what was in their mutual best interests—a safe and healthy delivery (or, in some instances, good advice and practice for safe sex or a safe termination). The pattera were able to ease tensions that many pregnant women felt about going to the doctor, by helping them understand the value and importance of a regular checkup. Tan Liang characterized this assistance as maolek and essential for averting possible complications: "You find it very, very maolek advice to the pregnant women sa' [because] you can spot the high blood pressure you know, any symptoms like for the first three months ... [and] for the second three months, since like some develop hypertension and eclampsia ... like mañågu [to give birth] and they're like swollen. So I think it's very important to have them see the doctor first before they come to me."[95]

Tan Liang's use of the word *maolek* to describe i che'cho' i pattera invokes a tåddong meaning in CHamoru—the performing of what is good and right for the achafñak, familia, clan, village, and community, with connotations of balance and harmony under the terms of inafa'maolek. The pattera's labor to do the maolek thing vis-á-vis modern practices of health also gives us a glimpse into new, gendered CHamoru reinscribed notions of health and well-being. Clearly, a significant part of the pattera's labor was to translate the idea and significance of prenatal care (routine visits and monthly checkups), to monitor conditions like high blood pressure and eclampsia, and to assure patients they would be with them throughout their pregnancy even if it meant at times putting the patients' needs before family obligations.[96]

Before turning to certain American naval health practices that the pattera considered not so maolek, I return to the social spaces that existed between the pattera, enfetmera, and navy nurses. Navy nurses often served as mediators between CHamorus and naval doctors. In an oral history, Wilma Leona Jackson (assigned in Guåhan from 1940–41 and 1944–45) recalled an incident in which she was able to solve a communication and cultural problem involving a rather technical issue a young trainee was having. The problem involved having to properly set and determine the correct volume for a bottle of baby formula to ensure sufficient caloric intake for an age group different from which the standard volume had been set. The CHamoru nursing student took the initiative to ask for help from the naval hospital's doctor, Michael McKenzie, a Harvard-trained physician, but the trainee's sixth-grade-level education prevented her from understanding the doctor's explanation, one involving the concept of formula ratio to adjust for age. When the student approached her for help, Jackson realized that she too did not know how to solve the problem and so spoke directly with "Michael." Jackson pointed out that the problem lay in the explanation furnished by Harvard types like Michael and students with a basic command of English. This is how Jackson, who later became director of the Navy Nurse Corps (1954–58), figured it out. After speaking with the doctor, she returned to her student:

> "Well, now, here's your problem," I said. "The formula that Dr. McKenzie gave you will not be sufficient nutrition for [a] child that is more than nine months old." I said, "You remember that down here at about five to six months you're beginning with very soft foods, like mashed potatoes or applesauce or something like that. You're beginning to give them some food and this takes up part of the calories in your diet. You don't take them completely off the formula right away." ... And then I showed her how to figure the child's needs in calories. Well, the next day she came over, and she had the nicest routine set up, all she needed.... She didn't have the background, you see, for some of this, but she could learn. She had the ability to learn. As soon as I went over the whole thing, she knew it and she knew it for good.[97]

Through common cause around solving technical matters, CHamoru and American women also began to bond around mutual interests in doing things properly, whether to make things maolek for a baby and her mother or for serving the island community or the needs of the empire. Of such bonds of affection, Jackson recalled a touching moment with the chief Native nurse Joaquina Siguenza (1948–51), who you may recall as the trusted senior nurse and aunt who recruited Emeteria Duenas into nursing:

> I remember ... Juaquin Sequensa [sic] ... an excellent nurse, a very nice person.... A sister of Juaquina's had a very bad heart condition. She had had too many babies and too close together, and when she came in to us, we knew the thing was inevitable. She was on Juaquina's ward. I made it my business every day to see her as I made rounds, and the day that she died, Juaquina was at her bedside. I stayed with Juaquina until her sister took her last breath, and then she started to prepare to be taken out of the

ward. I said, "Let me help you, Juaquina," and I closed her sister's eyes. She said, "You have been so good to her," and she was on the point of tears. I said, "Juaquina, if she had been my sister, you would have done the same wouldn't you?" She said, "Yes, I would." But I didn't leave Juaquina alone to meet that grief, because . . . I had developed a closeness to the native nurses, and they felt close to me. This was her reaction, the fact that I had stopped by every day to see that everything was being done. I knew Juaquina would do it anyway, but it was simply to give Juaquina reinforcement, don't you see. . . . I helped her, and together we prepared the body to be taken home and prepared for burial.[98]

There are not very many examples better than genuinely grieving with another person's loss for forging authentic bonds of love and kinship, though helping the loved one with the technicalities of dressing the body must rank highly and be even more rare. Just as CHamoru nurses and nurse-midwives developed intimate ties with American navy wives, so too did they forge strong relations with navy nurses through their common tasks of caring for other women and for each other. These ties could also smooth tensions that often came with the job. At the same time, there were situations that required the pattera to put social, physical, and discursive distance between themselves and the clinics, hospitals, and even American navy nurses and wives.

Pattera Notions of Progress and Propriety

The pattera appear to have enjoyed relative freedom in that, in addition to working at the clinics, dressing stations, and hospitals, they worked independently, in the homes and villages, away from the constant gaze and surveillance of navy nurses and doctors. This mobile place, as well as "dwelling-in-travel," allowed pattera to negotiate American naval ideology and modernity somewhat on their own terms.[99] At the same time they enjoyed a certain freedom of movement, the pattera were not necessarily free from the naval gaze. And as a consequence of their mobilities, neither were their patients exempt—patients whom the pattera treated in the privacy of their own homes and in villages that took the pattera's bull cart days to reach. As an extension into CHamoru homes of the U.S. Navy's "hand," to switch back to another metaphor that is appropriate to this history, the pattera were expected to plant the American seeds of hygiene and child birthing, to be the eyes and ears of the navy's modernizing and colonizing efforts to ensure CHamoru compliance with naval regulations. Some pattera, like Tan Marian Dogi', were also

Red Cross nurses who, in advising patients about their health and diet, conducted home and school inspections.[100] This doubling up of jobs enabled a colonial multiplier effect in which the twin dynamics of two other colonial entities—the Department of Education and the Department of Health, from where the pattera/Red Cross nurses were dispatched—worked in tandem.

Much like the kottot made of woven akgak or kaffo', in which the pattera, donning white uniform, cap, and shoes, carried their surgical gloves, stethoscope, scissors, forceps, and other modern implements, the labor of pattera could not be judged by its exterior or interior but by its effects, a result of the mixing of American naval and CHamoru practices and beliefs and insistence on CHamoru ways when deemed right and appropriate. It was not simply that American modernity supplanted indigeneity or that CHamoru traditions existed in isolation from modernity and the United States. One site of tension involved the pattera's reliance on CHamoru beliefs and practices surrounding childbirth and pregnancy and their use of åmot CHamoru. These beliefs and practices, contrary to what Laura Thompson claimed, were not practiced *simply* because they did not clash or conflict with the "modern methods" (read: American practices) or because they were harmless but because CHamorus insisted on their validity and efficacy, and insisted that they were maolek. Nor was it simply the case that many of the "old practices" surrounding medicine, pregnancy, and childbirth were "dying out" due to the increased role of the pattera in attending to deliveries. This repudiates commonplace claims, based on the binary opposition between tradition and modernity, that the process of licensing replaced tradition and women trained by the navy had become less authentically CHamoru.[101]

Indeed, even the most modern or liberal pattera prevailed on åmot CHamoru, just as some healers—pattera, suruhåna, and suruhånu—clashed (and continue to clash) with Western medicine in their conviction that åmot fresko (a well-known treatment in cases of difficult delivery, for restlessness, and to spur conception) is efficacious.[102] According to Tan Liang, there were medicines that they "didn't tell the navy" about, like atmagosu, used to decongest the newborn.[103] Tan Liang, recall, was of the class of pattera that championed the need to send women to the hospital for the purpose of monitoring high blood pressure, eclampsia, or hypertension but that also continued practices handed down by their manåmko' and mañaina healers. Like Tan Ånan Siboyas, Tan Liang advised patients to adhere to beliefs that modern medicine would scoff at or dismiss as primitive old wives' tales or Native superstitions: for example, how the expecting mother's position under or near a doorway affected different factors of the baby's delivery. In Tan Liang's own words, "Anggen mapotge' i palao'an [when a woman is pregnant] ... tumotohge i petta, standing by the door, nai ... then the old people says you go back, because if you [keep] standing by the door, the baby will be born in ... ayu mappot ma fañågu [a difficult delivery]." Potentially troubling to modern medicine as well was advice like the following, which she gave husbands, partners, or fathers, and which was considered to affect the delivery's outcome or character: "Go out[side] and walk around or run ... [so that the] deliver[y] is faster anggen anåkko' i puti-ña ... makkat ma fañågu [If her pain is long ... [and] she's having a hard time delivering]."[104] In contrast, Tan Kina'—who entered nursing school as one of the older and presumably less "pliable" (to colonial influence) trainees—was one of those who flatly rejected such old beliefs: "When the time of your cervix not [ready] to be open," no amount of walking could facilitate the onset of labor and delivery, "no matter you walk from here to Umatac."[105] As Thompson recorded, many CHamorus believed that a woman should get up and walk around immediately after giving birth to her first child as a way of rendering the woman insensitive to pain. This old childbirthing custom of "walking" was called *gupu*, which means "to fly."[106]

Other pattera emphasized the relationship between an expecting mother's bodily position and direction relative to certain spatial markers and the character of the delivery, despite such beliefs being dismissed as superstition. Tan Ånan Siboyas explained, for example, that the position of an expecting woman's head and feet affected the baby's position and determined whether a woman would need a cesarean section: "Yanggen sino hekngok ... ayu ilek-ña hekngok, ayu anggen para u fañågu an umå'sson i palao'an ha na'huhuyong i dos patås-ña gi i pettan apusento pues ayugue' na manhunggok i patgon ni'ayu" (When a woman sleeps or lies down on her bed and her feet face the door of the bedroom, then this induces a possible breech presentation because the child hears this). Amid skepticism, Tan Ånan Siboyas still advised women to take precaution: "Ayu nai este ni manmapotge' na ma chachatge yu' yanggen hu sangåni na mungnga ma na'talakhiyong i patås-mu gi i pettan kuåtto, na'talakhiyong i ilu-mu gi i petta sa' eyague' påtgon para ma fañågu i ilu-ña fine'nena'" (That's why sometimes these pregnant women laugh at me when I tell them not to lie down with their feet facing the doorway and that their head should face the doorway, the way a baby's head exits first from the mother's body).[107] The same convictions, care, and measured caution obtained in cases of breeched deliveries. Tan Ånan Siboyas would massage the woman's stomach to turn the baby, but Tan Liang chose not to because of the risks, such as the apuya' getting wrapped around the baby. For the same reason, Tan Kina' shared Tan Liang's view, though she acknowledged the skills in the hands of Tan Ånan Siboyas and their efficacy. For Tan Kina', women like Tan Ånan Siboyas were maolek kannai-ña, which is why she took a niece who was having trouble conceiving to see her and affirmed that Tan Ånan Siboyas's massage worked!

As discussed earlier, one practice from which this book draws its principal inspiration is the burying and planting of the placenta, the ga'chong i patgon. From revered saina in her own genealogy—a belonging of accountability that included her parents and extended to her great-grandparents and into the early 1800s and so would have constituted a formidable oral history archive in its own right—Tan Liang learned to carefully wrap and bury the "child's friend" (also called the påres) and umbilical cord, the tålen apuya'. It is also worth noting that in her genealogy is her tiha, Tan Concepcion Leon Guerrero (Tan Chong Arugon), among the first of the navy-trained pattera who hailed from the "modern" town, not "rural" village, where Thompson claimed these "conservative" traditions no longer existed.[108] According to Tan Liang, the proper burial of the ga'chong and apuya' under the stairs or floor of the house in the påpa' såtge or near the house ensured that the påtgon would not fall down and would be protected from injury or other harm as they grew older. From her interviews, Thompson recorded that CHamorus practiced this so that when the påtgon grew up, they "will not run away from home."[109] This insistence on properly caring for the ga'chong and apuya' (against the navy's orders to burn them), I suggest, was also about ensuring proper cordage and directionality.[110] Not all pattera practiced this protective measure and tradition. Tan Kina' did not; although, in the same way that she acknowledged the efficacy of skilled massaging even though she chose not to practice it, she always honored a family's wishes to abide by this precautionary measure.

The contestations and tensions surrounding just how pattera handled compensation and money are also revealing. Though they identified the opportunity to earn money as a reason for entering the field, the pattera often accepted other forms of compensation. In fact, naval law stipulated a set fee for pattera services: in 1925, between $2.50 to $10.00, which by 1936 was set at a minimum of $10.00.[111] Even then, the pattera did not adhere to the system. Tan Dolores Mesa Sablan of Barigåda, who was paid anywhere from $2.00 to $5.00, explained: "I never asked for more, because I knew how the people were. They had many children and often the father was jobless. Sometimes I felt sorry for them and I wasn't paid anything at all."[112] Tan Ånan Siboyas recalibrated the value as that which came "from the heart":

Hunggan, ma apåpasi yu' anggen hu na'åtta. Ma apåpasi yu' ni iyo'-ña nu i minagof-ña i taotao. Annai ma faisen yu' kuånto, ilek-hu, "ti hu tåtasa yu' månu ha' minagof-mu." Pues anggen guaha salappe'-ña ma nå'i yu' guaha na trenta pesos. Ennao ha'.

I get paid when they [the mothers are] well. It's usually from the heart. Sometimes when I'm asked how much do I charge, I say, "I don't really charge for my services, but whatever you're happy to give me." That when they can afford it, I'm sometimes given thirty dollars. That's all.[113]

These practices militated against the navy's efforts to establish a cash-based economy in Guåhan as part of the broader project of modernization through the transformation of the CHamorus into productive wage earners. Even though the law gave the pattera the right to refuse service if they had reason to think that a family could or would not pay, they rarely if ever withheld such services. To do so would have been culturally inappropriate.[114] The oral histories confirm what is generally known about economic life before World War II, that the majority of CHamorus were self-sustaining farmers and harvesters of food and resources from the land and seas and did not have much cash. Pattera were part of this society, so it was unthinkable—indeed, tai respetu or tai mamahlao (having no shame)—to refuse a delivery over the inability to pay with cash. Pattera were more concerned about helping families and thus extended the practice of fa'taotao, to treat someone as a person or human, which is to say, with dignity and decency. Under certain circumstances, fa'taotao also demanded that the pattera reciprocate or fa'danche. Tan Ånan Siboyas explained, "If I know that they have plenty more children than I do, so I better [return] that money, and they give me three chickens or one small pig. My husband said, 'If you see that the patient [has] plenty children, then don't take anything.'"[115]

The ability of pattera to negotiate Native and naval spaces on matters concerning compensation points to a distinguishing trait of the pattera—the ability, according to Olivia Guerrero, to "assess not just the mother and the baby, but the situation of the family."[116] This is why the pattera may have also been considered yo'åmte (deep healers) beyond the bounds of the individuated body.[117] In the story below, we get a sense of Tan Liang's determination to do what was maolek, to reciprocate, her need to na'åhustao, yet another way "to adjust, set right, or put in order." Although they were grateful for whatever compensation could be provided, Tan Liang confessed, "I feel hurt when they know that I'm doing that pattera and if they come to me and ask me if I can delivery [sic] their wife. Why should I not if I'm available? I just want to take care of them. I don't care about money, because they are giving me something special besides money ... everything from the ranch ... especially people before, they're poor."[118]

Indeed, compensation for pattera services came in different forms of inagradesi (appreciation) that were "from the heart." The most common was in the form of produce from the låncho or guålo (small cultivated land or garden). Fred Diego recalled jumping at the opportunity to accompany his nåna, Tan Concepcion Paulino Diego of Inalåhan, on her excursions because it meant he would get to eat all sorts of fruits and gollai (vegetables) while waiting in the kitchen for her to finish her job.[119] Of one of her favorite forms of payment, Tan Ånan Siboyas said, "Ya-hu kåddon månnok" (I like chicken stew).[120] The stories are ubiquitous: Felix Perez comes home one day to find two large ayuyu (coconut crabs) on his kitchen table as payment to his nåna, Tan Rosa Taitano Perez (Na' Nai) of Yigu; Catalina Eustaquio Duenas, daughter of Tan Natividad Iriarte Eustaquio (Tan Da') of Yo'ña, described "payday" as coming home to a "bull cart of everything, from corn to bananas."[121] Whereas the navy saw it as primitive and unproductive and felt duty-bound to eradicate and replace it with a wage economy, the låncho self-sustaining economy constituted in the prewar years an integrated part of CHamoru society and culture, especially compelling when understood through pattera relations.

Pattera were also often compensated by being named matlina to the babies they delivered, which, again, would have been antithetical if not incongruous to the navy's pains to turn CHamoru society into a cash-based economy. A product of intricate relations between CHamoru and Spanish-Catholic practice and ritual, the kompaire system reflected both old and relatively new forms of political and social patronage. In the wake of the CHamoru-Spanish wars and introduced diseases, it reflected a useful and innovative way to reinvigorate and strengthen existing ties and recreate new kinship lines among surviving CHamoru families. As a system of patronage, the godparents are obligated to look out for the spiritual and material needs and well-being of their chosen (and given) godchildren, while the godchildren are obligated to pay respect and homage to their godparents, their patrons. The matlina (also known as "nina") in particular wields tremendous respect, power, and authority in the rearing of the child, in some instances even challenging the authority of the child's nåna or tiha, who, like the matlina, is also often considered othermother to the child. Besides the familiar hybridity of this form of compensation, it is also noteworthy that this form of payment for services rendered obligated the pattera to future services to the family and thus put the vendor further into social and economic debt. Tan Inga' was named matlina (or "nina") to Rosa Carbullido's child and thus became komaire or målle' to Rosa.[122] Tan Da' was also paid in matlina and målle'. Acknowledging the interesting turn of events, a spin on debt and obligation, Catalina pointed out that the pattera were still giving, because as matlina they were bound to many obligations, starting with the purchase of the båta' (baptismal gown).[123] Whatever form of chenchule' or nina'i (gift) was used to pay the pattera, it carried a degree of obligation that the recipient would reciprocate at a later date.

These reciprocal relations undergirded and evolved from the way pattera handled compensation. Along with how the pattera crossed back and forth between Native places and naval spaces and how they massaged tensions between the two (even at the risk of being labeled famalao'an chålan or worse, puta), the pattera can be understood as working and reworking Indigenous notions of child birthing and health alongside and against American naval practices. This tracking of indigeneity's persistence in the new spaces and new paths of consciousness in the pattera's work also begs the question of how CHamoru articulations and self-determinations of what is inafa'maolek might have contributed, wittingly or unwittingly, to their eventual phasing out in the postwar years. How was pattera labor rendered unnecessary for CHamoru progress after World War II? In her study of African American midwifery, Gertude Jacinta Fraser offers one possible explanation. The shift from home births to hospital births occurred simultaneously with changes in diet (from self-sustaining farming to store-bought foods) and the subsequent psychological changes in African American minds and bodies. With this "modernization" of land, body, and community—including the shift away from home-based remedies, herbs, and plants—came changes in the consciousness of a younger generation for whom older rituals, treatments, and ways of knowing no longer had the power to influence, heal, and inform.[124] More indicative of suitability rather than efficacy, clinical and hospital births were believed to be more appropriate for "modern" bodies than midwife-assisted births. Following Fraser, we might begin to appreciate how a new CHamoru valuation of what was appropriate and suitable for bodily entrance into the new world emerged, as evidenced by a new generation of CHamorus questioning the efficacy of the older ways and practices. Recall Tan Ånan Siboyas's observation about how some women laughed at her advice that they sleep with their feet facing the doorway.

The decline of pattera practice in the postwar system of health care (and to a lesser extent in theory and practice, because even today some of their methods continue under the suruhåna/suruhånu (and now yo'åmte) stemmed from a number of things: the outbreak of World War II in 1941, which interrupted nursing school instruction; the changes wrought by the navy's newly-established school in 1945, which became more closely modeled after approved U.S. curriculums; the closing of the nursing school after the passage of the Guam Organic Act of 1950, which transferred colonial administration of the island from a military-style government under the Department of the Navy to a civilian one under the Department of Interior; and the creation of a local, autonomous GovGuam that imposed its own forms of public health.[125] The Organic Act also granted U.S. citizenship to residents of Guåhan, which may have added a different dimension to the navy's efforts to transform CHamoru "minds and bodies," resulting in CHamorus conceding more to foreign forms of health care.

Long after the "decline" of the pattera (the last license was issued in 1967)— as a result of Guåhan's postwar development and modernization—deep affect, memories, and stories of the land and an Indigenous lay of the land, in which the pattera figure prominently as healers, mediators, and community leaders, continue to survive and thrive. As an illustration of this, consider the following archive story and "women as archive" story.[126] Once, my grandmother had accompanied me on one of my interviews with Tan Liang. Unbeknownst to me at the time I set up the interview, I learned that Tan Liang had delivered one of her sons, my uncle John, whose ga'chong i patgon, if tradition served, would have been buried underneath the påpa' såtge of the old house in Didige' (Hagåtña Springs). Nearly fifty years later (at the time of the interview), the terms of compensation still held firm between fa'fañågu'i (one who delivers, gives birth) and ná'fafañågu (one who helps one deliver)—the inafa'maolek relations, which Tan Liang reminded me of during one of our interviews.[127] My grandmother deliberated on whether to bring fresh gollai from the nearby produce stand or whether to bring frozen chicken from the deep freeze. This reflected a different form of a persisting indigeneity: a new kind of postwar inagradesi, respetu, and chenchule' in the form of frozen chicken.[128] This story also demonstrates how we cannot simply demarcate indigeneity along chronologies of prewar and postwar. This depth (and reach) of CHamoru relationalities of guinaiya and respetu became much more pronounced when, in my attempt to acknowledge the relations, I prodded, "I ga'chong-mu [your friend], no, Mom?" My grandmother retorted, as if to correct but also reprimand me for being disatenta: "Hey! That's my pattera!" In the next chapter, I follow the path of Susan Dyer, the navy wife whose labor and leisure established the Susana Hospital and laid the groundwork for the formal training and labor of the pattera. The Susana furnished a space through which the pattera would begin to transgress CHamoru proscriptions around gender and a woman's proper place and experience new forms of labor, leisure, and mobilities under the United States that would ultimately have them negotiating and working old and new ways of inafa'maolek in a changing but nonetheless CHamoru lay of the land.

CHAPTER TWO

White Woman, Small Matters
Susan Dyer's Tour-of-Duty Feminism in Guåhan

A month after arriving in Guåhan, the American navy wife Susan Hart Palmer Dyer contemplated the task of empire ahead. To her cousin Susie, she wrote: "These wards of the nation are so neglected by the Nation that a great responsibility rests on the few who do feel an interest in them. It is the only place, I am sure, in all the world, where our flag flies over a people where there is nothing done to teach them anything. . . . That we ever took any of these islands seems a horrible mistake to my anti-imperial mind, but now that we have them, we are bound to look out for them."[1] In a manner conveying the "reluctance of empire," Dyer deployed sympathy, concern, and obligation as a way of reconciling Guåhan's fate with her new-woman anti-imperial sensibilities.[2] In the eighteen months that she and her husband, Governor George Leland Dyer, and their two daughters were stationed in Guåhan from 1904 to 1905, Susan Dyer established the first hospital for Native women and children, which laid the foundation for the formal training of nurses and nurse-midwives under the U.S. Navy. As discussed in chapter 1, Dyer's imperial philanthropy helped furnish a new and different kind of materiality through which famalao'an CHamoru, the pattera, transgressed old and new boundaries and proscriptions and appropriated American health and childbirth practices while maintaining older Indigenous forms and practices in medicine. Dyer also became active in organizing socials beyond her domestic space of the governor's palace in the island's capital of Hagåtña. These socials—palace balls, dinners, afternoon tea, dances, charity fairs, moonlight excursions, and Guam Dramatic Club performances—were initially organized for the pleasure of military personnel in Guåhan but would eventually become some of the earliest social spaces under U.S. colonialism into which elite mestizo/a (in CHamoru, mestisu/a) and later nonelite CHamorus would enter. Dyer dubbed this labor and leisure of the gendered landscape the unofficial "small matters" in contrast with her governor husband's official "big matters."[3] These pet projects of the American naval governor's wife, of course, were anything but slight and insignificant; when examined as part of the racial and social hierarchy of U.S. imperialism, these white-woman small matters *did matter*, and thus they represent the new analytical possibilities for how novel forms of power operated and were reconsolidated through them.[4]

In this chapter, I examine Susan Dyer's small matters as part of her navy wife trajectory, in the context of an already evolving new-woman feminism on the rise—one that would be shaped by a tour of duty in tropical Guåhan. Following Antoinette Burton (in her study of British feminists and zenanas), I suggest that CHamoru women became the foil and "special political burden" (in Dyer's words "great responsibility") against which Dyer asserted her own difference and "social-imperial usefulness" and "rightful place" as a citizen of the nation.[5] In the case of Dyer, this white woman's sense of purpose featured a combination of urgency and exuberance (but also a lament over the need) to make an indelible mark and footprint in empire as the hallmarks of what she referred to as her "anti-imperial mind." These fused sentiments might also be recognized as telling markers of what can also be understood as a specific or distinct form of new white womanhood as it was forged in tropical tours of duty. This particular subjectivity and form of progressive white womanhood, what I call white women's "tour-of-duty feminism" in the tropics, stemmed from unsettling feelings of being constantly relocated and reassigned, either as wives of husband-officers or, later, as laborers—nurses and teachers—under contract with the navy. More importantly, I will argue that if there generally emerged a historically and culturally specific form of new womanhood in relation to overseas tours of duty with husband-officers or other jobs performed by women affiliated with or working for the navy, there was also something unique or at least sufficiently different in Dyer's experience in Guåhan from other white women's experiences in other tropical locales. This difference mattered for how Dyer conducted her work on the island, which continued to command her time and energies when she returned to North America. This difference had to do with what she encountered in the cultural and historical specificities of Guåhan's CHamoru people and landscape.

Drawing extensively on her letters to her cousin Susie and earlier letters between her and her husband, George, I explore how Guåhan's political, social, cultural, and physical landscapes shaped and were shaped by Dyer's new woman tour-of-duty feminism, including efforts to maintain her own version of what Amy Kaplan called the "imperial reach" while away—that is, in the double sense of being "away" from North America as she experienced Guåhan at the far reaches of American empire across the seas and also how Guåhan continued to shape the kinds of work she did when "away" from the island when she returned home to the continent. Kaplan traced this imperial reach and the "mobile and mobilized outpost that transformed conquered foreign lands into the domestic sphere of the family and nation" in the nineteenth-century writings of white American women Catharine Beecher and Sarah Josepha Hale, for whom the domestic was expanded in the way they envisioned other worlds and the mission of helping Native heathens.[6] For my purposes, the imperial reach is the encounter and the work (both cultural self– and other-fashioning), as it involved the gendered division of labor between the big and small matters that American men and women were supposed to perform overseas for American colonial purposes.

What Dyer encountered, what she set about to work with, and what shaped how she worked in Guåhan (and later back home) involved a distinct kind of tropical landscape and exotic culture that was unexpected, in the way Philip Deloria describes supposed anomalies about American Indians that did not reconcile with modern expectations.[7] Among CHamorus, Dyer found exoticism, but of a mixed kind. Instead of a people and landscape that was to be natural, Native, primitive, virgin, and untouched, Guåhan's difference was forged out of its unique history of racial and cultural mixing, coupled with a cultural and geographic distance from and proximity to the United States, Europe, and Asia, while still retaining presumably quaint traits, features, and patterns of CHamoru alterity. The difference in Dyer's specific forms of white new womanhood lay precisely in the terms by which she encountered and worked the anomalies of Guåhan's landscape and what she found to be exotic about CHamorus. These forms set the conditions and materiality for what we might view as a transplanted white womanhood that in turn provided new cultivated spaces through which CHamoru women would rework and refashion new selves in and for a different modernity under the United States. As a segue to exploring the new landscape of Dyer's labor and leisure—and as a reminder that nature, like the processes of hybridized cross-fertilization on which theories of cultural mixing have been based, is also a gendered cultural narrative—I flag the possibilities of "mixing" and of the "mixed" that are conveyed in metaphors of encounter in Guåhan's history.[8]

Four months into her tour-of-duty feminism in Guåhan, Dyer would write Susie about her unexpectedly busy life in the tropics. At first Dyer was (or appeared to be) disillusioned, because she "had hoped in coming to Guam to reach the land of the Lotus Eatus, where it would be 'always afternoon,' that is, the Land of Leisure," but realized that even in Guåhan, though "there was no pressure," there was also "never quite time enough to get through with the things one plans to do each day."[9] In other words, Dyer, it seemed, had looked forward to relaxing in the tropics, but that desire was countered by a prior investment in not just the "things one plans to do each day" but doing things that require the kind of time about which there was "never quite time enough to get through." Dyer's work ethic, even or especially out in the tropics (i.e., out in the "imperial reach"), undermined the modernist will or understanding to relax standards and go on a vacation. Being so busy in her small matters reminded Dyer that time, as was "always the case" back home (under modern civilization), cantered now (in the primitive tropics) along "nimbly, instead of striking a slow, steady gait."[10] This constancy had the effect of rendering Guåhan categorically different from what one expected to find in the tropics, but the difference also had something to do with Dyer's new-woman "temperament" and something about Guåhan and CHamoru culture that made them seem or feel closer to modernity than primitive indigeneity. Dyer's temperament differentiated her sufficiently from CHamorus of a time and place that, according to Anne McClintock, are rendered "anachronistic" by colonial discourse.[11] This residual and distinct form of authority (the new woman on tour of duty) was evidenced in her perceptions of the terrain in the "Land of Leisure," which she also referred to as her "island kingdom," where she reveled in daily walks, treks, swims, horse rides, carriage rides, bull cart outings (figure 2.1), tennis, bridge, and teatime.[12] In this way, in this place, tropical mornings and midmornings, afternoons and late afternoons, brought musings of sorts of leisure-turned-labor and labor-turned-leisure for the new woman in Guåhan.

As demonstrated in Dyer's musings, the lotus flower is an apt metaphor for the historical and cultural forces at work for Americans in the tropics and for an earlier racialized time-space of islands in particular. For Dyer, an avid gardener, the lotus signified the island's geographic marker of the exotic as associated with the tropics and with the Orient, with life at the edge of the familiar and of the radically different. The lotus also suggests vertical or layered depth to the surface-level cultural and political meanings that crossed cultural, racialized, gendered, and sexualized boundaries of geographic, imperial crossings. An example of this is in the very naming of the hospital as the Susana—a sign of not only Dyer's accomplishments but also of deep Indigenous ownership and control of the terms of colonialism by the CHamoru women who christened it *not* the Dyer or Susan Dyer but the Susana (in CHamoru, Susåna) Hospital. This naming was in keeping with temporally and discursively deep principles of CHamoru inagradesi and chenchule' inherent in inafa'maolek, even if the honorific employed the Hispanicized form of the name Susan. Even before Dyer and the first Americans arrived in Guåhan in the Marianas—indeed, one might argue, long before the arrival of Spanish explorers and missionaries before them—these islands and their peoples, like specific sites and identities within them (i.e., beaches and social halls, hospitals and garden

FIGURE 2.1 Susan Hart Palmer Dyer and Governor George Leland Dyer, between 1904 and 1905. Courtesy of George Leland Dyer Papers, Joyner Library, East Carolina University.

plots), had already become fertile places of historic and cultural encounters, borders, and contact zones, of transplantings and cross-fertilizations that ran deep in Indigenous time and substance.[13]

Relocating White Womanhood among the CHamorus of Guåhan

Upon hearing of her husband's latest assignment as naval governor in Guåhan, an elated Susan Dyer wrote, "I shall love it, for we shall be together" and able to "make life pleasant there."[14] Before their arrival on island, George and Susan occupied increasingly separate social spaces, particularly in relation to their respective roles in the U.S. Navy and the navy's part in U.S. imperial projects overseas. As a navy wife who followed the ship and her husband's tours for nearly thirty years, Dyer lamented over their separation but also relished the opportunity to travel to places like Uruguay, the Philippines, Hawai'i, Spain, Cuba, China, Hong Kong, and Japan.[15] In Guåhan, the Dyers had the "fine quarters" of the USS *Supply*, the iron steamer on which they would dine on the weekends and tour different scenic spots of the island or take jaunts to exotic ports of the Asiatic Station.[16] Of her husband's earlier assignment on the USS *Charleston* (1890–1893), Dyer told George, "What a fine ship she must be but alas—she is to take you away from me."[17] Not just coincidentally, the USS *Charleston*, different from the USS *Supply* in taking him away from her, also figured crucially in other gendered and racialized connections of dispossession between the U.S. Navy and Native Pacific Islanders and American Indians in the imperial reach of the United States; from its home berth as part of the Pacific squadron at Mare Island, California (home of the Patwin Indians), the USS *Charleston* would bring the remains of the Hawaiian monarch King Kalākaua back home to Hawai'i from San Francisco after his passing there in 1891, before the overthrow of the Hawaiian monarchy in 1893. Less than ten years later, steaming out of Honolulu Harbor upon the U.S. declaration of war against Spain in 1898, it was the same USS *Charleston* under the command of Captain Henry Glass that would capture Guåhan, thereby ending three centuries of Spanish colonial rule over the CHamorus and signaling the start of life under the benevolent and paternal terms of U.S. colonialism. It was not only a white woman that was dispossessed of a loved one through the comings and goings of American naval warships like the USS *Charleston*, even though her own interests were consolidated through the very presence and purpose of such ships in the Pacific.

The costs for Susan Dyer mattered especially early in the Dyers' relationship, when George was deployed overseas while she remained at home on the continent. The cost of being far from him doubled her commitment and energy to join him and assist him when the opportunity finally arrived with his promotion. As evidenced in letters between them, the separation took its toll financially, emotionally, and physically. George Dyer griped about the mundane work, inappropriate behavior of the brass, poor salary, and promotions, which were few and far in between. Writing from the Philippines in 1902, he expressed uncertainty about the military's mission there and contemplated his own role, especially at the expense of not being at home with his family. George confessed: "I am half surprised at times to see the same kind of emotions which we are subjected to in these dark skinned people. Who knows how little actual radical difference there is between the races!"[18] In her letters, Susan wrote about the emotional and physical hardships of being separated, raising three young children alone, and living a modest lifestyle on his modest paycheck. But Susan also had some sense of what was in store for her and what was expected of her as a wife of a career officer. Her father, Oliver Hazard Palmer, was a prominent New York lawyer and Civil War veteran, and her mother, Susan Augusta Hart Palmer, was a first-generation *true woman* whose life revolved around her husband and their children. From her parents, Susan learned it was her duty to support her husband's military career.[19] From her mother, Susan also learned that even as a navy wife living on modest means, she could still find ways to walk, talk, and dress the part of a New York socialite. Vexed, but understandably more optimistic in the prospects of his abilities and his career, George advised Susan to ignore her mother's concerns about their "poverty."[20]

While she and George were apart in the early 1890s, Susan occupied her time in progressive women's clubs and organizations like the Albany Society, the Women's Anthropological Society, and Navy and Army Auxiliaries. Here, she was introduced to expressions of new womanhood. Even George noticed the change, commenting that he need not worry about her solitude since she seemed "to have grown into a philosophically minded young person, quite independent in character."[21]

It was her involvement in the Cobweb Society, as one of its original twelve members, that suggests her embrace of bolder new-womanhood values even before she came to Guåhan. These values would inform her work in Guåhan. Her work and her values would in turn be shaped by what she encountered there, the sum of which could be viewed as the propagation of newer forms of womanhood as a result of transplanting, taking root, and being grafted in colonial relations with specific Indigenous peoples in specific places in a zone understood in binary opposition to modern American stateside homes and societies.

Established in January 1890, the Cobweb Club was an all-women's literary organization in Washington, D.C. Its founder and president was the author and philanthropist Margaret Jane Mussey Sweat, and its original membership included a cadre of elite women, such as Phoebe Apperson Hearst, Edith Horner Hawley, Aileen Adine Bell, Rebekah Black Hornsby, and Alice Worthington Winthrop.[22] The Cobwebs, as they called themselves, met weekly. At their preliminary meeting on January 11, 1890, which Dyer attended, the Cobwebs agreed to the "utmost freedom of discussion," which was to be "kept a profound secret from the public."[23] The club read, discussed, and published on a variety of topics: religion, history, patriotism, self-sacrifice, nature, literature, travel, hospital work, and women's suffrage. The club hosted new-women intellectuals, suffragists, and feminists, including leading thinkers on the so-called Indian question, anthropologist Alice Fletcher and Amelia Quinton, co-founder of the Women's National Indian Association.[24]

A highlight for Dyer was the club's private audience with Susan B. Anthony. In a letter to George, and amid a clash and complement of competing notions of white womanhood, Susan described Anthony's refinement and dignity (amid her force, wisdom, charisma, and authority), particularly as they were evident in her views "against man and man's oppression of women." She continued, calling Anthony a "very nice old lady" and saying that "the meeting was very enjoyable and suggestive.... Many bright things were said and the women were all so in earnest. Mrs. Anthony sat entranced in a big arm chair, dressed very nicely in black silk with the inevitable little shawl, she always uses one but this time it was white—not red, and displayed her feet in blue sensible laced shoes almost guiltless of heel in charming abandon."[25]

In fellow Cobweb Margaret Sweat's own retelling of Susan B. Anthony's visit, however, not all the members (including Susan) were as comfortable with the kind of womanhood that Anthony represented. The Cobwebs, according to Sweat, asked Anthony about what "home life" was like for suffragists. More specifically, they asked if these women lost "refinement and domestic attractiveness" on account of their spending time and effort on "the management of public and political matters." Anthony replied no, explaining as well that any decision on their part to express their opinions, to "contribute questions to daily life"—that is, rights that would be bolstered by women's right to vote—would not cause dissension in the family. Engaging in "public questions," she further assured them, did not mean "women would lose affectionate and sentimental influence."[26] Dyer may or may not have been among the anxious members who were prodding Anthony; for all her embrace of the ideals of the new forms of white womanhood, she grappled with these new forms that valorized speaking out (or at least sharing opinions) on women's rights in public. These moments and tensions can be discerned when Sweat's journals and the Cobweb annals are juxtaposed with Dyer's letters to George. Such tensions, for instance, on the question or value of subordinating or sacrificing one's own opinions or interest for the betterment of the whole would also manifest in her work among the CHamorus of Guåhan. Her views on the value of "self-sacrifice" appeared in a paper she wrote and presented to the group. According to Sweat, only Dyer and another woman maintained the position that "no individual has the right to demand his own happiness but should find his satisfaction in self-sacrifice and in aiding the advancement and development of the race."[27]

Dyer's resistance, or at least her ambivalence to certain strands of new womanhood and feminism on the rise, is palpable in her writings to George on two instances: the first, around the club's discussion of the British South African

Olive Schreiner's 1883 novel *The Story of an African Farm* and the second, on a short story about Commodore Oliver Hazard Perry's victory over the British at Lake Erie in the War of 1812. Though ostensibly about other political and military intrigues, both also implicate British and American settler and military colonialism in Indigenous lands and among Indigenous peoples who are erased from the narratives. Schreiner's work has been hailed as one of the first (white) feminist novels for what some describe as its bold centering of topics like women's political and social independence, divorce, and premarital sex. Though "all the other Cobwebs admired" it, Dyer told her husband (in the letter) she found the novel wreaked of "pessimism" and "was unhealthful in tone and unnecessary."[28] Dyer found the short story of Commodore Perry's victory at Lake Erie, for its part, interesting and "well written."[29] More substantively, she thought the story elicited "quite a discussion on patriotism"—a topic one of the Cobwebs insisted was a thing of the past but which Dyer "maintained was as much alive as ever."[30]

Dyer's hesitation—her preference to "self-sacrifice" individual opinion and interest for one's "race," which in the question of patriotism is conflated with one's "nation"—harked back to influences in her upbringing and the circumstances she was experiencing at the time. Not only was her own father a career army officer who became a successful lawyer and a judge and so was committed to serving the (U.S. nation-state's) laws of the land, but he was actually named after Commodore Oliver Hazard Perry, the hero of the naval battle at Erie and the principal subject of the story she had just read while her own naval officer husband was sitting on board the USS *Charleston* docked at Mare Island, and which, as we learned, played a prominent role in the United States' *anti-imperial* crusade against Spain, steaming into Guåhan's Apra Harbor and capturing the island in 1898, after which it joined Admiral George Dewey's fleet in Manila Bay. As the spouse of a naval officer on such overseas assignments and as a daughter taught to be the "good" military wife by her own father, Dyer unsurprisingly took the minority position to subordinate her personal opinions to that of the race/nation and defend American patriotism.

In the United States, this defense of patriotism was needed because there were many anti-imperialists challenging the integrity of the nation, while overseas there were yet different reasons for supporting the United States' imperial venture, or at least showing loyalty to the country. In a later letter to her cousin Susie (the one that opens this chapter), Susan defended her defense of American imperialism despite her "anti-imperial mind" by reasoning that the action had already been done and that the social and welfare needs of those unfortunate Natives who were now under the flag of the United States were not being addressed or cared for. Yet equally important, not all Natives overseas were "happy" and "smiling" toward American overtures.[31] The outward shows of hostility, moreover, were causes for concern and caution over whether women should be allowed to join their military husbands abroad. On one assignment off the coast of Cuba, George tried to convince Susan to postpone her visit because of anti-American sentiment there. George warned Susan of anti-American sentiment even on board American ships, like the USS *Yankton*, where Japanese servants defamed the U.S. flag.[32]

In the Philippines, George Dyer encountered similar anti-imperial sentiment when, during one theatrical performance, he witnessed Filipino male actors trampling on the American flag, while a female actor waved the Katipunan flag and declared its superiority.[33] Though the Philippine-American War had officially ended by the time George Dyer arrived in the Philippines, there was still much fighting and resistance. Unlike the picturesque tropical Guåhan landscape, where Susan found "tall trunks and wave plumed tops" of the coconut palms outlined the "darkening sky," and where she found "gentle brown people" at cabin doors "[standing and] singing together," the political, social, and cultural scenery that met George Dyer in the Philippines was far from quaint. Filipinos were not all "happy," "smiling," or "saluting" the United States, as Susan Dyer opined of the CHamorus.[34] In this particular "theater" of American empire, as such spaces of masculinist performativities are named in both military and cinematic discourses about the Pacific, the Natives were not only restless; they were openly defiant, through literal performances, like "seditious plays."[35] In these two similar yet distinct cultures of U.S. imperialism at the far ends of the United States' imperial reach across the Pacific Ocean, the CHamorus were figured as good or at least docile while the Filipinos were figured as unruly rebels rallying around their own flag. These differing perceptions and realities, coupled with a specific naval masculinist narrative around what constituted appropriate maleness or femaleness structured the experiences of white women in the tropics and on the continent.[36]

If the circumstances of Indigenous political and social restlessness in the Philippines were not enough to make the islands no place for American women, George Dyer speculated that in Cavite, the "poor girls" who come out as teachers "must have been pretty hard up at home" despite all the attention and "good time" they seemed to be enjoying "from a young woman's standpoint."[37] Although he did not elaborate on what he meant or what exactly constituted a "good time," we can be certain George Dyer was shaking his head reproachfully, whether over public displays or private affairs or perhaps simply over their sheer presence in Cavite away.[38] In any case, we can also be certain that how George viewed American women who ventured out to the tropics would have also mediated how his wife, Susan, would or could articulate tensions in her mind through the kind of work she would do both in Guåhan and back in the continental United States. The mediating or shaping power of George Dyer's and white American societal viewpoints over Susan Dyer's subjectivity and work can be gleaned in the judgments about the proper role and corresponding value of the status of white American women, initially in their capacities as teachers and later as nurses or just as wives. If teaching was, at least initially, the only acceptable profession that a white woman might find out in the tropics, the job of being a teacher there became an especially surveilled site for the likelihood of social and moral degeneration. Cavite, where Dyer was stationed, was a hotbed of Filipino resistance, and in the context of "unruly" behavior by the Natives there, white womanhood was scrutinized even more for its potential to be out of line. The site of intense battles during the Philippine revolution against Spain (1896–1902), and later during the Philippine-American War (1899–1902), Cavite was also home to Filipino revolutionaries like General Emilio Aguinaldo, who led his armies in both wars.

Moreover, gender-specific proscriptions were linked with a need for proper amenities for white women in the tropics, which stemmed from a cult of domesticity and a chivalrous sense of protecting women. In communiqués between George and Susan, the fraught debate between an unrelenting husband and a wife who could be obstinate—even independent thinking—over whether she could and should join him in Cavite also furnished additional elements that help us understand men's anxieties about women's presence and decorum in the tropics, which women had to work with. He told Susan that having her in Cavite would be "more of an aggravation than a comfort" and that, even in Manila, the "necessary outlay" would require a carriage for which they lacked the means.[39] Alongside Euro-American anxieties about the tropics (dust, mosquitoes, heat, monotony of life) and the political geography of such places, then, there were also naval patriarchal concerns over the availability of accoutrements of presumed civilization as a precondition for women's place and mobility across imperial circuits. While it could very well have been the case that there were "absolutely no quarters available in Cavite," in Manila, naval officers having "extra means" or the "means of borrowing" would play no small role in ensuring the proper respectability and femininity for women, but as regulated, dictated, or "naturally" qualified by such factors as age, marital status, and emotional and physical ability to survive the tropics. "The girls" (Dyer's daughters), for example, "could live in Manila," but Susan "would have to keep out of sight."[40] The need to shelter wives and mothers—what a carriage made possible—expressed a white male chauvinism duty bound to protect white women from the deleterious effects of the tropics and possibly even from Natives with wandering or peering eyes. George Dyer's inability to afford or acquire a vehicle was the equivalent of not being able to extend his "protective shield" over Susan and their daughters, of not being able to do his job on the domestic front.[41] George expressed this filial protection in letters to Susan during their separation when he lamented his longing "for a patriarchal house with every one around" and the bliss of returning to a good home, which meant a good wife.[42] But even for good wives, tropical tours of duty in exotic island settings had the potential to become sites through which unstable categories of white womanhood, if only in transit or transition, experienced alterity. Despite George Dyer not having the "entire disposition" of tugs, laundries, transports, horses, wagons, and "a fine house provided by the government" and all the "attention to his family" that a high-ranking officer always gets (or is always supposed to get), this predicament did not negate Susan's or their daughters' wanderlust.[43] The eldest, Susan "Daisy," looked forward to adventures occasioned by her father's overseas assignments. On the eve of the Spanish-American War, when the family's plans to join Dyer in Madrid were interrupted, Daisy looked past the city's ongoing riots and dangers with a suffragist lament of her own:

> This is the day that we were to have started for Madrid.... There has been a riot of officers in Havana, and there has been much excitement in Madrid—so Father has thought best to put off our going for a day or so.... He is afraid to have us in Madrid should there be a revolution—which seems not only possible but probably [sic]. Our presence there in a time of danger would embarrass him terribly—but... what an experience it would be!! It is so unbearable at times to think that one is a woman and has got to remain one, until the... Grim old Man emancipates one![44]

We might read the "Grim old Man" as a reference to father and country, except for the fact that the country is gendered female (mother country with founding fathers and fighting fathers and sons) and for the fact that white women have historically supported the paternal cause of white nation building, as Daughters of the Revolution or as obedient and dutiful wives and daughters, even as they have struggled with progressive forms of articulating these identities. Under the lens of colonialism at home and abroad, these articulations would also have to deal with the specifics of the encounter—in the landscape, in the peoples, and in the anxieties experienced by their husbands and fathers over their wives and daughters' presence and status in the imperial reach.

Unlike the Philippines and Cuba (and Madrid, in Spain, itself long imagined an anachronism as far as European nations go), tropical Guåhan seemed inviting. This explains why the Dyers reserved their fondest memories for Guåhan. It was only in Guåhan, wrote Susan, that the navy governor was "absolutely independent," his "own master entirely."[45] Once there, the Dyers had access and means to what Susan characterized as the very best of accoutrements and "all the pleasant, lovely things" that ever came to them. Susan likened George's newfound social status to that of the British statesman George Nathaniel Curzon, who may have had "400,000 for every one of George's people, but to his 10,000 George is every bit as important as Lord Curzon is to his four hundred millions."[46] Thanks to Guåhan, the Dyers were nothing short of the social and political equivalents of India's viceroy and his wife, Lady Mary Victoria Leiter. In Guåhan, they had a luxuriously furnished palace, a Steinway, menservants (and "plenty of them"), a Victoria, a pair of ponies, a vegetable farm, and a lovely garden where they had tea every afternoon.[47] Adding to their "royalty" was the fact that they had their own army (or so it seemed to Susan), their own band, and in effect their own iron steamer, the USS *Supply*. If she followed the ship and the flag dutifully, it seems the ship and the flag reciprocated the favors and the privileges.

At the same time, however, Guåhan's tropical landscape and the CHamoru people also furnished something for Susan Dyer that made her feel at times secure, affirmed, and in control of her mirroring roles as dutiful wife and vital helper of the national cause, albeit in the domesticated realm of the small matters, and at other times, not so much undone in these but the opposite, feeling particularly outside and above these domesticated realms. It was in how she experienced the residual vestiges of Spain's monarchical and royal accoutrements—in the palace gardens (built and maintained by the agents of a supposedly retrograde form of European civilization) and the palace socials—that she had experienced uplifting sentiments and affirmations that seemed to separate her from and even elevate her into a category above the social order of her own husband and what a white woman could possibly experience in tropical tours of duty. For this reason, she spent considerable time and energy working at activities associated with these sites. Ironically, it was also in the work that she did in these spaces that she encountered CHamorus and through which CHamorus themselves would find sites of new social and material practices to suit their own interests. In the palace gardens and terraces surrounded by exotic flora and fauna (figure 2.2) and at the palace socials in intimate and romantic settings, Susan Dyer described her experiences as "dreamlike" and "unreal" even as she continued to describe the island in familiar,

FIGURE 2.2 Susan Dyer, Governor's Palace, between 1904 and 1905. Courtesy of George Leland Dyer Papers, Joyner Library, East Carolina University.

canonical, and racist terms like the "backwater" into which she would drift momentarily.[48] In light of these discrepancies, we might understand this particular expression of backwaterness as something other than merely godforsaken. Here, backwaterness was a place of difference that birthed new cultural forms. In Guåhan, the spheres through which these differences could take shape were in the small matters and in the work of organizing leisure and recreation typically deemed as the appropriate and complementary role of the big matters of naval officers, though, in fleeting moments of dreamlike unrealness, they could also point to new and potent cultural and political possibilities for both white women in the tropics and Indigenous peoples, who have long histories of strategically engaging the things, ideas, and peoples who stumble or come rushing and crashing upon their shores.

Palace Mixers and a Mixing of Other Sorts

The place of women and wives in empire was not only dictated from the outset by Victorian notions of women's proper place and later by what scholars have recognized as the crisis of masculinity but by a particular sensibility of the military and the navy concerning women, especially the wives and daughters of naval officers.[49] The ease and unease in which women's abilities to move about the routes of empire depended on their husbands' military rank and title, along with certain technologies and provisions of empire, like a docked ship or horse-drawn carriage. A woman's place in empire was also determined by her physical and mental ability to withstand the tropics. Indeed, George often referred to Susan as a "Steady Old Reliable Pine Knot."[50] The genre of work that was expected in Susan Dyer's labor in leisure, along with her steady, hard, resilient but also flexible temperament, was considered crucial to the welfare of Americans if they were to do their part in bringing what they believed to be an enlightened colonialism to the CHamorus. This kind of work was considered so vital for combating the perceived adversities in the tropics that Governor Dyer in 1905 established the Department of Health and Charities for personnel in a place whose peoples he described as "poor, ignorant, very dirty."[51]

In Guåhan, Susan Dyer was charged with making life pleasant for the military, which entailed entertaining them and also helping the "poor people of Guam," which was a direct order from her governor husband and also required some innovation on her part.[52] Her labor to provide leisure and gaiety for the military and her leisure time spent on charitable and philanthropic work for the CHamorus in the domain of the intimate may have been examples of the unanticipated consequences of colonial practice in Guåhan. Though technically military and civilian matters were supposed to be handled separately, the reality was that the governor's civilian tasks often converged with his military tasks as commandant. One direct result of this coupling was that money used for civilian matters, like George Dyer's hiring of teachers, came out of the navy's treasury instead of the Island Treasury. George Dyer even declared the entire island a naval station, likening Guåhan to a ship "where the narrowness of the quarters and the object to be attained can only be accommodated by a single director."[53] In how she did the work of a navy wife, there were moments when Susan Dyer might as well have been the commander of the ship, or perhaps ruler of the high seas on which the ship and the nation coursed. In these transient moments, her "kingdom" of Guåhan was bigger than an island, a nation, or an empire.

This view had profound implications for the ordinary protocol of the military, which typically followed strict codes of conduct around rank, title, status, and gender. It also had significant impact on how the wife as helpmeet, a status assigned to missionary and military wives, handled civilian and military affairs.[54] As helpmeet or helpmate—or in keeping with the ship metaphor, first mate or shipmate—Susan Dyer also understood the need in Guåhan to be flexible. "Our society," she wrote, is "mixed, for in a little place like this, one cannot draw lines too closely."[55] But in doing her part to entertain the military and drawing from prior social circles in New York, Dyer perhaps "mixed" things up just a bit too much and blurred lines one too many times. While perhaps it cannot be said that Dyer disturbed the status quo drastically, it is nonetheless important to recognize how her palace socials and other leisure work paved the way for CHamoru entry into spaces ordinarily reserved for Americans, which would eventually become the domain of CHamoru women like Agueda Johnston (chapter 4), who worked her way into such elite social spaces. This work, especially the palace socials (or palace mixers, as I prefer to call them, for their propensity to blur or disrupt the colonial situation, if even a bit), required a coalescing and mixing of racialized and gendered bodies, given the navy's lack of resources from the federal government in its administration of the island.

Dyer's socials exemplified her efforts to transplant white womanhood, which drew from her earlier experiences and networks in elite New York circles. As Native studies scholars have demonstrated, these earlier spaces and networks were and continue to be the violent legacies of settler colonialism, which in that part of Indian country equates to Haudenosaunee land dispossession.[56] In Guåhan, she organized many socials in her home, the governor's palace. These included biannual balls, weekly dinners, frequent dances, and afternoon tea every day except Thursdays, which was reserved for other wives in their weekly "Ladies Day" mess dinners at the Service Club. With these wives, and also the enlisted men, Dyer established and organized social clubs and social events like the Guam Dramatic Club, which advertised monthly events at the Grand Opera House in Hagåtña, such as its "side-splitting Negro impersonations" and "high-class vaudeville" performances.[57] These racialized performances, organized in the first two months of Dyer's arrival in Guåhan, which did not feature CHamoru performers, were not of the same caliber or scale of performances staged in places like Australia, Hawai'i, and

New Zealand as part of the evolving Pacific circuit and expanding U.S. empire, but they do suggest an effort on the part of Americans and American women like Dyer to keep up to par with events happening elsewhere if only to make it into the island's local Colony Chat column of the naval-run *Guam News Letter*, which was sent to stateside family and friends. Susan Dyer coached and chaperoned the Guam Strollers, an offshoot of the Guam Dramatic Club, which featured her daughters, Daisy and Dorothy. Those who formed the mixed audiences for the Dyer performances—the marines, hospital corpsmen, and elite CHamorus—eventually became organizers and cosponsors of these events. Up until the club's fifth performance in June 1904, when a small group of CHamorus began to perform on these stages, Americans were the actors and musicians. Of particular interest is the entry of certain Americans, like the former U.S. marine and postmaster of Guam, James Holland Underwood, who served as head usher for the Guam Dramatic Club from September 1904 to May 1905 and later married into CHamoru families. These individuals and their marriages with CHamorus would usher in a new generation of elite political and cultural brokers, some of whose "mixed" children, like the "troublesome half-castes" Damon Salesa has described in Britain and New Zealand, posed problems for naval governors obsessed with preserving white racial purity, like Governor William Gilmer (1918–20).[58] In due course, CHamorus, mixed-blooded or not, "troublesome" or otherwise, would also come to invest heavily in social practices initially established by American military wives like Dyer for American military purposes in the tropics.[59]

The biannual governor's ball was something Susan Dyer was expected to do, however, this event was unique in that CHamorus, noncommissioned officers, and enlisted personnel were allowed to attend. There were conditions, though: only elite (and later mixed-blood) CHamorus and enlisted American men who wore coats were allowed—the relatively relaxed proscriptions and innovations that Susan Dyer claimed were her doing. Dyer boasted about these "firsts" to her cousin Susie: the first ball given by an American naval governor and the first one that enlisted men were invited to. The first invitees from the CHamoru side were members of the "Slipper Gang" and "Shoe Gang," and specifically not invited were those of the "Bare Foot Gang."[60] Little is known of these "gangs." It is not clear how formal they were, who definitively gave them their names, and how membership was determined. Although a handful of names are associated with the first two, the Slipper and Shoe Gangs, the third appears to be a tongue-in-cheek reference to the rank-and-file CHamorus, who tended not to wear any shoes at all. The Slipper Gang for instance might have referred loosely to an upper class of CHamorus who tended to wear slippers, called chinelas in Spanish. The Shoe Gang was the name supposedly given by American marines to the manakhilo' class of CHamoru-Spanish mestisa, many of whom married American men, and in at least one other historical reference, it referred to American men who married CHamoru women.[61]

Susan "Daisy" Dyer attributed these innovations to her mother's ability to make the best of any "transient situation" as a condition of being a navy wife and to "live in each new place as though it were her permanent home"—another way of saying that perhaps her mother had the ability to dwell in the present moment.[62] Insofar as each new place entailed imperial expansion, Dyer's mantra of replicating home permanently amounted to nothing less than a bid, in Julia Ann Clancy-Smith and Frances Gouda's terms, at "domesticating empire" as well as domesticating the colonies and its peoples.[63] Dyer tried to replicate the permanence of her own stateside home by bringing specific belongings, like books and pictures, which mirrored to a certain extent her importing of social events and styles from prior civilian and military circles in New York and Washington, D.C.[64] What was imported, however, had to complement or flex with local conditions and needs as determined by the navy's gendered view of the physical, social, and cultural landscape, which included but also excluded CHamoru determinations and perspectives.

This flexibility, which was tied to the uncertainty of transience and the payout of permanence, was the nuanced point of difference between the work of new-women navy wives in the early twentieth century and that of an earlier parade of missionary and settler colonial wives. In contemplating the establishment of a hospital, for example, Dyer paused to consider: "Will all our efforts be only temporary?"[65] These negotiations of the fleeting and temporary nature of the military wife's new-woman work are what laid the groundwork for white woman's tour-of-duty feminism.[66] We must also not forget what those close to Dyer described as her "temperament," especially in the tropics, where many (if not most) military wives believed "temperate-zone reared women" could not survive lest they become physically or mentally ill.[67] For safe measure, just to ensure her legacy lived on long after her departure, Dyer raised double the amount of seed money she estimated for the hospital project. The interest that accrued from the seed money, with help from subsequent fund-raising navy wives and CHamorus, continued to pay for the hospital's operations even when it was destroyed by an earthquake in 1909, and until it was destroyed completely almost three decades later, during, ironically, the bombardment of Hagåtña in World War II when the United States returned with a vengeance to reclaim turf it lost from the Japanese occupation of 1941–44. This relative permanence is evidence of Dyer's resolve, temperament, and determination to go beyond expectations. The biannual governor's ball, under her direction and held more than twice a year, was an example of this. In Dyer's work, we might say that new white womanhood informed the labor of leisure, but conversely the labor of leisure also reshaped white womanhood to the extent that Dyer's innovations involved and generated the interests of new subjects and subjectivities with their own determinations.

Family Mix-Ups

To get a better sense of the new forces and subjectivities manifest in Dyer's labor of leisure, I return to Daisy and her observations about her mother. Perhaps more a new-woman feminist than her mother—recall her sarcastic depiction of her father as the "Grim old" emancipator—Daisy once likened her mother's characteristic open-mindedness to new ideas to a "good port."[68] Perhaps like a "good port," Susan Dyer trafficked in new ideas in her participation in the domestic and in domesticating small matters, which in fact involved quasi-official functions in the public sphere. In this, Dyer exemplified vestiges of new womanhood. At the same time, Dyer, it seems, struggled with earlier forms of white mothering that focused on safeguarding the purity and sanctity of her family and home from the uncertainties of an exotic and unfamiliar locale, and also from the unanticipated effects of being in a place that required an unusual amount of social mixing and mingling on account of the navy's twin responsibilities of running a military base and administering Guåhan as if the island were a ship.

Dyer's own "mixed" position inside and outside the navy's colonialism in Guåhan is also evident in her simultaneous desire for the exotic and her anxieties over the racial and classed issues that came with it. These anxieties are nowhere more apparent than in the epistolary form in what Carroll Smith-Rosenberg calls the "female world of love and ritual."[69] While I have not yet found Susie's correspondences back to Susan Dyer, one can easily cull from Susan's writings that her cousin's letters during the Dyers' stay in Guåhan were important sources of comfort and inspiration. Susan thanks "dear" Susie often for keeping her up to speed with events back home and for keeping the letters coming, especially when others failed to write. In return for Susie's constancy and for sending books, magazines, toiletries, and seeds for the palace gardens, Susan indulged her cousin with stories of exotic life in Guåhan and occasionally sent pieces of dress cloth that Susan acquired on her trips to Asia. Susan also confided in Susie about her anxieties, fears, desires, and occasional indulgences. One particular anxiety she had, despite her "open-mindedness" and "flexibility," pertained to the "little community" on Guåhan.[70] "I should dread propinquity in this fascinating milien [sic]!" Dyer wrote. "[But] as it is, there are plenty of men to take the girls hunting, riding, walking, swimming, to have private theatricals and tennis, but not to be alarming."[71] For Dyer, the social mixing might be "fascinating" to a certain extent and, with an appropriate amount of mixing of men, even "alarming," enough at least to explicitly point out to her cousin that it need not be. But for Dyer, it still merited the "dread" of propinquity, and with that, anxieties about race and desires to manage too much intimacy and proximity within the colonial landscapes in Guåhan.

Dyer's efforts to control the floodgates are also apparent in her desire to homeschool the "girls," Dorothy and Daisy, at the time already eighteen and twenty-five, respectively. An overprotectiveness that first strikes the reader as a particularly intense case of the classical, if not compulsive, parental refusal to let go—Susan claimed that Dorothy was "too young to stop studying"— might be better understood as a maternal brand of white paternalism and patriarchy.[72] This paternalism and patriarchy involved the controlling power that women earned and wielded especially over their children by virtue of upholding and mobilizing patriarchal presumptions and rules about womanhood and femininity. Then again, Dyer's desire to homeschool the girls might also be understood properly as a generational clash between competing feminist notions of white womanhood as inflected by American and naval colonial discourse in the tropics. Evidence of Dyer's maternal patriarchy can be found in letter form to her cousin Susie wherein Dyer admitted that homeschooling might be "selfish on her part" since it was she who enjoyed the two hours of Spanish and music she gave the girls.

However, a sense of deep competition between women across generations, possibly even between upstart feminisms across generations and perhaps between patriarchy and matriarchy, emerges or becomes evident when we consider that the occasion that triggers the maternal desire to continue homeschooling is the girls' desires to find their own niche in empire. Suddenly, the tables are turned, somewhat, and the mother is now the father, the governor of the house and captain of the ship. As in the case of Daisy's adventurism in Madrid—one blocked by her "Grim old" emancipator father—in Guåhan, naval patriarchy continued to orchestrate the relationship between the Dyer girls and Susan Dyer's desire to homeschool them precisely because the girls were themselves answering the navy's call for contract "special laborers" to teach CHamorus. Interestingly, Susan Dyer's initial refusal to allow Dorothy to teach because she was too young differed sharply with the navy's own recruitment of CHamoru women who were younger than Dorothy.

George and Susan Dyer tussled over what was better for the girls. Their differences in this case seem to describe a displaced collision in Guåhan between two other enduring American colonial realities: patriarchy and matriarchy. The clash was compounded by the fact that it was George Dyer who created the category "special laborer," which prompted the Dyer domestic crisis and mix-up. With what Susan Dyer called her husband's "New England conscience" under "revolt at the state of affairs in Guam," Governor Dyer immediately saw the contracting of special laborers—the wives and daughters of American personnel and qualified enlisted men, like the marines—as an ideal way to address the educational needs of the Native population in the absence of sufficient funds for stateside teachers. The special laborer category (or "clerical special laborer") permitted Dyer to utilize naval station funds provided through the navy to appoint naval dependents and marines. And although Susan Dyer claimed her husband had agreed initially that Dorothy would benefit more by continuing her lessons with her mother, it was her husband's enlightened paternalism as naval governor, evidenced in his official and unofficial writings, which often infantilized CHamorus, that presented the Dyer women with the opportunity to teach in the first place.[73] These gendered footpaths followed an earlier path of opportunity to travel for the Dyer women that was occasioned and structured by George Dyer's career in the navy. Halfway through their stay in Guåhan, as it would turn out, the competing viewpoints reached an agreement in permitting the younger Dorothy the opportunity to teach in Guåhan. What is still not clear is whether it was the new woman in Susan Dyer (and daughter Dorothy) that prevailed over the true woman who desired to guard the integrity of the family or whether it was the true woman who ended up capitulating to the policy of an enlightened New England consciousness that the husband and naval governor George needed to deploy in tropical Guåhan.

Dyer's anxiety over the mixed society in Guåhan is evident in her more blatant and honest confessions to Susie about the palace socials. After bragging about being the first to open the governor's palace to enlisted men at least twice a year for the biannual extravaganza, she reveals to Susie another reason for doing what she did: "I could not see why I should open my house to the hoi polloi of Guam, brown at that, and not ask decent white men."[74] Dyer's anxieties about race would be tempered by the fact that she socialized predominantly with an elite mestisu/a or mixed CHamoru-Spanish class of natives with which she was particularly fascinated.

As with her faithful communication with her confidante and cousin Susie, Susan Dyer cherished the relationships she built with certain mestisa

CHamorus. To more effectively understand Dyer's affection for these women, we need to return to her labor and investments in the socials, the palace mixers, and the tensions and possibilities they contained for all involved. If Dyer's spaces back home in the States were with the likes of Susan B. Anthony, her spaces along the imperial routes would include "rubbing elbows" with royalty. Daisy explained that it was her mother's personality and also her fluency in Spanish, French, and German that brought her into "social prominence far beyond what she would have otherwise enjoyed as the wife of an attaché of small means" and that she was in "constant demand" at diplomatic dinners and "given a place of distinction in spite of the rigid diplomatic society etiquette."[75] Sometime between 1890 and 1891, the Dyer women met up with George Dyer in Honolulu. There, according to Daisy, they met Queen Liliʻuokalani, who invited Susan Dyer to ʻIolani Palace to sing duets with her. This begs the question: How did Dyer's anti-imperial mind reconcile the U.S. overthrow of the beloved Kānaka queen two or three years later?

Susan Dyer would go from being a guest to hostess of lower-profile but nonetheless gendered and racialized Native and colonial encounters. Capping off a premiere gala at the palace, Dyer wrote that the event "proved a howling success" and "gratified the men extremely" and that their "friends" the mestisa CHamoru women enjoyed themselves too. This, according to Dyer, had been a big improvement over the "solemn affairs of the past" when the Native women "sat in gloomy rows along the walls of the school house" and "men herded in corners." In this new setting that the new woman Dyer orchestrated, "every one moved about," "wandered in the gardens and on the terrace" lit bright with colored lanterns and sat in galleries. Indeed, for Susan, there was an "atmosphere of friendliness" and "good time" that a hostess feels "instinctively."[76]

Here, we can begin to gauge a return on Dyer's investments in palace socials. Affirming Dyer's claim that her ball "gratified the men," the commanding officer of the USS *Mohican* wrote in Dyer's guestbook that he would "carry away the most pleasant recollections" of the place and people, and CHamorus too expressed their enjoyment and attested to Dyer's accomplishments, such as the hospital fund-raising events.[77] Unlike Governor Dyer, Governor Edward J. Dorn (1907–10) did not enjoy the constant help of his wife, Syble, because she was unhappy and often too ill to involve herself. Thus, it was Dorn who emphatically continued the work begun by Susan Dyer. Dorn Hall soon enough became the central space in which CHamorus themselves organized and led socials and followed up on the hospital work.[78]

Mobile Mestisas and Dyer's Desires

Dyer's legacy was the establishment of social spaces, such as that captured in figure 2.3. As a result of her labor, colonial and Native worlds intersected, coincided, and collided in ways that extended and produced new forms of Native and American cultural and political consciousness. The socials begun by Dyer would also move into other more private, intimate settings like the palace gardens, the galleries, and the azoteas, or covered terraces. Dyer worked hard to fashion these specifically tropical settings into exotica, like when she planted banana and bamboo to "hide a bad place" or grew her favorite white native lilies, and simultaneously forge domesticated or civilized places out of jungle, as when she renovated the palace and had galleries installed.[79] It was in such intimate, domesticated, and exoticized settings that Dyer wrote of her equally exoticized (and seemingly eroticized) relations with the elite mestisa women. This relationship and its social consequences for Americans and for what can be understood as an emergent CHamoru modernity under U.S. colonialism is best illustrated in the case of a group of women known rather affectionately as the Shoe Gang because of their particular fondness for American fashion and specific femininity reminiscent of white American womanhood, with a mix of Spanish CHamoru in between. Though the name was also associated with a group of American men who married CHamoru women and who stirred trouble for Governor Gilmer, who, in response, passed a law prohibiting interracial marriage between CHamorus and Americans, the Shoe Gang is more widely associated with a handful of elite CHamoru-Spanish and later American women. These women began to challenge traditional CHamoru norms around dress, behavior, travel, and proximity to (and eventual union with) American men. These women often traveled with Americans on daytrips around the island or off-island shopping trips to the Philippines, Japan, Hong Kong, or China, which were especially popular among the wives of officers. Governor Dyer too had a fascination with the light-skinned mestisas, indicating that the "younger superior" ones with their "gentle manners" and "attractive appearances" added a "charming feature" to Guåhan's "intimate social purposes." That they owned sewing machines and read women's magazines like *Butterick* and the English publication *The Queen* were also for Dyer a plus.[80] The dance halls, and later Dorn Hall, were favorite destinations for these mobile mestisas, which troubled their staunchly Catholic CHamoru and Spanish fathers, particularly when the dances were no longer sponsored by the wives of the governors, like Susan Dyer, but by American men themselves, including governors like Dorn. These

FIGURE 2.3 "One of the Baile Crowds... taken in [Governor Luke] McNamee's yard," c. 1908: 1, [A. J.] Geiger; 2, [Governor Luke] McNamee; 3, Gardener; 4, Mrs. Moses; 5, Mrs. McNamee; 6, [H. D.] Lamar; 7, [J. A.] Minter; 8, Ava Martinez; 9, [Pedro] Duarte; 10, Amelia Martinez; 11, Maria Duarte; 12, Bowne; 13, Miss Hall; 14, [William L. F.] Simonpietri; 15, Magdalena Calvo; 16, Beatrice Moses; 17, Teddy Mayhew; 18, Major Moses; 19, unidentified; 20, Concepcion Calvo. Courtesy of George Leland Dyer Papers, Joyner Library, East Carolina University.

dances were also popular for CHamoru men, elite or not, as Governor Dorn himself recalled in his diary.[81]

Members of the Shoe Gang belonged to elite mestisu families of Hagåtña—the Duarte, Calvo, Martinez, Torres, and Herrero clans—who were politically influential. The patriarchs of these families had gained prominent status during the Spanish administration and held high government positions. When the Americans arrived, some, like the Spanish military officer Pedro Duarte, switched and swore allegiance to the United States and as a consequence continued to enjoy their elite status. Susan Dyer was especially fond of the wives and daughters of these manakhilo' men (while Governor Dyer seemed especially fond of the "younger" ones), whom she dubbed affectionately the "native 400" women, because at the time it was estimated that Hagåtña's elite population numbered that much. In her letters to Susie, Dyer wrote often of these women, whom she described as "fair women, very refined and desirable" compared to their male counterparts, among whom even the "unmarried" ones were only "fairly interesting."[82] More than an indication of her anxieties about CHamorus, the "hoi polloi, brown at that," Dyer's social solidarity with the mestisas of Hagåtña (they often had tea at one another's homes) represented a homosocial bonding with both kin and exotic Other. She wrote, "I like them very much for they are almost all convent bred, having been sent to Manila to be educated, and speak very good Spanish. They are widows of Spanish officers, of children of native women married to Spanish officers; are quite light in color, and some of them very pretty."[83]

In time, Dyer grew fonder of these women, who were educated but also capable of reciprocating emotion. "They are fine women, intelligent for the chances they have had, forceful, and they are all fond of me. Perhaps that's one reason I like them so much!"[84] The fifty-two-year-old Dyer saw herself in these women and aspired to be like them: refined, noble, desirable, pious, light-skinned, elite, forceful, and emotional. The mestisa challenged Euro-American and navy discourses of Pacific Islander women as bare-breasted dusky maidens; in the case of CHamoru midwives, a primitive menace; or in the case of other islanders in Guåhan, the "unclothed" and "unlovely heathen" Carolinians.[85] On the other hand, despite the fact that they were already well provided for in terms of their means, dress, and schooling, Dyer's mestisas were fundamentally and significantly still Native and exotic Other. For all of the troubled history of insisting upon and policing the boundaries of this category, I want to dwell on Dyer's continued attraction to them as a desire for a mixed, racialized exotic-erotic Other.[86] This desire was informed and shaped by Dyer's employment or flirtations with different forms of white womanhood, especially through the labor and leisure afforded through her husband's relocation and assignment in Guåhan.

I return here to the intimate spaces of the Hagåtña palåsyo (palace) gardens, where Dyer planted a mix of colorful flowers, domestic and native, as a metaphor for desired worlds and to the form of women's history in women's letters. She wrote of the exotic native lilies she was anxious to grow with the help of others: "I have two Japanese boys to help me, and often think as I watch their sturdy figures that they ought to be at home fighting for their country, but am glad they are not."[87] Like the lilies, the mestisas represented an exotic mix that Dyer was anxious to domesticate. The Japanese "boys" represented another exotic Other that Dyer desired, domesticated, and feminized. The two Japanese boys not only provided a service to help Dyer; they serviced Dyer to the extent that their "sturdy figures" were for Dyer's private delight in her garden, if not consumption. The bodies of Japanese men ("boys") are clearly marked here by Dyer as national boundaries. But unlike white women's bodies that are marked as national boundaries and sexually off limits to all but white men, Japanese men are, in these discourses, presumably within the boundaries of white women's desire and consumption.[88] Recognizing that they, like other ordinary boys, "ought to be at home fighting for their country" during the Russo-Japanese War of 1904–5, Dyer was instead "glad" that they were not. Empire and domesticity likewise afforded Mary Ellen Chenoweth Pownall, wife of the rear admiral and navy governor of Guåhan Charles Pownall (1946–49), an exotic encounter with the prominent and respected Māori anthropologist, physician, and political leader Te Rangi Hīroa (a.k.a. Sir Peter Henry Buck), who was part of a visiting University of Hawai'i contingency to Guåhan during the Pownalls' tour of duty there. For Mrs. Pownall, he was a "wonderful, great big, fine looking native."[89]

If in fact Dyer's leisure and labor were shaped by the landscape, including her hybrid garden, then we might also find in her garden uncanny hints or at least potent symbols—metaphors of the lotus, native water lily, and also transplanted zinnias, moonflowers, and four o'clocks—of new forms of consciousness and subjectivities evolving. Other than some of the apparent or obvious symbols, like transplants and hybrids, like the temporalities of the tropics, we might also recall Dyer's feelings or sensations of being in a dreamlike, surreal state of mind. Her boasting of the four o'clocks in her garden nods to the fact that it was typically at four in the afternoon that the island's "real social life" began.[90] Dyer herself acknowledged an uncannyness, what she described as a "delicious freshness," that came at four o'clock in the afternoon when she took her daily five-mile drive to Piti, along the island's western shoreline, where she had the "whole effect of the glorious sunset" over the exposed reef and the sea beyond.[91] By the time she and George returned to the governor's palace, where "the orderlies, one marine, and one native" stood at attention and greeted them, the Dyers always felt "calm, cool and peaceful."[92] Adding to the "lovely close" of the colonial order of the day, she would add that the navy band was in the nearby plaza playing its usual evening concert. That, according to Dyer, along with the dimming light of the day, reminded one of dinner and the "girls in their low-necked white gowns," which usually meant the nearby presence of "a young man or two waiting hungrily."[93] In this, the "whole effect" from her Victoria horse-drawn carriage, Dyer was much like other navy wives who were so struck at the natural beauty of the tropics but which they at times found difficult to put into words. This feat and labor of taming what is Native and natural into dimensions of empire is what Vicente Rafael describes as the workings of colonial domesticity and the "phantasms of home that were at once in and out of place."⁹⁴

"Me Here" in Guåhan: The Susana and Assertions of Moral Authority

Like the freshness that overcame her during late-afternoon sunset rides on dirt and kaskåhu roads, an overwhelming feeling of responsibility and authority also consumed Susan Dyer during early-morning horseback rides along the fina'okso' in the island's interior. For Dyer, this newer feeling, from which the "beauty of our island" emanated, came with the "force of a fresh revelation" every day.⁹⁵ Dyer's rides along undeveloped roads reminded her of the lack of resources and lack of interest for Guåhan. On these leisurely rides outside Hagåtña, Dyer encountered another kind of CHamoru (other than the mestisa), whom she found to be the "gentlest, most friendly folk" (by virtue of being "far afield"). These "folk" for Dyer were the underclass, rank-and-file CHamorus who spent most of their time outside Hagåtña and Sumay (Guåhan's two principal towns) in rural villages or especially in their låncho and small dwellings, where they raised livestock and produce. With the "force of a fresh revelation" and a sense of purpose, the Susana became her resolve to look out for the health and welfare of especially these CHamorus. Dyer's time and energy to build this hospital, like her labor of leisure, provided the means through which Dyer claimed and reconsolidated new forms of white womanhood, which also provided the means through which CHamoru women would rearticulate modern American and tåddong values and ideas of CHamoru indigeneity, in the work that is of the pattera. Through the hospital work, Dyer asserted "moral authority" against a racialized and infantilized CHamoru.⁹⁶

Dyer's work involved education of a highly circumscribed type supposedly appropriate to the intelligence level of CHamorus and also in accordance with labor needs of the naval government. These, too, were gendered accordingly. In line with Governor Dyer's establishment of an industrial arts and later agricultural school, Susan Dyer initially entertained the idea of opening an industrial arts school exclusively for CHamoru girls.⁹⁷ In these schools, boys and girls alike, but separately, were required to perform calisthenics, drill exercises, and recitations before the American flag. The boys were prepared for the militia and to play in the navy band. An industrial school for girls then seemed to fit the bill; it would teach an appropriate gendered education and division of labor. Susan Dyer described to her cousin Susie what that education looked like: "We quite agree with you about the folly of over-educating the Chamorros. George's idea is simply to teach them to read, write and speak English.... His idea is more an industrial education, with a tendency mostly to agriculture."[98] Not "over-educating" CHamorus was justifiable, according to Dyer, because they were already content in their ways. Describing what she saw in the common CHamoru as an "Arcadian simplicity of life," Dyer wrote that "there is nowhere a more contented, happier folk."[99] So that CHamoru women might come to appreciate and benefit from her endeavor to eventually establish a hospital, Dyer sought out the mestisa class because she believed they could learn quicker and lead by example. But more than beneficiaries, the common CHamoru functioned as a necessary foil against which Dyer could not only take her rightful place in U.S. empire but through which she might imagine other noble identities for herself. In Guåhan and in famalao'an CHamoru, Dyer had the *raw* materials. What she lacked was start-up funds for philanthropic work: "If Congress, or Rockefeller or Helen Gould, or Carnegie would only give me five thousand dollars!"[100]

In Dyer's declaration, we get a glimpse of a different kind of woman's sphere, one more official and public than the charity work that went into organizing palace leisure and other gaiety in Guåhan. To be sure, hospital work (in the trajectory of the work of providing basic education for CHamorus) was a continuation of Dyer's "business of benevolence" and philanthropy work but one that bolstered and was also bolstered by the recognition of women's "strengthened perception of their own collective status" and a profound reappraisal of the nature and terms of women's charitable work—in this case, in the specificity of women's issues and women's rights.[101] It is telling that Dyer would liken her work in Guåhan to the work of New York philanthropist Helen Gould, daughter of the financier and railroad magnate Jay Gould, whose patronage included $100,000 to the U.S. government in support of the Spanish-American War, $50,000 to build military hospitals for soldiers, and a library building to New York University. But in this renewed social and cultural subject position, and sensing a more urgent "feeble cry" particularly from the "lower class" of CHamoru women and children, Dyer opted in the final leg of her tour in Guåhan to expend all of her energies toward the building of a hospital rather than an industrial school for girls.[102] Perhaps she was inspired by former Cobwebs—Edith Hawley's work in establishing the Philadelphia General Hospital Training School for Nurses or the philanthropist and fellow suffragist Phoebe Hearst's travels to London and reporting back to the society on the history and mission of the Foundling Hospital. With other wives and American women of the station, and calling on her husband as the governor to help her in what then might have easily been dubbed "big matters," Dyer organized a fund-raising campaign to establish in 1905 Guåhan's first hospital for Native women and children. Dyer envisioned the hospital to augment the hospital established five years earlier by Maria Schroeder.[103] In a one-page circular titled "The Cry of the Little People," which Dyer distributed to friends in the United States, she discussed the overcrowded and unsanitary living conditions in Guåhan, a "little spot of land, so lonely in the great waste of waters." Racializing and gendering health, Dyer wrote that "little or nothing" had been done for the "brown-skinned, kindly, courteous, friendly race" in the way of health and their "bodies," and thus the neglected "Chamorro women shrink from being carried [sic] for in illness by men."[104] We know, of course, that for centuries and over time, traditional healers—the makåhna/kakåhna, suruhåna and suruhånu (and now yo'åmte), and pattera—have always attended to the physical, mental, and spiritual well-being of CHamorus; from chapter 1, we also know that the pattera continued to care for women and assist them in their reproductive health needs on inafa'maolek terms, employing åmot CHamoru and other CHamoru knowledge and practice (while adopting U.S. naval health standards).

From fellow New Yorker Margaret "Olivia" Sage, wife of the wealthy financier and philanthropist Russell Sage, came $10,000. In articulating the need for a hospital, Dyer inventoried the conditions of the existing one: "While neat and airy, clean as a pin ... [the existing hospital was] sadly inadequate in size and appointments.... The convalescent and the dying have to be all together; the operations have to be performed in the gallery.... The nurses sleep in the gallery; the laboratory is in the gallery, and the natives, who come every day for treatment for various skin and other diseases, have an open court at one side of the building."[105] Dyer's definition of a more adequate hospital and her vision for a maternity ward exceeded the expectations of naval officials. These men had to catch up. For while Dyer's vision involved a championing of Native women and children's health, the wider story of improving Native health and well-being, no less in the realm of maternal care, rested on white, middle-class American notions of what constituted "proper" health care. And out in the colonial circuits, the "benevolent" burden of modernizing health care was also inextricably linked to the welfare and well-being of American settler or military colonists in the tropics in general, and the specific needs of white American women who might suddenly and unexpectedly find themselves in need of adequate maternal health care. If the project seemed excessive to them initially, the naval officers realized soon enough the advantages to "looking out" for CHamorus and also the necessity for Americans stationed in Guåhan to do so.

However linked the Susana Hospital was to white male naval authority and the benevolent gendered landscape down the long road, we must also recognize the equally important gendered dimensions that structured and animated the establishment of the hospital. The Susana, Anne Hattori argues, can indeed be read as a "symbolic assertion" of American women's power over that of CHamoru women, of American ideas of maternity and childcare over those of CHamorus, "in the interest of the naval government, male authority, and modernity."[106] To the extent that the Susana Hospital Corporation, or "Civil Society" as it was also referred to, was comprised mainly of American men, and that naval men handled the money and the subsequent Sage Foundation donation, Hattori's assertion is correct. However, by equating modernity as the exclusive preserve of the navy and male authority, even when that male authority included Guåhan leaders, we not only uphold the experience of white navy men in Guåhan as paradigmatic but also run the risk of losing the nuances in the means and formations of gendered and gender-diverse subjectivities, including the diversity of CHamoru and American women's historical experiences of modernity. The "administrative junta" (i.e., governing body) of the corporation included Påle' Jose Palomo, the first CHamoru Catholic priest, and Pedro Duarte, who was married to Maria Anderson Millinchamp and was the patriarch of the manakhilo' Shoe Gang daughters.[107]

In identifying the need for the hospital, Dyer spoke from a different vision of modernity, one that was woman centered. Of the contemporary practices, Dyer observed, "government looks out for sick men, but makes no provision for women, beyond having doctors here who will attend to them, and do—but at a disadvantage."[108] At this time, "modern" medicine and the subfield of tropical medicine were already transitioning from a philanthropic and social reform project to a more advanced scientific project. Though it was clearly linked to the kind of philanthropic work associated with early tropical medicine (in Guåhan the services were also free), Dyer's vision entailed early feminist elements insofar as it concerned itself specifically with the issue of women's health and well-being, as was the case with systems of prenatal care in the United States that were established *not* by doctors but by nurses.[109] This woman-centered vision was also expressed in Dyer's organizational plan (the flow-of-power chart, so to speak) of the proposed governing board, which would eventually be called the Susana Hospital Aid Association. The board was purposely organized so that the governor's wife, starting with Dyer, would head the association. Furthermore, Dyer stipulated that she would reserve the right to name subsequent women residents and chairmen or delegate that right to another woman of her choice. Dyer had found and identified her suc-

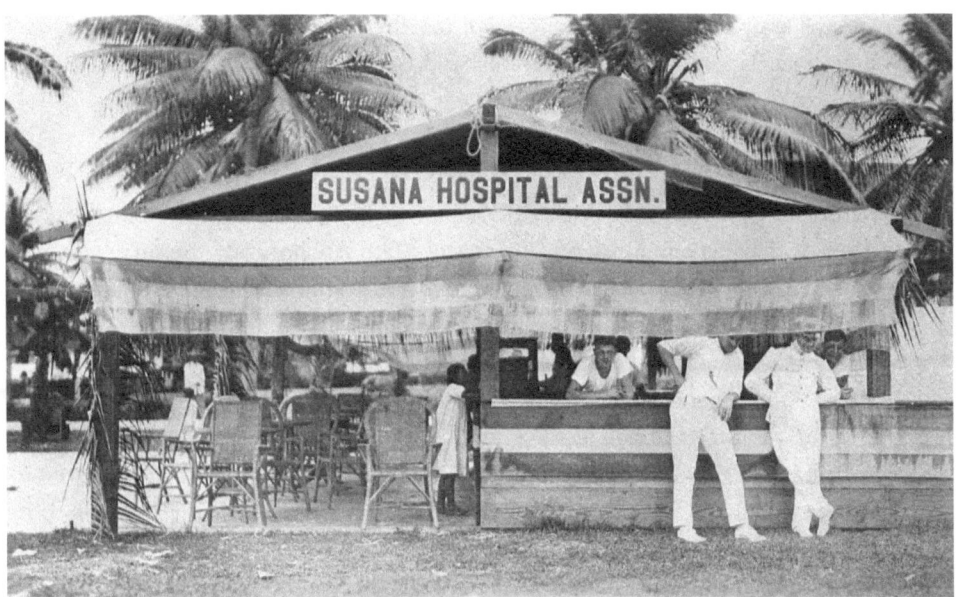

FIGURE 2.4 Fundraisers for the Susana Hospital often took place at the annual Industrial Fair, where this photograph was taken between 1917 and 1918. Governor Roy Smith Collection, box 24, folder 3 "Photographs of Guam." Courtesy of Naval Historical Collection Archives, U.S. Naval War College.

cessor, Bertha Cheney McLean (a.k.a. Mrs. McLean), whom she found to be "young and earnest" and whose "keen sense of duty" she attributed to McLean's "New England" roots.[110] Dyer also named ten CHamoru women of the mestisa class, the aforementioned "native 400," to an executive committee of the Susan Hospital Aid Association, whose duty it was to seek out CHamoru women for treatment.[111] For reasons as yet unknown, the association—and more importantly, its women-oriented vision—would be renamed the Susana Hospital Association (figure 2.4) and run by American and elite CHamoru men years after the Dyers' departure.[112] Eventually, the designation of the Susana as a hospital for Native women and children would also change, as evidenced in the correspondence between Olivia Sage's attorney and executor, Robert de Forest, and Governor George Dyer. In a discussion of another Sage fund, de Forest stipulated the new terms: the Susana would be for the "medical treatment of *all* women and children, native and foreign, irrespective of color" to which Governor Dyer, by then retired in the states, would agree.[113] Dyer's tour-of-duty feminism—precisely for how it became structured by the gendered landscapes of colonial and Native relations of power in the tropics and in the fleeting and peripatetic nature of military overseas assignments—can also be tied to other feminisms, namely, that of Olivia Sage. Upon the death of her husband, Sage began directing her philanthropy to women's causes. The Susana was one of Sage's favorites.[114]

Maternal Modernity's "Structures of Feeling"

Writing from her home in Winter Park, Florida (where the Dyers eventually retired and which they referred to as the "The Anchorage"), Susan Dyer thanked Olivia Sage for a second "generous gift" to the Susana. Dyer's letter, penned a decade after her departure from Guåhan, is no mere thank-you to an important benefactress whose generosity helped institutionally memorialize Dyer's own beneficence. Writing from the "very depths" of her heart on behalf of "far away and helpless women and children," Dyer thanked Sage, to whose name CHamoru "thoughts and prayers" would be linked.[115] Noteworthy here were the affective ties that comprise colonialism's "structures of feeling," particularly in the relations between Dyer and the CHamoru women employed at the Susana.[116] Contrary to what the navy had hoped and claimed, the women who worked at the hospital as lay matrons, pattera, and enfetmera were not exclusively of the elite class, yet they were fully capable of reciprocating emotion. In a letter to Susie, in which she described the night before and morning of her final departure from Guåhan, Dyer again invoked the "cry of the little people," which even Daisy recalled as "lines of weeping" CHamorus: "I had a most sorrowful parting from Senora Rosa, the hospital Matron and the six girl nurses the night before, and now here were all these friendly, kindly faces bathed in tears. I cried too as you may imagine. All the officers' wives of course were there—these I might expect to see again—but these dear brown people!"[117]

Shortly after the Dyers' departure, the lay matron Rosa Perez commenced a series of letters with "Doña Susana" intended to keep her abreast of the island's progress and that of the Susana.[118] More than a transmission of news and information, the letters were filled with love and affection, with "good wishes" and "affectionate memories" between CHamoru women and Dyer. After listing specific cases by which the Susana continued to be "the asylum for the ill that it was meant to be," including an American wife's successful delivery, a typhoon that destroyed the hospital's walkway, and the fact of no change in personnel, Perez turned to news of how Dyer's "daughters" (i.e., the nurses, lay matrons, shown in figure 2.5) were faring back in Guåhan. Perez even named specific women—Maria Roberto, Maria Guevara, Maria De Leon Guerrero, Felicita San Nicolas, Maria Flores—who "continue to be happy" and send "great hugs and kisses."[119] Striking features of this letter merit further attention, starting

FIGURE 2.5 CHamoru nurses and lay matrons on the steps of the Susana Hospital, 1905. Courtesy of George Leland Dyer Papers, Joyner Library, East Carolina University.

with competing notions of what the Susana was intended to be. For Perez, it was an "asylum for the ill," something different from what Dyer envisioned when she described it as a place for specialized care and maternity care, where sick women and babies could be "properly cared for." Also, Perez's letter reads like one to a family member, and what figures prominently therein are mother-daughter relations: between Dyer and the nurses and lay matrons, possibly between Perez and the nurses, and between other mothers and daughters (like Mrs. Kemp and her baby girl). Most of all, like Dyer's grateful letter to Sage, Perez's letter is saturated with deep, heartfelt gratitude and affection.

The Susana Hospital was a physical manifestation of what Raymond Williams has called potent "structures of feeling," which in colonial contexts fused the domestic and the foreign through affective bonds between colonizer and colonized.[120] We might start with the naming of the hospital. According to Dyer, the "people here asked George to have the hospital named for me ... but Dyer seems rather a grewsome [sic] name for a hospital, doesn't it? So as I am known here as Dona Susana, they have called it the Susana Hospital, which means me here, and isn't too personal away from here."[121] When CHamorus claimed Susan Dyer as one of their own, as "Dona [Doña] Susana [Susåna]," they were in fact keeping things very personal. In the end, even Susan Dyer continued to take the Susana personally, keeping tabs on the hospital ("me here" or me there, however you look at it). This intense personal bonding between structure and namesake is what animated or informed the sentiments that Dyer conveyed so gratefully to Sage on the occasion of Sage's second contribution.

Margaret Jolly has offered the metaphor of the "maternal body" as a critical concept for rethinking white women's roles and the ties that bind in the colonial histories of Oceania. The figure of the historical maternal body involved the mobilization of Victorian ideas, including true womanhood, as fundamental components of the colonial project, demonstrated in colonial health policies and also in how Native men and women were feminized and infantilized. For Jolly, the metaphor also crystallizes the multiple subject positions and subjectivities at stake in white women's and Native women's complex participation in these imperial projects.[122] In a critical response to Jolly, Aileen Moreton-Robinson argues that in attempting to complicate and historicize the nuances of women's roles in the colonial project, Jolly equalizes the fundamental differences between white women's and Native women's differential and uneven positioning to colonialism and thereby understates the historical and political relations of power between the two, while also misconstruing and therefore eliding the specificity and difference of Indigenous women's perspectives and lived realities. Moreton-Robinson's contention is that the maternal body is incommensurate with the historical experiences of Indigenous women, who not only do not regard middle-class white women in Australia as mothers but who insist on white women's direct implication in the ongoing legacy of racism and sexism, assimilation and domestication, land dispossession and stolen children.[123] To be sure, white women (feminists) in Guåhan must similarly be held accountable to colonialism. There is no denying, however, at least in this letter, the affective ties, if even only between Dyer and Rosa Perez, which imply Native complicity with colonialism and kinship with the colonial new-woman agent, Susan Dyer. On the eve of her departure, Susan Dyer lamented to Susie that she wished she were younger and able to stay longer in Guåhan, to do more work on that which preoccupied her "whole heart and soul." This preoccupation would be the hospital. Even the leisurely "path" down her garden would eventually be diverted to the vegetable garden, as a site and metaphor for labor, because, as she admitted to Susie, "this is what has been bringing in money to help pay for teacher's salary."[124] Dyer's new womanhood in Guåhan would eventually be relocated back to the States, to her work with the Colored Women's Club and women's suffrage movement in Winter Park, Florida. On Dyer's passing, the Colored Women's Club president Sallie Williams intimated similar (to Rosa Perez's) bonds of affection: "In sad and loving memory of Mrs. Dyer, who worked so faithfully with us to foster our club work. She is gone, but will not be forgotten."[125]

Nearly a decade after the Dyers left Guåhan, their youngest daughter, Dorothy (whose husband's orders brought them back to the island) wrote a detailed account to her mother (whose imperial reach extended from back on the continent), because, as Dorothy had put it, "I know that all of you are just waiting on the edge of your chairs to hear about it."[126] Dorothy reported on the island's progress (a new wharf) and the same pleasantries—the channel, the capital, the plaza, palace doors, and the familiar sight of CHamoru boys waiting at the dinner table. Dorothy noted however that this time the "boys" were Dorothy's former students, Vicente and Manual. She drew attention to old and new faces and places: Påle' Jose Palomo (a.k.a. Påle' Engko'), the American teacher Mrs. Constanoble, and the usual drive along the beach. And when the view became "too dark to see anything," Dorothy relied on familiar colonial senses (and sentiments) of the tropics to reconnect. "I would know where I was by the smell," wrote Dorothy, who had been "suddenly transported [back] there" to the Dyers' time in Guåhan. Three years later, their good friend Pedro Duarte would also help to transport Susan Dyer back.

In 1916, following the flag and also the ship, or more appropriately its "anchorage" in Winter Park, Florida, Duarte sent a postcard reminding the Dyers of their standing as two individuals "never [to be] forgotten by the good people of Guam."[127] The postcard featured what by then would have been an image or sight familiar to the Dyers: against a Guåhan sunset, an American military man dressed in white uniform stands on the shore and gazes upon a CHamoru fisherman and his family at the water's edge as they set off in a traditional galaide, or outrigger paddling canoe. This image captures a number of things beginning with the mutual but unequal relations between the military man gazing on the Native, while the image of the Indigenous canoe evokes a number of other different themes, such as CHamoru cultural survival. At another abstract theoretical level, it serves as a powerful metaphor for decolonization and vehicle for rethinking the terms of indigeneity through mobile watercraft and histories of Austronesian linguistic and human dispersal.[128] If the canoe can signify Indigenous mobilities, it also has the capacity to signify Indigenous mobilities forged in relation to imperial mobilities, as those described in this chapter. In the next chapter, I follow the image of the CHamoru canoe on the Guåhan flag and the American new woman associated with its design, Helen Paul, for a more focused attention on how Guåhan's natural landscape became the optics through which another white woman would conduct work that would also become emblazoned—literally, nostalgically, and contentiously—in the hearts and minds of CHamoru political consciousness.

CHAPTER THREE

Flagging the Desire to Photograph
Helen Paul's "Eye/Land/People"

In 1948, the prominent CHamoru educator Agueda Iglesias Johnston narrated a brief history of the Guåhan flag in which she attributed its design in 1917 to the "beautiful and charming American navy wife" Helen Paul. According to Johnston, while Lieutenant Commander (LCDR) Carroll Paul carried out his duties for the navy's public works projects, "his artistic young wife busied herself in the interest and welfare of the people by teaching school, conducting shows and plays for benefits and recreation, and by reproducing the natural beauty of Guam by the many drawings and sketches she made of the different sceneries around the island." For Johnston, one of the most "outstanding" of these sceneries was the image that would be used as the central figure of the Guåhan flag: a picturesque composition of a lone coconut tree at beachside, along a stream, with the ocean and a sakman (CHamoru outrigger sailing canoe) against the backdrop of the island's familiar northern coastal landmark, Litekyan (or Ritidian) Point. "What a fine tribute it would be to the designer" and "all others responsible in its making," wrote Johnston, if Guåhan representatives made resolutions to have the flag recognized as the island's "Official Flag" in a "similar manner as the State Flags in the U.S."[1]

In this endearing praise of a former teacher, Johnston captured a sense of the intimacy between CHamoru students and their American teachers, a sentiment not unlike what we encountered between nurse-midwives and navy nurses in chapter 1. But in calling attention to "others" who contributed labor to the actual production of the flag—including Lillian A. Nagel, the home-economics teacher and wife of an American marine, who she claimed sewed the flag—Johnston may have also indirectly flagged the historical erasures and tensions involved in its making. As discussed in this chapter, there are counterclaims from the alternative annals of Guåhan's oral histories contesting the earlier official narratives that credit Helen Paul as the sole or even chief designer. While it has been important to resolve the Guåhan flag design in order to give credit where credit is due, I also want to take up Johnston's observation of the collective and contentious nature of the making of the flag as an emblem of the complicated coconstruction and coconstitution of Guåhan's modern political and cultural history. In this case, the messy entanglement involves the specific work of a different generation of new women that also did not dismiss CHamoru imaginings and agitations for political autonomy. In this chapter, it is the work of Helen Paul's photographic eye on Guåhan's landscapes and CHamoru bodies and faces that provides the materiality for demonstrating these enmeshments. In addition to being noted (if even contentiously) for her role in the design of the Guåhan flag, Paul is also remembered as a teacher at the Guam Normal School, where she trained CHamoru educators and community and political leaders like Johnston. Less known is that she was a trained architect and avid photographer, one who was consciously drawn to and in turn drew and drew out a visual aesthetic, "the picturesque," in her sketches and photographs of the island's natural landscape and the culturescape of the CHamorus. She went looking for, found, and captured—through photography and sketches—visually appealing material in Guåhan and among the CHamorus.

In this chapter, I analyze Paul's explicit attention to picturesque "sceneries" and other cultural and visual texts, including her contribution to the design of the flag, as another form of duty that also now included what was classified as "diversion" or nonwork, rest and recreation activities that preoccupied a later generation of new women as they traveled the military circuits through the United States' tropical colonies, as wives of naval officers and as college-educated nurses and teachers. In Paul's case, this form of new womanhood in the tropics is evidenced in what I suggest was her desire to photograph. Just what was this desire to photograph, and how did this yearning converge with other colonial and Native sentiments? What sentiments emerged and diverged from Helen Paul's colonial gaze through her desire to capture the picturesque, and in what ways did this affect shape Native desires? Conversely, how might CHamoru desires have shaped Helen Paul's sentiments, her own photographic eye as it produced images about Guåhan and the CHamorus?

By working a body of essays and writing assignments by her CHamoru students alongside a reading of her photography and sketches, I follow this picturesque along and off the beaten path of her visual colonial optic. This larger colonial optic, I argue, trained and directed Paul's own eye in that it involved the machinations of a broader paternal and patriarchal gaze forged earlier in her life (her father was a surveyor of Indian lands in northern Michigan). Framed (and shuttered) in this colonial optic were a range of sentiments, from what colonizers coveted of Indigenous bodies and more intangible psychic and cultural qualities and traits presumed to be appealing to Native fondness for the unfamiliar and novel. The sentiments also included a complex and changing terrain of emotions, such as sympathy and nostalgia, that physical, social, or cultural traits and characteristics of Native peoples evoked in navy personnel like Paul. But the desires also included explicitly political wishes, expressed mostly by CHamoru male leaders, for political autonomy from the wide-ranging and unchecked powers of the successive waves of naval officers who also doubled as the island's governors during their stints. These wishes, articulated as early as 1901, were also bound up with matters involving the Guåhan flag when political changes occurred in 1950, as will be gleaned shortly. This complex entanglement of naval and Native desires is captured in the form and content of Helen Paul's optic and comprise what Ann Laura Stoler calls the "intimate landscape of affective ties and asymmetric relations" between colonizer and colonized.[2] Paul's colonial optic can also be understood to effectuate what Laura Wexler calls the "innocent eye" or "averted gaze," the capacity by which certain kinds of photographic practices are able to mask the structural violence of empire.[3] Wexler finds this form of colonial disavowal in late nineteenth- / early twentieth-century women's photography. Trained and directed by a larger, gendered colonial gaze, the affect (and effect) of Paul's eye on CHamoru lands, bodies, and psychic and cultural interiorities betray both colonialism's disavowals, the ruses of its power relations, and traces of CHamoru investments and determinations in colonial interests in Guåhan.

In Agueda Johnston's narration of the history of the Guåhan flag, for example, we get a glimpse of the political and cultural stakes for CHamorus on the eve of the passage and signing, in 1950, of the Guam Organic Act. Celebrated in Guåhan's canonical history as a political milestone, the Organic Act was the federal law passed by the U.S. Congress that (1) terminated formal naval rule over the island by transferring administrative oversight to the Department of Interior, (2) granted a circumscribed form of U.S. citizenship to the "native inhabitants," (3) established a structure of local governance (i.e., "GovGuam"), and (4) declared Guåhan's political status as that of an organized "unincorporated territory" of the United States by reaching back to an esoteric legal doctrine, known as the Doctrine of Territorial Incorporation. Formulated through a series of Supreme Court cases (in)famously known as the Insular Cases, the Doctrine of Territorial Incorporation supposedly settled the question of whether the U.S. Constitution "followed the flag"—that is, whether it applied fully and on its own accord to "insular" (overseas) lands and peoples that had come under and within the embrace of American political control after the Spanish-American War of 1898. Through the Insular Cases, the Supreme Court ruled that, with exception to matters pertaining to basic human rights (namely, the Bill of Rights), it was congressional authority, not the Constitution itself, which possessed the inherent power to determine the extent and scope of the Constitution's applicability to these places and peoples. It was in this technical sense that the Supreme Court ruled (and continues, to this day, to uphold the ruling) that in matters pertaining to overseas territories like Guåhan (and the other "insular territories" of Puerto Rico, American Samoa, and the Virgin Islands), U.S. Congress possesses "plenary" (i.e., exclusive and ultimate) power.[4] In short, through the aforementioned four conditions of these forms of democratic "inclusion," the Organic Act consolidates American colonial power over CHamorus, even though each of these changes (with the exception of the Doctrine of Territorial Incorporation) had also been agitated for by a generation of CHamoru leaders when they began to realize how much unchecked power the naval governor wielded over the island's civic affairs. Formally adopted by the Guam Congress in 1948 (and approved by then naval governor Charles Pownall) as the island's official territorial flag, the Guåhan flag is required by law to be flown in subordinate status (either below or to the right of) the U.S. flag. For that very entanglement, contestations over who designed the flag continue to resurface in postwar histories, particularly in flash points when CHamoru nationalists brandish and uphold the flag as the key symbol with which to decolonize the island from the clutches of both military and federal rule and from those GovGuam political leaders who might be viewed as puppets of or sellouts to Washington, D.C.

In examining more fully the messy entanglements of Native and naval desires that can be spied in Helen Paul's optic in Guåhan, I offer counterreadings of photographs and sketches of Guåhan's landscapes and CHamoru bodies and facial "looks"—candid and spontaneous snapshots of nature and Native peoples that ostensibly captured in a seemingly transparent way a natural beauty or quaint feature of their subjects but which betrayed the disavowed workings of colonial rule and agitations against it. In what might otherwise be construed as ordinary, mundane, and even banal moments of existence, these photos of CHamoru faces and bodies are better understood as having been posed in repose by Paul's eye within the gaze of U.S. colonial modernity. Annoyed at the paternalism of such staged posings, as well as their capacity to disavow contemporaneous political agitations, I also actively interrogate their semiotics to gauge to what extent these seemingly quaint photographs might also belong to another class of transparent and everyday photographs that Craig Campbell calls, appropriately enough, "agitating images," which have the power to trouble the relationship between photography and historiography through the ways their content invites meaning making in multiple forms.[5] Inasmuch as these images have become part of the colonial archive, I understand the act of rescripting their possible meanings as helping to build a CHamoru "counter-archive" for the political and cultural purpose of reclaiming history and place through what Jolene Rickard and others have theorized as the Indigenous goal of attaining "visual sovereignty."[6]

Duty, Diversion, and New-Woman Photography in Guåhan

When Helen Paul arrived in Guåhan in 1917, well over a decade after Susan Dyer had left the island, she brought with her a level of technical training, skill, education, and talent in the visual arts and sciences that rendered her and women of her generation (like the professionally trained nurses brought to Guåhan discussed in chapter 1) a sort of "newer" new woman, at least compared to Dyer, who was old enough to be her mother. The daughter of a surveyor, then Helen McGraw Longyear graduated with honors from the Massachusetts Institute of Technology (MIT) in 1909 with a degree in architecture. Shortly after, she worked for a leading landscape and architectural firm in New York City. In New York, she also became involved in "settlement work," an early form of social work (of which a main objective was the establishment of settlement houses) through which women like Paul lent their skills and talents to assist immigrants and poor or disenfranchised individuals to better "settle" into their new lives in the United States. Though a lighthearted social announcement of her wedding to the U.S. Navy civil engineer Carroll E. Paul quipped that "Dan Cupid ... finally won her from architecture and the immigrants," the fact was that neither love nor marriage nor relocation to the other side of the world could conquer Mrs. Paul. That is, she did not have to abandon her passion for her profession: drawing, sketching, photography, drafting, designing, or her desire to be engaged in social work.[7]

As demonstrated in the previous chapter in the case of Susan Dyer, white patriarchy and naval hierarchies of race, gender, and class and specificity of place in the tropics certainly dictated the terms of domesticating empire, including establishing the parameters around which white womanhood felt "at home." But, as Jane Simonsen argues, imperial domesticity could not also simply be exported; the process of "making home" involved a "pattern of working relationships" wherever these women went or were directed toward, and these patterns and relations, as she puts it, "took work."[8] And part of the work in the making of imperial domesticity in women's public and cultural work—whether as anthropologists, nurses, teachers, or, in Helen Paul's case, photographers—often relied on or at least featured both the rhetoric and the imagery of sentimentalism. If the labor and leisure of Susan Dyer, the new woman who built Guåhan's first hospital, was informed by a moral authority of new women in the tropics that in turn shaped a specific kind of feminism that I (in the last chapter) called a tour-of-duty feminism, then the social space making of Helen Paul nearly two decades later would involve a new kind of authority and gaze that developed through her teaching at the Normal School and was given further exposure through the art and science of the conventions of photography and image production.

Arriving on board the U.S. Army Transport *Sheridan* on June 25, 1917, Helen Paul followed her husband, LCDR Carroll Paul, to his overseas assignment in Guåhan as the navy's chief civil engineer (1917–19).[9] He was tasked with the Agaña Springs and Agat-Sumay water systems project and the construction of a road connecting the central and southern parts of the island. Of this feat one anonymous writer in the *Guam News Letter* poetically remarked, "God help the man who builds that road from Inarajan to Ordot: He'll slip into a ten-foot hole of Mud, and there he'll be forgot."[10] Prior to his naval career and fresh out of Dartmouth in 1904, LCDR Paul worked three years for the U.S. Reclamation Service on irrigation projects in the U.S. West. One might say he had already been "knee deep" in an earlier civilizing and modernizing project, one that was also predicated on the removal and dispossession of Indigenous peoples.[11] In Guåhan, Helen Paul would do her share working as a teacher at the Normal School in the island's capital. The Normal School was established in 1916 to provide a three-year teacher-training program for CHamorus, in subjects ordinarily taught in secondary education in the United States.[12] Today, Guåhan schools bear the names of some of Paul's students and esteemed educators, such as Agueda Johnston, Jose L. G. Rios, Simon A. Sanchez, and Maria A. Ulloa—some of whom I shall return to shortly.

While in Guåhan, Helen Paul explored other forms of new womanhood as an enthusiastic photographer in search of the picturesque. Paul's desire to photograph and her yearning for the picturesque, like Susan Dyer's desires for labor, leisure, and mixing, placed her on a continuum with the larger U.S. civilizing project, but it also brought her slightly out of step with colonial proscriptions, including unspoken codes and caveats by other military wives.[13] Following the earlier footsteps into appropriate spaces and duties reserved for military wives and women, Paul devoted her time in Guåhan to philanthropy and charity work. Paul sketched and photographed island landscapes for postcards for Red Cross fund-raisers. She designed props for other fundraising events, including vaudeville performances. One prop, a canvas backdrop, told an interesting saga.[14] Helen Paul's cousin, Mabel Tibbitts, the Red Cross director in Guåhan at the time, told the story of how Paul painted the canvas for a Red Cross event in Hagåtña. Tibbitts described that it was a "gay display of Pierrots and Pierrottes dancing beneath a full moon, and it was used again and again for stage shows."[15] In her details of the event, we also get a glimpse into CHamoru investments. Tibbitts recalled that, "when the canvas became too chipped and dingy for further decorative use, Mrs. William G. Johnston, Guamanian wife of an ex-marine and friend of Mrs. Paul stowed it away in her home." Johnston, continued Tibbitts, wanted to keep it for "sentimental value," indicating that Johnston, in her own words and with a "smile," claimed that the canvas was "too good a piece of canvas to throw away." During the Japanese invasion of Guåhan, Johnston "clung to the canvas" and with her bull cart and other family possessions carried it back into the hills. Eventually, according to Tibbitts, Johnston used it as a porch roof for her family's hideout during the two and half years under Japanese occupation. Shortly after the U.S. Marines returned to "liberate" the island in the summer of 1944, Tibbitts and Johnston returned to the jungle dwelling where Paul's canvas backdrop once hung and found that its "latest occupants were still using it as a roof despite all the bullet holes."

Paul's extracurricular activities (like painting beautiful stage backdrops on canvas for social events in Hagåtña) reveal how the individual and personal interests of the new woman in Guåhan had the potential to be understood in terms of their own potential service to Native desires, much like how a canvas stage prop that could hold sentimental value for one CHamoru could also double as shelter after World War II, despite the bullet holes, for another. For Johnston, the painted backdrop had "sentimental value" and was simply "too good a piece of canvas to throw away." In fact, there are deeper or at least additional layers to both the utilitarian and affective values of artifacts like the painting. Precisely because it was used for performances that proved to be both popular and significant in efforts to modernize Guåhan and build relations between navy personnel and CHamorus, it was worth collecting for future display, at least until the war broke out and it was determined it could be used for something else. But before the war, Johnston had already become involved in the establishment of a Guam Museum and in overseeing collections.[16] As for the seemingly harmless gesture of simply having the canvas to use at the outbreak of the war and during the Japanese occupation, such an act was in fact a direct violation of the Japanese army's orders for CHamorus to surrender all relics of the United States.[17] By holding on to it, Johnston risked her life and the lives of her family; it was also an act of defiance and of holding on to a tangible object of life under the United States for the value that such an intangible sentiment could play in maintaining one's faith under trying, desperate, and dangerous times.

Like her paintings, Paul's sketches and photographs afford us different and competing valences of colonial and Native sentiment. The tours of duty and diversion that new women like Paul traveled, through racialized and gendered pathways of colonialism out in the tropics, were marked by the dutiful *following* of the guidelines prescribed by the navy, but they would also include *diverting* from them. Paul's detour was the desire to photograph the exotic tropics and its peoples, both of which were presumed to offer an abundance of natural and cultural diversity and alterity. As evidenced in the writings of duty-bound nurses, assignments in Guåhan presented one with leisurely activities set in the tropical landscape. These leisurely pursuits—trekking and photography—were and continue to be diversions for military tours of duty and what Teresia Teaiwa described as the historical and conjoining forces manifested in "militourism," a phenomenon by which military and/or paramilitary forces facilitate the successful operation of a tourist industry while the same tourist industry masks the violence of militarism in the Pacific Islands.[18]

These leisurely activities present another dimension of the specific forms of gender that evolved overseas in the imperial reach out in the tropics. In a 1918 article titled "Duty and Diversion in Guam," American navy nurse Frederica Braun called attention to the "excellent" things one can do while off duty in what by then was already officially christened as one's "tropical tour-of-duty."[19] These diversions included swimming, dances, automobile rides, and walks. Braun considered the walks, especially those taken "just as the sun goes down" and when "darkness comes," particularly enchanting, like being in a "fairyland" or placed under a "spell not soon forgotten." Moonlit picnics were "the best of fun," and tennis courts were "simply the best" because balls would be "picked up and brought to one by the little native boys."[20]

Braun arrived on Guåhan aboard the USS *Logan* eager to work. Her assignment provided exactly what she sought and desired: experience in public health and welfare work in tropical diseases. The diversions that tropical Guåhan also offered provided not just recreation and leisure but emphatically their best forms. In part, their superiority or excellence stemmed from the availability and use of modern accoutrements that luxuriated the kinds of activities of leisure that one would expect to encounter on tropical tours. What also made playing in the tropics simply the best was the supposed eager labor of "little native boys," whose diminutive presence in the narrative (Were they in fact young boys, or was she referring to men in the way colonial officials often infantilized male servants?) bespoke how duty and diversion for white women was further racialized and gendered in the tropics. In her own recollection of her tour of duty in Guåhan, chief navy nurse Sue Dauser recalled a favorite pastime along the nature path among a group of Natives whom she gendered male and singularized into a racial typology in one part of the sentence: "When walking about the island one sees the simple, humble, primitive life of the native and always finds him friendly, kind, generous, and respectful." But in the following sentence, when she explains why it is that an American woman might "see" and "find" such appealing qualities in the figure of the Native man, she suddenly switches to the plural form as if to multiply or play up the sentiment and rationale: "The natives are always ready to demonstrate their love for Americans."[21]

As a particular form of leisure and rest and relaxation, walks or hikes in the tropics called explicit attention to and perhaps symbolized multiple, varied, and even competing meanings in colonial and military assignments and their "projects," which included photography.[22] For the most part, these American women's accounts of their tours of duty repudiate competing views of the tropics as only debilitating sites of degeneration, decay, and wilderness. On the contrary, the positive, almost tonic, descriptions of tropical charms and of happy little Natives who are eager to please comprise a long-standing Western desire for primitivism, paradise, and noble savagery supposedly found in these parts of the world, the likes of which one no longer is able to find back home in the modern world. The sexualization of tropical Pacific land- and bodyscapes, as found in Dyer's palace garden in the previous chapter and as we shall glean from vaudeville performances in this chapter, are more than mere Guåhan and CHamoru examples of the workings of a particular colonial gaze in the Pacific, which Margaret Jolly characterizes as the "erotics of the exotic"; that is, the inextricable entanglement in colonial optics of sexual attractiveness of radical difference or, the reverse, difference that is sexually appealing because it is different (or far from home).[23] The examples in Guåhan, thus, are more than mere local examples of such erotica and exotica; they are the erotics of CHamoru exotica that, in racialized and sexualized encounters and exchanges with new women engaged in temporary diversions from their official duties, also conditioned the kinds of work these women performed in these specific places. To be sure, such newfound diversions—walks and hikes in the hålom tåno' along the paths with eager, loving Natives ready to assist—are good examples of the way prior domesticities that are transplanted in new Indigenous settings and in sexually and racially charged encounters with Indigenous bodies also became reshaped or, in the words of Julia Clancy-Smith and Frances Gouda, became "warped beyond recognition."[24] In the case of Helen Paul, the encounters involved her technically skilled "eyeings" of Guåhan's lands and CHamoru bodies and faces.

Though Helen Paul's passion for photography had been technically developed through enrollment in private photography courses after she graduated from MIT (she had attended Smith College after graduating from the all-girls Burnham School in Massachusetts), her exposure to technologies of image and the picturesque began much earlier under the aegis of her father, John Munro Longyear.[25] The senior Longyear was a professional landlooker who made a fortune for his family by surveying Michigan's Upper Peninsula (UP) for its value for the timber and copper-ore mining industries.[26] He was also an amateur photographer who spent much of his time surveying and photographing the UP's own picturesque landscape. In close pursuit, the younger Longyear turned to photography as a mode of exploring and asserting new forms of white womanhood. Paul's membership in the Huron Mountain Club—a 20,000-acre privately owned campgrounds established by her father in 1889—may also explain her interest in photography and nature and "roughing" the landscape in Guåhan. Paul's mother, Mary Beecher Longyear, was a teacher, philanthropist, and member of the Daughters of the Revolution. She was also involved in historic preservation work, such as funding the first King James Version of the Bible in braille, working with the Longyear Foundation, and helping develop collections for Christian Science.[27] Upon returning to Marquette after Guåhan, Paul took up similar historic preservation work, such as the Fort Wilkins project and Henry Rowe Schoolcraft (Indian Agency) House in Sault Ste. Marie, Michigan.[28] In what follows, I examine the landscape of Paul's desire to photograph in Guåhan and her work as a teacher in the Normal School for how they shaped and were in turn reshaped by the island's landscape and Native desires. Before turning more fully to this work, however, we need to explore the aesthetic of the picturesque in the history of photography for flux in how the genre has been defined and redefined historically and into the present, in terms of shifting ideas about what constitutes nature, human artifice, and beauty. Ultimately, efforts to define the picturesque can also index how we understand history itself.

According to Geoffrey Batchen, the genre of the picturesque has roots in the emergence of a "desire to photograph" that can be traced back even decades prior to the invention of photography in 1839, and more specifically to the work of protophotographers who yearned for the inscribed image—a term Batchen uses to refer to the technical precursor to the camera proper in which images could be written onto special parchment through controlled exposure to light. In his history of photography, Batchen acknowledges the importance of poststructuralist analyses of the inherent instability of the meanings of photographs and images, of the need to analyze these artifacts in terms of the discursive practices that govern their production but do not guarantee definitive meanings. But Batchen is also interested in historicizing photography's central aesthetic (the picturesque), one that is best expressed in the art's historical desire to capture, often spontaneously, that which is inherently or intrinsically visually appealing. Initially, these were thought to reside exclusively in nature and landscape but later could also be found in anything said to be inherently beautiful, visually appealing, or romantic. In historicizing photography through this aesthetic, Batchen traces this specific desire in the writings of early nineteenth-century photographers—"from an occasional, isolated, individual fantasy to a demonstrably widespread social imperative"—and especially highlights the multiple manifestations of its (the desire for the picturesque) continuity into the vocabulary of early twentieth-century photography. Batchen also finds and outlines a strong link between drawing and photography, including the formal training in both that is required to capture the picturesque spontaneously in nature and especially in landscape and noting a deep bias toward photography as better able than drawing to capture true nature.[29] He writes that, regarding content and genre, the picturesque lent itself to the capture of landscape and "provided its adherents with a widely recognized set of conventions and aesthetic standards by which to make and judge landscape images."[30] For the implications of this judgment on how we think about history, we will return later to Batchen. For now, we turn to one particular "adherent."

An Emotional Landscape of Desires

Armed with formal training and professional experience in architecture and photography, Helen Paul set out to find these conventions, standards, and aesthetics in Guåhan and put them to use. In time, in the tropics, she too would become a landlooker, though her discerning and her own version of the picturesque would extend beyond the physical and into the social and cultural landscape. In tropical Guåhan, Paul's own desire to photograph helped justify the navy's civilizing and modernizing mission, but it also at times became out of focus with it. As Jane Lydon writes, "In photography's tactile and excessive transcendence of its authenticating function, in its expression of the colonizers' own uncertainties regarding their project, and in its assertion of indigenous

FIGURE 3.1 Photograph of Hagåtña Bay by Helen Paul. Courtesy of the Helen Paul Collection 1917–19, Richard Flores Taitano Micronesian Area Research Center, University of Guam.

objectives, the visual archive reveals a more dynamic and intimate relationship" between colonial photographer and Native subject than has been allowed."[31]

A third of the body of Helen Paul's photographs of the picturesque is of nature and landscape sans humans or human-made artifacts (figure 3.1). Most feature what Mary Louise Pratt calls the "imperial gaze" of the panorama. Pratt defines this gaze as the "seeing of the spaces of others and otherness" within colonial systems of knowledge, value, and beauty—an inscription that made possible the "dispossession of New World territories for capitalist consumption."[32] Of course, the absence of human subjects and human-made objects in Paul's panoramics or other photos of nature does not signal the absence of human presence. We perceive these in a given photographer's *agency* in considering any number of aspects involved in *taking* a picture: choice of subject matter, framing, lighting, composition, and in the invention of the camera and its precursors. Moreover, the idea of nature itself is, by definition, a human concept. So, too, is the picturesque.

As Batchen argues, the picturesque and efforts to theorize the picturesque (i.e., picturesque theory)—like nature itself (or theories of nature)—were in constant flux, expanding at times, contracting at others. At other times, the effort to define the aesthetic experienced moments of existential crisis: Did it or did it not inhere in nature and hence have to exclude anything human-made? Where and how did one draw the line between what is nature and what is human-made? At different times in different historical moments, the picturesque might include only nature or nature with certain categories of man-made objects, like buildings, provided they met certain criteria involving what constituted beauty, itself a notion in flux and always contested. For Batchen, above all else, the import of understanding the history of the picturesque was that the changing definitional landscapes of the aesthetic were "signifiers of history."[33] Following Batchen, I view Helen Paul's collection for insights into the traces of its cultural moments in which larger historical and structural narratives get inscribed or imprinted in images that are likewise conditioned by the particularities of CHamoru landscapes and bodyscapes as they are captured by the eye or optics of the latest generation of new women with the kind of technical training in photography's central conventions.

Consider, for example, how the choice and composition of figure 3.2 (*The Ancient "Capilla" of Anigua*) of an otherwise nondescript white stone building of Spanish-era architecture set against a coconut grove backdrop offers a visual and textual narrative of Guåhan's past in how they themselves provided a cultural and historical setting for the dominant or primary image of a CHamoru woman and (presumably) her children. Placing the Natives in the foreground against this backdrop, the photograph "tells" a cultural story of CHamoru female subjectivity in relation to its children against the historical tension between nature in Guåhan and Spanish-era artifice. The visual narrative suggests a gradual story of CHamoru severance from nature through a history of European encroachment. There is, I suggest, more than a tinge of nostalgia for the days when a camera or a sketch might include only Native women and children and nature to convey the picturesque of real beauty and truth. To assist in the interpretation of this photograph, as with the remaining two-thirds containing humans and artifices, Paul often furnished captions that named the historical significance or the cultural truth of the subject matter, as if the picturesque, visually appealing, and momentous were still not self-evident or sufficient, or perhaps to thwart a potential crisis in interpretation or representation. Captions provide what Susan Sontag called the "missing voice" of a photograph's expectation "to speak for truth."[34] The caption in this case named the historical (i.e., human-made) context through its age ("the oldest") and its

FIGURE 3.2 *The Ancient "Capilla" of Anigua.* Courtesy of the Helen Paul Collection 1917–19, Richard Flores Taitano Micronesian Area Research Center, University of Guam.

particular function and significance (the first chapel "built by the first missionaries"), which is still used by the devout locale. Another important detail is that the only concession to modernity is "its new roof made of corrugated iron."

Insinuated in this desire to photograph and to narrate the historical significance of the picturesque is another range of desires that can be characterized as ambivalently sympathetic toward both the CHamoru other and the self's broader civilizing and uplifting project among them. For my eye, this photograph conveys the paternal and benevolent sympathy that U.S. colonial officials in Guåhan and in other former Spanish colonies felt toward the victims of an antiquated, antimodern, and stagnant Spanish Catholic order. To justify the wider modernizing project, the U.S. Navy constructed a particular colonial sympathy for former subjects under Spanish colonialism. It was not just that former Spanish colonies lacked civilization, but they needed to be saved from Spanish misrule—hence the navy's naming of the specific mission in Guåhan as the "long road to rehabilitation."

Paul's Normal School students would articulate this pre-American-era misfortune and misery under Spain. In an essay entitled "Can the Guamanians

Govern Themselves?" Miguel Salas wrote that, "before the Americans came to this place [Guåhan,] they [the CHamorus] did not know how to get clean and eat regular nutritious food, they sat on the floor before the stove and ate their food with their uncleaned [sic] hand." According to Salas, and indicative of the deep hold of kostumbren CHamoru, Catholicism was the only improvement to come out of Spain. Under the United States, in contrast, there were many examples of progress: civilization, cleanliness, high buildings, good roads, bridges, good clean water, sanitary toilets, hospitals and good doctors, "more crops," "lots of money," government employees, good schools, great stores, and "shops of all kinds."[35]

Four years later, in 1921, a student of Agueda Johnston would convey similar misfortunes. In a letter-writing assignment to an American pen pal, one Margie Fraker, Ana B. Charfauros wrote that, "since when the Spanish took position [sic] of Guam. They did not increase the island. But when the America took position [sic] of it. The island looks beautiful everything get increase nowaday [sic]."[36]

This pro-American (or thoroughly schooled) sentiment by CHamoru students of all that is "beautiful" and "good" (though not necessarily maolek in the CHamoru language context) may have been scripted to give the American teacher, and later the Native teacher, what they wanted to hear and feel, or perhaps even to get an A on assignments. In a visitor study of an exhibit (2003) that I curated on Helen Paul's collection, respondents gave similar explanations to account for the pro-American and sentimental writings by Paul's Normal School students.[37] The students' writings furnish an early record of a new class of CHamorus investing in progressive rituals, like literacy and modern education, in the interest of constructing new economic and social opportunities for themselves and their families that took place amid an already two-decade-old elite CHamoru male-led political movement, to gain U.S. citizenship as a way to terminate American naval military rule.

Meanwhile, other CHamorus fashioning similar new mobilities through English and the epistolary form seized on other opportunities. In 1922, another student of Johnston, Beatrice Perez, asked Fraker (who seems to have had her hands full with pen pals from Johnston's class!) if she would purchase items she and her sisters were "crazy to have" but could not acquire in Guåhan. Perez inserted advertisements of the requested items: one black eyebrow pencil, one rouge lipstick, Madame La Fontaine's *How to Write Love Letters*, and a book on "telling fortunes by cards." She closed with another request to Fraker: "Please don't mention in your letter that I told you to buy those things for me because my daddy is reading the letter first then he gave [sic] it to me when he got [it] from [the] P.O."[38] In a follow-up letter to Fraker, Perez wrote, "Please don't tell anybody about these things that I told you to buy for me." Afraid that her father or someone else might still find out, Perez included this postscript: "Please tear this letter if you finish reading it."[39] This may explain why some CHamoru parents were opposed to sending their girls to school: for fear that they would learn to write love letters.[40] From Perez's letter, we get another glimpse of how young CHamoru women began to explore new forms of American modernity while working spaces opened up in the intersections and interactions with white women. Indeed, we get a glimpse of a gendered version of the CHamoru picturesque—the expressed new desires and longings (for wearing make-up and writing love letters) amid and against CHamoru-Spanish Catholic patriarchy's strong chokehold on women's behavior, sexuality, and aesthetics.

In another iteration of Helen Paul's picturesque (figure 3.3), this time of how the aesthetically pleasing was writ on the body, two CHamoru schoolchildren, "Jesus and Dolores," appear innocent and solemn, dressed in white. One might also surmise from the boy's half smile a general sense of Native satisfaction and contentment. What also stands out in the photograph is the contrast from the interstices of brown (faces and appendages) amid the bleached and bleaching effects of the contents and composition of the photograph (the clothing, the wall, the ground, and objects the children are holding). Thanks to the caption, one learns the boy is making a basket and the girl is making lace. One also learns that they are at school and are taught courses and trades along a gendered division of labor. The navy implemented this curriculum to help CHamoru children become industrious citizens who would eventually reverse a situation in which the island's "wealth of material" went to "waste" and for which Governor Roy Smith in 1917 established the first Guam Industrial Fair (held on July 4) for the purpose of showcasing and selling artisan crafts and agricultural "yields."[41] But the caption also reveals what the visual does not: that in addition to the U.S. Navy inculcating CHamoru children in handicraft and vocational skills, such as basket weaving and lace making, the navy also taught the three Rs in terms of a specifically American education. And though we get a sense from the caption of the tensions between what colonial authorities desired for the CHamorus—a good balance between vocational skills and an American education—and what CHamoru children themselves presumably wanted (to make lace more than learning to read, write, and do math), neither the visual nor the caption gives any inkling of the subjugation if not violence of the presumably benign gift of U.S. colonialism and an American-style education in Guåhan. Determined to break this discrimination imposed

FIGURE 3.3 *Jesus and Dolores at School.* Courtesy of the Helen Paul Collection 1917–19, Richard Flores Taitano Micronesian Area Research Center, University of Guam.

on an already strict CHamoru-Spanish Catholic code of proper place, one Maria Perez went off to school in the United States in 1920 claiming, "Women in Guam must all plow the fields with oxen . . . I want to do something different, but there are no schools there [in Guåhan] to prepare us for anything except basket weaving and cooking."[42]

Hiding behind the photograph and the text are the austere reality and lived experience of CHamoru children not only prohibited from speaking fino' CHamoru in the classroom but punished and fined for doing so. Instead, we are given a sentimental treatment of Native contentment and what Wexler describes as a "solution to a clash of forces that we must learn to see."[43] Indeed, as Wexler argues, the "theater of force founded in sentimentalism's power to naturalize the violent text is nowhere more evident . . . than in the work done by photography in institutions such as schools, missions, hospitals, agencies, and armies."[44] In this regard, the work of white new-women photographers in denying the structural impact and forced assimilation of United States overseas expansion is especially insidious. As Wexler reminds us, these denials and acts of "tender violence" developed "not as a matter of conscious policy but as a matter of gender—that is, as a matter of course . . . theirs was a seemingly natural way of seeing that did not imagine itself as misrepresenting."[45]

Though not a professional photographer, Helen Paul was a trained and avid one whose images revealed her eye for the picturesque, which also came with the ability or desire to obfuscate structures of power through its sentimental and nostalgic longing for natural beauty and truth in the landscape and, if needed, American-era buildings like schools and hospitals and the good things that transpired in them, such as "modern" education and public health. So, even amid potential effacement and misconceptions, Paul used captions to bring attention to what was good. These desires by the good navy wife to show the good Native were especially timely (or perhaps touchy, depending on the angle or proximity) given that CHamorus had already begun to challenge the legitimacy of military rule in Guåhan.[46] Though Paul's photographs may not have been intended to go public, at least not originally, they convey a picturesque deemed expressive of a peculiar but nonetheless agreeable kind of beauty that is brought into focus through the caption.

Thus, in another photograph (figure 3.4), the word *dandy* in the title was used to connote agreeableness and goodness. Elsewhere in her collection the term was intended as a compliment to a student, Simon Sanchez, on an assignment about a love-struck lancheru, Juan, who one evening while walking along the Apotgan kanton tåsi (beach) in his Sunday best—"an open coat, a beautiful

A YOUNG CHAMORRO DANDY.

The young Chamorro is usually a sleek, muscular fellow, very vain of his good looks-- and indeed, he is generally taller and better looking than his Tagalog cousin of the Philippines.

FIGURE 3.4 *A Young Chamorro Dandy*. Courtesy of the Helen Paul Collection 1917–19, Richard Flores Taitano Micronesian Area Research Center, University of Guam.

Panama hat, and a diamond ring"—met the elegant Carmen in her fine attire "whistling merrily" under a breadfruit tree.[47] In this photograph, the caption also distinguishes the CHamoru of Guåhan from the Tagalog of the Philippines. Perhaps for Helen Paul, like Susan Dyer before her, the Filipino armed insurgency (rather than described as a continued struggle for independence) against Americans only a decade before the Pauls' assignment in that archipelago was what made the CHamoru appear to be good, sleek, muscular, taller and "better looking" than his "Tagalog cousin." Opposite and as opposed to the Philippines, Guåhan is posed and reposed as pacific, obedient, welcoming of American rule and order. But the idea of the dandy has other, sexual connotations. In his analysis of the construction of whiteness and a nineteenth-century working class consciousness, David Roediger traces the racial origins of *coon* and *buck*—terms that feature importantly to the figure of the dandy. A buck of the American Revolution era meant a dashing, young, virile man, ostensibly white. A century later, the term became associated with the dandy and meant a "self-proclaimed fascinator of women."[48] During the mid- to late-1800s Reconstruction era, both terms—*buck* and *dandy*—referred specifically to black men. The racialized black dandy, writes Monica Miller, is a threat because he is at once masculine and feminine, also "aggressively heterosexual yet not quite a real man."[49] In her "most amusing recollections" of her travels during the early 1900s, the American navy wife Edith Crose painted a colorful image of one such dandy. Crose recalled how Willie was an "uneducated" but faithful and funny "house servant," indeed "the best looking darky boy," whose one ambition was to be known as a "sport" and who kept a suit nearby at a friend's house because, according to Crose, "He wouldn't ask no lady to go walking with him" in his uniform pants but also "wouldn't go with no lady who wasn't a swell dresser."[50] As with Crose's Willie, perhaps Paul's *Young Chamorro Dandy* was a specific kind of amusement and "animatedness" to be found and had in the imperial circuits.

At the same time, Paul's use of the word *dandy* and by association dandyism also connected with links between dandyism and *rowdyism*. Rowdyism, or the potential of CHamoru men in Guåhan to become restless or idle and to cause trouble, was something the navy cautioned against in the 1920s and 1930s. Governor Edmund Root (1931–33) in his annual report of 1932 raised concerns that young CHamoru men who walked about the streets in a state of rowdyism were becoming too proud and arrogant and too concerned with leading a "dressed up life" rather than toiling in work that "soiled their hands."[51] Though navy officials expressed these concerns explicitly in terms of the island's economy, the problem of rowdyism (and dandyism) that emanated from being too educated and not performing enough physical labor—at least not the right kind of work that the navy taught in agriculture and industry courses under its training-for-life curriculum—was also about anxieties and fears around CHamoru male masculinity and sexuality.[52] In Paul's caption, perhaps the fear is that CHamorus might possibly become too educated or, worse, become too much like the infamous Filipino *ilustrado*, the learned elite, who only decades earlier led the rebellion against Spanish and U.S. rule.[53] Ironically, in labeling the CHamoru a "dandy" in supposed stark contrast to the Filipino, Paul's textual addendum to the visual text of her optic also runs the risk of making key links (and kinship) between the two Austronesian cousins. In labeling the young brown CHamoru man a dandy, even in the seemingly innocent realm of the family souvenir scrapbook or concerted attempt to conserve, she also unwittingly and in unmarked ways runs the risk of placing the racialized and sexualized Native man between white woman's virtue and honor and white men's chivalry and compulsion to defend that virtue and honor, as perhaps it was emboldened under the navy. It is precisely in Paul's attraction to CHamoru dandyism, its agreeableness, its goodness, its picturesque, through the "I" or specificity of her photographic eye on the specificity of CHamoru islanders, that we begin to get a sense of the dangerous and racialized liaisons between navy wives and Native lives. These dangerous links—the other side of the willingness or eagerness to work with white women—are evident in the Native recoil in the mere mention of the term *navy wife* in hypermilitarized places like Guåhan and Hawai'i that trouble boundaries prescribed by patriarchy, paternal colonialism, and domesticity.[54]

The visual and textual narrative in figure 3.5 offers something of a female and feminine counterpart to the CHamoru dandy in that it also rallies around the significance of good physical appearance in women as shaped now (in contrast to the past, under Spanish influence) by good modern political aspirations under American tutelage. Beauty (and conviviality) here were of a particular kind of racialized and sexualized breed and breeding of the CHamoru woman—that of a young, fair-skinned, and American-flag-donning heterosexual woman that we might now call the "new mestisa." In this photo, we get a lingering sympathy for an earlier colonial disorder, as it was bolstered or corrected en route to being replaced by an American racialized and sexualized iconography. Traditionally, the term *mestiza* (or *mestisa*) refers to a woman of mixed heritage, but it also commonly relates to an early CHamoru style of dress, such as the one worn by the woman in figure 3.2. Literally and discursively a mix, the mestisa evoked a cultural and genealogical "amalgamation" between CHamorus and Spaniards or other mestisus/as from elsewhere in the

MESTIZA BEAUTIES OF GUAM.

These young ladies, posing as "The Allied Nations" in an amateur vaudeville performance, fully justify the long standing reputation for good looks and good breeding that is the heritage of the mestiza (Spanish- Chamorro) girls of Guam. Throughout Micronesia they have been much sought after as wives, traders from the Bonin Islands and from distant Yap vying for their favor.

FIGURE 3.5 *Mestiza Beauties of Guam*. Courtesy of the Helen Paul Collection 1917–19, Richard Flores Taitano Micronesian Area Research Center, University of Guam.

Spanish empire and their mixed investments and vestments of multiple origins. In drawing and staging attention (Paul not only photographed but also organized vaudeville performances) to the women's mixed-race heritage, Paul's *Mestiza Beauties* may have also established an early visual archive of the American desire to thwart political grievances of the time—among them, as we gleaned earlier, political clamoring for self-government and a petition for U.S. citizenship.[55] But Paul's text and image were of a different kind of mestisa, as signified by the draping of the American flag and the staging of internationalism and diplomacy. More importantly and disturbingly, the photograph asserts CHamoru women's long-standing availability throughout the region as, in Paul's own words, the class of women who were "much sought after as wives."

Precisely because of how colonial discourse can so easily erase CHamoru women's determinations (and Native lands) as well as disavow the historical violence involved in such discursive machinations through more specific practices that valorized their status as beautiful (objects to behold) or available (objects to be held or possessed), it is important for me to pause and name specific CHamoru women whose historical reputations—their "value" for recordation in the archives—have been based precisely on their status as "wives" and wives of white men because of the terms of what supposedly constituted their beauty and/or agreeableness.[56] In what might seem a diversion from the main path of this chapter, I pause here in order to disrupt, for the record and for posterity, the extent to which these famalao'an CHamoru and hagan Guåhan (daughters of Guåhan) have been diverted from Indigenous orders through their gendered and sexualized marginalization as beautiful and pleasing objects of marriage. In her specific reference to "traders" and "wives" in the Bonin Islands and Yap, Paul draws attention to earlier histories of travel involving most likely the CHamoru women Maria de los Santos y Castro (Maria Castro de los Santos), Joaquina de la Cruz, and Bartola Garrido. I shall return to these women alluded to in Paul's caption shortly. For the moment, however, and as a way of further bringing CHamoru women out of obscurity, I furnish additional information from a January 1919 article in the *Guam News Letter*. From the article, we learn that this vaudeville performance was a two-day Red Cross fundraiser in Dorn Hall, put on by the ladies of the station, and that Helen Paul directed the event and designed the set, curtains, and "Oriental" backdrop.[57] We also learn the names of the "young girls" and their dramatic roles—the "prettiest of the native girls," that is, who provided the "climax to an evening of fun." They are Isabel O'Connor (America); Jesusa Blaz (France); Maria Leon Guerrero (Portugal); Josefina Unpingco (China); Isabel Perez (Serbia); Rosa Veneziano (Greece); Concepcion Leon Guerrero (England); Remedios Leon Guerrero (Italy); Maria Gutierrez (Brazil); Magdalena Unpingco (Japan); Pilar Calvo (Romania); Julia Martinez (Belgium); and Maria Perez (playing the part of Columbia, the "Goddess of Liberty").

In the few historical accounts of Maria de los Santos (b. 1828), we know that she departed Guåhan in 1843 on board the schooner of an English merchant, Henry Millinchamp, bound for the Bonin (now Ogasawara) Archipelago, which lies between Japan and the Marianas. Ogasawara had been colonized by the British via Hawai'i in 1827 as a new whaling settlement. There, Maria was married three times. One of those was to the American whaler Nathaniel Savory (b. 1794), with whom she had eight children. Most accounts say she boarded the schooner to bid farewell to another CHamoru woman, Joaquina de la Cruz. The sources vary as to whether Maria was held on board against her will or left Guåhan on her own accord. Noteworthy also is the story of de la Cruz (her aunt) and her connection to Millinchamp. In these accounts, Millinchamp convinced Maria's aunt, Joaquina, to leave an abusive relationship in Guåhan and start anew in the Bonin Islands.[58] If it is in fact the case that Maria had been abducted, the sin of Paul's visual text of CHamoru women as mere "sought after wives" can be understood as an unconscionable generalization that basically valorizes specific historical incidences of violence against famalao'an CHamoru. On the other hand, if Maria had left of her own accord, encouraged by her aunt, we might still read Paul's caption as a glossing over of an earlier history of kinalamten famalao'an through desires for new adventures or perhaps even to flee abuses and violence back home.

The Guåhan-born Bartola Garrido was another woman alluded to as one of those "much sought after as wives" who ended up where they did. Her story, even what little is known, needs to be freed from the disavowed violence of such picturesque visual narrativities, in this case, from how the very category of "wife" for Indigenous women in particular rests on their value as somehow more naturally rooted to land and family such that venturing too far from home might incur for them the wrath and reputation of abandoning their cultures. What is known of Garrido (b. early 1800s) is that she was educated by Augustinian Recollect priests and left Guåhan in 1875 on board the schooner *Arabia*, which at the time was commandeered by the notorious blackbirder and pirate William "Bully" Hayes. The *Arabia*, some say, was lost and eventually drifted to Palau (Belau) in Micronesia. According to some accounts, the American whaler Crayton Philo Holcomb rescued the ship, and from there, Holcomb and Garrido eventually ended up in Yap, where they continued his business ventures.[59] For her part, as one of the earliest CHamorus to reside in Yap, Garrido would gain prominence (or notoriety) during the German-Spanish struggle to control the island. In August 1885, after the Germans *beat* the Spanish by raising the German flag over the island first, Garrido promptly tore it down and defiantly raised the Spanish flag, which she reportedly had sewn herself and hung on a tree at the highest point of the coastline. She continued to fly the Spanish flag for several months, even during the formal German occupation of Yap.

Like de los Santos and de la Cruz before her, Garrido gets subsumed beneath narratives, images, and captions, which do not just privilege European and American husbands but do so by valorizing these women as covetable objects whose worth emanated intrinsically from the supposed physical and cultural beauty and truth that resided either naturally in the bodily landscape of their identities as wives or in the landscaped identities improved upon through the man-made labor of their husbands or paternal parentage. In either case, the valorized reduction of these specific CHamoru women to the status of wives, or, in Garrido's case, "mistress and helpmate," forecloses on the future trans-Indigenous political and cultural possibilities that can be imagined through a critical understanding of Native histories of travel, mobility, and the various transgressions these histories intimate.[60] That there is a seaside locale in Yap called Chamorro Bay, for example, or that in the British-held Japanese Bonin Islands, de los Santos refused to give up on her CHamoru-Spanish Catholicism, suggests there was a CHamoru woman's side to the heteropatriarchal history of American whalers, merchants, and traders and the Indigenous herstory (and theirstory) domiciled in the new woman's captioned photograph.

It is imperative to not lose track of Native determinations, however entangled they were in the colonial picturesque, in images of the dandy or visually appealing, and in the landscape of colonial desires, contentment, repulsion, fears, and anxieties. From this context, Helen Paul's position as a teacher at the Normal School and, more specifically, her writing assignments on subjects often pertaining to CHamoru custom and culture (and in the fino' håya) must also be examined as excursions into the picturesque of CHamoru cultural and political consciousness. These excursions, or perhaps dabbles, into the Native picturesque, into the tåddong CHamoru knowledges and traditions, featured information on such subjects as the phases of the moon, planting, miracles, spirituality, and child-birthing customs. Even though the navy may have encouraged wives to cultivate civilian contacts and "show an interest" in the customs, culture, and religions of different people, there was also a point at which navy wives had to be careful not to overstep accessible "safety zones" (of physical, social, and affective spaces in which *difference* was deemed unthreatening) lest their interests be deemed as counterproductive to the navy's civilizing efforts.[61] These intersections between Native lives and navy wives may have been especially troubling given racial anxieties and tensions in the United States and those brewing in Guåhan, which resulted in the island's first antimiscegenation law, passed by Governor William Gilmer in 1919.[62] In the same year that the Pauls arrived (1917), Governor Smith proclaimed English as the official language and prohibited the use of the CHamoru language in public, except for the purposes of translating it into English.[63] Or perhaps such excursions were, for Paul, continuations of or reversions to the settlement work she had begun in New York shortly after her graduation from MIT.

Colonial Nostalgia and Native Sentience in the Guåhan Flag

Helen Paul's diversions and excursions into the exotic realm made for another interesting sentiment—nostalgia, which would in turn work its way into CHamoru nationalist discourses. We return to a familiar photograph of landscape and nature (figure 3.1) and juxtapose this with Helen Paul's sketch of the Guåhan flag (figure 3.6). The nostalgia that structured the iconic representation of a particular picturesque scene in Guåhan is similar to but not identical to the affectionate recollections that Paul's former students expressed for their beloved teacher. It is somewhat ironic that the same affections seem to inhabit present-day CHamoru nationalist feelings around the Guåhan flag as a symbol of a proud CHamoru heritage. The image in figure 3.1 shows a picturesque shoreline with a palm tree and an oceanic backdrop. Recall that this was one of those landscape photographs in Paul's collection whose self-evident beauty did not have a caption and thus was not thought by Paul to require one.

In comparing the image of the Guåhan seal, the central feature of the Guåhan flag design (figure 3.6), to the photograph and nostalgic imagery on which the seal was based (figure 3.1), one notices in the flag the erasure of the thatched house and the inclusion of a sakman under sail. In his video narration of the semiotics of canoes in Micronesia, Vicente Diaz points out the troubling affinities between the presence and absence of canoes and what they stand for in prevailing conceptions of culture and history. Diaz explains that the absence of the sailing canoe among CHamorus in Guåhan in conventional historiography had been equated with the absence of Indigenous culture after centuries of Spanish colonialism, while the presence of canoes in a place like Polowat is equated with the survival of culture but the absence of history. In another words, CHamorus "get to have history but no culture" while Polowatese "get to have culture but no history."[64] In Guåhan's waters around the time of Paul's presence, one would no longer find traditional sailing canoes, although the smaller paddling canoes, the galaide, were still common. More importantly, around this time, the narrative of the disappearance of authentic Native traditions was already well established. Thus, any allusion to sailing canoes for which CHamoru were marveled at in the sixteenth and seventeenth centuries bespoke a nostalgia for the precolonial days and constituted what Renato Rosaldo describes as "imperialist nostalgia" or longing even for what Susan Stewart calls a "prelapsarian" experience.[65]

Indeed, it is imperative to keep track of Indigenous determinations, however enmeshed they were in colonial sentiment, in the picturesque nostalgia.

140 Chapter Three

FIGURE 3.6 Blueprint of the Guåhan flag, 1917. Courtesy of the Helen Paul Collection 1917–19, Richard Flores Taitano Micronesian Area Research Center, University of Guam.

Also in 1917, during Paul's time in Guåhan, Governor Roy Smith established the Guam Congress in response to CHamoru clamoring for political autonomy and U.S. citizenship. The Guam Congress, whose members were elected to the Guam House of Council or Guam Assembly had no lawmaking powers, and served only as an advisory body to the naval governor. Governor Smith also established the first annual Guam Industrial Fair in 1917 as part of an effort to keep CHamorus in line with the navy's prescribed training and education for the purposes of providing labor for such public works projects as building better roads, adopting a Protestant and industrious work ethic, and developing agriculture. The event was held in July and was intended for CHamorus to showcase their agricultural produce and livestock and to sell Native arts and crafts.[66] On the closing day of the first annual fair, Governor Smith delivered a speech that was intended to encapsulate the fair's success and boost morale. He told CHamorus that Guåhan "had a habit of hiding its light under a bushel" and that the objective of the fair was to "make the light shine in the open."[67] Governor Smith then proceeded to instruct CHamorus on proper ways to breed cattle. In a proud nod to selective breeding (and lesson in agricultural eugenics), but what for some CHamoru farmers may have brought feelings of na'mamahlao/shame (particularly since many of them may have been older than Smith), Governor Smith encouraged farmers to abandon their "old habits." He specifically told them to set "aside their strongest and finest animals for breeding" and work the inferior ones and that they should visit the navy's agricultural experiment station, where they could learn to breed their cattle with American-imported "blooded stock."[68] A writing assignment by one of Paul's students, Carmen Leon Guerrero, offers an interesting counternarrative to Governor Smith's lecture to CHamoru farmers on not recognizing their full potential. Leon Guerrero delineated inafa'maolek seasoned and old habits as they related to the different phases of the moon: planting, crab and deer hunting, and the cutting of coconut leaves for new roof thatching.[69]

Paul's student assignments and conversations she had with the CHamoru teacher and later paymaster Atanacio Perez, seem to indicate her interest in Native desires and aspirations. Wanting to engage, or perhaps just gauge, the sentiments of her CHamoru students (ages eighteen to twenty-five), Paul instructed them to write about the Guam Industrial Fair of 1919. Paul would have been keen to hear what students might say because she was directly involved in its organization. She drew up blueprints and sketches, including one that was used at the fair to illustrate how to breed and raise pigs. Though nowhere near the caliber of the architecture of American pastoralism that Rebecca McKenna traces in Baguio in the Philippines, these industrial spaces at the annual fair in Guåhan's capital represent American colonial efforts to domesticate and breed out an inferior Native stock.[70] Paul was also elected as chairperson of decorations and was involved in the selection of the Guam Industrial Fair queen of 1919, which might explain Paul's interest in (and close-up photo of) then-queen Josefina Pangelinan—a "picturesque" image (figure 3.7), which did not require a caption.[71] Like Dyer, whose imperial reach kept her in the loop with the Susana, Paul kept an eye on the picturesque (and pastoral) landscape of the Guam Industrial Fair, as evidenced from a photo in her collection taken a year after her departure from Guåhan. In the imperial reach of the caption that she furnished in this 1920 photo, Paul brought attention to the opening day of the annual fair and the crowning of the queen, in that year, a "CHamoru belle" named Maria Perez.[72]

Paul's CHamoru students wrote about the fair, both its desirable and undesirable qualities. Their desires differed from those of Governor Smith from two years earlier. Some suggested ways to improve the fair, as evidenced in their concerns for how to accommodate the manåmko', especially those

FIGURE 3.7 *Guam Fair Queen.* Courtesy of the Helen Paul Collection 1917–19, Richard Flores Taitano Micronesian Area Research Center, University of Guam.

who traveled a long way from northern and southern villages to Hagåtña to attend the festivities, which lasted two to three days. Rosario Perez expressed concerns about the pressure the fair put on southern farmers. As if dry seasons and typhoons were not stressful enough, now farmers were expected to produce and exhibit each year at the venue and for observers. Perez cautioned: "I want to suggest to you about how to bring their minds back to the Fair, those Inarajan people because they are so disappointed this year, that they are not going to take another trouble for nothing like this year. The dry season tried their nerves very much."[73] Others focused on the more picturesque elements. Carmen Leon Guerrero wrote of "all the pretty things, the big sports and parades, the big crowd of people, and the Guam Queen," which made her feel like she was "taking a trip to a foreign country."[74] The best example of the "pretty things" for Baltazar Carbullido was also the queen.[75] The queen's coronation was part of the annual ritual, and it was often the case that the queen and her royal court were of the mestisa class. Governor Gilmer too boasted about the ritual and hoped that "many *fair* daughters" would continue to be crowned.[76] While Gilmer was most likely referring to light-skinned mestisas, the word *fair* also connotes innocence and an "agreeable" disposition, both of which, like mestizas, nod to the racialized and sexualized desire for the picturesque. In Gilmer's observation, connotations of the word *fair* also condition or qualify the peculiar choice for designating candidates for the crown ("daughters") who will vie for the title Queen of the *Fair*—the Guam Industrial Fair, that is, whose purpose is to elevate Guåhan away from being steeped in semidarkness under Spanish rule to modern civilization under American tutelage, education, health, and public works. Maria Ulloa, who would become one of the island's leading educators, confessed that, though the best part of the fair was the queen's coronation, she also liked the parade because it featured boys from the navy band and cadets who composed the Guam Militia.[77]

Maria Ulloa's reference to the Guam Militia in her writings on the Guam Fair is telling and timely since, like the recruitment of Native teachers and nurses and the establishment of the all-Native navy band, the enlistment of Native boys into the Guam Militia was an important part of the naval government's efforts to modernize Guåhan not just through Americanization but through the regimen of military culture. Governor Smith established the Guam Militia in 1917 in preparation for World War I. Service was mandatory for CHamoru men between the ages of sixteen and twenty-three.[78] Once the militia was formed, Governor Smith deemed it only fitting that Guåhan should now have its own flag, even if the island's male leaders had been agitating for self-government and U.S. citizenship since 1901 and had been continuously thwarted in that agitation by the naval government of the island.[79] At any rate—or, to be more precise, to calibrate or measure the rate and standard by which the island could collectively imagine its political future as an entity—Governor Smith put out a call in the *Guam News Letter* for a Guåhan flag design contest. Helen Paul, the stage-designing, coronation-organizing, student-teaching, landlooking, photo-taking, sketcher-of-all-things-picturesque navy wife, entered the contest and won, with a design of a panoramic landscape whose only human-made object was a sakman. If the design evoked colonial nostalgia for the purity of an earlier CHamoru people and culture, the winning picturesque image was also not, as many contend, an original work by Helen Paul.

Guåhan Flag Contest-ations

At the closing of the Guam Fair festivities in 1918, Governor Smith witnessed the culmination of his desires for the Natives of Guåhan when the Guam Militia, brandishing the Guam Militia flag, marched by the grandstand. It was the first time the Guam Militia flag was displayed (figure 3.8). In his concluding

FIGURE 3.8 First Guåhan flag displayed, Guam Industrial Fair, 1918. Governor Roy Smith Collection, box 24, folder 3 "Photographs of Guam." Courtesy of Naval Historical Collection Archives, U.S. Naval War College.

remarks, Smith called attention to the significance of the militia, whose "smart appearance, military bearing, and correct drilling made a fine impression." "The inhabitants of the Island," he continued, "see in the Cadets the first fruit of universal military training, which they themselves petitioned the Governor to establish. On this drill they bore for the first time, along with the national colors, the Island Flag of Guam."[80]

Two different iterations of the visually appealing in the Guam Cadets (also known as the Guam Militia)—the first, as observed lovingly by Governor Smith, and the second, by "the inhabitants of the Island" themselves who, we are told by the governor, were gathered "to see" the uplifting spectacle—would congeal in another picturesque image (figure 3.9) taken not by Helen Paul (who is pictured in the front kneeling) but by someone else. It is tempting to wonder if it was taken by her husband, LCDR Paul, or a CHamoru. In any case, Helen Paul felt compelled to narrate the picturesque, the visually appealing in what she saw in the photograph, and she did this with what else but a caption that called specific attention to traits in the CHamoru subjects of the photograph. The

FIGURE 3.9 *Fashion Show in Umatac Village*. Courtesy of the Helen Paul Collection 1917–19, Richard Flores Taitano Micronesian Area Research Center, University of Guam.

traits she saw in the photograph that was taken by someone else were, first, a "look" or, more specifically, a group of "fashionable"-looking CHamorus, who, incidentally, also hailed from down south in Humåtak, a rural, seaside village that to this day enjoys the reputation as one of the island's more famous picturesque villages; second, a sentiment of a particular technology (as in, the CHamorus "love to have their picture taken"); and third, for the fact of their "love" of having their picture taken, a sense of self-absorption, namely, their "vanity." Had the photographer been CHamoru, what would the picturesque be? My rhetorical question stems from two interests, an academic one and a more immediate, ongoing political one. The first is prompted by the question, what CHamoru in 1917 would own a camera? Or what CHamoru would be trusted by navy officials (or their wives) to operate one? One answer might be a CHamoru who had been traveling abroad. The seriousness of the second, political motive for the rhetorical question is prompted by the playful flight of the imagination of the first: What political and cultural possibilities are enabled when we center Indigenous desires for beauty, truth, and perfection, particularly through definitions and conventions that do not romanticize and sentimentalize purity and stasis in ways that erase and preempt competing alternatives? In fact, in the same way that rereading the essays of CHamoru students can offer counternarratives to those that are presented by colonial teachers, we can also take a second, closer look at photographs of Native peoples and Native landscapes for traces of such alternative possibilities that go against the grain of surface meanings intended by the photographer's eye.

Following Helen Paul's eye, as it zooms with textual assistance by the caption, we are led to a young member of what Paul calls the "Glorious Guam Militia." A closer look will show that this cadet is only one of two people in the frame who appear to be gazing back at the camera. Just why Paul might be drawn to the member of the "Glorious Guam Militia" is understandable given its link to the desire for a Guåhan flag, which prompted Governor Smith to call for a flag design contest, which in turn gave her the opportunity to do what she loved and was trained to do best. But, as will be shown in detail shortly, though canonical histories of the Guåhan flag attribute its design to Helen Paul, oral histories contest this claim. Interested in CHamoru reclamations of history and icon, as much as in the form and content of competing narratives swirling around the Guåhan flag, I now turn to a flurry of discourses and desires—Native, naval, local—and to early twentieth-century CHamoru longing and imaginings for a political picturesque and a CHamoru aesthetic that comes with it.

In another postwar rendering of the Guåhan flag (also referred to at one time as the Guam Militia flag), another one of Helen Paul's students recalled her teacher's own account of what inspired the drawing. In the recollection furnished by Remedios Perez (née Leon Guerrero), we can discern the picturesque that inspired Paul, or at least the picturesque of a post–World War II CHamoru woman's memory: There was a tall and lonely coconut tree standing at the mouth of the Såddok Hagåtña, which flows into the sea. The trunk of the tree was so bent and its roots were all so bare that it looked as if a slight breeze might cause it to topple into the water. Then a destructive typhoon in, 1918 hit the island, destroying many houses and uprooting many trees; yet when the typhoon abated, there stood the lonely coconut tree showing its firm determination to live in spite of the adversities. It continued to bear fruit and to be useful. Thus, this incident caused the artist to use the coconut tree as a symbol of courage, strength, and utility.[81]

In Remedios Perez's version, as well as Agueda Johnston's, Paul's inclusion (or co-optation?) of the CHamoru sakman was based on her desire to recognize the prowess and courage of the CHamorus. According to Perez, the famous landmark was Puntan Dos Amantes, or "Two Lover's Point," which represented "faithfulness." According to Johnston, Two Lover's Point for Helen

Paul symbolized "romance." Another point of difference is that Perez called attention to the shape of the seal, whereas Johnston made no mention of it. For Perez, the shape of the seal "resembled that of a Guamanian sling stone."[82] She explained, "For many years this was their only weapon in hunting and in warfare against the white man's firearms. It is a symbol of protection the people find in their home government." For Paul, the slingstone was an example of "'heliolithic' culture of the savage islanders" of Guåhan. This is the description she gave in a caption to a photograph she shot of a set of slingstones *discovered* (taken?) from Malesso/Merizo, perhaps while on one of her many treks around the island. Noteworthy in Perez's passage is the mention of the symbolic association of the slingstone, the traditional CHamoru weapon, with the protection that "the people find in their home government." It is important to ask, in the interest of tracking the question of whose nostalgia is at work here, which "white man" (the Spanish or the American) was the traditional slingstone aimed at in this post–World War II CHamoru recollection of a prewar white American woman's story?

Purging the Guåhan Flag of Naval Colonial Origins

Barring slight variations, Johnston's and Perez's renderings of the meanings behind the Guåhan flag have, for the most part, carried the day, although many say the cliff is Puntan Litekyan rather than Puntan Dos Amantes. In a 1968 GovGuam employee newspaper, *The Tablero*, the authors again attributed the design to Helen Paul. And again, the flag is said to represent perseverance, prowess, loyalty, and now also "sustenance."[83] CHamoru and local narratives have even, again for the most part, appropriated Johnston's description of the flag's tincture and heraldic colors: "Over a field of 'marine' blue was yellow, representing the sand, brown the tree's trunk, green its leaves, white the canoe's sail, grey the distant point, and red for G-U-A-M."[84] One thing is definite: Governor Roy Smith's equation of the lone coconut tree as a symbol of "agriculture" rather than determination and the canoe as a symbol of "commerce" rather than prowess—that is, his version of the picturesque and what constituted a proper flag—would not take root in postwar narratives of the Guåhan flag.[85]

Debates on whether the Guåhan flag truly represented Guåhan and the CHamorus and contestations over who really designed the flag emerged in the late 1970s. On January 17, 1977, the local American attorney Senator Howard Trapp and CHamoru businessman Thomas V. C. Tanaka introduced legislation to acquire a new design for the flag. In their legislative findings, Trapp and Tanaka found that the flag was "uninteresting," that its details were small and "impossible to distinguish at any distance."[86] In an effort to acquire a more original and "aesthetically pleasing" representation, the legislature appropriated $19,000 for a new design and looked to the Flag Research Center of Winchester, Massachusetts, to help. The director of the center, Whitney Smith, who considered himself a foremost authority on vexillology, reassured Guåhan that the center would merely serve as consultants and that "the people themselves" would "design and create a symbol which they believe truly represents the island and its people."[87] Though Smith did not make it clear who "the people" were that he had in mind, Native CHamorus would take center stage in the debate over the next several weeks.

On March 15, 1977, the legislature held a public hearing on the bill. Smith and his assistant, Anne Del Prado, acting as consultants only, testified in support of the bill. They decided that "nothing in the present flag ... truly represents the Guamanian people and their history."[88] One by one, CHamorus testified. Monsignor Vicente Martinez, testifying on behalf of Bishop Felixberto Flores, intimated the bishop's support of the bill and desire for a new design that would represent the "three glorious eras" of CHamoru, Spanish, and American influence. The noted historian and educator Pedro "Doc" Sanchez testified against the bill, taking issue with the labeling of the flag as "uninteresting," but felt the field of blue could be slightly modified. Two other CHamoru educators, Sylvia Guzman and Mary Elaine Cadigan, opposed the bill, saying the flag evoked a strong emotional sentiment.[89] Tomas R. Santos testified that all five hundred members of the Guam Association of Retired Persons were against the bill. Also testifying against the bill was an elderly CHamoru woman, Maria T. Garrido. She nostalgically recalled how as a child she often played at the mouth of the Såddok Hagåtña near the famous coconut tree, which, like the CHamoru people, had survived a terrible typhoon.[90] She told a familiar narrative of the flag representing the courage and endurance of CHamorus and offered a new/old kostumbren CHamoru spin: the flag "means the love of the land and the love of the people to help each other." For many, including the petitioners of Chamorro Fandaña ya u ta satba i Bandera-ta (Chamorros in support of keeping our flag), this would be reason enough to keep the flag, no matter who designed it—that is, until CHamoru activists in the early 1990s determined that a more appropriate symbol of CHamoru nationalism was needed to help usher in a new era of decolonization and independence struggles.

On February 19, 1992, in a heated public hearing on the flag, Nasion CHamoru (CHamoru Nation) leader Angel Santos and member artist David Sablan showed up to present a very particular and pointed perspective and an altogether different flag, whose iconographies would, in their opinion, be appropriate for what Guåhan's flag should really stand for. Santos declared that the island should have a flag designed by a CHamoru.[91] In addition to calling into question the legitimacy of the Guåhan flag design because it had been designed by a non-CHamoru, Santos also pointed out the incongruity of having a nationalist symbol, the Guåhan flag, adopted for the island by a colonial agent, the navy governor Willis Bradley—who adopted the flag's seal as the official seal of the U.S. naval government of Guam.[92] Unlike the previous CHamorus two decades earlier, Santos knew exactly the design he wanted: one by David Sablan that would "really have meaning for the Chamorro nation." The central figure in Santos and Sablan's flag was the figure of a CHamoru chief, who, for Santos, symbolized the island's Native "forefathers," "ancestry," and "roots." The gold border around the figure of the ancient chief, also in gold, was in the now familiar shape of the ancient CHamoru weapon, the slingstone, except now it symbolized "talent" and "skill." The slingstone also resembled the sinåhi (new moon), which, according to Santos, represented the forefathers' "closeness to nature and the workings of the moon."[93]

Pursuing what he believed to be a more authentic or at least appropriate iconography of indigeneity in the movement and struggle for decolonization and *land back*, Santos explained that the gold border of the slingstone around the chief symbolized the "fencing in" of CHamoru rights against a field of black representing struggles and "hard times." Santos proclaimed that the color gold also represented the birth of the CHamoru nation and CHamorus' continued fight for independence. Had it not been for the testimony of Bernadita "Benit" Camacho-Dungca at the same hearing, Sablan and Santos's design might have been adopted. Camacho-Dungca confirmed that a navy wife designed the Guåhan flag but that it was a CHamoru artist who designed the central figure of the flag, the seal. According to Camacho-Dungca, between 1912 and 1913, Francisco Feja "Tun Kiko" painted the famous scene along the Såddok Hagåtña and gave the painting as a gift to a navy wife when she complimented the painting.[94] After that, no details are given as to how the seal came into Helen Paul's possession between 1917 and 1919.

In more popular accounts and contestations over the true designer of the Guåhan flag, one thing is definite: Helen Paul designed and sketched the blueprint for the flag, whose central icon is the Guåhan seal, which has been recognized by many to be the design of Tun Kiko Feja. In the 1980s, the Guam Legislature would pass a resolution acknowledging Tun Kiko as the artist behind what Agueda Johnston referred to as the "most outstanding" scenery of the Guåhan flag. In the next chapter, I look at the CHamoru educator Agueda Johnston, who could very well have been one of the American-flag-donning famalao'an CHamoru in Paul's photograph *Mestiza Beauties of Guam*. Or she could have been the one photograph that Paul never got around to capturing: that of a CHamoru woman donning both the U.S. and Guåhan flags. In what follows, I focus on the complex negotiations of new CHamoru womanhood in the work of Agueda Johnston.

CHAPTER FOUR

Giniha yan Pinilan Guåhan
Agueda Johnston and New CHamoru Womanhood

On July 3, 1945, the Columbia Broadcasting System (CBS) aired a fifteen-minute special broadcast of events overseas in Guåhan, where July 4 festivities were already underway in the war-torn capital of Hagåtña. A year earlier, the island was the site of intense battles of the Pacific theater during World War II. On this day, outside the demolished colonial governor's palace, military personnel and civilians gathered around the flagpole to commemorate the island's own independence (from Japan) and to witness the U.S. flag being hoisted for the first time since the Japanese occupation in 1941. Setting the stage for a display of CHamoru-American patriotism thousands of miles from home, CBS pointed out to its listeners that the familiar "Star-Spangled Banner" in the background was being played by the all-Guamanian (CHamoru) band. In another staging (if even belaboring) of CHamoru loyalty to the United States, CBS then went to the "heart of a great symbol," the nearby George Washington High School, where students were saluting the American flag and reciting the Pledge of Allegiance.[1]

At the center of this commemoration was the beloved fafa'na'gue and principal Agueda Iglesias Johnston. She described her students' perseverance despite having only a building shell for classrooms, salvage lumber and empty boxes for chairs, and American magazines like *National Geographic, Reader's Digest, Time,* and *Life* for textbooks.[2] She captured this postwar CHamoru endurance and spirit in her vivid detailing of boys donned in GI uniforms and girls in dresses made from curtains and homemade wooden clogs determined to take back the American-style education they had lost under Japan and the Greater East Asia Co-Prosperity Sphere. In lockstep with Johnston's patriotism and sentimentality, eighteen-year-old Teresita Perez recalled how she once pined for "golden school days" and a reunion with her "dear familiar Comrades" and was finally living the "great happiness" of liberation.[3]

Conventional and popular narratives of Agueda Johnston, such as this, revolve around her wartime efforts, especially in harboring George Tweed, a U.S. Navy radioman who successfully hid out in Guåhan's jungles and caves throughout the duration of the Japanese occupation. Conventional historiography views him as a symbol of the United States' survival and eventual return to the island, and for this reason, Tweed was assisted by CHamoru families, many of whose members, like Johnston herself, were severely beaten and some even killed for being suspected of hiding or assisting him. We will return to Tweed later, to Johnston's fraught relationship with him, and to her postwar representations and their role in narrativizing, commemorating, and institutionalizing the moral lessons of Guåhan's liberation by the U.S. military from Japanese tyranny and wartime atrocities.

This chapter endeavors to tell a more nuanced and gendered history of the prominent CHamoru educator and the multifaceted dimensions of her work. To be sure, Johnston was a symbol of modernity in Guåhan under the United States and even today remains at the center of national commemoration, but she is often misconstrued as *simply* a product of U.S. naval colonial education and remembered *principally* for her staunch patriotism. I argue that Johnston was a key figure in the construction of an early twentieth-century new CHamoru womanhood whose investments in the United States under military tutelage revealed a complex set of negotiations around education, progress, civic duty, and citizenship, in the interest of advancing the island and the CHamorus. The complexity in and of Johnston's political, cultural, and social work and the competing interests staked therein are perhaps best exemplified in her assertion that she was "Guamanian-Chamorro by birth but American patriotic by choice."

My retelling of Johnston's self-scripting as simultaneously Guamanian-CHamoru (by lineage) and American (patriotic, by choice) is informed by critical historiography and literary texts that have begun to complicate the terms of CHamoru loyalty and patriotism, especially regarding the memory of Japanese occupation and the United States' return as one of "liberation"; my restorying is also based on a reading of her record of activities, and especially from wading through complexities and contradictions in her unpublished writings.[4] This unpublished body of work consists primarily of sets of writings: a collection of thoughts, which she called her "Chamorrita Notes," and coauthored memoirs with one Clyde Myron Cramlet, whom she recruited to assist her. Though we know that Johnston furnished the details of her lifestory and events in Guåhan and Cramlet ensured the accuracy of larger historical contexts and facts—or, as the foreword put it, she furnished the "personal and historical narrative" while Cramlet provided the "bookish historical and scientific background"—the memoirs help to tease out what Johnston meant when she self-described her identity as a Native woman of Guåhan by being CHamoru by birth, American patriotic by choice.[5] This moniker can be and has been misleading in that it shortchanges CHamoru investments in the United States and affixes Johnston as an acculturated, assimilated, or worse, co-opted, colonized Native. For example, Johnston often used the term *Guamanian* to refer to her Indigenous identity. Today, the term connotes something of an intentional downplaying of Indigenous CHamoru political struggles to right an historical injustice, as if to self-identify as CHamoru and especially to advocate for CHamoru rights (for example, for CHamoru self-determination and the return of ancestral, traditional, and contemporary lands) were a racist and exclusionary sentiment. Here, the term *Guamanian* is presumed to be more inclusive of the "civil rights" and interests of non-Indigenous residents of Guåhan as all should be treated equally under the American flag and political system. But in Johnston's usage in the pre- and immediate postwar years and up to the 1970s—when the term *Chamorro* (now officially spelled *CHamoru*) began to be embraced with greater frequency by Indigenous inhabitants to self-identify—the term *Guamanian* was for all intents and purposes synonymous with the term *Chamorro* to refer to the people with Indigenous ancestry in the Mariana Islands.[6] For reasons that will become clear shortly, CHamorus of Guåhan would also soon embrace the term *Guamanian* over *Chamorro* after the war, precisely to differentiate themselves from CHamorus of the Northern Mariana Islands. As will be discussed later, Johnston was a leader in the movement to hold a plebiscite in which the public voted *Guamanian* over two other options, *Guamerican* and *Guamian*.

There were two reasons why CHamorus of Guåhan even underwent a process that led to the adoption of the term *Guamanian* to self-identify: the first was to celebrate a new political and social era under more formal American political affiliation after World War II. In 1950, after decades of political advocacy, CHamorus of Guåhan gained U.S. citizenship by virtue of federal organic legislation that also clarified the island's political status as that of an organized "unincorporated territory" of the United States. The Organic Act of Guam also created local home rule and transferred administrative oversight of the island from the Department of the Navy to the Department of the Interior. The second motive was less celebratory: choosing the term *Guamanian* would differentiate CHamorus of Guåhan from CHamorus of the Northern Mariana Islands—Saipan, Tinian, and Rota. Unlike Indigenous CHamorus of Guåhan, who became political wards under U.S. naval rule and American hegemony following the Spanish-American War of 1898, Indigenous CHamorus of the Northern Marianas came under German colonial rule (when Spain sold these islands to Germany) and later Japanese rule, at the outbreak of World War I. When World War II broke out, CHamorus of the Northern Marianas had already been classified as third-class

Japanese citizens and served the emperor loyally as translators and also especially as enforcers of Japanese military policies, including the most brutal of orders during the Japanese occupation of Guåhan. CHamorus of Guåhan have bitter memories of the role their relatives played during the occupation years. Thus, the bid by CHamorus of Guåhan to self-refer as *Guamanians*, at least in the three decades following World War II, was both an effort to differentiate and distance themselves from CHamorus of the Northern Marianas and a gesture of marking and commemorating a new postwar political, social, and economic future for Guåhan under the United States.[7] In neither case did the term *Guamanian* in this period register for the CHamorus of Guåhan the termination or repression of one's Indigenous identity in the same way that the choice between *Guamanian* and *Chamorro* would come to signify by the last quarter of the twentieth century and into the twenty-first century, when the island experienced profound social, economic, and cultural transformation through modernization and development that witnessed, by the 1970s, Indigenous CHamorus falling to under 50 percent of the population, a new generation no longer fluent in fino' CHamoru, and the apparent eclipse of kostumbren CHamoru values in favor of liberal American norms, expectations, and aspirations.[8]

In Johnston's unpublished "Chamorrita Notes" and memoirs, which together span a period from the prewar years to the 1970s, there is a noteworthy, clearly detectable ambivalence and even lament at times about the social and cultural transformation under the United States at the expense of CHamoru culture. This uncertainty is especially palpable in Johnston's stories about the nature of postwar militarization and growth. These differences and sentiments indicate that leaders like Johnston could not or may not have had the ability to foresee or even imagine a day when modernizing under the United States and being CHamoru might come at the expense of the latter. Hence, in her "Chamorrita Notes," Johnston often referred to herself as "Chamorro," "Guamanian," or "Guamanian-CHamoru," while in the memoirs, she, in third person, was described as the "Last Chamorro" or sometimes as one "of a vanishing race," both of which might be regarded as racialist observations projected onto her by the non-CHamoru coauthor, although usage of such language could also have been an effort on her part to play up a tragic distinction between how Johnston herself recalled the CHamoru world åntes di i gera and the acculturated world of the late twentieth century. Notably, the difficulties in parsing out who authored which markers of identity and what they might mean get even more complicated when they are more explicitly Orientalized, gendered, and sexualized. In one moment, Johnston is a "woman on the crossroads of West and East, loyal to both," and in another, she is a "dusky native girl."⁹ Did she in fact author these words and see herself through such a racialist and Orientalist lens? Did she internalize American colonialism, and if so, to what extent? Was she helplessly or hopelessly modern? No longer CHamoru? In my estimation, Johnston's words, and the words of a white American man (Cramlet) whom she chose as a trusted co-author, reveal an Indigenous modern ambivalence and nostalgia for an authentic world that was rapidly disappearing. In English, these sentiments can only be couched in the available terms and discourses, and so long as they are articulated in English and not in the vernacular, over which Johnston retained command, any Indigenous alterity or difference could only be so contained in the connotations and denotations, the tropes and contexts, in which they are uttered or written. What appears certain is that Johnston wrote from sensing the apparent negative and damaging effects of the pre- and postwar investments in the modern United States and did not always like what she saw. In her twilight years, she doubled up her efforts to giha yan pulan Guåhan, to steer and steward her island, to point out the way and lead the way, but in the direction of caring for the land, community, and its more vulnerable people, the manåmko'.

Indeed, I examine Johnston's patriotism historically, at a time of flux, and not simply as a matter of *being* patriotic or *being* CHamoru. To historicize her loyalty to the United States is to attend to what motivations went into her enactments and performances of patriotism and to sense the discursive thresholds or limits to such articulations of indigeneity, which are always subject to change. If CHamorus embraced American modernity before the war in ways that did not preclude being Indigenous, the wartime occupation—or at least the hegemonic memory of that period as one of unmediated brutality and oppression by the Japanese occupation forces—would also combine with the sentiment of witnessing the returning American forces as liberators. These sentiments would conspire to forge a narrative of CHamorus as steadfastly patriotic Americans, and Agueda Johnston would be one of the most celebrated examples of this loyalty. These sentiments were born out of the crucible of wartime trauma, but they were also urged, often legislated, along by an intensive prewar campaign to modernize (read: Americanize) the island under the tutelage of the U.S. Navy—one that also furnished a public discourse, if not vernacular, that claimed a monopoly over any and all forms of progress and beneficence. This was a prewar period when the principal form of protesting naval rule was to call for U.S. citizenship in the understanding that citizenship would come with the protection of the U.S. Constitution and thus check or curtail what often seemed to be the unfettered political, if not tyrannical, power of the naval governor. However, pre- and postwar discourses of CHamoru loyalty and patriotism to the United States, whether expressed through the U.S. citizenship movement in the case of the former or as forged in sentiments of the bitter and painful memories of the Japanese occupation and gratitude toward the returning liberators in the case of the latter, were also driven by personal and social desires and resolve for the novel and for mobility, as we learned in the case of the pattera and will also observe in the case of mamfafa'na'gue like Johnston. These instances of women's work describe, as I have been arguing, something akin to CHamoru notions of progress and modernity, and new ways of embracing social and cultural forms that did not automatically or necessarily dispense with deeper Indigenous values. As demonstrated later in this chapter, Johnston's writings about the wartime experience also marked these sentiments in terms of rebirth and rejuvenation, which I read as determinations for new ways to refashion CHamoru womanhood. Hence, this chapter traces elements and progressions in Johnston's "modern girl" and new-woman consciousness and desires for political, economic, and cultural freedoms, especially in the context of a stringent and stifling CHamoru-Spanish Catholic patriarchy struggling to hold firm amid a colonial, but nonetheless progressive, liberal United States under the navy.[10] Johnston's efforts to push and transgress the boundaries of CHamoru women's education and other causes and safeguard the well-being of girls, like when she cofounded the Guam Women's Club and Girl Scouts, represented what I am suggesting was an incipient CHamoru feminism.

The Guam Legislature's eulogy to "Tan Agueda" in 1978 (written and delivered by the CHamoru educators Robert Underwood and Katherine Aguon, respectively) aptly captured the complexity and paradox of her work: "Johnston symbolized the struggle for adaptive and progressive change in the modern world, yet without losing the dignity and aura of her Chamorro roots.... She symbolized Chamorro struggle in the Chamorro fashion."[11] Invoking the notion of adaptability—one that diverged from the navy's narrative of the assimilation of the pattera under the United States—this local tribute instead focused on Johnston's "persevering CHamoru womanhood" alongside modernity.[12] Johnston herself described the initial growing pains of this subjectivity as the simple fact that "she and the Island were growing up together."[13]

This persisting CHamoru womanhood, or "strength of Agueda," is reflected in her many monikers: "Patriot," "Maestra," "First Lady of Guam," "First Chamorro Lady," "Queen Bee of Guam," "Friend of the GIs," "Guam Matriarch," "Godmother of Education," and "Maga'håga."[14] Two in particular—godmother or *matlina* and *maga'håga*, names associated with her in postwar oral histories and counternarratives and in political and cultural resurgence movements and decolonization struggles—give us a glimpse of Indigenous women's minesngon (endurance, resistance) and metgot determination to advance and watch over, to poksai and pulan, Guåhan and the CHamorus. The first, *matlina*, captures more than her leadership in the history of U.S. colonial education. An explicit reference to an important cultural subjectivity of CHamoru-Spanish Catholicism, *matlina* underscores her connection to a longer history in which famalao'an CHamoru figured prominently in the indigenization of kostumbren CHamoru.[15] In other words, Johnston was not just a leader under U.S. naval tutelage but an important interlocutor and intermediary, whose direction and giniha in modern education and other ostensibly American spheres would extend a longer story of CHamoru cultural survival through a new colonial order. The name *maga'håga* evokes an older, gendered subjectivity of early CHamoru matrilineal society, whose obligations to not only control clan resources but to pulan and poksai land and life centered on CHamoru siblingship and extended reciprocal kinship relations in the face of enduring colonialisms. Examining gender and indigeneity through Johnston's story and Johnston's story through the framework of indigeneity and gender—that is, the distinct but not mutually exclusive figures of the matlina and maga'håga—helps us to appreciate Johnston's otherwise patriotic work in more embodied CHamoru terms, especially as dictated by relations and responsibilities to taotao and tåno'. This analysis helps to push beyond the singular narrative of CHamoru patriotism that confines the complexity of Johnston's history even as she herself may have believed that her success, and by extension, the island's progress, also rested on "her admiration of both men who built steel ships and her seventh grade teacher, Mrs. Peck."[16]

The Education of Agueda: Metgot Determinations in U.S. Naval Teachings

> Study hard, Agueda, and keep ahead of your class
> you'll have no difficulty whatsoever.
> —Captain Edward J. Dorn, USN

Writing over fifty years later in her unpublished "Chamorrita Notes," Tan Agueda Johnston recalled her humble beginnings as a teacher and student under the U.S. Navy. Taking the advice of Governor Edward Dorn (1907–10) and heeding the lessons from navy wives and teachers like Eva Belle Peck at the Leary School and Helen Paul at the Guam Normal School, Johnston worked diligently, excelled, moved ahead to the front and top of her class, and became one of the island's distinguished educators and community leaders.[17] Johnston was born in 1892 and was among the first cohort of children in Guåhan to undergo formal education under the U.S. Navy, which assumed administrative control over the island in 1899. On January 22, 1900, the first naval governor, Captain Richard Leary, established compulsory education for children between the ages of eight and fourteen. It was not until 1904, however, that twelve-year-old Agueda—who had spent much of her youth living at the family låncho in Fineguayoc-Machinao (in northern Guåhan)— would begin her formal schooling at the Leary School in Hagåtña (in central Guåhan), where the navy first established schools. Johnston recalled her strong desires to attend the American schools and speak English like other young, well-dressed CHamoru women.[18] She described the speed bumps, roadblocks, and (sometimes) detours that she overcame: a small (but justifiable) lie to her nåna (Nånan Iglesias) that she had been ordered by the navy to report to school, the navy's new age limit in 1904 (from fourteen to twelve) that considered Agueda "too old" for school, and the tussle among saina—between the family matriarchs who wanted to keep her at home and a loving tåtan bihu (grandfather), "Tåtan Gue'," who was a stalwart to Agueda's cause to continue her education.[19] Agueda's tiha, "Nånan Ita'," figures notably here (along with Tåtan Gue' and Agueda's nåna) in terms of extended family dynamics and authority as well as the local politics between Hagåtña and outlying villages. According to Johnston, Nånan Ita' had the standing and authority over her not only because she was older sister to Agueda's mother but also because she helped support the family's livelihood in Hagåtña through her own physical and cultural self-sustaining work (and kostumbren CHamoru upkeep) of the låncho. The låncho, to be clear, was not typically understood as the large plantation of the rancheria, upon which the CHamoru word *låncho* was based. A CHamoru låncho was more often than not a small plot of farm space. For Agueda, it was an important space for learning and socializing, and for the disciplining and cultivating of Indigenous sensibilities, which she did not take for granted even in her modern training under U.S. naval colonial education. She described the lessons and technical learning of the låncho and extended kin—"Tåtan Ingo''s Fusiños" and the "Academy of Nånan Samba"—in affectionate, embodied, grounded, and modern terms and expressions.[20]

Compulsory education, along with the expulsion of Spanish Catholic priests, was the navy's first step in Americanizing and modernizing CHamorus.[21] The navy took extra steps in stamping out vestiges of Spanish colonialism and religious instruction. For his part, Governor Leary banned village fiestas, which honored patron saints, and ordered the removal of all crucifixes and pictures of saints in schools.[22] Even the CHamoru women's Spanish-style clothing, the mestisa—with its long-flowing gown that would occasionally touch the ground—was regarded as an impediment to the navy's attempts at cleanliness and progress. In 1907, Governor Dorn passed a law that forbade students from wearing the mestisa in schools—a policy that, according to Johnston, CHamoru women sarcastically remarked had more to do with the superintendent's desires to "get a peak" at their ankles.[23] American schools under the navy offered girls and young CHamoru women like Agueda, those coming of age who were sottera (pubescent) and po'dak (adolescent), a different kind of tutelage from that found under Spanish colonialism. Although Spanish colonial education in Guåhan was erratic and CHamoru experiences differed—contingent on, for example, geography (whether one resided in Hagåtña or the other villages), the training and tenets of specific Catholic orders (Jesuits or Augustinian Recollects), and the political agendas of Spanish governors—schooling revolved primarily around two types of instruction: eskuelan påle' and eskuelan rai (king's or government schools). Within this system, often religious in nature and under the tutelage of the påle', education was reserved for the "best and brightest" and the manakhilo' families of Hagåtña, and extended to only a few girls and young women.[24] The first and longest running institution, the Colegio de San Juan de Letran for boys, was established in 1669, a year after the founding of the first Catholic mission in Guåhan by San Vitores. In 1674, the Escuela de las Niñas for girls was established also in Hagåtña but received less attention and funding from Spanish colonial administrators in Manila.[25] Of these two elite institutions, Rose de Freycinet (during her three-month stay in the island's capital in 1819), wrote that the Colegio was "very wisely placed at the far end of the town" from the "house . . . that serves as a school for the girls."[26] Although schools under the navy were also established along a gendered divide, both pedagogically (in terms of the type of instruction) and physically (with boys and girls attending school at different times of the day), Freycinet's observation may perhaps have been an indication of how much wider and more demarcated the gulf was between the boys' and girls' schools under Spanish colonialism.

In his study of education in Guåhan, Robert Underwood has argued that with the onset of U.S. colonialism, CHamoru lives were interrupted by a harsh school system whose main agenda was to modernize young CHamorus and turn them into loyal and patriotic American wards. American schools, through the formal and informal policies of the navy, were major agents in the assimilation to the American way of life and in the decline of the CHamoru language

FIGURE 4.1 Postwar radio show featuring Agueda Johnston and students of George Washington High School, 1945. Courtesy of the Guam Public Library System.

and culture. American-style education focused on four subjects: English, health and hygiene, citizenship, and training for life or "life on the farm," which included instruction in agriculture.[27] The navy's measure of success, according to Underwood, was based not on how American one was but how "un-Chamorro" one had become.[28] This process of civilizing and modernizing by subtracting rather than adding resembles the "overweening surveillance" that K. Tsianina Lomawaima and Teresa McCarty describe of Indian boarding schools in what is now the United States—the primary means by which Native languages, cultures, and identities were pounded out and reshaped.[29]

In Guåhan, under the U.S. Navy, modernizing meant Americanizing, which meant socializing CHamorus to become loyal and patriotic so that they would in turn self-exhibit loyalty and patriotism through activities such as prewar health parades, Christmas pageants, agricultural and industrial fairs, postwar liberation celebrations, and radio broadcasts like the one featured in the opening paragraph (figure 4.1). Within this militarized landscape of paternalism in education, CHamorus performed what Saidiya Hartman elsewhere describes as the terror (but also resistance) in "scenes of subjection." In her study of racial subjugation during slavery and its aftermath, Hartman describes these scenes as quotidian forms of jollity and simulated contentment in the making of black identity. Comparable simulations would obtain in CHamoru routinized subjections and performances of daily callisthenic drills, flag rituals, and hygiene inspections in addition to being banned from speaking CHamoru and fined for doing so or fined for even missing school.[30] Governor George Dyer gave a glimpse of these routinized scenes in 1905 when he reported that the navy assigned men and women to school restrooms to inspect students' "habits of order and cleanliness"; if found "soiled in person or dress," they were sent home.[31]

Like the pattera, who were expected to impart American colonial perceptions of health, hygiene, and childbearing, CHamoru teachers were required to inculcate American-style education, and "cheerfully and harmoniously cooperate with the teachers of English" in this regard.[32] Like the pattera, who served as the long arm of the U.S. Navy, especially in the villages, CHamoru teachers and educators did their part in scrutinizing other CHamorus. Johnston herself noted several occasions when she and another CHamoru educator, Remedios Perez—both of whom, you may recall, narrated histories of the Guåhan flag in the last chapter—drove around the island conducting school inspections.[33] The aforementioned Dick Taitano, a graduate of George Washington High School, where Johnston served as principal (1936–46), recalled being on the receiving end of these inspections. In his 1937 valedictory address, the then fifteen-year-old Taitano described the "many advantages" of an American education but also conveyed that he and his peers did not appreciate the "frequent visits," particularly the rounds administrators made on bikes checking on tardy students.[34] But just as the pattera resisted certain elements of their training, such as the English-only policy in the Susana, or American nurses' and doctors' instructions to burn or discard the ga'chong i patgon, the teachers who trained under the navy did not so readily abandon being CHamoru. Indeed, as Underwood writes, despite the invasive and far-reaching colonial agenda, several factors, including the navy's lack of resources, would have the effect of blunting the "reality of domination."[35] This would be the case particularly in the first two decades, before the navy's efforts in the 1920s to professionalize the island's educational system through curriculum reform and teacher training. Only a few elite teachers, Johnston among them, would cultivate the navy's "forward look."[36] Johnston and Simon Sanchez, superintendent of public schools, would later help secure and prepare the island for the postwar reopening of schools in August 1944, and for the return of

American-style education. In general agreement with Underwood's analyses, I also think that, like or even exemplary of the zeal of these teachers who held firm to CHamoru values, Johnston's own passion for American-style education also did not automatically mean that she abandoned her cultural allegiances to values born out of her upbringing and sensibilities as one who had grown up on the låncho. Though she had elite lineage (Tåtan Gue' was Spanish), she also had not grown up in these influential manakhilo' circles. Hence, championing modern American education did not automatically mean forgetting her CHamoru roots that she was rerouting up, over, and across the various walls of change.

To be sure, Agueda Johnston and the Filipino educator Simon Sanchez were star pupils who later became known as the architects of Guåhan's postwar public educational system, which was modeled firmly on American ideals and standards. Both studied together at the Normal School under Helen Paul. Though Johnston no doubt was considered one of the island's political, economic, and social elites at the time, her upward and outward mobility was enabled and explained by circumstance, proximity to white American military men and women, marriage, and, perhaps most of all, her metgot, dogged (or sheer) determination.

To understand Johnston's determination and investments in the United States—her rise from promising to stellar student and, in due course, model fafa'na'gue and onward and upward to prominent administrator and community leader—we must consider other facets of the political and socioeconomic landscape and milieu out of which Johnston emerged, starting with the navy's lack of resources and teacher shortage in the early 1900s. Unlike in the Philippines at the time, where U.S. colonial officials sent hundreds of American teachers (so-called Thomasites), there were far fewer qualified teachers in Guåhan. Of the dozen Protestant missionaries who sailed from Manila to Guåhan on board the American schooner *Bessie B. Stevens* in March 1899, only a handful remained to serve as teachers, and then only for the handful of American children and the few CHamoru children of the first converts to Protestantism. This was before the arrival of the first naval administration in Guåhan in August of that same year. Over the next several decades, naval governors appealed to both the Department of the Navy and U.S. Congress for funds to hire stateside American teachers. To the chagrin of naval governors, these requests were not met.[37]

It was in this milieu that Agueda Johnston came under the tutelage of Eva Peck ("Mrs. Peck"). Mrs. Peck and her husband, the naval education superintendent Leo Peck, were stationed in Guåhan from 1904 to 1909. The navy had contracted her as a special laborer, a bureaucratic category that, as discussed in chapter 2, Governor Dyer created, which allowed the navy to hire the wives and/or daughters of officers as teachers. Although Agueda held her other teacher, Helen Paul (who was only seven years her senior), in high regard, it was her seventh-grade teacher, Mrs. Peck (fifteen years older), whom she greatly admired as a mother figure and confidante in "matters relating [to] conduct and propriety" and to whom she expressed deep inagradesi.[38] Mrs. Peck's hire was significant because it was this contracted navy wife who inspired Agueda to become a teacher. For its part, the special laborer category just barely permitted the navy to do its job, having had to rely, early on, for example, on hiring enlisted marines, which it did as early as 1899 when the first unit arrived in Guåhan with Governor Leary on board the USS *Yosemite*.[39] The hiring of marines to serve as teachers was also significant in other, more intimate ways that bolstered Agueda's social standing, a point to which I will return shortly. Subsequent navy governors continued to detail marines, especially when American women and navy wives were unavailable, but some did so reluctantly.

Faced with the lack of funds and labor, the navy was forced to hire from circles not directly under its command even as it sought to maintain its authority and sensibilities. In its civil administration of the island through the challenges of establishing an educational system, the navy also soon came face-to-face with a socioeconomic class hierarchy in which it found itself having to navigate local CHamoru leaders on one side, an up-and-coming class of erstwhile teachers on another side, and a group of marine teachers whose own allegiances did not always align well with the naval hierarchy. Still, a sense of the prevailing order (and contestation) became evident in the educational system that emerged: CHamoru teachers oversaw entry-level classes, marines instructed intermediate classes, and navy personnel or their dependents (e.g., wives and daughters) tutored advanced classes. In his autobiography, Jose R. Palomo, the first CHamoru to receive a PhD, described one of the advanced classes in Hågatña, Class Number 3, as "the playground for the intellectual elite."[40] Palomo was in Class Number 2, taught by a marine. By the mid-1920s, as more schools were established in the villages, CHamorus already comprised the majority of the teachers.[41]

This distribution gives us a sense of the navy's challenges in hiring stateside teachers and a glimpse into how it viewed CHamorus from outside the island's capital. By extension, this distribution also tells us of the clustering of the intermediate and intellectual elite in Hågatña and, through these groupings, the concentration of, and the social relations between, marine and naval teachers. This racialized and classed hierarchical military terrain around education also brings us back to how individuals in these different classes—students and teachers alike—viewed and navigated the island's changing physical and cultural landscapes.

In his memoirs, Reverend Joaquin Sablan describes the clash in Hagåtña between expectations and values that underwrote the navy's compulsory education and the sensibilities and expectations of a well-established local CHamoru order. Reverend Sablan wrote that by the time he entered fourth grade at the Intermediate School in Hagåtña, most of his teachers, with the exception of two navy officers' wives, were CHamoru. These were Agueda Johnston, Julia DeLeon, Eugenia Duenas, and Maria Leon Guerrero. Assuming perhaps that CHamorus living in Hagåtña were homogenous, the navy collided with a long-standing class system that was divided and socially hierarchized into barrios or districts, the oldest being San Ignacio, where the manakhilo' resided. The manakhilo' were the mestisu/a class, the elite CHamorus who married into the ruling Spanish and later American class. Even in 1905, after the navy established compulsory education, the manakhilo', according to Reverend Sablan, "still kept their children from attending schools ... so as not to mingle with the 'lower' class of Chamorros who, by the sheer fact that they resided in Hagåtña, were now afforded newer spaces."[42] As indicated earlier, Johnston occupied something of a liminal space between the elite and the "lower" classes that resided in Hagåtña. Though her maternal lineage was mestisu and resided in Hagåtña, she was raised on the låncho where a majority of the families of Hagåtña spent most of their time even if they had residences in the capital.

Sablan describes an island society on the eve of social transformation, one in which the small but influential CHamoru-Spanish aristocracy began to sense its power on the wane and the rise of the new elite CHamoru-American class. Agueda is the best example of the girl from the låncho who would find new mobilities and experience novel freedoms. Sablan also points out that the Såddok Hagåtña, which ran the length of the capital city before the navy rerouted it, delineated the lower class of CHamorus from the upper class. Even still, wrote Reverend Sablan, the social divide symbolized by the såddok was no match for the one that divided men and women in CHamoru society along thick gender lines, or walls, at that time—an indication of just how entrenched Spanish Catholic patriarchy had become in CHamoru society.[43] It merits pointing out that this is the same såddok that Helen Paul captured photographically from various angles during her time on Guåhan, the same såddok that juts out into the Philippine Sea and also made its way picturesquely into the Guåhan seal and Guåhan flag, as discussed in chapter 3. It is also the same såddok that Tan Maria Garrido recalled, with equal nostalgia, playing along as a child and where she saw the famous coconut tree that she interpreted to stand for CHamoru endurance. For CHamorus who did not belong to the elite class, like Reverend Sablan, the river indicated gender, class, and privilege and for this reason did not evoke the picturesque the way it did for Paul.

Though Johnston did not belong entirely to the "lower class" of CHamorus that Reverend Sablan referred to, she was not of the prominent large land- and business-owning CHamoru-Spanish manakhilo' class. Johnston's social standing, at the time at least, helps us appreciate how CHamoru society was far more complex and fluid than a binary case of lower and upper classes. In power relations between CHamorus and the U.S. Navy, where the principal binary between Native and non-Native tended to obfuscate other uneven power relations that flowed along gender and class (and religious) lines of not only colonial but Indigenous CHamoru divides, Johnston rose from what she described as "humble roots."[44] Her memoirs might be read as her tracing, indeed, her mapping, of these up and across the physical and figurative walls and fences of Hagåtña in ways analogous to how Mishuana Goeman has demonstrated in her own countermapping reads of Indigenous women writers of fiction, nonfiction, and poetry whose stories "mediate and refute colonial organization of land, bodies, and social and political landscapes."[45] In her memoirs, Johnston herself mapped the social lines and hierarchies that she sought to transcend. For example, she described her family's little two-room thatched home, which was made from the traditional materials of the dokdok, ifit, and gago from trees native to the island, and the smaller, unattached kusinan sanhiyong (outside kitchen), as was characteristic of CHamoru dwellings then and now. She also recalled the furniture of the prewar days: two benches, a wooden bed, and a special chair reserved specifically for the påle' who made the rounds to hear confession. This home, in which she lived with her nåna and tåtan bihu, sat in "quaint dissonance" behind (and in stark contrast to) the mamposteria (tiled-roof homes) that faced the Plaza de España, to the south, with only the plaza (plåsa) between these "elegant buildings" and the naval governor's palace. Johnston carefully surveyed the walls around her home: the first, directly south of her grandfather's home, belonged to the Augustinian priest Påle' Lasa; another belonged to the American botanist and naval lieutenant governor (under Leary), William Safford; and a third made of bamboo belonged to a CHamoru neighbor.[46] Johnston's story can be read as that of a rural CHamoru girl whose smarts and grit allowed her to eventually redirect her time and energy "in town," as opposed to the family låncho. Hers is a story of being attracted to, learning about, mastering, and transcending tangible and intangible walls that existed between the manakhilo' and manakpåpa' (lower) classes as well as the gradations within the elite and privileged class. As for the physical and figural walls that emerged and reinforced the divisions between the modern (American/navy) and traditional (kostumbren CHamoru) society—walls that enclosed the American schools, the English language, the house with the crystal kerosene lamp in San Ignacio District, the socials at Dorn Hall, the Elks Club, and the Gaiety Theater—these represented for her openings and vistas from the limits of the låncho and their towering figures of authority, like her Tåtan Ingo' (uncle) and Nånan Samba (aunt), whose values and perspectives she would continue to honor and respect for their own deep Indigenous wisdom and sensibilities. Tellingly, perhaps unlike Reverend Sablan, Johnston was also drawn and attached emotionally to the Såddok Hagåtña, where she spent afternoons with her ga'chong Rosalia Perez. Perhaps the såddok that flowed through social and economic divides also symbolized, for Johnston, passage across the classed and gendered lines without losing its deeper value in Indigenous CHamoru socioecology. Johnston described this sense of place in detail: playing along the riverbanks lined with håyun dokdok, akgak, and niyok (breadfruit, pandanus, and coconut trees), listening to the women singing and conversing in CHamoru while they did their laundry, and watching the men catch the asuli (freshwater eel) that swam downstream whenever the river overflowed during the fanuchånan. She also lamented that *this place* after the war had been "covered over by the rubble and debris after the destruction of the town by the American reoccupation forces."[47] Here, Johnston's unpublished writings reveal deep, embodied human and other-than-human relationalities between taotao, tåno', såddok, håyun, and asuli. In the prewar days especially, I argue, one cannot so easily detach these attachments and articulations from the preponderance of stories of Johnston's proclivity for the United States and patriotism and loyalty to it. At the same time, however, Johnston's writings as well as her postwar actions and decisions, especially later in life when she began to perceive the unintended and perhaps completely unimaginable (for CHamorus of her generation) social, political, and cultural costs of modernization and Americanization on CHamoru land and people, also begin to reveal deep ambivalences that reach the level of anger and disapproval at postwar developments. These affective reversals were most evident in instances that involved care for the manåmko' in modern society and in the navy's mistreatment or abuse of land. The work of teaching and educating by Guåhan's modern Godmother of Education did not in her mind or intent entail the termination of Indigenous values and wisdom. Johnston's memoirs furnish not only a story of survival and resistance, or "survivance," to borrow the Anishinaabe writer Gerald Vizenor's oft-used word, but the means (and meaning making) for CHamoru self-refashioning.[48] For Johnston, one such moment of rebirth came one postwar morning, inside a military tent in the American camp at Hågat. As she contemplated a war-torn Guåhan, gazing up at the canvas roof, Johnston fixated on other forms of lina'la' around her—the guåli'ek (lizard) going about its way and the ababang (butterfly) emerging from its cocoon.[49] This revelation and new lease on life bound "with religious zeal" Agueda to the United States. But it was even more than that. For Johnston, it was "Japanese cruelty in separating my husband from his family by interning him in a Japanese prison camp [that] securely fixed my loyalties with America."[50] Before turning to Johnston's wartime experiences and revisiting her links to the aforementioned navy radioman, George Tweed, I explore Johnston's prewar mobilities, her metamorphoses and transformations along new routes and into new political and social circles, through metgot determinations of her own and through her propinquity to white American military men and naval wives.

New Forms and Flights of CHamoru Consciousness and Mobility

American education in the first half of the twentieth century offered nonelite CHamorus and women opportunities for social mobility. For Agueda Iglesias, that opportunity came in 1906, when she was fourteen. Mrs. Peck had recruited her top student, Agueda, to stand in as a substitute for the CHamoru teacher, Mr. Calvo.[51] On the spot, Agueda was detailed to take over. Through Mrs. Peck's influence, as well as her own determinations, Agueda was hired by the navy as a special laborer to fill the position permanently. Under Governor Dorn, Agueda was officially sworn in as a teacher, and her monthly salary then was ten dollars. She continued her studies in private and evening classes and earned her high school diploma through a Chicago correspondence school.[52] Agueda eventually sought out a private teacher, William Gautier Johnston, an American marine, who arrived in Guåhan via the USS *Thomas* in 1907. William tutored Agueda after her regular day classes, and they fell in love and married in 1911. Love, however, was not the only reason for Agueda's outward and upward mobility. She had already been working closely with the navy, as one of the first CHamoru teachers in Hagåtña (at $0.35/day) in 1907 and later, in 1911, as the first CHamoru woman special laborer (at $2.56/day).[53] Working thus gave her important proximity to absorb and learn new ideas and practices from socializing with military wives and elite CHamorus, like the enviable mobile mestisas of the Shoe Gang (to whom I'll return shortly), who had already allowed her entrance into and experience over new spaces that were occasioned and structured by American naval colonialism. Her marriage to an American marine seems to have been both an expected outcome of and additional booster to her trajectory.

In her interaction with navy wives, as a student and "daughter" of Mrs. Peck and later pupil and friend of Helen Paul, Agueda's own career and civic paths branched up and out in ways that continued to intersect with and map out new CHamoru destinations from colonial ones. That mobility was built through her deep labor on many different projects with American women who were rerouting white womanhood in Guåhan. One American observed that Johnston was the "leading woman in civic affairs." As head of the island's chapter of the American Red Cross, Johnston helped raise funds for the Susana Hospital, which served elite CHamoru women and naval wives and opened up new opportunities for the pattera. In 1917, the *Guam News Letter* reported that Johnston had made available the use of the family-owned Cine-Gaiety Theater for a Red Cross vaudeville fund-raiser, as part of the larger campaign to support the hospital.[54] While Guåhan's first hospital for Native women and children served the interests of American women (like Susan Dyer and Margaret Sage) and American men (like Governor Dyer), its success was owed to Johnston's (and other CHamoru women's) labor and investments. In turn, this work by famalao'an CHamoru, exemplified best by Johnston, helped reconsolidate earlier forms of white womanhood and assertions of higher moral authority. It was precisely because she found Eva Peck, her first teacher, to exemplify the "finest in American womanhood" that Johnston wished to dedicate a portion of her memoirs to Peck.[55]

Indeed, Johnston's vita with naval wives was long and remarkable. She, along with other CHamorus, helped Esther (aka Hester) Von Preissig (wife of the U.S. Navy paymaster Edward Von Preissig) produce a CHamoru-English dictionary. In 1937, she helped establish the Guam Museum with Margaret Higgins, a scholar and the wife of Captain Spencer Higgins, and other members of the American Legion Mid-Pacific Post. The navy later hired Higgins as curator, and it was in this capacity that Higgins produced and serialized English translations of the 1683 publication of Father Francisco Garcia's *The Life and Martyrdom of the Venerable Father Diego Luis de Sanvitores*.[56] Higgins also worked with the CHamoru teacher Maria Gutierrez Brunton, who, like Johnston, also married an American marine. Maria's husband, Foster Brunton, and William Johnston donated their stamp collections to the Guam Museum. William Johnston oversaw the museum's collections from 1937 until the outbreak of war in 1941 during which time Agueda handled the CHamoru collections.[57] Maria and Agueda were also among the few CHamorus to operate a radio during the war as part of the underground resistance to the Japanese occupation.[58] Writing to her longtime friend from her home in San Diego after the war, Higgins informed Agueda that she would send cotton dress material, needles, thread, and toiletries and explained that the little bamboo basket "hanging in a window facing the Pacific all these years with fresh flowers every day" served as a lovely reminder of their stay in Guåhan.[59] Johnston's affectionate relations with American officers and their wives gave her, in other words, access and means to other goods and services that arrived in the immediate postwar era—excess Army Quonset huts, buses, and jeeps for performances.[60]

With the navy wife Frances Darr, Johnston started the first Girl Scouts troop in Guåhan and served as its first president. In 1935, she helped establish the first beauty shop in Guåhan. Margaret's Beauty Shop in Hagåtña, run by her daughters, first Margaret (the owner) and then Marian, advertised itself as being "just west of the Officer's Club." Margaret's provided services to navy wives, CHamoru women, and, later, Japanese comfort women. Though her daughters would run the shop, Johnston continued to be involved in beauty culture and trained at the Max Factor School in Manila (while Marian, like her sister Margaret before her, trained at the Aguinaldo Institute).[61] On weekends, Johnston shared cosmetic tips she learned from beauty schools in the Philippines. The arrival of the first permanent wave machine and solution on board the USS *Chaumont*, according to Johnston, marked the beginnings of what CHamoru women would refer to as "getting a Margaret," the CHamoru version of the Toni (the name of the popular U.S. brand that in the 1940s introduced the first home permanent solution).[62] As a leader in beauty culture in Guåhan, a pursuit she attributed to Mrs. Peck, Johnston also helped organize fashion shows, pageants, and other performances for the navy, following in the footsteps of Susan Dyer, who had put on socials for the military four decades earlier. The military even dubbed her "Friend of the GIs" because she brought "busloads of beautiful woman" to perform for them during the war.[63] In this instance, we learn how being matlina extended beyond education and into how CHamoru women might also (like her) refashion themselves and their notions of beauty and aesthetics.

Before considering her proximity to white men and American patriarchy and the question of how her desires and dreams of outward and upward mobility and activities wittingly or unwittingly aided and abetted U.S. colonialism, it is worth exploring the link between Johnston's leading role in promoting beauty culture and organizing shows for military men as cultural performances in and of themselves.⁶⁴ Johnston's performances and displays of beauty can be linked to patriotism and loyalty during the war and postwar years, which in turn can be linked to an earlier yearning for and investment in beauty culture. Agueda's "dreams and ambitions" were to dress like members of the Shoe Gang— the Martinez, Duarte, Torres, Calvo, and Herrero girls—and attend the same parties as them: "At the time I was growing up, there were prominent families on the island whose daughters were not only beautiful but the best dressed. These families had come from parents of means and education and were looked up [to] by the people of the community. They either owned large tracts of land, stores, or held prominent positions in the government. They were also of closer Spanish ancestry than the rest of the people. They dressed in European costumes and wore shoes."⁶⁵

Determined to fulfill these dreams and ambitions, in 1907 Agueda spent her first paycheck on luxuries from Montgomery Ward: six pairs of stockings (blue, pink, yellow), "shiny" leather high-heel patent shoes, and a parasol.⁶⁶ In 1913, Agueda Johnston was the highest paid CHamoru teacher, at fifty-four dollars a month. By then, Johnston's sartorial style included not only the American fashions but the custom-designed mestisas as well. She was well on her way to becoming one of the island's beautiful and well-dressed elite CHamoru women she once secretly admired, as would be captured in a 1916 photograph (figure 4.2) of Johnston and other CHamoru women employed with the navy's Department of Education.⁶⁷ Even Johnston's wedding dress—the lace, silk, and spangles of which were purchased in the Philippines by the American captain E. L. Bissett of the USS *Supply*—was custom made by one of the "pretty and accomplished" Shoe Gang girls, Dolores Herrero, before her own marriage to the American Earl Schmitt.⁶⁸ The gifts that Johnston received from her husband, like a Russian blue mink coat from Saks Fifth Avenue, were indicative of a status enjoyed only by American military wives or elite CHamoru women. Johnston's mink coat was a sign of just how much traveling she had done and was expected to do to the states or to Japan and China on the USS *Goldstar*. Figuratively speaking, being fashionably wrapped in fur also brought her in closer proximity to white women of the temperate zone, which is to say it helped symbolically close the gaps between the supposed differences that were said to exist between women of the tropics and women of temperate zones—a point of obsession in the writings of Euro-American and military personnel. The navy wife Shirley Lehman, for example, noted that "white children stay well here and ours have not been seriously ill since arriving in Guam. White women do not take it as well. Most women are in any of the stages of 'nerves' and as I understand it is most

FIGURE 4.2 Department of Education, December 23, 1916. From left to right: (sitting) Lieutenant Commander M. G. Cook, Governor Roy Smith, Jacques Schnabel; (standing) Hester Von Preissig, Maria Gutierrez, Remedios Leon Guerrero, Maria Rosario, Maria Perez, Ignacia Butler, Agueda Johnston, Carmen Leon Guerrero, Rosalia Duarte, Rosa Perez, Rosario Perez, Joaquina Untalan, Catalina Eclavea, Alice Herrera, A. P. Manley. Governor Roy Smith Collection, box 24, folder 3 "Photographs of Guam." Courtesy of Naval Historical Collection Archives, U.S. Naval War College.

because temperate-zone reared women cannot stand the tropical climate. Physically or mentally."[69]

Johnston's other dreams—to attend the same socials as these girls—were also becoming realized. One need only look through the naval-run *Guam News Letter*, the only newspaper at the time, to notice that Johnston was already socializing with both American and elite CHamoru women. She joined weeklong excursions on board American ships to Manila and swimming parties hosted by Americans in exotic sounding spots like "Piti-by-the-Bay," which CHamorus called simply Piti.[70] A typical outing or diversion of such kind might have entailed a morning sail, a noon "shore dinner," a two-hour swim in the channel, and, later, a clambake.[71] With such "thoroughly enjoyable" New England–style clambakes, it is no wonder that an anonymous writer exclaimed, "Newport had nothing on Guam!"[72] These outings also began to fill the pages of the *Guam News Letter*, which troubled naval authorities. Concerned that family and friends back in the States would see their relatives' tours of duty as all fun and play, the navy urged military personnel to get back to charitable and civic work. Civic work included the annual Christmas celebrations in the schools and Christmas pageants in the plaza, organized by military women and elite CHamoru women, including Johnston, where every CHamoru child in attendance received a gift.[73] The novelty of giving and receiving gifts at Christmas had become so popular that once, when news that the transport carrying gifts would be delayed, the navy decided to postpone Christmas; the tradition continued in the postwar years with fresh trees flown in.[74] The annual Christmas pageants, begun in the 1920s, were so large a feat that only the most capable of administrators were tasked with carrying them through. First among this class was Agueda Johnston, whose annual pageants and entertainments were, wrote an observer, a "monument to her ability."[75]

Johnston's stellar performance as an organizer of pageants and other annual entertainments resulted in a reputation that had her booked even in the midst of cleaning up a war-torn island. She held the fort for battle-weary soldiers, so to speak, until the arrival of the United Servicemen's Organization (USO), the famous social organization that dutifully followed U.S. ships, flags, and airplanes in an effort to entertain and boost the morale of U.S. servicemen abroad. In the immediate aftermath of the United States' bloody recapture of Guåhan in July 1944, even before World War II officially ended, the island was already teeming with hundreds of thousands of military servicemen (compared to its population at the time of about thirty-five thousand). In those moments when the USO was not able to furnish the celebrated and much anticipated celebrity pin-up girls for which it was world famous, it could count on Johnston's trained eye for talent and beauty and her organizational skills to round up and furnish CHamoru proxies, famalao'an CHamoru as "pin-up girls," a status and image I will return to shortly. Johnston recalled her first booking when the island was still literally in shambles and ruins. Her shows' audiences included the marines aboard the USS *Arkansas* returning from Iwo Jima. Marine Sergeant Little, who had seen the Christmas pageants and other school entertainments Johnston had directed, asked her if she would organize similar performances for members of his Third Marine Division stationed in Yo'ña. She informed him that all the entertainers she could think of were scattered and that there was no way of contacting them. He promptly furnished at Johnston's "disposal" a jeep and a truck.[76]

Johnston's performances had become so popular among the armed forces that her troupe, which initially included her son and daughter and two other teachers, went camp to camp for two months, following the ships in the harbor.

Fifty-one years old at the time, Johnston served as chaperone for these performance troupes, which eventually solicited the help of Shoe Gang members.[77] Her troupe included the Velarde sisters, who sang "after the fashion of the Andrew sisters"; ten-year-old Juanita Calvo, who performed solos; and Kitty Tenorio, who performed the CHamoru stick dance. Five-year-old Pauline Calvo, who imitated Shirley Temple and sang Autry tunes, was a "hit with the men."[78] Johnston's efforts continually "warmed the hearts" of men of the Third Marine Division, the unit that stormed and "liberated" the island on July 21, earning her the accolade "Friend of the GIs." Johnston's troupe continued to entertain the armed forces until the USO arrived and until her time was needed for the auspicious November 10, 1944 reopening of George Washington High School, auspicious (for Johnston) because the date coincided with the establishment of the marines in 1775.[79] These performances, which also included Polynesian hula and which trafficked on exotic Pacific Island maiden stereotypes, showcased another now familiar trope of performativity: CHamoru-American patriotism, especially as it was forged out of the ashes of two and a half years of Japanese occupation and tempered by overjoy and gratitude toward the return of Uncle Sam in the form of the heroic marine.[80] Johnston described a special tropical number called a "Night on Guam," which boasted attractive Native pin-up girls and "belles of the island."[81] That Guåhan's matlina, Johnston, already an important leader and maga'håga in the island's community, chaperoned the "busload" of CHamoru women, cannot and must not be underestimated.

Rewriting and Recasting the Colonial Scripting of the CHamoru Pin-Up

In CHamoru displays of American patriotism in Guåhan, which were already distinguishing themselves from Native displays of loyalty to the United States elsewhere in the Pacific, CHamoru women were often held to different standards and registers than CHamoru men. As one army sergeant told a reporter with *Yank, the Army Weekly*, "I've been through three campaigns ... and I'll be goddamned if anybody ever threw a flower in my jeep or gave me a drink of wine," but in Guåhan, there were many "smiling" Native women in their "ragged best" honoring the troops.[82] Two of these women were Agueda Johnston and her daughter Marian. Included in every *Yank* magazine were feature stories like this one, cartoons, and a "Yank Pin-Up Girl." In its references to physical good looks and features, patriotism, and correct union with the correct men, this story about "Pacific Liberation" could also have served as visual text of the Yank Pin-Up Girl but with a *CHamorita* twist. The article opened by introducing the mainland reader to a "destitute" but loyal and appreciative "Mrs. Johnston," who was "an attractive Chamorro woman."[83] The reader learned a sad story. She fell in love and married an American marine, but when the Japanese invaded and occupied the island, they captured the American and exiled him to a concentration camp in Japan, where he died a year later. Enter Marian, a "21-year old belle of Agana," whose story also involved a romance with an American, Ensign Robert Gabriel White, of the U.S. Naval Reserve. Marian was on a date with him not long before Japan's attack of December 8, 1941 (December 7 in Hawai'i and the United States), which led to his heroic death on board the USS *Penguin*.[84] A third CHamoru woman was introduced, a "girl, almost equally attractive, but one who was not entirely unresponsive to the advances of Jap [*sic*] officers." Not much more substance or interest is provided about her. She is not even named. She is as good as the Japanese officers to whose advances she responded. Through stark contrast and opposition, her betrayal throws into sharper focus, or relief, the patriotism of mother and daughter through their tragic love for American soldiers. Also staged here was the drama between a form of Native beauty and patriotism that pivoted around male soldiers of competing nations and races—love for the right, white American soldier linked true beauty for correct country, while love, or at least submission, to the wrong soldier was not simply incorrect but was tantamount to betrayal or treason and lesser forms of "beauty." When situated alongside other stories in military magazines like *Leatherneck* or popular American magazines such as *Collier's*, *Life*, and *The Elks Magazine*, the *Yank* article begins to highlight the specific kinds of registers associated with CHamoru women during the war and also afterward. These registers would inhere in what I am suggesting was a specifically gendered wartime and postliberation construction and narrative of CHamoru women as exotic, grateful, and loyal pin-ups of patriotism.[85]

It is worth pausing for a moment to consider some examples of how narratives about romance, beautiful island maidens, and vulnerable but heroic GIs comprised a larger recurring narrative about Native CHamoru patriotism and loyalty to the United States, which in turn bolstered an even larger self-conceit about the righteousness of the United States' entry into the Pacific theater and the legitimacy of its newfound and hard-fought political and moral place atop the nations of the world. While magazine and even radio coverage furnished countless examples of beautiful, grateful island women and romantic allusions to military men as a kind of allegory for this self-congratulatory American self-possession, Agueda Johnston's story was to serve as exemplary.

In a May 1945 issue, *Collier's* would contrast Johnston's supposedly diminutive stature as a five-feet-two-inch Native woman to her six-feet-two-inch American marine to secure for her (through her marriage to him) an elevated status as the island's "uncontested First Lady." In sizing up the contrast in physicality and spatio-racialized identity of the petite (read: delicate) Native woman from Guam and her tall (read: strapping) marine from Tennessee, the magazine actually inverted the supposed power of a helpless island maiden to convey a particular kind of loyalty engendered through loving gratitude of a type forged through the terms of romance consummated even before the outset of conflict—Johnston's "soft dark eyes, her rippling laughter and her fragile beauty completely won the big Marine" over.[86] The couple would go on to have seven children, but in the magazine, readers would learn that during the occupation, when William Johnston was exiled and imprisoned in Japan, Agueda Johnston's worst fears were of not being able to protect her daughter, the "vivacious beautiful Marian," from the Japanese, who had forced CHamoru women into sexual servitude as comfort women.[87]

To be sure, immediate postwar descriptions that explicitly connected the tropes of the natural and alluring beauty of Native women with wartime victimhood and gratitude toward returning GIs in highly romanticized and sexualized terms were commonplace, though, again, Agueda Johnston's particular stories seemed to serve as exemplary. Examples of this ubiquity abound: In the same year, *Yank* featured a photograph of Ignacia Quintanilla, a Bank of Guam accountant, who was identified simply as "Gnacia" while the caption furnished all that was needed for the American reader to make sense of the pretty face: "Here is somebody it was nice to liberate."[88] Not to be outdone, *Leatherneck* published the article "Glamour on Guam," which featured twelve "representative young women" from the island's various villages as if it were some kind of directory listing of island pin-ups and where they might be found: six from Agana (Hagåtña)—Toni Martinez, Victoria Leon Guerrero, Harriett O. Chandler, Irene Bordallo, Ignacia Leon Guerrero, and Barbara Bordallo; three from Agana Heights (Tutuhan)—Elizabeth Perez, Toni Terlaje, and Ana Leon Guerrero; and another three from "Telefofo" (Talofo'fo')—Josefa Ulloa, Lucy Taitague, and Antonia Mendiola.[89] *Life* got in on the action when the magazine highlighted five of the aforementioned women and introduced four new ones with a lede that said that American marines "have long felt that somewhere, somehow, romance could be found in the fabled South Seas" but that war had instead yielded "discomfort, disease and death."[90] But GI perseverance and grit prevailed, and "at last" these women appeared, a sight for beleaguered and sore eyes—and somewhat surprised eyes, for instead of dark exotic maidens of the fabled South Seas, many of the beauties featured in what the magazine called the island's "bouquet of pin-ups," like Harriet Chandler, were of mixed race and possessed physical features that also made them "indistinguishable from the girl from Toledo." Even then, it was the mixture of races that a GI would find in Guåhan in particular that furnished these tropical belles their distinct type of beauty and charm, even if it had also been augmented by some of the women's mimicry, like the one assumed by Ignacia Leon Guerrero, of an already classic "glamour pose" as seen in American movies before the war. If the aforementioned Chandler could not be distinguished from an American midwestern beauty from Ohio, Ignacia Leon Guerrero and Toni Terlaje, on the other hand, posed what the magazine identified as an "Asiatic appearance" and a "strain of Polynesian, mixed with Filipino," while another, identified simply as "the girl with a new lipstick," sported a "distinctly Malayan cast of features."[91] The magazine went on to account historically for this outcome: under Spanish misrule, the island came close to complete depopulation but, thanks to rehabilitation and a campaign of health and hygiene under naval governance since 1898, the CHamorus rebounded, or more precisely, "multiplied." The "girls" had the "remote" ancestry of "handsome, light-skinned, warrior Chamorros" to thank for their bold, exotic looks. Ending on the "impeccable cleanliness" of the island's young women, the article proceeded to introduce the reader to Agueda Johnston as the "first CHamoru lady of the island" and "wife of an American marine." Here, as in many stories about her in this period, Johnston—and her (deserved) fame and reputation as a prominent woman leader—are never dissociated from narratives of pre- and postwar romance between island belles and military men within longer histories of the island's natural and social despoliation and the United States' redemptive presence (or return, as in the case of its "liberation" of the island). Here, it is precisely the role of exotic CHamoru women as loving and loyal partners and intermediators to white men that makes for the real beauty and truth of these glamorous CHamoru women.[92]

In its September 1945 feature story, *The Elks Magazine* delved into the life of Johnston, now nicknamed, "the Queen Bee of Guam," highlighting her role in helping George Tweed by bringing him food, magazines, and cigarettes as he hid in Guåhan's jungles during the occupation. This saga of Tweed—whom the war correspondent Coles Phillips and others referred to as the "Ghost of Guam"—was so well known in the United States that Phillips predicted it would one day be made into a movie and that Dorothy Lamour would play the part of Agueda Johnston.[93] Though Tweed's story was eventually cinematized as *No Man Is an Island* (1962), Lamour was not cast to play Johnston.[94] Though Lamour never did feature as Agueda in the movie—nobody did, since, for reasons unknown, Agueda Johnston's persona is completely absent—the presumption or expectation that Lamour would or should be cast as Agueda only reinforces the linkage between exotica and erotica through racialized and gendered representations of island women, glamour, and how they wend into narratives of war and redemption. Lamour was especially famous for her "sarong" films of the 1930s and 1940s, which earned her the reputation as queen of the Hollywood islands and silver screen goddess. According to Sean Brawley and Chris Dixon, Lamour represented the idealized image of South Seas sexuality and by 1943 was the number-one pin-up girl.[95] While Lamour never played Johnston in a film, she modeled how famalao'an CHamoru like Johnston would get to "play" in narratives of America's wartime efforts and its meanings for both contemporary and present-day Americans as well as CHamorus. The allure of Johnston's beauty as a Native woman pin-up lay also in how it sentimentalized the supposed truth of the United States' place in the Pacific and in the world, especially after World War II.

The "pinning up" of Native CHamoru women's determinations around modern American and patriotic notions of beauty through exoticism and eroticism as imagined and as imaged in and by white Americans through white women in islander drag (Lamour as island maiden in sarong) was also captured in other terms and images of Native Pacific Islander women like the "island belle" and "dusky maiden."[96] The latter, especially, harkens back to a common representation of American Indian women in feature-length films that M. Elise Marubbio calls the "Celluloid Maiden." The culmination of the Indian princess and sexualized maiden, this image is one of a female "conquerable body" willing to sacrifice herself in the name of white men and the U.S. nation, one that becomes colonized and expendable in the name of imperial expansion.[97] As Adria Imada argues of similarly imagined Hawaiian women dancers in World War II hula circuits, Native women performers were not simply "two-dimensional magazine pin-ups" or "passive commodities in the constraining order of empire; they improvised tactics to subvert colonial scripts that insisted on primitivist eroticized roles ... and presented themselves as modern Native women and cosmopolitan tourists."[98]

Johnston's wartime and postwar recollections and activities are indeed steeped in American patriotism but of the sort that needs to be understood in terms of Indigenous interest, resolve, and purpose. Like the pattera who, as I argued in chapter 1, embraced modern delivery practices without abandoning ancient CHamoru practices of stewarding Native well-being, Johnston's patriotic practices did not automatically cancel out loyalties to Indigenous

CHamoru values. In time, as I have argued, their simultaneity, their ability to coexist without contradiction and tension, would be tested and challenged, and Johnston herself would be among the first to notice the price that being modern CHamoru would have to pay in its wager with also being American. Yet we need not cite only her perspectives that explicitly reconsider the unexpected or unanticipated outcomes of CHamoru investments in the United States. In other words, her "dutiful" performance of ostensibly patriotic activities can also be read as performances of duty to the island's postwar needs.

Johnston's creation and production in 1946 of the weekly radio show *The Guam Hour* is an example of the multitasking she performed for the military and in the interest of CHamorus. The impetus originated as a favor to then-naval Commander Martin Carlson.[99] At the time, Johnston was superintendent of education, a position she held from 1946 to 1953. During her tenure as superintendent, she witnessed the 1950 transition of the Department of Education out from under the navy to its new home under the newly established GovGuam (now under the Department of Interior). The radio show, she claimed, was a way of keeping the community abreast of all things pertaining to public education. Even to this day, public education remains one of the major sectors of GovGuam, and its weekly activities are common fare in the island's print and electronic media's coverage of community events.

Another event in which Johnston played a leadership role, as part of the Guam Teachers Association, took place in the 1960s and involved the public plebiscite on a new name and identity for CHamorus. As discussed earlier, motivation for the plebiscite hinged on two circumstances: a desire to celebrate a new political and social era under the United States following the Japanese occupation and to distinguish CHamorus of Guåhan from CHamorus of the Northern Marianas, many of whom were loyal to the Japanese and served as interpreters during the war. The three choices for the Indigenous people of Guåhan were *Guamian, Guamanian,* and *Guamerican.* Johnston's personal preference was the last, but most favored the second option. The term *Guamanian,* until around the 1970s, became the preferred way for one or two generations to refer to CHamorus, to all things CHamoru. It was not only until the 1970s that a new generation of CHamoru intellectuals and leaders began to openly question the island's status as a "colony" of the United States and express reservations about the increasingly marginalized status of CHamorus in their own homelands and the weakening of values and practices of kostumbren CHamoru. From the 1980s onward, there was something of a concerted effort to readopt the term *Chamorro* but reserve it for referring specifically to Indigenous peoplehood, language, and culture and use the term *Guamanian* for any resident or aspect of Guåhan regardless of racial or ethnic lineage. It is also primarily in the cultural politics of the island since the 1980s that leaders like Agueda Johnston began to be regarded by some as simply assimilated or acculturated or, worse, colonized or coapted CHamorus whose loyalties to distinctly Indigenous values and peoplehood might be rendered suspect. But such views would ignore the fact that, like many of her generation, Johnston's embrace of an American future for the "people and island she loved so dearly" could not have imagined or foreseen the deleterious effects it would have for CHamoru indigeneity.[100] We might say that for leaders like Johnston, on whose shoulders, minds, and energies would rest in part the future of the island, even a term like *Guamerican* did not automatically or necessarily mean only a privileging of America in that future. Even the term itself prioritizes *Guam* over *America* in the order of placement.

Johnston's vita of patriotic duties was first and foremost to advance the island, albeit under a political system that had, for leaders like herself, offered compelling, if even monopolizing, narratives and vehicles of and for CHamoru progress and prosperity, for democracy and freedom, for exposure to a world beyond the låncho or the walls of a racially classed Hagåtña beyond the såddok; this much is certainly evident and celebrated in Johnston's five-month "Victory Tour" in 1947 across the United States. The tour revealed just how far and deep ran her many ties to the United States—which now included kinship relations with Americans who had been to Guåhan and with CHamoru family who had moved to the states. Traveling in style on board the USS *Mann*, an upgrade compliments of Mary Chenoweth Pownall, wife of the navy governor Charles Pownall, Johnston visited with friends and family abroad. She also toured the Girl Scouts headquarters as well as that of the Elks Lodge in New York City. Both were important American institutions in whose transplanting in Guåhan she played a major role. She also visited with military brass like Rear Admiral Lawrence E. Tull, Homer Votaw, who was in charge of the postwar refugee camps, and Rear Admiral George McMillan, who had had the misfortune of being appointed naval governor of Guåhan before having to formally surrender the island to the Japanese in 1941. In Franklin, Tennessee, Agueda visited William Gautier Johnston's mother and sister, a meeting that surely was bittersweet given that her beloved husband had passed away while imprisoned in Japan and also because it would be the first time she would meet her mother-in-law (and sister-in-law). In Baltimore, elsewhere on the East Coast, and in the Midwest, Agueda Johnston was able to visit her son and daughter who had moved stateside before the war, when the navy began to evacuate military dependents. Johnston also traveled to Montgomery, Alabama, to visit with the American marine "Carey," her first boy "crush," whom she had met in 1907 along the wall that divided her home and Lieutenant Governor William Safford's home in Hagåtña. In San Diego, Johnston reunited with her longtime mentor and friend Eva Belle Peck.

In between these personal and social trips across the states, Johnston continued to perform more civic duties, delivering public lectures with titles like "That Chamorro Race" and "What the Flag Means to an American When His Country Is Occupied by an Enemy."[101] For Johnston, these two topics were deeply intertwined and precisely a lesson that an island people under enemy occupation could teach Americans about what the American flag could mean. As discussed in the previous chapter, the meanings of flags can be hotly contested, especially, as we noted in the Guåhan flag (which served for a time as the official flag for the U.S. Navy), when the flag's very iconography and design entail Indigenous landscape and Indigenous workings and aspirations. The interconnection between these two topics of Johnston's lectures abroad also helps explain the depth and range of her civic duty to Guåhan and to the United States in the same way that, by 1947, her visiting of family, friends, and former supervisors in the continental United States also constituted essential components of her duty as a CHamoru woman to her kinship relations under the terms of inafa'maolek. These entanglements are evident in one visit to California with Rear Admiral McMillan that emblematizes just how freighted Johnston's patriotism and inagradesi was. Not surprisingly, that visit concerned the actual American flag that was first unfurled and flown in Guåhan when the Americans returned to reoccupy the island in 1944, one that reportedly had been sewn during the occupation by a CHamoru woman. A purpose, if not outcome, of that trip for Johnston then was to bring *that flag* home.[102]

Bringing That Flag Home

My effort to continue to complicate the terms of Johnston's loyalty and patriotism by displacing the monolithic and singular terms of the United States as the undisputed and supreme referent now involves calling attention to matters *back home*; that is, in Guåhan's soil proper. This effort requires examining the CHamoru cultural politics of domesticity and femininity as they become embroiled in CHamoru women's aspirations for the new contra the stifling, but also in flash points after the war and moments of tension during the war. These tensions, registering in social and personal relationships and also evident in existing political orders, help destabilize monolithic understandings of CHamoru patriotism to the United States in general, and it is my contention that how they played out with respect to Johnston's story, in particular, can also illustrate the residual concerns for CHamoru indigeneity that are enmeshed in these tensions of patriotism.

To understand the complexity of this kind of patriotism, we can return to the prewar period that featured and shaped Johnston's intricate social and even intimate relationships with American officials and the scorn she received from certain CHamorus because of them. In the question of the importance of her relationship to American men, second only to her husband, Gautier, was the case of Governor Edward Dorn. Recall that it was under Governor Dorn's administration that Johnston first took her oath as a teacher and public servant under the navy. From her notes, we discover that Dorn was a first in many life-changing ways for Johnston. From her notes and Dorn's diary, it was also evident that "Guam's Patriarch of ex-Governors" was fond of "the pretty little teacher" and concerned about her welfare.[103] Evidence of deep affection and admiration, but not of romantic love—which by all accounts was faithfully reserved for Gautier—Johnston's recollection of the "most impressive and lasting" of all her "many pleasant" acquaintances with the American governors, which included civilian governors like Ford Elvidge (figure 4.3), also illustrates, as discussed earlier in this chapter, the hierarchy of naval, marine, and CHamoru teachers.[104] Here, however, we gather how the social and the intimate played out and how these bring the question of interest and loyalty to all things American back to their proper place in Indigenous CHamoru values, priorities, and aspirations. Hence, at the top of the hierarchy sat the governor, one whom Johnston deemed to be the "most appealing," because, while he wielded the most authority on Guåhan, he showed "no disapproval" upon learning of Gautier's interest in Agueda and turned out to be "most cooperative" when Gautier wished to buy out the rest of his enlistment in the Marine Corps so that he could marry Agueda. Well aware of Governor Dorn's fondness for her, Johnston conveyed admiration and appreciation over the fact that Dorn could have easily halted or at least seriously impeded a relationship that proved life changing for her. Johnston described this respetu and inagradesi in familiar terms and relations: "If Governor Dorn were a teacher I'd easily consider myself one of his pupils."[105]

In an incident, a smear campaign, involving a series of poetic barbs by CHamorus directed at Agueda, the loyal Governor Dorn came to her defense.[106] From Johnston's recollection of the incident, an indication of just how far up

FIGURE 4.3 Agueda Johnston with Governor Ford Elvidge (right), 1956. Courtesy of the Guam Public Library System.

and out her humble roots branched, we are given a glimpse of a deep kind of conflict and tension in CHamoru cultural politics as they were implicated in intimate relations with agents of American naval colonialism:

> For the youngster it could be a kite, a top or jumping road fads. At a certain time there was a "poetry fad." This fad would have had its merits but ... the "poets" would poke fun at or ridicule people, at parties or gatherings. The poems would be typed or hand written and thrown into people's windows or doors. Everybody concerned was angry but no one knew who the poet or poets were. I was not to be exempted as a recipient of these poems as I knew already that I had aroused disapproval for selecting an American to be my suitor. So it wasn't very long before some of these cleverly written verses reached my house. For awhile [sic] they were mild and childish mostly making fun of my sudden transformation. Then I received one which was very personal. I thought then that perhaps this might be the time to put a stop to it. I took all the copies of the poems that I had received to the Governor. The typewritten ones were found to

be done at the court house typewriters. But who did it nobody could tell as everyone at the court house had access to the typewriter from the judges to the messengers. Anyway, the Governor issued an order that anyone using Government paper and typewriter for other purposes than Government business would be punished and discharged.[107]

In this instance, as with the instance where Gautier was able to buy out the rest of his enlistment, the question of U.S. naval authority can also be redirected or rerouted in the interest of serving certain CHamoru political and personal aspirations, interests, and desires. In the case of the "poetry fad," we learn that CHamoru interests are not monolithic or uniform; they compete and contest, somewhat like sibling rivalry. Hence, ostensibly about Agueda's outward and upward social mobility, about her new and "sudden transformation," these new criticisms may also have had more, or at least as much, to do with Agueda's decision to marry an American, her desire for an American "suitor," her desire (we might say more bluntly) to control the terms of her own sexuality. I am presuming here that her principal detractors were CHamorus with similar investments in American modernity, like new clerical jobs in the naval government offices. For instance, they could type and employed new literary forms like poetry and poetic barbs and the power of the pen. But through these modern practices, they were no less CHamoru. Perhaps they were CHamoru men who bristled out of jealousy or insecurity, personal or professional. Maybe it was because of spurned or unrequited interest, or maybe a reaction to the success of a Native woman who was not even of their class or who, as a member of their class, showed them up. Either way, Agueda Johnston clearly was transgressing her place as a CHamoru woman. Perhaps the sharp-tongued poetry came from rival CHamoru women. Perhaps the poems, her access to the governor, her marriage to an American (a Marine, at that, if the detractor was of the manakhilo' class), were modern day slingstones, to recall the historic and contemporary CHamoru contestations over the Guåhan flag's multiple meanings. Perhaps the poetic lines, especially the too "personal" ones over which she finally drew the line and solicited the help of the governor, were actually lines drawn by the detractors when it came to marriage to a white man. Even her mother had initially disapproved of Agueda's interest in American men. Yet, although her mother "cried" and hoped to keep her chaperoned from the dangerous "women loving Americanos" who were "too much after Chamorro women," too aggressive in their pursuit of them, Agueda was "too intrigued by the new fair and handsome young men on the Plaza to be alarmed." In her teens, on her way back home from the Leary

School (site of the old Escuela de los Niños)—which was a block north of the plåsa, on the west side of the Calle de Pazos, and faced the end of the road where Agueda's house sat—she chose not to take the shorter route down Chålan Isabela la Catolica, which ran along the east side of the plåsa past the church, but instead took the "more interesting" route home past the jail and the marine barracks.[108] The marines, according to Johnston, took more notice of the older, well-dressed "beautiful girls circulating about town," the Shoe Gang. The paths home might have been a bit circuitous, longer, and more indirect than they had to be, but Johnston always returned home.

Godmothering and CHamoru Patriotism

In her 1939 campaign speech for the Guam House of Council, Agueda Johnston told residents of Hagåtña that she never intended to run for office but that because her friends had placed her name in the contest and because she was accustomed to rendering public service, she agreed to run. Atop her platform was a topic of recurring interest and agitation: the fixing by formal clarification of Guåhan's political relationship to the United States as it was understood by Guåhan's political leaders to be secured through the granting of U.S. citizenship for CHamorus:

> The people of Guam can obtain progress and the granting of more privileges easier, by a friendly, harmonious and co-operative attitude toward the Government than by any other method. The legal status of the people of Guam has been defined as being "neither aliens nor citizens but wards of the Government." This means that we stand in the same relation to the United States as a child does to his guardian or, I might go so far as to say, "a child to his parent." The government the United States has bestowed on us has been parental in every respect and it behooves us to show our appreciation by giving consistent and loyal support to those in authority. By doing so we can win their favor and secure more than by creating a feeling of antagonism.[109]

Johnston was referring to the growing tensions between CHamorus and the navy around the CHamoru movement for U.S. citizenship. Although CHamorus first petitioned for citizenship in 1901, the height of the movement came before the war in 1936 when then Guam Congress representatives Baltazar Jerome (B. J.) Bordallo and Francisco Baza Leon Guerrero (Tun Kiko Suilo) traveled to Washington, D.C., to petition Congress. For Johnston, CHamorus could achieve "progress" and be granted "more privileges" if they cooperated with the navy. She also couched the relations in terms of a child's obedience to a parent and so appeared to have accepted the paternalism of U.S. colonialism and her lot as that of a child, which is to say that she acquiesced to the racialized and gendered discourse that infantilized CHamorus as helpless children in need of parental supervision and guidance. If the governor was her father, the patriarch, then the United States was her mother (country). This loyalty and patriotism was writ across her platform for education and in what might be understood as a CHamoru women's "politics of respectability," a phrase coined by Evelyn Brooks Higginbotham to describe late nineteenth- and early twentieth-century black women's roles in their forging of the church as a powerful institution for social and political change in the black community.[110]

For Johnston, as articulated in her campaign address, the foundation that would bring about the island's progress and advance CHamorus was education. Johnston, whose speech read as if she were thoroughly schooled by white American male administrators and their agents of U.S. education—marines, military spouses, and dependents who doubled as teachers and special laborers—explained it this way: "Naturally, having spent the greater part of my life as a schoolteacher, I am a firm believer in education." She continued: "No people can progress far without education. I do not mean education of an impracticable nature, but education that will best fit the child for the work of life later on—education that will make him a better citizen and that will make him an economic asset to his community. A program for the practical education of the youth of Guam within the bounds of money available has been my platform and always will be whether I am a member of Congress or not."[111] As critical scholarship on colonial education and colonialism in general has demonstrated, a lesson planned and taught by the colonizer does not guarantee that the student will simply learn it, much less apply it toward the same effects and outcomes that might have been intended by the teacher.[112] There is no guarantee, in other words, that Johnston's faith in practical education or her aspirations for progress for Guåhan were identical with those of the U.S. Navy. Furthermore, it would be nothing less than acceding to U.S. colonialism if we were to presume that the United States or the West possessed exclusive ownership over ideas of education, progress, practicality, or modernity."[113]

As I have argued of similar or analogous investments in American modernity by other CHamoru women, like the pattera, Johnston's assertions of the kind of education best suited for Guåhan were also grounded in a larger belief in what was maolek under the United States. We can get a better understanding of how this conviction or loyalty informed Johnston's story by taking substantively what CHamorus meant when they referred to her as Guåhan's "Godmother of Education." As discussed in chapter 1, in CHamoru, the term for godmother is *matlina*, the Indigenous pronunciation of the Spanish term *madrina*, a highly cherished and respected title that comes from kostumbren CHamoru, the historical CHamorucization of Spanish-Catholic religiosity and sociality. Even though the name appears to have originated in CHamoru postwar recollections of Tan Agueda to honor her over half-a-century commitment to the island's education, it effectively captures the way Johnston was able to act as public servant and civic and community leader. This honorific title, I would also suggest, helps us reread and thus rescue her from hegemonic narratives that use her story to legitimize Guåhan's further integration into the United States' political system or to justify (through her brand of patriotism) further military development and land takings in the twenty-first century. It is worth considering key examples of that rhetoric as they invoke, in particular, her steadfast patriotism and loyalty to the United States in the most perilous of conditions during the Japanese occupation. In turn, we will also understand how her recollection of that experience, particularly with respect to her tense relationship with the American war hero George Tweed, can also serve to undermine the stability of those hegemonic narratives. I argue that it is in the tension between Tweed and Johnston that we can begin to appreciate the substance of her matlina cultural politics that do not simply align with the monolithic narratives. This matlina politics can also inform what it means to pulan and poksai Indigenous lands and peoples at the limits of colonial modernities under the self-serving heroics of U.S. militarism.

Along with education, citizenship and greater self-government were also maolek and vital to nurturing, steering, and advancing the island, and so in September 1949, then-assistant superintendent Johnston traveled to Washington, D.C., to meet with American congressmen and federal officials to help the cause. As Doloris Coulter Cogan recalls in her own memoirs of the Guam Organic Act, Johnston's style of fighting for CHamoru civil rights was in a "genteel manner."[114] This manner, which some might say was actually Johnston's korason fåha' (softhearted, peaceful nature), included her hosting of federal officials in her home, a maneuver that some speculated helped to garner the support of federal officials for legislation that many American officials, beginning with the Department of the Navy, still refused to support.

Johnston's style of patriotism, with which the push for CHamoru educational and political advancement were not incongruous (at least not then), had become so prodigious that even posthumously, it is used to advance the island politically. In 1997, the U.S. Congress heard testimony on the Guam

Commonwealth Act, CHamoru-initiated legislation that failed in its bid to change the island's political status from an unincorporated territory to a commonwealth, one similar to the Northern Mariana Islands. At the hearings, the American veteran Darrell Doss of the Third Marine Division tesitified in favor of the bill: "I wish time would permit me to tell the story of a few of these brave people and what they endured because of their love for the United States, a love which I feel has not been returned in the policies of our government." Doss named Agueda Johnston in that cohort and continued,

> I am sure that some of you would have tears in your eyes, just as we liberators had tears in our eyes when we liberated the concentration camps. These are the people I am asking you to support and allow them to have a closer and more democratic relationship with America. . . . I ask you to please vote for true justice on this very important issue. . . . In doing so, the members of this Congress shall share the honor we have as "Liberators of Guam." Your vote can accomplish that which we, 75,000 strong, and backed with massive military arms, were apparently unable to do in 1944.[115]

In including Johnston in this small cohort of CHamorus who truly know the meaning of American democracy, Doss also emplaces her at what is often taken to be the spatial, temporal, and cultural arbiter of that truth and knowledge: survival during the Japanese occupation through undying faith in the United States' return. For Agueda's story, her occupation in this site entangles and implicates in complex ways two American men: the first, her beloved husband, who was imprisoned in Japan, and second, George Tweed, whose escape from Japanese soldiers made him an instant hero. But Johnston's story also does not abandon the centrality of CHamorus, as is usually the case in conventional historiographies of Guåhan's liberation, when Indigenous narratives and interests do not necessarily align with the United States' political interests or when CHamorus themselves had major conflicts with Americans. It is then worth pursuing such tensions that Johnston recalled with Tweed.

Her loyalty to the United States (and responsibility to the island) would be put to the test because of her contentious relationship with George Tweed, who in dominant U.S. narratives is a national hero. Many CHamorus saw Tweed as a symbol of the United States and risked or sacrificed their lives to protect him as he hid in Guåhan's jungles for two and a half years. For Johnston, Tweed symbolized the return of the Americans. Most tellingly, Johnston also saw in Tweed's survival the prospects of Gautier's eventual freedom and safe return from a prisoner-of-war internment camp in Japan. Her own family was on the line. But as Johnston had put it, Tweed was kept alive "not for any personal interest in him but because of the flag he represented."[116] But where a reader might perceive this ordering as a privileging of the American flag, I argue that the flag had also by then, and under circumstances of war, come to represent Johnston's cultural, political, and social commitments to her island and her familia. Moreover, as we shall learn shortly, Johnston's rhetorical decision to prioritize national allegiance over personal interest was understandable since the tension with Tweed centered on his (baseless) charge that Johnston, like other CHamorus who helped him, could not place selfish interests over U.S. national ones. In effect, he was questioning Johnston's loyalty and patriotism when she expressed concern over the number of CHamorus who were being killed or brutally beaten over allegations of assisting him. In working our way to that tension, it is also worth keeping in mind just how high the tensions ran here. Johnston and Tweed knew each other and socialized in the same circles before the war. It was Gautier who had initiated Tweed into the Elks Club. Agueda believed this was the reason Tweed kept her abreast of his whereabouts during the occupation.[117]

In his autobiography, Tweed recounted how early in the occupation, Johnston conveyed to him in secret messages hidden inside soap bars (from the Johnston family's soap factory) that he needed to keep himself alive, for the sake of CHamorus whose hopes and dreams he carried.[118] Toward the end of the war, when Japanese soldiers began beating, torturing, and executing CHamorus suspected of harboring Tweed, Johnston and her three children were arrested, and she was beaten. After the incident, Johnston instructed Tweed never to write her again, but he ignored her request and wrote her again. In his version of the story, Tweed conceded that despite the beatings, Johnston did not divulge information. He had received word from another CHamoru, Tun Antonio Artero, who had been hiding him, that Johnston's nerves were shattered and that she told Artero to ask Tweed whether he intended on "staying in the bush while the rest of us got killed."[119] According to Tweed, as relayed to him by Artero, Johnston had even suggested that Tweed should surrender. Moreover, as Tweed wrote, Johnston had warned him that she did not know whether she could "hold her tongue" if the Japanese were to beat her again.[120] Tweed wrote that he sent a return message to Johnston informing her that he refused to surrender but again conceded that he had been assured that Johnston would never betray his whereabouts. Against Johnston's wishes that Tweed no longer contact her, he wrote her after the beatings, and Artero delivered the letter. In his letter, Tweed threatened her.

As the search for Tweed continued and Japanese atrocities against CHamorus (especially those suspected of sheltering him) intensified, Tweed feared Johnston would reveal to Japanese authorities his whereabouts in a cave in Urunao, in northern Guåhan. In a letter dated August 31, 1943, disguised and addressed from J. C. to J., Tweed reminded Johnston of her possible fate should she reveal Tweed's whereabouts even amid Japanese torture and violence. He told her that a "comparable form of violence endured by those persecuted by the Japanese" would come to her "not at the hands of the Japanese ... but at the hands of the Americans." "U.S. Army officials," Tweed declared, would "have no compunction against shooting a lady" for a military offense. "Even if you were fortunate to escape such a tragic end," Tweed continued, it would mean "long years in prison for you. Your own self-respect would be gone, also the love and respect of those whom you love and who love you, especially the love and respect of one who is now absent."[121] The absent one Tweed referred to of course was none other than Gautier. In reading Johnston's wartime accounts alongside Gautier's, it becomes even more evident just how many competing meanings the U.S. flag could contain and just how much Tweed's survival could also represent what that flag symbolized, regardless of how one felt about the man. So tensions between Johnston and Tweed are also bound to trouble or upset that containment. In his diary entry of June 14, 1943, written just a few months before Agueda received Tweed's infamous last letter, Gautier intimated (from an internment camp from afar) what the flag meant to him: "The 14th was our Flag Day and I lay awake at night thinking of past Flag Days in happier days, and the dance that followed, and I could see, in my mind's eye, my wife and the girls in their pretty new dresses and (sons) Herbert and Tom at the bar. When will we be together again?"[122] In most local and national commemorations of Tweed, in stories about the relations between Johnston and Tweed, these threats, not surprisingly, are left out or downplayed respectably, if not assuaged. According to Johnston, she "hurriedly wrote a note back telling Mr. Tweed" that his "threats were not appreciated," but "Antonio refused to take it [her reply], saying that he had no way of delivering it as Tweed had already left his premises."[123]

A CHamoru version maintains that Johnston told Tweed he needed to surrender because Japanese soldiers were planning to kill B. J. Bordallo, who they suspected was hiding him.[124] Bordallo was a prominent CHamoru political and civic leader who, as mentioned earlier, joined Tun Kiko Suilo in Washington, D.C., to petition the Congress for U.S. citizenship for CHamorus. More importantly, Bordallo was a family man and father of twelve. Here, amid the terror and atrocities of war, deeper CHamoru values and codes of responsibility surface. We might recognize this obligation as a marker of kostumbren CHamoru womanhood and the role of women to safeguard the family, and the even deeper workings of inafa'maolek and mañelu relations between Johnston and Bordallo and Johnston and Artero. Johnston wrote: "I was deeply troubled in knowing where Tweed was and allowing Bordallo to be killed and at the same time if Bordallo were spared, Antonio Artero would be killed."[125]

The matlina, to be sure, wields tremendous authority and is a potent manifestation of kostumbren CHamoru, and I assert that what animated Johnston's confrontation with Tweed and her deeper assertion of being "Guamanian-Chamorro by birth but American patriotic by choice" were competing allegiances between the United States and CHamoru indigeneity in exceptional moments when these tended, in otherwise normal circumstances, to not necessarily conflict. There would be other touchstones or flash points in Guåhan's postwar history when it would be clear that being CHamoru and investing in the United States could no longer appear to be seamless or without contradiction. In those moments, Guåhan's godmother of education would register ambivalence and even regret in contradictory moments in her memoirs even when she claimed otherwise.

It is widely known that Johnston, one of Guåhan's leading matlina and civic leaders in the postwar reconstruction, was the mastermind behind what is now celebrated annually as Liberation Day, the island's most important secular holiday. Since 1945, every July 21, the island has held its biggest fiesta in honor of the returning liberators who freed CHamorus from the Japanese. In recent years, critical scholars have questioned the underlying narratives of the annual celebration and have called attention to the religiosity that permeates the memories and commemorations surrounding Liberation Day. In his analysis of World War II memories in Guåhan, Keith L. Camacho writes that Johnston's original intentions for Liberation Day were for it to serve mainly as a fiesta to Sånta Marian Kåmalen, for looking out for the welfare of the CHamorus. However, this religious intention, which included a procession around Hagåtña, became co-opted when, in 1950, Liberation Day adopted "loyalty" as a commemorative theme.[126] It would also be a mistake to reduce Johnston to religious fundamentalism hiding in liberal clothing. If there were another deep dimension to Johnston, I would prefer to call it a latent or proto-CHamoru feminism, one best exemplified in CHamoru oral histories of an incident pertaining to the matter of wartime prostitution, as recalled by Reverend Joaquin Sablan.[127] This story concerned a CHamoru woman who was found guilty of such charges. Shorn of her hair and forced to sweep the streets of Hagåtña in the hot sun, the woman collapsed. Heeding this in tåddong ways and asserting her role as matlina and maga'håga, Johnston confronted the governor, who informed her that it was a CHamoru priest who recommended the punishment. Johnston, according to Reverend Sablan, chided the American governor, and "really laid into him," telling him that he should have known better, certainly better than a priest. But Johnston also did something truly radical at the time: she promptly marched to the kombento (convent) and demanded that the påle' fa'maolek and make things right.[128] By the postwar years, when this event happened, Johnston, who by all accounts was raised Catholic, may have also already given the Church grief. In 1915, she and Gautier had opened the first movie house in Hagåtña. Though working women may have participated in this new urban American experience of consuming motion pictures and "occupying the spaces of streets" and the chålan in new ways, some staunch Catholic families regarded the practice, along with dances, as inappropriate activities for women.[129] If not feminist, then Johnston's action was at the very least a demand to act on behalf of CHamoru women's well-being, according to what is proper or right in CHamoru terms, but her actions also did not simply acquiesce to Catholic or other CHamoru confining dictates that inform kostumbren CHamoru.

CHamorita Reawakenings: Between Matlina and Maga'håga

We CHamorus, we love our land.

—Dick Taitano

In August 1944, shortly after Guåhan's liberation from the Japanese, six CHamoru leaders, including Agueda Johnston, sent a letter of "heartfelt thanks" to Admiral Chester Nimitz for the U.S. recapture of the island by the "strong and invincible forces" under his command.[130] Writing on behalf of CHamorus, they wrote: "The recapture of Guam was opportune. Had it been delayed longer the native inhabitants would have barely withstood the ill-treatments and atrocities received from the Japanese. What kept us up throughout the thirty-two months of Japanese oppression was our determined reliance upon our mother country's power, sense of justice, and national brotherhood."[131] In the new opportunity of the United States' highly militarized return in 1944, Johnston herself returned—this time, with her mañelu: Francisco B. Leon Guerrero, Vicente P. Camacho, Pedro P. Martinez, Jose C. Manibusan, and Jose Roberto. Here, the United States is figured as "mother" to the CHamorus, who are in turn figured as national brothers to the Americans. Expressed in terms of kinship and notably of equality (i.e., American commanders are not paternal fathers but brothers), the letter also conveyed, like the institution of the matlina, another dimension of inafa'maolek denoting goodness and balance, inagradesi.

Later that year, in a different but reciprocal display of gratitude, the island's first lady would be invited by the newly decorated Fleet Admiral Nimitz to do the honors of turning on the lights at the navy's tree lighting ceremony at Fonte (renamed Nimitz Hill).[132] This gesture—resminiscent of earlier Christmases when the navy would call on Johnston to put on a show—in some ways was also a symbolic reminder of brighter days ahead, of renewed kinship between CHamorus and the U.S. military, and of seemingly mutual interests in Guåhan's postwar development. Despite the shared sentiments of gratitude and hope, a contrapuntal reading of CHamoru and military writings also reveals a discord, especially with regard to feelings for the tåno'.[133] In his wartime writings, Nimitz would refer to Guåhan (like Midway, unfortified) as a "liability."[134] For Johnston of course, Guåhan was not simply a geopolitical space on an American military strategic map and its negative condition. At the outbreak of war, when she had the opportunity to join other military wives on board the USS *Henderson*, as the wife of an American military man, she chose not to abandon Guåhan; because of her tåddong guinaiya for the land—like that which Tun Dick Taitano (her former student) expressed earlier —she chose to stay.[135]

Indeed, Johnston's postwar leadership in the field of education cannot be dissociated from her leadership in the civic and patriotic activities of boosting the morale of battle-weary troops, and these in turn cannot be dissociated from her staunch guinaiya and convictions for her homeland. Her immediate postwar efforts in the field of education, along with her fellow educator Simon Sanchez, could also be understood in terms of preparing the island and islanders for the return of the United States, now in the form of the return of American-style education, with herself (and extended kin and mañelu like Sanchez) at the figurative helm. In this sense, the joint letter put her in the brotherhood of CHamoru and American military leaders as they set out to rebuild Guåhan and CHamoru society from the rubble and ashes of World War II.

But of course, there was tension, and even early in the postwar reconstruction, amid the flurry of patriotic activities, Johnston also began to register ambivalence in what was unfolding. It was concern for the land and the people and the U.S. military's postwar condemnation of more than 85,000 acres (more than 60 percent) of land in Guåhan that proved to be a turning point for her or, just as importantly, a moment of critical pause.[136] Johnston expressed ambivalence, at times disapproval, of the military's incessant and relentless bulldozing of the hålom tåno' and the låncho, a space where she had not only spent her childhood but which held or contained her strongest memories of Indigenous alterity. Johnston lamented the loss of "hundreds of acres of the finest farm land" that lay buried under the "asphalt" of "unnecessary air fields."[137] She referred to the ubiquitous bulldozer as the "dulldozer" for the routine and banal way that it chugged over every landscape, "pushed over acres of palms and shrubs and forests, half of the Island, in leveling for airstrips, hangars, machine shops, storage depots, living areas for 200,000 military personnel, and roads and highways to every section of the Island," and how it was replacing the fusiños, the CHamoru farming implement that worked the tåno' into food and social space for CHamorus.[138] On one occasion, she confronted a marine, a "Captain Smith," who had come too close to the Torres låncho in Jalaguac: "You wouldn't dare to touch this house.... How far west are you pushing us Indians, Captain 'John' Smith?"[139] Here, Guåhan's matlina reached back to and reasserted the value of stewardship and protection of the land to her routine and modern form of protecting the familia. She did so, interestingly, by likening the marine and the bulldozer to the history of American Indian land dispossession, beginning with the arrival of the first settlers and embodied in the figure of Captain John Smith.[140] Though Johnston's confrontation did not ultimately challenge the military's destruction and development of lands (in the end she acquiesced and relocated to Anigua/Aniguak), at the very least Johnston's pause and ambivalence challenge the otherwise unconditionally patriotic CHamoru narratives that deem the destruction and loss of lands as nugacious. On the one hand, Johnston claimed in her memoirs that she "had no regrets for the loss of a sentimental past" despite being lost to progress "dictated by a Bulldozer"; on the other hand, she wrote that even though the "island was filled with young people who would attest to the defense she spent her energies on" in bringing them "into the modern world," she still "felt lonesome in her lifelong realm."[141]

Like the majority of CHamorus during the occupation, Johnston spent much of her time at the låncho, which she did not abandon even when she moved to Hagåtña before the war to be closer to the novelties the town could offer her, novelties like an American education. One day, Japanese soldiers arrested her at the låncho. They proceeded to question her and then beat her over Tweed's whereabouts. What she told her captors about Tweed's survival in the hålom tåno' rises above the "anything" a victim who undergoes torture would say to the perpetrator to get the perpetrator to stop the meting out of pain. What she said also rises above the lofty ideals of American freedom and liberty for which Tweed himself and for which the American flag for that matter also symbolized, especially, as Johnston once argued, for "a people under enemy occupation." What Johnston managed to tell her tormentors in-between the beatings was that it was the land, not the people, that kept Tweed alive, citing as typical and not singular or exceptional her own experience as a CHamoru who knew the tåno': "I could walk alone into these lush jungles and live indefinitely on its fruits and nuts and edible plants."[142] Though her immediate point was that Tweed did not need CHamoru assistance (and so, she hoped, they would stop punishing CHamorus whom they suspected of assisting him), I suggest that we can read in her recollection and perspective the ultimate primacy of the ability of the tåno' to care for humans, even those on whose survival rests the highest ideals for which the United States and its flag stands. In this sense, Johnston was not capitulating but rather educating. She was speaking from the vantage point of having traditional and embodied ecological knowledge of the land: dokdok, lemmai, chotdan galayan (large cooking banana), kamuti (sweet potato), dågo (yam), suni (taro), mendioka (cassava, tapioca), ilotes (corn), påhong (edible pandanus nut), manha (soft meat of the young coconut), kalamasa (pumpkin), lalanghita (tangerines), and papåya (papaya).[143] As well, she was godmothering. I would also suggest that, for any possible "miseducation" of Johnston in the prewar years, the idea that Johnston's embrace of American-style modernity might one day come at the expense of what she knew and valued as a CHamoru woman was something she and others like her had no real way of even imagining. If anything, her determination to get an education, to excel in it, and to carry it through to the changes it could bring for her and the island was also predicated on retaining knowledge of the sustaining value of the tåno' and the need to return and care for the tåno'.

Robert Underwood has observed that the success of American colonial education under the navy was predicated not on how American one had become but on what he called "the degree of CHamoru unbecoming." As Johnston often proclaimed, she *chose* the United States—and clearly became one of the most celebrated icons and advocates of American patriotism for CHamorus—but the degree to which her education under naval rule unmade her CHamoru indigeneity is a subject that requires further study, analysis, and narrativization. Clearly, for whatever success and prominence she gained, Johnston also chose to hold on to her CHamoru language and culture, and this choice put her at odds with Americans, both soldiers and officials, much as how her embrace of modern American institutions and values and culture put her at odds with CHamorus, including the priests.

Johnston's enduring CHamoru womanhood—her sense of obligation and efforts to maintain fino' håya and elements of kostumbren CHamoru and inafa'maolek—presented tensions and challenges on the homefront. Certainly, Johnston's mesngon values and metgot determinations placed pressure on relations with Gautier, whom Johnston affectionately called "Papa." Papa, she wrote in her memoirs, preferred to attend socials that were comprised of the roughly two dozen American white men and their Native wives (spaces that she also begrudged for she often felt like the "lone Chamorro" at these American parties) over those attended largely by CHamorus and at which the vernacular was the choice of medium. These tensions also occurred in private, where the women, including Nånan Iglesias and two others who helped Agueda with house choirs and with take caring of the family, Nånan Tona' and Ana, collectively "swung the Chamorro balance in the home" and wherever CHamoru language instructions prevailed for the children, "contrary," wrote Johnston, "to Papa's wishes."[144]

The tension, strain in relations, and moments of disconnect were not confined to the home. In his farewell address in 1910, Governor Dorn, second only to Gautier for Johnston in influence and affection, predicted this trajectory of progress for CHamorus: "With time, your language will be replaced by English; when your small children become grandparents, only a little Chamorro will be in use."[145] In a letter to the organizers of a Chamorro Studies Convention held in Guåhan in January 1977, the eighty-four-year-old Tan Agueda essentially reiterated Dorn's prediction but proffered it as a warning, not an upbeat desire, and lamented the thought of CHamoru children not being able to "communicate freely" with their saina. For Tan Agueda, this condition was "sad" because it "discourages the beautiful relationship that should exist between the grandchildren and their grandparents"; in her conference address, she commended CHamoru language advocates on their worthwhile efforts and encouraged them to continue to "preserve" the "culture, history, mother tongue and heritage of the Chamorro people!"[146] Her audience then was primed for that tone, since the early 1970s stood as a key moment of mounting recognition of the plight of fino' CHamoru and the fate of the CHamorus in the midst of the tumultuous growth that the island had begun to experience. By the 1980s, the U.S. federal census revealed that CHamorus had fallen from over 95 percent of the island's resident population (not counting transient military personnel) in 1950 to under 50 percent of the total population. The children of CHamoru baby boomers, though conversant, were not fluent in fino' CHamoru, as their parents were, and had learned English as their first language. The term *Guamanian* no longer signified

CHamoru peoplehood and was embraced by anybody who chose to call Guåhan home. The låncho became "real estate," public housing, industrial parks, recreational areas, public land, and, of course, military land.

In December 1977, in a milieu of cultural anxiety that marked the start of a CHamoru cultural, linguistic, and political rebirth and resurgence—that in the late twentieth and early twenty first century would evolve into a robust decolonization movement, in which even the term, and more precisely the spelling, *CHamoru* is replacing *Chamorro*—Agueda Iglesias Johnston passed away. Even in the twilight of her life, however, Johnston's spirit of grit, resolve, and determination, her championing of progress for and service to her beloved island and people, never wavered. And just where she chose to put her energies is also not at all surprising and is also predictable, for her most noteworthy project in this period was to help establish the organization, Servicio Para I Manåmko, which catered to the daily activities of the elderly at village community centers. Traditionally revered, the manåmko in modern Guåhan had also begun to be forgotten and neglected—a condition, which, in inafa'maolek context, is understood as tai mamahlao and tai respetu. It was a generation to which she not only belonged but with which she empathized deeply. In keeping with the classed hierarchy of the prewar years, this generation grew up primarily on the låncho and spoke English as a second language (many were not fluent). They lived kostumbren CHamoru and inafa'maolek even if they also embraced modern American values and institutions. Like Tan Agueda, they were of the generation for whom, it seems flirting with the United States did not mean not being CHamoru. That the island even needed a government agency to care for them was a sign of tremendous transformation that did not bode well for CHamoru indigeneity under the United States.

In a portrait of her mother, Cynthia Johnston Torres once described the flair with which Tan Agueda worked with her fellow manåmko'. "My mother," Torres said, would encourage the manåmko to "take your clothes and your jewelry out of where you're hiding it and put it on... we're not gonna sit around and wait for our death. No more babysitting, no more rocking chairs. Get out and let's have fun."[147] This jovial flair also evidences Johnston's metgot determination with more than a hint of defiance, especially of a type that is common among proven leaders who refuse to spend their remaining days being cared for or retiring in obscurity. Here, Johnston still took charge in her care of the elders. In this, her godmotherly charge and her fiercely progressive demeanor recall an even deeper CHamoru female subjectivity, the maga'håga. It is from the maga'håga's takhilo' authority to care for kin and land (and water and sky) and their manifestations in Guåhan's pre- and postwar narratives of famalao'an CHamoru confronting the gendered landscapes of American modernity—evidenced in the hands-on work and footpaths of women like the pattera Joaquina Herrera, Rosalia Mesa, and Ana Rosario and the educator Agueda Johnston—that I gain inspiration and cull materiality to imagine a placental politics that can inform an Indigenous feminist theory in the context of a new round of militarization in Guåhan and CHamoru women's activism.

Conclusion

Following the Historical and Cultural Kinship "Where America's Day Begins"

Somewhere in the Pacific they say that men have wings while women have only feet.

In other parts of the Pacific they say that women belong to the land while men belong to the sea.

Have you ever seen and heard a woman stand on the beach and wail, wail at the sea and sky?

—Teresia Teaiwa, excerpt from "For Salome"

Litekyan is not just a piece of property—it is our life, our beautiful history, and a way for us to connect with our ancestors. Our ancestors were also buried there before the war . . . such sacred grounds. Our nephew Rain Flores San Nicolas drowned at Litekyan saving his cousin's life a few years back. So to think of bullets going into that part of the ocean makes our stomachs turn and our hearts ache in pain. Those are sacred waters . . . .

—Lou Flores Bejado, descendant of original landowners and stewards of Litekyan

In the new and ongoing forms of U.S. empire, settler colonialism, and militarism in Guåhan, similar but also different registers involving CHamoru women's embodied knowledge and sacred practice with the land abound. Redolent of the historical and cultural positions assumed by prewar CHamoru women laborers, famalao'an CHamoru of the twenty-first century have redefined the political and cultural terms of CHamoru womanhood, gender, and indigeneity, and have staked renewed roles as stewards and protectors over lands, peoplehood, and communities in a new and unprecedented hypermilitarization of the island. Unprecedented too, is the potential killing power of the military arsenal and technology to be deployed to Guåhan as part of the pivot and rebalance in American statecraft and U.S. foreign policy, which former secretary of state Hillary Clinton envisioned and dubbed "America's Pacific Century."[1]

At an August 12, 2007 oversight hearing on the U.S. military buildup, members of the multiethnic women's organization Fuetsan Famalao'an ("strength of women" or "strong women") invoked an image of CHamoru stewardship even deeper and older than the matlina—that of the maga'håga. Drawing on this minetgot, Fuetsan representative Ann Marie Arceo, founder of the island's first fino' håya immersion school, Chief Huråo Academy, insisted that any discussion of the buildup be "accountable to the needs of women and children and to the health of the land and sea.[2] A day later, at a hearing overseen by Virgin Islands delegate Donna Christensen, then chairwoman of the U.S. House Committee on Natural Resources (Subcommittee on Insular Affairs), manmaga'håga (women leaders) reminded federal officials and local leaders of the U.S. military's historical and ongoing destruction and contamination of the island. They called specific attention to the devastating environmental effects on the southern and northern villages of Santa Rita (near Naval Base Guam) and Yigu (near Andersen Air Force Base), whose residents suffer the highest incidence of cancer and death rates.[3]

A form of Indigenous feminist truth telling, inagången famalao'an (women's testimonio), unlike other testimonies at public hearings on the buildup, also highlighted the unresolved issue of Guåhan's political status as an unincorporated territory (colony) of the United States and the federal government's continued denial of CHamoru self-determination.[4] Much like the way prewar pattera were duty-bound to ayuda yan adahi women and children before, during, and after birth—recall Tan Kina''s insistence with Tun CHu' that it was her job to accompany her patient or Tan Ånan Siboyas's point about forgetting to call her husband because she was busy caring for her patients—or the way Tan Aguedas concerns for a CHamoru woman forced to work manual labor in the scorching sun required that Tan Agueda confront a naval governor and CHamoru påle', famalao'an CHamoru in the historical present practice and act on inafa'maolek and assume responsibility to fa'maolek. As a reminder of this obligation, CHamoru women of the movement to protect the island against further military destruction and desecration prefaced their opposition to the buildup with the adage "Isao-ña i tumungo' ya ha sedi, ki ayo i mismo umisagui hao" (Greater is the fault of he who allows the injustice upon himself).[5]

At a time when the U.S. military insists it is "committed to being a good steward of the environment" in supposed equal partnership with GovGuam and the island's leadership and the local tourism industry—under a new brand of militourism that embraces, co-opts, and deploys CHamoru culture—women of different generations themselves pivot, readjust, kalamten (move, call to action); they reassert older and deeper political, social, and cultural roles and embodied relations with the land and the sacred while challenging (together with their mañelu, manhoben, extended kin, and allies) the U.S. military's new "road" to realignment and the colonial, patriarchal, local, and settler state narratives of national security and economic growth.[6] During a gathering of women against militarism in Guåhan in 2010, the former teacher and now Guåhan senator Sabina Flores Perez declared that "genuine security does not come from military security, [but] from healing and nurturing our communities."[7] Such counternarratives also begin to unsettle the familiar and seemingly benign adage "where America's day begins." The slogan, a reference to Guåhan's position on the other side of the international dateline (fifteen hours ahead of Washington, D.C.) and its geopolitical location as the westernmost American "soil" and "gateway to Asia," is also associated with the island's tourism industry and a joint marketing campaign between the Guam Visitor's Bureau and Continental Airlines in the 1970s. The motto's origins, as Camilla Fojas argues, can be traced to a long-range economic plan of the Department of Interior (Office of the Territories) to develop Guåhan as an exotic tourist destination and stopover around the same time the island was being developed by the U.S. military as a key site of the nuclear arms race and where President Richard Nixon announced his Cold War Doctrine in 1969.[8] In her opening address at the aforementioned congressional hearing, in which she claimed kinship (and sisterhood) with Guåhan delegate Madeleine Bordallo (as fellow U.S. representatives of nonvoting territories), Christensen recalled in benign ways the insidious collusion between militarism and tourism and Guåhan's legacy as a colony and now "tip of the spear" of the United States: "It is truly an honor for me to be on this beautiful island of Guam where America's day begins and where our nation's westernmost border also begins. As our country better prepares to protect our people and our homeland, we are all challenged by change. Nowhere though is a challenge greater than on Guam, as we look to the potential military buildup plan for this island paradise, this piece of America closest to Asia."[9]

On October 5, 2017, at yet another public hearing, this time to discuss the military's plans to build a marine live-fire training range complex on lands overlooking the village of Litekyan (Ritidian) along Guåhan's northern coast, Maria Hernandez of the direct-action group Prutehi Litekyan countered the military's claims of being a good steward. A descendant of original clans and stewards of Litekyan (which in CHamoru means, a "stirring place"), Hernandez confronted the military's highest in command, Rear Admiral Shoshana Chatfield, commander, Joint Region Marianas (JRM). Hernandez called out the military's blatant and continued use of the term *mitigation*:

We all came here today because we care about our community. We don't want any more harm to our communities. And speaking about mitigation, I hate that word mitigation, because I keep hearing it over and over and over. But we don't care about your mitigation. We don't want this firing range at Northwest Field. We don't want it over Ritidian. We want it taken off the table. And if you don't agree with us and if you can't work with us to come to a solution that we can all agree on, then the only way that you would build this range is over our dead bodies.[10]

In asserting "we don't want any more harm to our communities" and demanding that the military take Ritidian "off the table," Hernandez changes the rules of engagement, refusing partnership and kinship with the military; as well, she asserts an Indigenous stewardship and cordage willing to lay its life on the line and on the land, willing to resist and rise for the tåno' yan tåsi. Hernandez's inagångi (testimonio) and confronting of the navy admiral is an example of what Aileen Moreton-Robinson (in Australian Indigenous contexts) has called "talkin' up" to the white woman; like her mother Lou Bejado's inagångi above, it is an illustration of how stories of the sacred and the historical experiences of Indigenous women "speak to the intersubjectivity between white women and themselves where incommensurabilities operate in communicative exchange."[11] In a keynote address one month earlier inaugurating the new admiral to the post of JRM, the former senator and secretary of the navy James Webb noted that in the change in command what the military was doing was simply "following a long line of military tradition.... The people may rotate, but the continuity will not rotate."[12] Despite his blatant glossing over of the obvious break with "military tradition"—in the rotation in of one navy woman, Chatfield, and rotation out of another, the Filipino-American Rear Admiral Babette "Bette" Bolivar, to the highest military post on island—Webb also downplays perhaps unknowingly the historical and cultural legacy of white women and military women in Guåhan and in the broader U.S. current political milieu.[13] As this book demonstrates, CHamoru women now and then have always confronted the work and "tender violence" of American navy wives and military women in new and old forms of power.

In another instance of protecting the CHamoru sacred against new forms of colonialism, manmaga'håga on August 14, 2011, convened a gathering at Gokña in central Guåhan. Commonly referred to as Gun Beach, because of the presence of a World War II Japanese antiaircraft gun there in the island's tourist sector of Tomhom, Gokña is the site of Lina'la', the island's first cultural and ecothemed park. The eight-acre Lina'la' boasts a nature trail, a zoo, and an authentic CHamoru village. The village, in vintage natural history form, exhibits primitive, static depictions of CHamorus. The park traffics literally on CHamoru culture, from its name, Lina'la', to the fact that it sits on top of a CHamoru burial site. In the process of building a cultural, heritage, and ecological park, the developers not only disturbed human remains and artifacts, including funerary objects, but also left the remains in an unmarked and nondescript pit adjacent to a nearby parking lot. The developers' desecration of a burial site is legitimized through a prior history of land condemnation and disturbance by the military. This they did for a park that would subsequently boast a living diorama where tourists and visitors can experience Native life and culture of Guåhan from five hundred years ago. Once again, Indigenous depth of a place, in this case Gokña, and CHamoru concerns for inafa'maolek furnished the occasion and material for CHamoru women to fa'maolek, to correct and make things right. In a sunrise ceremony called Chinachålanen i Mañaina-ta' ("creating pathways for our ancestral spirits") to rectify the recent desecration of a burial site, the former senator and educator, community leader, and farmer, Hope Alvarez Cristobal, explained that because the gravesites were disturbed so too were the aniti (spirits). Women, she maintained, "as mothers and daughters," needed to "offer peace and tranquility" to saina who passed down "sovereignty and human rights."[14] In what might now be understood as a placental practice of maintaining genealogical cordage to tåno', tåsi, yan manmofo'na, Cristobal merged ideas of Indigenous political self-determination and sovereignty with a long tradition of inafa'maolek and stewardship and CHamoru women being responsible for the well-being of the community and the land. The presence of another maga'håga, the CHamoru educator and language advocate Bernadita "Benit" Camacho-Dungca, is also noteworthy. In 1991, Dr. Dungca composed the "Inifresi," a "pledge" to protect and defend the beliefs, culture, language, air, water, and tåno' i CHamoru, from "i mås takhilo' gi hinasso" (the uppermost thoughts) and "i mas takhalom gi kurason" (very deep within the heart). A renewal of this commitment, as Senator Therese Terlaje asserts, is urgent for the "preservation of our sacred sites and ancestral villages, and the empowerment of our people to be the true stewards of our lands."[15]

To be sure, CHamoru women activists, along with queer CHamoru artists and writers, have deployed inafa'maolek and a form of placental politics evocative of an earlier practice rooted in Indigenous conceptions of self in relation to land and community, one that is up against new forms of U.S. militarization, modernization, and settler colonialism. In this book, I have privileged the work of pre- and postwar CHamoru women laborers—the pattera, Tan Kina', Tan Liang, and Tan Ånan Siboyas, and the fafa'na'gue, Tan, Agueda Johnston—in their obligations as matlina and maga'håga, especially as they intersect with the work of white U.S. naval wives and nurses and also for their insistence on ancient, tåddong and takhilo' practices like the planting of the ga'chong i pagton and apuya' for the powerful and enduring meanings that such practices have for Native conceptions of self, land, and propriety in modern and colonizing contexts. Together, such images embody the historical and political forces and motives that, as Teresia Teaiwa speculated, have driven Indigenous women across the Pacific to come to political consciousness and take up activism after the bodies of their loved ones become affected and infected by large and previously mysterious forces like nuclear contamination.[16] Placental politics adds to this history and possibility. Placental politics names a history and a futurity by which Indigenous women have consciously chosen to act as stewards of Guåhan, CHamoru peoplehood, and place. In Guåhan's history, CHamoru women's practice of planting the ga'chong i patgon and the apuya' connected CHamorus to the land in order to ensure proper growth and directionality. Implanted in their own struggles against reckless development and militarization, famalao'an CHamoru also continue to steer and steward CHamoru peoplehood and land in efforts to keep things right and balanced and to sustain what is maolek. Perhaps what has also driven CHamoru women to protect lands and waters are the physical and psychological effects of watching military manuevers over our children's ga'chong in addition to the bodies of our manmofo'na and loved ones. The reciprocal relations of women's work, of which the sacred practice of planting and safeguarding the child are one dimension, inhere deep in the hearts and minds of CHamorus and their stories about the land and lands lost. I once had a conversation with the late, Hågat mayor Antonio "Min" Cruz Babauta about what he remembered growing up in the southern village of Fena, what is now U.S. Naval Base Guam.[17] He recalled that the first house leading into the village belonged to a pattera, an aunt. He remembered that the land on which the house had been built had been given to her as chenchule', a form of payment, and as an expression of inagradesi for her help in delivering babies. Stories like these remind us of the reciprocal relations of women's responsibilities to giha, pulan, and poksai peoplehood and place; indeed, they remind us of how CHamoru women's histories are rooted in the land and how the land becomes routed through the histories of CHamoru women's work.

Glossary of CHamoru Words

The CHamoru spellings and meanings furnished herein draw from the knowledge of first language speakers, manåmko', mañaina, members of Kumisión i Fino' CHamoru, and individuals from various agencies and organizations engaged in CHamoru language, culture, and genealogy work—many of whom have been named in the acknowledgments. The book also draws from Donald M. Topping, Pedro M. Ogo, and Bernadita C. Dunga's *Chamorro-English Dictionary*, Rev. P. Roman Maria de Vera's *Diccionario Chamorro-Castellano*, and the PSECC's Hale'-ta publications.

ababang • butterfly
achaffñak • familia, family, extended kin, clan
åcho' • rock
adahi • take care of, guard, protect (n. inadahi)
afa'maolek • collaborate, help out, cooperate, work together to make good
aguayente • distilled liquor made from fermented fruit
akgak • pandanus (also kaffo')
åmot CHamoru • CHamoru medicine
åmot fresko • medicine (drink) used to help one conceive, treat restlessness
åmot palai • ointment
åmot para mungga mapotge' • medicine to prevent pregnancy
aniti • spirit
åntes di i gera • before the war
apuya' • umbilical cord (also tålen apuya')
asuli • eel
åtes • sugar apple, sweetsop
atmagosu • CHamoru medicine used to treat decongestion
ayuda • help, be of service, collaborate (n. inayuda)
ayuyu • coconut crab

båta' • baptismal gown

chålan • road, street, path
che'lu • sibling, sister, brother (plural: mañelu)
chenchule' • gift or donation, often in monetary form, that is part of a system of reciprocity and social exchange
cho'cho' • work
chotdan galayan • large cooking banana

dågo • yam
despues di i gera • after the war

disatenta • disrespectful
dokdok • seeded breadfruit

enfetmera • nurse
eskuelan påle' • priest school, catechism
eskuelan rai • king's or government school
estorian taotao tåno' • CHamoru history

fa'danche • correct or make right
fafa'na'gue • teacher, educator, one who teaches (plural: mamfafa'na'gue)
fa'fañågu'i • one who delivers, gives birth
famalao'an • women (singular: palao'an)
famalao'an chålan • women of the road (singular: palao'an chålan)
famalao'an CHamoru • CHamoru women
fa'maolek • make good, reconcile
fañågu • deliver, give birth
fangguålafonan • time and place of full moon
fanihi • fruit bat
fañinahi'an • time and place of new moon, crescent moon
fañomnåkan • time and place of sunshine, the dry season
fanuchånan • time and place of rain, the rainy season
fa'taotao • literally, to treat someone as a person; to treat someone with respect, decency, and kindness
finañågu • progeny, product, result
fina'okso' • hilly place
fino' • word, speak, language
fino' CHamoru • CHamoru language
fino' håya • CHamoru language, a specific reference to directional south
fo'na • ahead, in front, go ahead, be first
Fo'na • CHamoru sibling sister of creation
fusiños • farming implement, hoe, used for weeding and clearing grass, shaping the soil

ga'chong i patgon • companion or friend of the child, placenta (also påres)
ga'chungi • accompany
gådao • type of fish
gago • ironwood tree
gai mamahlao • to have shame, save face, which implies being sensible and discerning
gai minetgot • to have strength
gai respetu • to have respect
galaide • canoe, general term for dugout outrigger canoe
Gåni • original Indigenous name of the northern Marianas, islands north of Saipan
giha • guide, steer, direct, point out the way (n: giniha)
gi hilo' • from above (hulo': above)
gi iya mo'nana • of the past, present, future
giniha • the guiding, steering, and directing of (v. giha)

gi papa' • from below
gi talo' • from center
gi tano' • in/on the land, ground, earth, soil
gineftao • generosity
gollai • vegetable
guåfak • woven mat
guaha • to have
gualåfon • full moon
guåli'ek • small outdoor lizard
guålo' • cultivated land, small-scale farm or family garden
gua'ot • steps or ladder
guihan • fish
guinaiya • love
guma' • house, home, or dwelling
guma' uritao/guma' ulitao • bachelor home of early, ancient CHamoru society
gupu • to fly, a CHamoru custom of walking immediately after childbirth

håga • daughter
hagan Guåhan • daughter of Guåhan
haggan • turtle
håle'-ta • our roots
haligi • pillar or post
hålom åcho' • (among the) rock(s)
hålom tåno' • jungle
hålom tåsi • shore
håyun • tree
homhom • dusk
hutu • seed of the breadfruit

i che'cho' i pattera • the work of the pattera
ifit • official, native tree of Guåhan; hard, heavy wood used for carving posts and pillars in early CHamoru homes and churches
ilotes • corn
i maloffan na tiempo • the past
i manfåyi • the wise ones
inadahi • caretaking
inafa'maolek • a CHamoru system of ideas, values, and feelings denoting goodness and balance and based on mutual assistance, cooperation, reciprocity, interdependence, obligation, reconciliation, and peace; literally, a state or condition in which goodness or goodwill has been established or improved upon (based on *maolek* ["good"] and *fa'maolek* ["to make good"]).
inagången famalao'an • women's testimonio
inagångi • testimonio, testimonial
inagradesi • appreciation, gratitude
inayuda • help, service, collaboration (v. ayuda)

inangokko • trust, dependence
inifresi • a pledge
i pattera siha • the midwives

kaffo' • pandanus (also akgak)
kåhna • spirit, energy, life force
kalamasa • pumpkin
kalamten • move, mobilize, set in motion, call to action, progress (n. kinalamten)
kamuti • sweet potato
kånta • chant, sing, song
kåntan CHamorita • traditional call and response, poetic CHamoru song
kaskåhu • crushed limestone, gravel
kinalamten • movement, mobility, progression (v. kalamten)
kombento • convent
korason fåha • soft, sweet, and spongy heart or kernel of the young coconut; used to describe someone who is softhearted, kindhearted, and peaceful, with a good nature
kostumbren CHamoru • CHamoru custom and culture, representing a mix of Indigenous CHamoru and Spanish Catholic tradition
kottot • woven basket of akgak or kaffo'
kuåtta • belt
kompaire/komaire • godparenthood system
kusinan sanhiyong • outside kitchen

Låguas • original Indigenous name of southern Marianas islands of Guåhan, Rota, Tinian, and Saipan (refer also to Gåni)
lalanghita • tangerines
lancheru • farmer
låncho • ranch, farm
långet • sky
lasa • massage
latte • large stone carving used in the construction of early CHamoru homes, sacred burial place of CHamoru ancestors
lemmai • seedless breadfruit
lina'la' • life, living being, existence
lisåyu • rosary

maga'håga • highest daughter, high-ranking daughter of early CHamoru society who wielded tremendous authority and power, daughter of chief, political leader, governor (plural: manmaga'håga)
maga'låhi • highest son, high-ranking son of early CHamoru society, son of chief, political leader, governor
maggem • quiet and cautious, discrete
makåhna • CHamoru healers of ancient CHamoru society who were skilled herbalists mediating between physical and spiritual realms (also referred to as kakåhna)
måktan • gutter or downspout

målle' • term used to describe the special relation between matlina and a child's parents
mamåhlao • ashamed, embarrassed
mamposteria • tiled roof
mamfafa'na'gue • teachers, educators (singular: fafa'na'gue)
mañaina • parents, elder relations (singular: saina)
manakhilo' • elite or upper class
manakpåpa' • lower class
manåmko' • elders (singular: åmko')
mañelu • siblings (singular: che'lu)
manha • soft meat of the young coconut
manhoben • young people, the youth (singular: hoben)
manmaga'håga • high-ranking daughters, women leaders (singular: maga'håga)
manmofo'na • ancestors, people before
manakhilo' • elite, upper class
mannginge' • the sniffing or smelling of an elder's hand as a sign of respect
manulitao • young men of the ulitao
manungo' • knowledgeable
maolek • good
maolek kånnai-ñiha • good with their hands
matan hånom • "eye of water," spring
matlina • godmother
mattingan • deep ocean, sea
ma ulitao • young women of the guma' ulitao
mendioka • cassava, tapioca
menhalom • wise, sharp (n. minenhalom)
mesngon • enduring, lasting, resisting (n. minesngon)
mestisa • woman of mixed-race ancestry; traditional CHamoru dress
metgot • powerful, strong, tenacious (n. minetgot)
minenhalom • wisdom (adj. menhalom)
minesngon • endurance, persistence, resistance (adj. mesngon)
minetgot • power, strength, tenacity (adj. metgot)
mo'na • front, in front of, forward, or before
mo'nana • present, future

na'åhustao • adjust, set right, or put in order
nå'fafañågu • midwife (also pattera), "one who helps one deliver"
nai • interjection, exclamation
nå'i påtte • share and impart
na'mamahlao • shame
nåna • mother
nånan biha • grandmother
na'påranñaihon • suspend
nina'i • gift
niyok • coconut
nubena • novena, nine-day prayer vigil

påhong • edible pandanus nut
palao'an • woman
palao'an chålan • woman of the road (plural: famalao'an chålan)
palåsyo • palace
påle' • priest, but also used to address one as "father"
påpa' såtge • space below the floors of CHamoru homes built above ground on haligi
papåya • papaya
påres • placenta (also ga'chong i patgon)
påtgon • child
pattera • midwife (also ná'fafañågu)
pineksai • raising, nurturing, adoption; steering, paddling, propelling (v. poksai)
pinilan • watching and guarding over (v. pulan)
plåsa • plaza
po'dak • adolescent woman, at a specific stage of sexual maturation (refer also to sottera)
poksai • raise, nurture, advance, paddle a canoe forward (n. pineksai)
Pontan • CHamoru sibling brother of creation
prubleman famalao'an • women's problem, having to do with women's reproductive health
prutehi • protect
pulan • moon, also to watch, guard over (n. pinilan)
puntan • qualifier based on the root word *punta* (point), as in Puntan Litekyan (Litekyan Point)

respetu • respect

sabåna • savanna
såddok • river
saina • parent, elder relative (plural: mañaina)
saina ma'åse • another, newer form of expression for thanking someone, with direct reference to parents, elderly relations, and ancestors as being merciful
sakman • large, ocean-going canoe
sesonyan • swamp
si • article used with proper names
siha • plural marker
sinåhi • new moon, crescent moon
sinangan famalao'an CHamoru • CHamoru women's story
si yu'os ma'åse • thank you (emphatically expressed as dångkolu na si yu'os ma'åse, thank you very much); literally "God have mercy" or "God is merciful"
sottera • pubescent woman, single woman (refer also to po'dak)
suni • taro
suruhåna • female traditional healer
suruhånu • male traditional healer

tåddong • deep, profound, below the surface, age-old
tai mamahlao • no shame

tai respetu • no respect
takhilo' • high, in a high place, uppermost
tålen apuya' • umbilical cord (also apuya')
tåli • rope
Tan • A term of respect used to address female elders
tåno' • land, ground, earth, soil
taotaomona • ancestors, spirits, people of before, front people
taotao sanhiyong • people of the outside, outsider or foreigner
taotao tåno' • person of the land, often used to mean people of the land or the CHamorus, Indigenous people of the Marianas
tareha • chore, assignment
tåsi • ocean, sea
tåta • father, dad
tåtan bihu • grandfather
tiha • aunt
tinifok • weaving
totot • Marianas fruit dove
Tun • A term of respect used to address male elders

utak • mythological bird

yan • and
yo'åmte • deep healers, traditional healers, another name for suruhåna/suruhånu

Notes

Preface

1. Notes on spelling: In keeping with the intent to center indigeneity and decolonize CHamoru histories, I have chosen to use Indigenous place names when possible. Many of these have been recorded in Onedera, *Nå'an Lugåt Siha*. I use the original Indigenous name *Guåhan* over *Guam* except in references to official entities, documents, and sayings, or when using actual quotes that use the word *Guam*. Guåhan, which means "having," usually in the context of having an abundance of something, derives from the root word *guaha* (to have). Throughout the book, I use two spellings to refer to the Indigenous people of the Mariana archipelago: *Chamorro* and *CHamoru*. The latter is the official spelling adopted in 2017 by the Kumisión i Fino' CHamoru yan i Fina'nå'guen i Historia yan i Lina'la' i Taotao Tåno' (Commission of the Chamorro Language and Teachings of the History and Life of the People of the Land). Except when quoting or citing sources using *Chamorro* or other forms of the word (such as *Chamorrita*), I follow the Kumisión's spelling. As much as possible, I adhere to the Kumisión's orthography, including its rules on leaving intact the official spelling of names (without diacritical marks). I have also chosen to leave intact the spelling of earlier fino' håya (CHamoru language) translation work for the sake of preserving the integrity of that work. Because certain CHamoru words (like *pattera*) appear more frequently in the transmission of oral histories, I continue to use these and their older CHamoru terms (like *nå'fafañågu*).

The Marianas, in the western Oceanic region of Micronesia, consist of fifteen volcanic and coralline limestone islands and are divided into two administrative units of the United States: the unincorporated territory of Guam, the largest and southernmost of the Marianas, and the Commonwealth of the Northern Mariana Islands, which includes Saipan, Tinian, Rota, Agrihan, Alamagan, Anatahan, and Pagan. *Las Islas Marianas* was the name given by the Spanish Jesuit missionary Diego Luis de San Vitores in 1668, in honor of the Queen Regent of Spain, Maria Ana of Austria. The original CHamoru names of the archipelago are Låguas (the southern islands of Guåhan, Rota, Tinian, and Saipan) and Gåni (the islands north of Saipan).

The concept of "storied sites" comes from Goeman, "From Place to Territories." The idea of "land narratives" is from Basso, *Wisdom Sits in Places*, and Fitzgerald, *Native Women and Land*.

2. Forbes, "Chamorro Expressions."
3. Guam Legislature, Public Law 20-99, October 13, 1989; Césaire, *Discourse*; Said, *Orientalism*.
4. R. Underwood, "Teaching Guam History," 4.
5. Underwood, 4.
6. Warrior, *Tribal Secrets*, 124.

7. Goodyear-Kaʻōpua, *Seeds We Planted*. Aloha ʻāina literally means "love of the land" but has deeper meanings conveying the mutually beneficial relations between ʻāina (food production) and Native Hawaiians as well as Native Hawaiian obligations to and caretaking of the ʻāina.

8. PSECC, *Haleʻ-ta: I Manfåyi*; DeLisle, "Tumugeʻ Påpaʻ"; Trouillot, *Silencing the Past*.

9. Hattori, "Textbook Tells," 181. Here, Hattori refers mainly to the PSECC publications *Haleʻ-ta: Hinassoʻ: Tinigeʻ Put Chamorro* and *Haleʻ-ta: I Ma Gubetna-ña Guam*. Other historical re-framings include Goetzfridt, *Guåhan: A Bibliographic History*; Kushima, *Historiographies of Guam*.

10. L. Smith, *Decolonizing Methodologies*, 30, 142.

11. Diaz, *Repositioning the Missionary*; Huhndorf and Suzack, "Indigenous Feminism"; Simpson and Smith, *Theorizing Native Studies*.

12. T. Teaiwa, "Militarism, Tourism and the Native."

13. Diaz, *Repositioning the Missionary*, 18; Dennison, *Colonial Entanglement*.

Introduction

Epigraph proverb from M. Ramirez, *Los Ehemplus*.

1. My understanding of a more holistic and expansive view of Oceania is informed by Hauʻofa, "Our Sea of Islands"; and Diaz, "Oceania in the Plains."

In 1565, the Spanish explorer Miguel Lopez de Legazpi claimed the islands now known as the Marianas for the Spanish crown. For many historians, *formal* colonization commenced in 1668, when San Vitores arrived in Guåhan to establish the first permanent Catholic mission (the first in Oceania). I am mindful of how this demarcating of colonialism's origins has the potential to downplay earlier forms of colonial violence in first encounters (like the one between CHamorus and Ferdinand Magellan's crew in 1521) and through rituals of discovery—the planting of flags, the symbolic proclamations over Indigenous lands and bodies, and, in the case of the aforementioned Legazpi, the offering of a Catholic mass (Said, *Beginnings*; M. Jackson, "James Cook"). I am grateful to Debra Harry, Tina Ngata, and Marisa Duarte for the opportunity to discuss the implications of such rituals at a NAISA conference roundtable on "the Doctrine of Discovery," Waikato (Hamilton), New Zealand, June 27, 2019.

2. The term *moʻna* means "front," "front of," "forward," "be first," "that which lies ahead of us or behind us," or "that which came before us." Moʻna can be understood as that which is in the past, present, or future, or all of these at once, and hence is a circular conception of time, space, and place. The word *manmofoʻna*, which means "people who came first," refers to CHamoru ancestors (Russell, *Tiempon I Manmofoʻna*). Given the circular meanings of moʻna, the term might also signify ancestors yet to come. For the multiple meanings of moʻna and their implications for CHamoru ways of knowing and ways of being, I am grateful to R. Underwood, "Chamorro History."

3. Diaz and Kauanui, "Native Pacific Cultural Studies"; T. Teaiwa, "Yaqona/Yagona." The sense of roots to place does not foreclose on mobility, much as diaspora as an analytic teaches us that people can move and still have deep connections to their origins. Indigenous sense of roots and routes involves historical, discursive, and geographic mobility. In diasporic studies, the sense of mobility is often geographic in the sense of movement away

from one's homeland. In this book's study of the tensions of roots and routes of CHamoru women across time (i.e., past, present, future) and discourse (i.e., Indigenous precontact, Spanish Catholic, modern liberal American), I am also examining *internal diasporic* movements within the geographic homeland of Guåhan—that is, movements between spatial and discursive sites (the låncho and town) in ways that reveal similar productive tensions in what is now called trans-Indigenous scholarship that looks at Indigenous accountabilities at home in relation to being accountable to Indigenous concerns in the diaspora, in someone else's Indigenous lands. Allen, *Trans-Indigenous*; Diaz, "Oceania in the Plains." For me, such concerns and tensions raise the possibilities for a trans-Indigenous placental politics.

4. A discussion of the paratextual apparatus of the footnote is in Hanna, Vargas, and Saldívar, *Junot Díaz and the Decolonial Imagination*. The idea of footnotes to history transcended into footnotes as history is from Grafton, *Footnote*. For similar discussions of the footnote in CHamoru contexts of colonial erasure, including Guåhan as "footnote island," refer to Bevacqua, "My Island"; Craig Perez, "Guam and Archipelagic American Studies."

5. Tadiar, *Things Fall Away*, 4.

6. Aguero, "Forum on Guam's Pattera." Throughout the book, and as is customary in CHamoru culture, the terms *Tan* (for women) and *Tun* (for men) are used as a sign of respect when referring to or addressing elders.

7. DeLisle, "Tumuge' Påpa'."

8. PSECC, *Hale'-ta: Inafa'maolek*; Natividad, "CHamoru Values."

9. Althusser, "Ideology."

10. As Robert Underwood suggests, a prewar history of the island would necessitate looking at the pattera and teachers like Agueda Johnston as important community leaders. R. Underwood, "Teaching Guam History," 9. On oral histories as an Indigenous feminist method for challenging binary narratives; reconnecting (through shared transmission) researchers with kin, community, and language; and upholding Indigenous sovereignty, refer to Denetdale, *Reclaiming Diné History*; Anderson, Hamilton, and Barker, "Yarning." Scholarship on CHamoru women includes Anita Johnston, "Ethnic Identity Experience"; Souder, *Daughters of the Island*; Hattori, "Feminine Hygiene," in *Colonial Disease*, 91–123; DeLisle, "Delivering the Body"; Santos-Bamba, "Literate Lives; Naholowa'a, "Beyond Matrifocality'."

11. Million, "Felt Theory," 55. In her study of the diverse decolonization movements throughout Oceania, Tracey Banivanua Mar argues that imperial powers employed the rhetoric of decolonization as a new form of imperialism. Mar, *Decolonisation and the Pacific*.

12. Diaz, "Stepping in It," 90.

13. For a historicizing of Kiowa women's creative beadwork and the changing processes of trade goods that challenge simple binaries of reservation and postreservation Kiowa society, refer to Rand, "Primary Sources." In "Status, Sustainability," Rand calls for more historical work on Native women's adaptive strategies rather than their status or roles (based on preconceived ideas of universal gender oppression).

14. Tuck and Yang, "Decolonization Is Not a Metaphor," 21. On women's resistance to militarization along the settler state borders, refer to Tamaz, "Our Way of Life." On the legacy of white women in histories of settler colonialism and Indigenous (cultural) genocide, refer to Jacobs, *White Mother*; and L. Simpson, *As We Have Always Done*.

15. Deloria, *Indians in Unexpected Places*. CHamoru resistance to Spanish liberal reform at the end of the nineteenth century provides a glimpse into an even earlier episode of CHamoru political modernization before American rule. Madrid, *Beyond Distances*.

16. Moreton-Robinson, *Talkin' Up*; Trask, "Feminism and Indigenous Hawaiian Nationalism"; L. Smith, *Decolonizing Methodologies*; and Pihama, "Tihei Mauri Ora."

17. Examples in Pacific history include Dening, *Beach Crossings*; Hanlon, *Making Micronesia*; Hattori, *Colonial Dis-Ease*; Diaz, *Repositioning the Missionary*; K. Teaiwa, *Consuming Ocean Island*; Dvorak, *Coral and Concrete*; and Cook, *Return to Kahiki*. New imperial histories include Amos and Parmar, "Challenging Imperial Feminism"; Chaudhuri and Strobel, *Western Women and Imperialism*; Lewis, *Gendering Orientalism*; Burton, *At the Heart*; and Levine, *Gender and Empire*.

18. McCallum, *Indigenous Women*, 225. Other Indigenous women's histories include Child, *Holding Our World Together*; Harris, "History with Nana"; S. Hill, "Women Who Make," in *The Clay We Are Made Of*, 53–66; Ackley and Stanciu, *Laura Cornelius Kellogg*; Arista, *The Kingdom and the Republic*; and Nickel, "I Am Not."

19. An example of one of the few monographs to focus on the relations between American Protestant missionary wives and Native Hawaiian aliʻi through reciprocity and gift exchange is Thigpen, *Island Queens*.

20. Haggis, "Gendering Colonialism"; Haggis, "White Women and Colonialism." Recuperative histories from the Pacific include Knapman, *White Women*; and Grimshaw, *Paths of Duty*. Patricia Grimshaw (along with Regina Ganter) would later write that one of the risks of focusing exclusively on white women's complicity with settler colonialism is that it obscures the richness of cross-cultural interactions. Ganter and Grimshaw, "Introduction." On the continued struggles of writing about the entanglements of colonial white women and Indigenous women in Australia, refer to Cole, Haskins, and Paisley, *Uncommon Ground*.

21. Carroll Smith-Rosenberg defines the new woman as a social formation of middle-class white women who, starting in the mid-nineteenth century, defied the ideological domestic spheres of public and private and Victorian ideas of proper female behavior. This new subjectivity and formation was wrought by profound structural and cultural changes like finance capitalism, mass production, and international markets. Smith-Rosenberg, *Disorderly Conduct*, 26.

22. Burton, *Gender, Sexuality*, 2; Mani, *Contentious Traditions*, 6.

23. "Instructions to the Military Commander of the Island of Guam, Ladrones, Pacific Ocean," Official Orders to Richard P. Leary from William McKinley and Secretary of the Navy, John D. Long, January 12, 1899 box 12, folder "Guam and the Mariana Islands," Library of Congress Manuscript Division, Washington, D.C., John L. McCrea Papers; Rafael, *White Love*, 54.

24. Office of the Chief of Naval Operations, *U.S. Navy Report on Guam, 1899–1950*, 5.

25. Office of the Chief of Naval Operations, 3.

26. Office of the Chief of Naval Operations, 1, 3.

27. Johnston, "Medical Services for Guam."

28. Naval Government of Guam, General Order No. 18, May 12, 1900, RG 80, Box 383, 9351-10, General Records of the Department of the Navy, National Archives and Records Administration, Washington, D.C. (hereafter, NARA); Salman, *Embarrassment of Slavery*; S. Miller, *Benevolent Assimilation*, 3.

29. Richard P. Leary Proclamation, January 1, 1900, Department of the Navy, Isle of Guam, Broadsides. Clements Library, University of Michigan, Ann Arbor; Safford, "Addresses Delivered," 57.

30. Examples of Indigenous "othermothering" are in Lavell-Harvard, Memee, and Anderson, *Mothers of the Nations*. Refer especially in this issue to Brant, "Rebirth and Renewal"; and Charbonneau et al., "Storying the Untold."

31. Naval Government of Guam, General Order No. 5, September 15, 1899, RG 80, Box 383, 9351-10, General Records of the Department of the Navy, NARA; General Order No. 11, January 19, 1900, RG 80, Box 383, 9351-10, General Records of the Department of the Navy, NARA.

32. Bederman, *Manliness and Civilization*. According to Bederman, this new rugged masculinity proved earlier Victorian manhood premised on self-restrained manliness to be unprofitable during the late nineteenth-century depression. For Bederman, Theodore Roosevelt exemplified this ruggedness as a model for the age of U.S. empire and at the onset of the Spanish-American War—through his own aggressive lobbying along with other imperialists like U.S. senator Henry Cabot Lodge and the navy's Admiral Alfred Thayer Mahan. Roosevelt left his post as assistant secretary of the navy to lead the *legendary* Rough Riders in the Battle of San Juan Hill. For a demystification of the legend, refer to A. Kaplan, "Black and Blue"; H. Green, *Fit for America*.

33. Moreton-Robinson, *White Possessive*, 191.

34. Hattori, *Colonial Dis-Ease*, 193, 93.

35. Wolfe, "Settler Colonialism." As I am suggesting here, the term "settle" would seem to indicate the beginnings of settler colonialism, the systemic structure that replaces Indigenous peoples with new populations while seeking to expropriate Indigenous lands and resources. However, I am also suggesting that a large presence of settlers need not be the only marker or condition for thinking about settler colonialism in Guåhan, especially if we consider the role of the U.S. military overseas in maintaining the structural forces of settler colonialism in Turtle Island. Case, *Relentless Business*.

36. Arvin, Tuck, and Morrill, "Decolonizing Feminism," 15.

37. Kameʻeleihiwa, *Native Land*. Governor Leary's General Order No. 3 prohibited CHamorus from selling or transferring "property" without first obtaining the navy's permission. Naval Government of Guam, General Order No. 3, August 21, 1899, RG 80, Box 383, 9351-10, General Records of the Department of the Navy, NARA. Under General Order No. 10, Leary abolished the Spanish system of land taxation (based on monies earned from the use of land) and established a new land tariff under the navy (based on size and type of property), which required CHamorus to register their lands. Lands not registered became part of the Spanish Crown lands, which, by order of the Secretary of the Navy, John Long, became property of the U.S. government. Naval Government of Guam, General Order No. 10, January 5, 1900, RG 80, Box 383, 9351-10, General Records of the Department of the Navy, NARA. Phillips, "Land." For a study of the Chamorro Land Trust as a vehicle through which CHamorus have responded to colonial expropriation of land, refer to Rojas, "Navigating Contested Terrain."

38. "A Little Civic Pride."

39. P. Hill, *Their World*; Robert, *American Women in Mission*; Enloe, *Bananas, Beaches and Bases*.

40. Margaret Mead, "Field Bulletin," 5, September 14, 1925, box N1, Margaret Mead Papers, Library of Congress, Washington, D.C.

41. Laura Thompson (hereafter, LT) to family, November, 13, 1938, box 7, folder: Guam and Orient, Trip, Laura Thompson Papers, National Anthropological Archives, Smithsonian Institution, Suitland, Maryland (hereafter, Thompson Papers).

42. Naval Government of Guam, *Annual Report of the Governor*, 1901; Naval Government of Guam, General Order No. 24, August 14, 1900, RG 80, Box 383, 9351-10, General Records of the Department of the Navy, NARA.

43. E. Johnston, "Medical Services"; "New Hospital Buildings"; N., "Susana Hospital," 1–3; "Susana Hospital," 2–3; "Susana Hospital Needs Help."

44. "Woman's Section [July]," 23. The reference to CHamoru women in the third person may have indicated that the column was intended mostly for an English-speaking American readership followed by a select group of CHamorus who could read English.

45. "Woman's Section" (August), 34.

46. Cahill, *Federal Fathers and Mothers*.

47. Bowman, "Navy Nurse Corps," 689; Lovett, *Conceiving*.

48. "Charity Fair," 10. "Conclusions Reached," 21; "Red Cross Work," 26.

49. LT to family, December 14, 1938, box 7, folder: Correspondence: Personal Letters from Guam, 1938–39, Thompson Papers. Thompson wrote about a Red Cross benefit organized by the governor's wife, Mrs. Alexander, and a Mrs. Winecoff.

50. Evelyn G. Nelson, "Navy Wife," folder: Evelyn Nelson Writings, Frederick J. and Evelyn G. Nelson Papers, Richard Flores Taitano Micronesian Area Research Center, University of Guam, Mangilao, Guam (hereafter, Nelson Papers).

51. Nelson, "Following the Ship," folder: Evelyn Nelson Writings, Nelson Papers.

52. Bassett, *Realms and Islands*.

53. Potter, "A Lass Who Loved," 603.

54. Scharff, *Twenty Thousand Roads*, 6.

55. Jose Torres, "Following the Flag"; DeLisle and Diaz, "Itinerant Indigeneities."

56. *The Guam Recorder* 11, no. 5 (October 1938): 1.

57. LT, Journal entry, June 10, 1939, box 8, folder "Guam," Field Journal, Journal and Field Notes, 1938–39, Thompson Papers.

58. Marcus and Fischer, *Anthropology as Cultural Critique*, 95. Laura Thompson, *Guam and Its People*; Thompson, *Archaeology*. Critical treatments of Thompson's work include Stade, *Pacific Passages*; Diaz, "Reclaiming Culture"; Petersen, "Politics in Postwar Micronesia."

59. For an analysis of the kåntan CHamorita, including a discussion of Thompson's work assisting Hans and Gertrude Hornbostel, refer to Clement, *Kustumbre, Modernity and Resistance*.

60. Teves refers to the way indigeneity vis-à-vis Kānaka Maoli performers resists and recodifies itself against settler colonial-state logics in Hawaiʻi and nonnative appropriations of "aloha." My marking of a defiant indigeneity refers to the way CHamoru women in this instance defied cultural, social, and religious traditions and norms and eluded Thompson's ethnographic authority. Teves, *Defiant Indigeneity*.

61. Souder, *Daughters of the Island*, 63.

62. Poehlman, "Culture Change and Identity," as quoted in Souder, *Daughters of the Island*, 69.

63. Souder, *Daughters of the Island*, 43.

64. Thompson, "Women of Guam," 413. For anthropological anxieties over modernity, Mavis Van Peenan's salvage ethnography, and "movie-going" as a sign of demise of CHamoru culture, refer to Diaz, "Simply Chamorro."

65. Here, I draw from a history of modern Burmese *khit kala*, or "women of the times," which similarly works to rectify women relegated to the footnote. Ikeya, *Refiguring Women*, 4.

66. LT to family, November 13, 1938, box 7, folder: Correspondence: Personal Letters from Guam, 1938–39, Thompson Papers. The reference to "hubs" is from Ramirez, *Native Hubs*. In Thompson's appendix (based on the island's 1930 census), we learn of the "gainful occupations" for CHamoru women: the highest were cooks and other domestic workers, 625; the next were teachers, 66; followed by nurses and midwives, 51. Laura Thompson, *Guam and Its People*, 290–91. For prewar perceptions of barmaids and the support of CHamoru men of the Guam Congress in this profession, refer to Hattori, "Textbook Tells."

67. Jorgensen, *Guam's Patroness*, 141, 125. On rearticulations of Pollapese womanhood and women's traditional work of taro cultivation vis a vis Christianity and the December 8 Feast of the Immaculate Conception in Pollap, refer to Flinn, *Mary, the Devil, and Taro*.

68. Viernes, "Chamorro Men in the Making."

69. Garcia, *Life and Martyrdom*, 171, 439.

70. Coello de la Rosa, *Jesuits at the Margins*, 319.

71. Ballantyne and Burton, *Moving Subjects*, 2.

72. Barrett and Ferenz, "Peacetime Martial Law," 2.

73. Taitano, interview by author, May 21, 1993. Before his appointment with the Office of Territories, Taitano served six terms as a senator of the Guam Legislature.

74. Memo from the Civil Administrator to the Island Command Provost Marshall, June 18, 1946, box 1, folder L20 "Travel and Transportation of Personnel," RG 313, Records of the Naval Operating Forces, National Archives and Records Administration, San Bruno, California (hereafter, Naval Operating Forces).

75. The term is so fraught that even the CHamoru country singer Bobbie DeGracia Rebanio in her 1990 rendition of Kitty Wells's "It Wasn't God Who Made Honky Tonk Angels" would capture in the song's title the CHamoru equivalent of the wild, negligent, and stigmatized woman in two words: *palao'an chålan*.

76. A minibiography of Tan Inga' is in PSECC, *Hale'-ta: I Manfayi*, vol. 1.

77. Moraga, "Long Line of Vendidas." On the virgin/whore dichotomy in other women-of-color, Indigenous, and transnational feminist contexts, refer to R. Green, "Pocahontas Perplex," and Naber, "Arab American Femininities."

78. Coello de la Rosa, *Jesuits at the Margins*, 311.

79. T. Teaiwa, "Articulated Cultures"; Diaz, "In the Wake of Matå'pang's Canoe." Other interlocutors in Native Pacific roots and routes include: Clifford, "Indigenous Articulations"; DeLoughrey, *Routes and Roots*; and Whimp, "Interdisciplinarity."

80. Wendt, "Towards a New Oceania"; Hau'ofa, "Pasts to Remember"; Diaz, "Sniffing"; T. Teaiwa, "For Salome"; Mallon, "Against Tradition"; Te Punga Somerville, *Once Were Pacific*.

81. Harris and McCallum, "Assaulting the Ears."

82. DeLisle, "Placental Politics"; Souder, *Daughters of the Island*.

83. K. Cruz, *Pattera: Midwives*, 2001.

84. Driver, "Account of a Discalced Friar's Stay," 17.

85. My idea of stewardship draws from what Sandy Grande and colleagues describe as the "metaphysics of Indigenous stewardship" and how this ethics and obligation forces us to reckon with the way that "land is both spirit and sovereign" and "sentient, alive, and watching us." Grande et al., "Red Praxis," 254.

86. DeLisle, "Placental Politics"; Stivens, "Modernizing the Malay Mother"; Merrett-Balkas, "Just Add Water"; Lukere and Jolly, *Birthing in the Pacific*; Jolly and Macintyre, *Family and Gender*; Kahn, *Tahiti beyond the Postcard*; Ram and Jolly, *Maternities and Modernities*; L. Simpson, "Birthing an Indigenous Resurgence"; P. Gonzales, *Red Medicine*; Connor, "Māori Mothering"; Fontaine et al., "Nimâmâsak"; Simmonds, "Honouring our Ancestors." On "reproductive anticolonialism," refer to Reilly, "Placental Politics."

87. My work draws from early and important articulations of feminism in Oceania and the later and emergent Indigenous feminist and critical Indigenous studies theorizing of women's (including mothering and othermothering) relations to land, and the legacies of white women and white feminism in, for example, Souder, "Feminism and Women's Studies"; Te Awekotuku, *Mana Wahine*; Foerstel and Gilliam, *Margaret Mead Legacy*; T. Teaiwa, "Microwomen"; Emberson-Bain, *Sustainable Development*; L. Hall, "Navigating"; L. Ross, "From the 'F' Word"; Simmonds, "Mana Wahine"; Moreton-Robinson, "Indigenous Women's Standpoint"; Goeman, "Indigenous Interventions"; Daigle, "Tracing the Terrain"; Kim, "Nesor Annim, Niteikapar."

88. R. Underwood, afterword in Hofschneider, *Campaign for Political Rights*, 211; DeLisle, "Indigenizing Environmental Thinking."

89. Brandon Lee Cruz, "Rediscovering Fo'na and Pontan," Guampedia, https://www.guampedia.com/rediscovering-fona-and-pontan/. This entry in Guampedia is based on the video production "I Tinituhon: Rediscovering Fo'na & Pontan," directed by Manny Cruz and produced by Brandon Lee Cruz, June 18, 2016, https://www.youtube.com/watch?v=yQPM1Iayq7s. Research from the video suggests that the site of Fouha rock may actually be in Hågat. For a critique of the distinctions made between oral tradition and oral history, and a discussion of oral histories as legitimate historical accounts critical to Indigenous identities and relations between individual and collective narratives, refer to Mahuika, *Rethinking Oral History*.

90. The terms and titles *maga'håga* and *maga'låhi* are used today to more generally describe someone of prominent standing and authority who wields tremendous respect from the island's community. The terms are also used to refer Guåhan's female or male governor.

91. K. Camacho, "Fuetsan Famalao'an"; Bevacqua and Bowman, "Histories of Wonder"; Hattori, "Textbook Tells."

92. Coello de la Rosa, *Jesuits at the Margins*, 331.

93. Jaye Sablan, "åpuya." Melanie Yazzie and Cutcha Risling Baldy define radical relationality, the "ethos of living well" (for CHamorus, inafa'maolek), as the interdependency and respect of "all living things." This ethos, they insist, "brings together the multiple strands of materiality, kinship, corporeality, affect, land/body connection, and multidimensional connectivity." Yazzie and Baldy, "Introduction," 2.

94. Midwife.

95. Roughly translates as "and so it came to be that."

96. Fruit dove and fruit bat.

97. Sugar apple and coconut.

98. Fish and turtle.

99. L. Simpson, "Islands"; Tallbear, "Making Love and Relations"; Yazzie and Baldy, "Introduction." On the power of Native Hawaiian mo'olelo (story) as a reminder that Kānaka Maoli are extensions of the land and that in their declaration of aloha (i.e. "deoccupied love"), Kānaka Maoli will resist and rise, refer to Revilla and Osorio, "Aloha," 128.

100. K. Cruz, *Pattera of Guam*, 2, 37. K. Cruz, *Their Story and Legacy*.

101. Benavente, interview by author, May 8, 1994.

102. Atienza and Coello de la Rosa, "Death Rituals," 468. An exception to this, according to Atienza and Coello de la Rosa—one accounted for by a CHamoru mortician, Adrian Cruz (with no explanation as to why)—is that at a certain time in Guåhan's history, those who committed suicide were buried with their feet facing the interior.

103. Le Gobien, *History*; Lévesque, *History of Micronesia*; Lawcock, "Guam Women."

104. Joannis Joseph Delgado, *Historia general sacroprofana, politica, y religiosa de las yslas de el poniente lamadas Philipinas, Escriviala un Religioso de la Compañia de Jesus* (Microfilm of partial printout from Biblitéca Nacional, Madrid, Spanish Documents Collection, Micronesian Area Research Center, University of Guam), 1751 (folio 83, trans. Marjorie Driver) as cited in Rubinstein, "Culture in Court," 36.

105. Juan de la Concepcion, Historia general de Philipinas, por el Hermano Balthasar Mariano, Donado Francilcano, Manila, 1788, (tomo vii, pp. 48–49, trans. Marjorie Driver) as cited in Rubinstein, "Culture in Court," 36. Another reference to Juan de la Concepcion is in Thompson, *Guam and Its People*, 167.

106. Laura Thompson, *Guam and Its People*, 194. Rosario, interview by Karen Cruz and author, June 1, 2000. Traditional healers in Guåhan who rely on herbs and plants to treat patients are known as *suruhåna* (female healer) and *suruhånu* (male healer). The names derive from the Spanish word *cirujano*, which means "surgeon." In pre-colonial CHamoru society, these traditional healers were referred to as *makåhna* (also *kakåhna*), revered spiritual leaders who relied on their skills as herbalists and their ability to communicate with the aniti to treat patients. Because Spanish colonizers regarded the work of the makåhna as sorcery and pagan practice, particularly the worshipping of ancestral skulls, they outlawed the makåhna. Discussion of these clashes, transitions, and the survival of earlier CHamoru healing practices are in Cunningham, *Ancient Chamorro Society*; Hattori, *Colonial Dis-ease*; Hattori, "Cry"; Lizama, "Yo'åmte." These clashes indicate a messier transition under Spanish colonialism to American colonialism than is represented in the simple old and new binary of lay pattera and nurse-trained pattera. A similar history and melding of the cirujano practices is found in Ortiz, "History of Midwifery."

107. The real-life story of an enslaved black woman, Margaret Garner, who killed her daughter to prevent her from entering a life of slavery, is the inspiration for Toni Morrison's *Beloved*.

108. Cruz, "Rituals of Continuity," as quoted in Atienza and Coello de la Rosa, "Death Rituals," 469. Note: In the article, *måktan* is translated as "shadow of the roof"; I follow the definition provided by Topping, Ogo, Dungca, *CHamoru-English Dictionary*.

109. For similar references to stillborn babies given a specific kind of burial next to the house because they had not been baptized, refer to Ortiz, "History of Midwifery."

110. Lukere, "Conclusion," 196.

111. Simmonds, "Honouring our Ancestors."

112. Lukere, 196–97.
113. Barclay et al., *Midwives' Tales*; Cassidy, *Birth*.
114. Lauer, "Hawaiian Law."
115. Kahn, *Tahiti beyond the Postcard*, 65. Refer also to Bardwell-Jones, "Placental Ethics."
116. Tengan, Ka'ili, Fonoto, "Genealogies."
117. Teaiwa, "Review."

Chapter One

1. The other CHamoru word for midwife, *pattera*, is derived from the Spanish word for midwife, *partera*. The term for more than one pattera is *i pattera siha*. I use *pattera* and *ná'fafañågu* to denote the singular and plural. Although historical accounts and oral histories of the ná'fafañågu and pattera describe them as *women*, I recognize the possibility of gender diversity within midwifery, especially given the gender bias of colonial and CHamoru archives and sources.

2. On the shift in charitable models of public health to more scientific paradigms in the nursing profession through the cultural institution and category of "domestic science," refer to Bashford, "Domestic Scientists."

3. Teaiwa, "On Analogies."

4. Bruyneel, *Third Space of Sovereignty*. This social and cultural massaging is akin to the work of Indigenous rearticulation in other modern, colonial, military, and patriarchal institutions in Guåhan like the "new multicultural local" in sports. Diaz, "'Fight Boys'"; Diaz "Tackling."

5. R. Underwood, "American Education"; Souder, "A Not So Perfect Union"; Hofschneider, *Campaign for Political Rights*; Hattori, *Colonial Dis-Ease*; DeLisle and Diaz, "Itinerant Indigeneities"; Bevacqua, "Chamorros, Ghosts."

6. Hattori, *Colonial Dis-Ease*. For similar American anxieties (and desires) in the Philippines, refer to Isaac, *American Tropics*.

7. Office of the Chief of Naval Operations, *U.S. Navy Report on Guam*; Carano and Sanchez, *A Complete History*; Sanchez, *Guahan Guam*; Rogers, *Destiny's Landfall*.

8. For a discussion of colonial banality in the context of CHamoru patriotism and high enlistment in the U.S. military amid ongoing U.S. colonization and occupation of one-third of Guåhan, refer to Bevacqua, "The Exceptional Life."

9. Naval Government of Guam, *Annual Report of the Governor*, 1927, 10.

10. Piatote, *Domestic Subjects*, 5–6. Though the topic is beyond the scope of this study, there are other important points of difference between the terms of U.S. benevolent (and malevolent) colonial rule over Indigenous peoples overseas and in the continent toward the end of the nineteenth century. The biggest difference has generally to do with the legal and political forms of existence under federal administration and law. In Guåhan's case, there have been no treaties struck between the United States and the CHamoru people, and the island's political status as a U.S. unincorporated territory has been established and maintained through a series of Supreme Court cases in the first two decades of the twentieth century known as the Insular Cases. At the end of the day, however, American Indians and CHamorus remain under the plenary power of the U.S. Congress. A discussion of the

guardian-ward relationship and plenary power is in Wilkins and Lomawaima, *Uneven Ground*. For a discussion of the abusive domestic arrangement between CHamorus and the federal government, refer to Souder, "Psyche under Seige."

11. Seth, *Difference and Disease*.

12. For a similar rhetoric of "safe motherhood" meant to eradicate *hilots* (traditional birth attendants) in the Philippines, refer to Kadetz, "Risk and Resistance." For an earlier history of powerful Indigenous women healers in the Philippines under Spanish colonialism, refer to Brewer, *Shamanism*. In Puerto Rico, Native women came under a U.S. civilizing project that employed a rhetoric of overpopulation in contrast to the one of depopulation in Guåhan. Briggs, *Reproducing Empire*. On racial formations of "decency" and "disreputability" in antiprostitution campaigns, marriage reforms, and working-class "free love" in Puerto Rico, refer to Findlay, *Imposing Decency*.

13. Naval Government of Guam, *Annual Report of the Governor*, 1906, 5.

14. Bashford, *Purity and Pollution*.

15. Herrera, interview by author, May 7, 1998.

16. Simpson, *Mohawk Interruptus*.

17. J. O'Brien, *Firsting and Lasting*. References to specific ages of the older lay midwives (often described as over fifty) and younger nurses (mainly between eighteen and twenty-five) can be found in K. Cruz, *Pattera of Guam*; Hattori, *Colonial Dis-Ease*; Jackson, "I Was on Guam."

18. Naval Government of Guam, General Order No. 28, November 1, 1900, RG 52, E-11, box 140, 66735, Bureau of Medicine and Surgery, NARA.

19. Examples of reproductive justice scholarship on colonial, state, and white male usurping of Indigenous and women-of-color healing, birthworth, and motherwork traditions include Lavell-Harvard and Anderson, *Mothers of the Nations*; Theobald, *Reproduction on the Reservation*; Ross and Sollinger, *Reproductive Justice*; and Oparah and Bonaparte, *Birthing Justice*. My understanding of the "midwifery problem" and the campaign to eliminate the midwife is also informed by early and important feminist critiques of the male medicalization of women's bodies, including Rich, *Of Woman Born*; Daly, *Gynecology*; Poovey, "Scenes"; Ehrenreich and English, *Witches, Midwives, and Nurses*; Ginsburg and Rapp, *Conceiving*; Lee, *Granny Midwives*; Ettinger, *Nurse-Midwifery*; and Davis-Floyd and Johnson, *Mainstreaming Midwives*.

20. Hadley, "A Brief History of the U. S. Naval Hospital."

21. Naval Government of Guam, *Annual Report of the Governor*, 1901, 4. Other references to unclean methods and high mortality rates are in Braun, "Duty and Diversion," 650; Johnson, "Guam—before December, 1941," 994; and *U.S. Navy Report on Guam, 1898–1950*, 6.

22. Naval Government of Guam, *Annual Report of the Governor*, 1901, 9, and 1902, 5; Hattori, "Cry," 11.

23. An example of the navy's rhetoric of cleanliness and specific attention to hands can be found in Reed, "Health Notes," 9.

24. Herrera, interview by author, May 7, 1998. Elsewhere, I argue that the island's prewar pattera hybridized Indigenous CHamoru and colonial practices while simultaneously resisting and participating in the U.S. Navy's efforts to establish its hegemony on the body and cleanliness in Guåhan. DeLisle, "Delivering the Body."

25. Quoted in Cunningham, *Ancient Chamorro Society*, 96. Fray Antonio de los Angeles was the first clergyman to remain in the Marianas (on route to the Philippines). Driver, "The Account"; McGrath, "The Capuchins."

26. Lizama, "Yo'åmte, 5," Workman, Cruz-Ortiz, and Kaminga-Quinata, "Use of Traditional Medicine," 203.

27. The navy had "taught Guam to wash her face" so well that the navy had "let her forget how to feed yourself." *Guam News Letter* 3, nos. 3 and 4, September–October 1911, 2. Reference to the more methodical system of feeding and cleansing is in [L]eonhardt, "Letters from Navy Nurses III," 655.

28. Naval Government of Guam, General Order No. 71, December 7, 1903, RG 52, E-11, Box 140, 66735, Bureau of Medicine and Surgery, NARA.

29. Susan H. P. Dyer (hereafter SHPD) to Susie, November 20, 1905, box 340.17.b, George Leland Dyer Papers, East Carolina Manuscript Collection, Joyner Library, East Carolina University, Greenville, North Carolina (hereafter Dyer Papers); Guerrero, "Growth of Nursing," 14. According to Dyer, there were six nurses. According to Guerrero, there were eight nurses and one woman, Rosalia Ojeda, who had been recruited to translate English to CHamoru at the Susana. Knight, "Maria Roberta: A Tribute"; Workman, "Native Nurses in Guam," 127.

30. Bennett, "Nursing Service of Guam." Another example of the naval discourse on "adaptability" in Guåhan can be found in Naval Government of Guam, *Annual Report of the Surgeon General*, 1912, 25.

31. Bhabha, *Location of Culture*. For a similar colonial mimicry in U.S. public health projects in the Philippines, refer to W. Anderson, *Colonial Pathologies*.

32. Bowman, "History and Development," 358; Jackson, "I Was on Guam," 1245; Knight, "Maria Roberto," 282. References to Della Knight departing Guåhan and Josephine Bowman arriving via the USS *Thomas* are from *Guam News Letter* 7, no. 8 (February 1916), 4 and "By the U.S.A. Thomas," 4. For other discussions of the navy's desire to recruit a particular class of CHamoru women, refer to Bennett, "Nursing Service of Guam"; and Naval Government of Guam, *Annual Report of the Governor*, 1926.

33. Bennett, "History of Nursing," 888.

34. Bennett, 689.

35. Bennett, 689. The U.S. Navy nurse Laura Hartwell reiterated the same favorable conditions in Samoa because of the "very best" stock of nurses as daughters of the chiefs who attended the London missionary school in Atauloma. Hartwell, "Impressions of Samoa," 397.

36. Howe, *Quest*. On the association of Polynesians (Mormons) with the Lost Tribes of Israel, refer to Aikau, *A Chosen People*.

37. L[eonhardt], "Letters from Navy Nurses III," 655; L[eonhardt], "Letters from Navy Nurses" (November 1913), 126. Reference to the "mongrelized" race in Guåhan can be found in *U.S. Navy Report on Guam, 1898–1950*.

38. Jackson, "I Was on Guam," 124–25; Bowman, "Navy Nurse Corps," 690; L[eonhardt], "Letters from Navy Nurses" (November 1913), 126; J. Flores, "Dress of the Chamorro."

39. Bowman, "Navy Nurse Corps," 690.

40. "Department of Red Cross Nursing," 597–98.

41. Johnson, "Guam—before December, 1941."

42. Herrera, interview by author, April 2, 2001.

43. L[eonhardt], "Letters from Navy Nurses" (January 1914), 296. The image of the "Sairey Gamp" (or Sarah Gamp) was a stereotype with which American nurses were all too familiar, certainly the readership of the *American Journal of Nursing*, as evidenced in another reference to the drunken night nurse character from the Charles Dickens novel *Martin Chuzzlewit* (serialized 1843–44). Wead, "Lighting of the Seven Candles." Annette Summers has followed the prevalence of the image as a way to delegitimize the community nurse in Australia. Summers, "Sairey Gamp."

44. Higbee, "Letters from Navy Nurses"; Bowman, "Navy Nurse Corps," 689. On the Sacred Twenty, refer to Naval Historical Foundation, *U.S. Navy*; Sobocinski, "Sacred Twenty," Sterner, *In and out*.

45. United States Navy Department, "Funeral Services"; Guerrero, "Growth of Nursing," 14; Perry, "Governor Calls," 364; "Native Nurse Corps," 27.

46. Seaton, *The Seaton Family*.

47. Johnson, "United States Naval Hospital"; Hattori, *Colonial Dis-Ease*; .

48. Guerrero, "Growth of Nursing," 14; Perry, "Governor Calls," 364; "Native Nurse Corps," 27.

49. A mini biography of Elisabeth (a.k.a. Elizabeth) Leonhardt is provided in Glakas, "Remembering Herndon's History." On the duties of the navy nurses to train Native nurses, refer to Bennett, "History of Nursing"; "Red Cross Nursing"; "Native Nurse Corps."

50. "Susana Hospital Needs Help"; "Native Nurse Corps," 27; L[eonhardt], "Letters from Navy Nurses" (November 1914), 152. For references to "Miss Leonhardt," "Miss Coonan," and "Miss Turner" attending various social events together, refer to *Guam News Letter* 2, no. 12 (June 1911): 1, 4–5.

51. K. Cruz, *Pattera of Guam*, 31.

52. "Naval Hospital Notes," 15.

53. Wilbur, "Florence Nightingales," 4; "Uniform Requirements," 12.

54. Higbee, "Letters from Navy Nurses," 248. At the time of Higbee's writing, she was serving as the second Superintendent (1911–22) of the Navy Nurse Corps. Drew, "Lenah Sutcliffe Higbee."

55. Herrera, interview by author, June 12, 1998.

56. Herrera, interview by author, May 9, 1998.

57. K. Cruz, *Pattera of Guam*, 38; Guerrero, "Growth of Nursing"; Rosario, interview by Karen Cruz and author, June 1, 2000.

58. Mesa, interview by author, June 24, 1998.

59. K. Cruz, *Pattera of Guam*, 22.

60. Duenas, interview by author, June 13, 1994.

61. Guerrero, "Growth of Nursing," 14.

62. Herrera, interview by author, May 9, 1998.

63. C. Santos, "Guam's Folklore." With the exception of the apostrophe, which has been replaced with the glota symbol or glottal stop, Tan Carmen's translations and spellings remain intact as a way of preserving her work.

64. From the English translation, or from the surface, one might understand the song to be more about a seduction and the enrolled nurse's naiveté. When I inquired with CHamoru women, those who are first-language speakers, they used the word "rape" to describe the song's meaning.

65. Although such places are known for being tourist and/or military rest and recreation areas, Tomhom and Dadi are steeped in a prior history of what the Yellowknives Dene scholar Glen Coulthard refers to as "grounded normativity" in which CHamorus engaged in land- and ocean-based activities as evidenced in prewar stories of the låncho, hunting, and large fishing parties. Coulthard, *Red Skin, White Masks*.

66. Valentine, "Geography of Women's Fear."

67. Souder, *Daughters*, 43.

68. Rosario, interview by Karen A. Cruz and author, June 1, 2000; Guevara, "I Pattera."

69. K. Cruz, *Pattera of Guam*, 5.

70. Souder traces CHamoru women's independence and relative sexual freedom prior to Spanish Catholicism and American patriarchy and argues that following colonial rules governing sex and marriage, CHamoru men "seized the opportunity to gain control" over CHamoru women. Souder, *Daughters*, 45–49; Souder, "Unveiling Herstory," 144–48.

71. Workman, Ortiz, and Quinata, "I Che'cho Suruhåna," 9.

72. Bordallo, "The Nurses."

73. DeLisle, "Delivering the Body."

74. The other two wards of the naval hospital in Guåhan were Ward 1, known as the Maria Schroeder Hospital, and Ward 2, for enlisted men. K. Cruz, *Pattera of Guam*, 30. The Barrigåda pattera, Tan Dolores Sablan, recalled the old naval hospital to be in the vicinity of where the Nieves Library (Guam Public Library) is currently located. Guevara, "I Pattera," 61.

75. PSECC, *Hale'-ta: I Manfåyi*, 273; Duenas, interview by author, June 13, 1994.

76. Knight, "Maria Roberta," 516–17; Ventura, "Maria Anderson Roberto." After Roberto, the following women held the position: Dolores Lujan, Rita Garrido Blaz, Maria Duenas Sablan, Consuelo Terlaje Pellicani, Amanda Guzman Shelton, and Joaquina Siguenza. This information was provided by the CHamoru nurse Antonia Salas Sanchez in Guerrero, "Growth of Nursing in Guam."

77. In 1924, Roberto contracted Hansen's disease while working at the naval hospital. A year later, the U.S. Navy deported her to Culion Leper Colony in the Phillipines (where other CHamorus had been deported earlier) —a policy that ran counter to inafa'maolek and CHamoru families' desires to have their loved ones struggling with the disease remain at home in Guåhan, where families could care for them.

78. Rosario, interview by author, June 1, 2000. On the birth certificate as technology and biopower of the state, refer to Foucault, *Birth of Biopolitics*.

79. Herrera, interview by author, June 12, 1998.

80. Herrera, interview by author, May 7, 1998.

81. Rosario, interview by Karen A. Cruz and author, June 1, 2000.

82. For similar references in Fiji to hospitals as sites of death, refer to Jolly, "Introduction," 6.

83. Clifford, "Indigenous Articulations," 469.

84. Herrera, interview by author, June 12, 1998. By the eve of the Japanese invasion and occupation of Guåhan (from December 1941 to July 1944), CHamorus had seemed to acquiesce on the navy's preferred technical distinction, but one which centered instead on the difference between trained and certified nurses (enfetmera) and trained and certified nurse-midwives (pattera) rather than between "old" (self-made) midwives and "new," young, and supposedly malleable nurse-midwives, who were required to undergo naval certification. By this time, there also seemed to be another distinction among those who had midwifery

licenses: between those nurse-midwives who worked independently and were assigned to work either in their respective villages or island-wide, and those nurses who had midwifery licenses but worked predominantly in the hospital.

85. Herrera, interview by author, June 12, 1998. The word *lanña'* is an expletive that has multiple meanings and is used to express a range of emotions, the milder of which I have conveyed here.

86. J. Sablan, *My Mental Odyssey*, 106.

87. Te Punga Somerville and Justice, "Introduction: Indigenous Conversations about Biography."

88. Naval Government of Guam, *Annual Report of the Governor*, 1907, 8.

89. Manderson, "Shaping Reproduction," 37. Nurse-trained pattera can also be likened to Japanese midwives, whose role as cultural brokers and birth attendants for the Issei were contemporaneous with the transformation of midwifery into a new woman's profession as part of Japan's modernizing quest for empire and with the rise of Japanese immigration to the United States. Susan L. Smith, *Japanese American Midwives*.

90. Naval Government of Guam, *Annual Report of the Governor*, 1905, 10.

91. On the facts that only 2 percent of deliveries took place in the hospital and that most CHamorus regarded the Susana as for the manakhilo' class of CHamoru families, refer to Hattori, "Cry," 13.

92. Herrera, interview by author, May 7, 1998.

93. Mesa, interview by author, June 24, 1998.

94. Laura Thompson, Journal entries of December 27, 1938; December 28, 1938; and December 29, 1938, box 8, Field Journal: Journal & Field Notes, 1938–1939, Laura Thompson Papers. For a reference to åmot para mungga mapotge' as a method of birth control and a discussion of the Ma'ina suruhåna Tan Maria Namauleg Gutierrez Tuncap as a healer of prubleman famalao'an, refer to Workman, Ortiz, and Quinata, "I Che'cho Suruhåna," 36, 64–65. In 1990, Guåhan governor Joseph F. Ada signed into law one of the most restrictive anti-abortion statutes in the United States. For an analysis of the law and its later unconstitutional ruling, refer to Dames, "Chamorro Women."

95. Mesa, interview by author, June 24, 1998.

96. Dawley, "Campaign to Eliminate," 53.

97. Captain Wilma Leona Jackson, interview by Paul Stillwell, September 26, 1986.

98. Captain Wilma Leona Jackson, interview.

99. Clifford, *Routes*, 44. On the spatial dynamics of gender, work, and affect in the field of critical and feminist geographies, refer to Massey, *For Space*; Bondi and Davidson, "Situating Gender"; and Beebe, Davis, and Gleadle, "Introduction." Beginning in 1925, the U.S. Navy granted nurse-midwives a license in one of two categories of practice: general or district/village. Cruz, *Pattera of Guam*, 33.

100. "Red Cross Workers," 12; PSECC, *Hale'-ta: I Manfåyi*, 296; Soledad Pablo Tenorio, interview by author, January 18, 1994.

101. Laura Thompson, *Guam and Its People*, 191.

102. Workman, Ortiz, and Quinata, "I Che'cho Suruhåna," 16, 64; Workman, Cruz-Ortiz, and Kaminga-Quinata, "Use of Traditional Medicine." On other ways Indigenous health care endured Western medicine and colonial assertions of whiteness and authority, refer to Rutherdale, *Caregiving on the Periphery*.

103. Mesa, interview by author, June 24, 1998.
104. Mesa, interview by author, April 16, 1998; June 24, 1998.
105. Herrera, interview by author, June 12, 1998.
106. Laura Thompson, *Guam and Its People*, 196.
107. Rosario, interview by author, June 1, 2000.

108. Laura Thompson claimed not only that CHamoru traditions existed only when they did not conflict with the navy but also that they were practiced "before the war in conservative families" in the island's "rural" south. Laura Thompson, *Guam and Its People*, 191.

109. Mesa, interview by author, April 16, 1998; Laura Thompson, *Guam and Its People*, 196. The proper care and burial of the placenta and cord for similar protective measures is practiced in many other Indigenous cultures, for example, among the Plains Cree and James Bay Cree, as discussed in Anderson, *Life Stages*. This ritual is often preserved by women elders, as discussed in P. Gonzales, *Red Medicine*.

110. Un dångkolu na si yu'os ma'åse to Ann Marie Arceo for her provocative discussion of the three life stages and roles that CHamorus assume: påtgon, che'lu, and saina. It makes sense to think of these, along with the role and obligation of manmofo'na, as important elements of inafa'maolek and CHamoru directionality that are ensured through the proper care and planting of the ga'chong and apuya'.

111. K. Cruz, *Pattera of Guam*, 34.
112. Guevara, "I Pattera," 61.
113. Rosario, interview by Karen Cruz and author, June 1, 2000.
114. K. Cruz, *Pattera of Guam*, 34.
115. K. Cruz, 26.
116. Guerrero, interview by Karen Cruz and author, June 1, 2000.
117. Lizama, "Yo'åmte."
118. Mesa, interview by author, June 24, 1998.
119. Diego, interview by Karen Cruz and author, June 1, 2000.
120. K. Cruz, *Pattera: Midwives of Guam*.
121. Perez, interview by Karen Cruz and author, June 1, 2000; Eustaquio, interview by Karen Cruz and author, June 1, 2000.

122. PSECC, *Hale'-ta: I Manfåyi*, 94. Jose Blas, interview by author, October 5, 1994. For an analysis of the matlina (as othermother) in the CHamoru legend of Serena, refer to Naholowa'a, "Beyond Matrifocality."

123. Eustaquio, interview by Karen Cruz and author, June 1, 2000.

124. Fraser, *African American Midwifery*, 164, 168. Because of the robust CHamoru decolonization and independence movement happening in Guåhan, land back struggles and Indigenous resurgence are also now about reclaiming food sovereignty and traditional birthing practices. An increasing number of CHamoru women and their families are planting their child's ga'chong and apuya'.

125. K. Cruz, *Pattera of Guam*.

126. Burton, *Archive Stories*; Harris, "'I Wouldn't Say.'" On family history as "central to any reckoning of Indigenous studies," refer to J. O'Brien, "Historical Sources," 20.

127. Mesa, interview by author, June 24, 1998.
128. Kauanui, "A Structure, Not an Event."

Chapter Two

1. SHPD to Susie, June 19, 1904, 5, box 340.17.b., Dyer Papers.
2. Caronan, *Legitimizing Empire*.
3. SHPD to Susie, July 12, 1905, box 340.17.b., Dyer Papers; SHPD to Susie, August 21, 1905, box 340.17.b.
4. Frankenberg, *White Women, Race Matters*.
5. Burton, *Burdens of History*, 10.
6. Kaplan, *Anarchy of Empire*, 25.
7. Deloria, *Indians in Unexpected Places*.
8. Young, *Colonial Desire*; Haraway, *Primate Visions*.
9. SHPD to Susie, September 14, 1904, 16, box 340.17.b, Dyer Papers. Dyer's references to the "Lotus Eatus" and "always afternoon" appear to have originated from Alfred Lord Tennyson's 1832 poem "The Lotos-Eaters," in which "always afternoon" appears in the first stanza. Dyer drew inspiration from Tennyson, as evidenced in a letter to George in which she shared Tennyson's last poem, "Crossing the Bar." SHPD to George Leland Dyer (hereafter GLD), March 1, 1890, box 340.6.c, Dyer Papers. For another reference to the "Lotus Eatus," which also marked radically different worlds of exotic Native others in "The Wild Girl of the Nebraska," refer to Webber, *Tales*, 271.
10. SHPD to Susie, September 14, 1904.
11. McClintock, *Imperial Leather*. On the gendering and cultural construction of patriarchal "father time," refer to Murphy, *Time Is*.
12. SHPD to Susie, September 20, 1905, 61, box 340.17.b., Dyer Papers; SHPD to Susie, July 1–20, 1904, 8, box 340.17.b., Dyer Papers; SHPD to Susie, n.d., 2, box 340.17.b., Dyer Papers.
13. Anzaldúa, *Borderlands*; Pratt, *Imperial Eyes*; Dening, *Islands and Beaches*; Goeman, "Disrupting a Settler-Colonial."
14. SHPD to Susie, n.d., 2, box 340.17.b., Dyer Papers.
15. In 1875, the year they married, George Dyer was assigned to the USS *Frolic* and the South Atlantic Station. Later, Susan Dyer would follow his assignments to the USS *Constitution*, USS *Despatch*, USS *Charleston*, USS *Mohican*, USS *Vesuvius*, USS *Stranger*, and USS *Yankton*. Before his final overseas assignment in Guåhan, he served on board the USS *Rainbow* and USS *Albany* in the Asiatic Station.
16. SHPD to Susie, n.d., 2, box 340.17.b, Dyer Papers.
17. SHPD to GLD, April 12, 1890, box 340.6.c.
18. GLD to SHPD, March 21, 1903, box 340.16.e.
19. For an early and important discussion of white woman's separate sphere ideology and its emphasis on the values of piety, purity, submissiveness, and domesticity, refer to Welter, "Cult of True Womanhood." A destabilizing of Victorian true womanhood is in Schuller, *Biopolitics of Feelings*.
20. GLD to SHPD, April 4, 1890, box 340.6.c, Dyer Papers.
21. GLD to SHPD, November 10, 1899, box 340.15.b. "Albany Society Awakes," 12; "Albany Society Dines," 9. With the Albany Society, a nonprofit organization in New York, Susan Dyer was involved in charity work for Episcopalian churches and the historic preservation of old mansions. Blair, *Clubwoman as Feminist*; Cott, *Bonds of Womanhood*.

22. Sweat, "Annals." Other members included Aileen Adine Bell, the sister of Alexander Graham Bell; Rebekah Black Hornsby, the daughter of Judge Jeremiah S. Black, attorney general and later secretary of state under President James Buchanan; and Minna Blair Richey, the daughter of Montgomery Blair, Dred Scott's attorney and U.S. postmaster general under Andrew Jackson. On the link among white women's philanthropy, white women's rights, and the work of Hearst, refer to J. Johnson, *Funding Feminism*.

23. Sweat, "Annals." Setting the club's tone and aspirations of public intellectual life and publishing, at its first meeting on January 13, the Cobwebs began with a conversation on the *salonnières*. On salon culture, refer to Goldsmith and Goodman, *Going Public*; Kale, *French Salons*; Vick, *Congress of Vienna*.

24. Jacobs, *White Mother*; Tonkovich, *Allotment Plot*; Leckie and Parezo, *Their Own Frontier*.

25. SHPD to GLD, March 20, 1890, box 340.6.c, Dyer Papers.

26. Sweat, "Annals," March 3, 1890, 45, 47. On the troubling links among marriage (as social contract), white feminism, and patriarchy, refer to Pateman, *The Sexual Contract*.

27. Kelley, *Learning to Stand*; Sweat, "Annals," March 24, 1890. This self-sacrifice on the part of Dyer is reminiscent of an earlier womanhood discussed in Kerber, "Republican Motherhood." My interest is not in espousing mutually exclusive tenets of "true manhood" versus "new womanhood" but in highlighting ruptures of white womanhood and the suffrage movement as discussed in Todd, *"New Woman" Revised*; Kraus, *New Type of Womanhood*; and Tetrault, *Myth of Seneca Falls*.

28. SHPD to GLD, March 17, 1890, box 340.6.c, Dyer Papers.

29. SHPD to GLD, March 17, 1890.

30. SHPD to GLD, March 17, 1890.

31. SHPD to Susie, at intervals from July 1 to July 20, 1904, 10, box 340.17.b.

32. GLD to SHPD, February 27, 1901, box 340.16.a.

33. GLD to SHPD, May 12, 1903, box 340.17.a.

34. SHPD to Susie, July 1–20, 1904, 10, box 340.17.b.

35. GLD to SHPD, May 12, 1903.

36. Domosh and Seager, *Putting Women in Place*.

37. GLD to SHPD, March 21, 1903, box 340.16.e, Dyer Papers.

38. Between 1901 and 1902, some one thousand American teachers were sent to the Philippines by way of the U.S. Army Transport, the USS *Thomas*; hence they came to be called the Thomasites. For a critique of the idea of the Thomasite mission as "benevolent," refer to Sianturi, "Pedagogic Invasion"; Pineda-Tinio, "Review."

39. GLD to SHPD, April 15, 1903, box 340.16.e, Dyer Papers.

40. GLD to SHPD, April 15, 1903.

41. In a letter to Susan, on the passing of George Dyer, Evelyn Wainwright (hereafter EW) recalled George Dyer's "protecting shield" over Susan. EW to SHPD, April 3, 1914, box 340.19.c, Dyer Papers.

42. GLD to SHPD, January 24, 1903, box 340.16.d; GLD to SHPD, June 11, 1899, box 340.15.a.

43. GHPD to SHPD, April 19, 1903, box 340.16.e.

44. Diary of Susan "Daisy" Dyer (hereafter Daisy), Entry of July 15, 1898, box 340.22.a. Cooper, "Diplomat and Naval Intelligence."

45. SHPD to Susie, n.d., 2, box 340.17.b, Dyer Papers.
46. SHPD to Susie, n.d., 5.
47. SHPD to Susie, June 19, 1904, 4–5, box 340.17.b.
48. SHPD to Susie, November 20, 1905, 66, box 340.17.b.
49. Bederman, *Manliness and Civilization*; Hoganson, *Fighting for American Manhood*; Greenberg, *Manifest Manhood*; Oriard, *Reading Football*.
50. SHPD to Susie, August 21, 1905, 57, box 340.17.b, Dyer Papers.
51. "Commandant Makes Report." A discussion of Dyer's establishment of a Department of Health and Charities is in "A Memory," 8. Hattori, "'Cry.'"
52. SHPD to Susie, n.d., 2, box 340.17.b, Dyer Papers.
53. Naval Government of Guam, *Annual Report of the Governor*, 1905, 3. R. Underwood, "Colonial Era," 75.
54. The term *helpmeet* is from Robert, *American Women in Mission*.
55. SHPD to Susie, July 1–20, 1904, 9, box 340.17.b, Dyer Papers.
56. Hill, *Clay*; Parmenter, *The Edge*.
57. Reference to "high-class vaudeville" is on page 26 of the Dyers' Guestbook, box 340.24.d. Reference to "side-splitting Negro impersonations" is in the Guam Dramatic Club's program of September 3, 1904, box 340.24.d.
58. Salesa, *Mixing Races*.
59. For references to CHamoru performances in the palåsyo during the Spanish administration, refer to Lévesque, *History of Micronesia*, Vol. 19.
60. SHPD to Susie, March 18, 1905, 40, box 340.17.b, Dyer Papers.
61. "The Shoe Gang," "Chamorrita Notes," box 16, folder 79, Agueda I. Johnston Papers, Richard Flores Taitano Micronesian Area Research Center, University of Guam, Mangilao, Guam (hereafter Johnston Papers).
62. Daisy to Edna, circa 1921, box 340.19.f, Dyer Papers.
63. Clancy-Smith and Gouda, *Domesticating the Empire*.
64. Daisy to Edna, circa 1921, box 340.19.f, Dyer Papers.
65. SHPD to Susie, February 24, 1905, 37, box 340.17.b, Dyer papers.
66. A fuller treatment, beyond the parameters of this book, would also necessarily require an examination of how *nonwhite* military women also pushed against the boundaries.
67. Dorothy Dyer to SHPD, c. 1913, box 340.18.f, Dyer Papers.
68. Daisy to Edna, circa 1921, box 340.19.f.
69. Smith-Rosenberg, "Female World of Love."
70. SHPD to Susie, June 19, 1904, 5, 7, box 340.17.b, Dyer Papers.
71. SHPD to Susie, June 19, 1904, 7.
72. SHPD to Susie, July 1–20, 1904, 8, box 340.17.b.
73. References to Daisy's employment as a "special contract" laborer in Guåhan at $2.50 gold/day are in Alli, "Susan H. Dyer."
74. SHPD to Susie, March 18, 1905, 40, box 340.17.b, Dyer Papers.
75. Daisy to Edna, circa 1921, box 340.19.f.
76. SHPD to Susie, March 18, 1905, 40.
77. Dyer Guestbook, 12, box 340.24.d. Examples can be found in Dyer's letters to Susie and the *Guam Newsletter* of CHamoru women's responses to Dyer's socials, including fundraising events for the hospitals.

78. Edward John Dorn (hereafter EJD), Journal entries of June 6, 1910, October 31, 1910, November 3, 1910, container 1, folder: Diary 1910. Edward John Dorn Papers, Manuscripts Division, Library of Congress, Washington, D.C. (hereafter Dorn Papers). Dorn also continued the hospital work of Maria Schroeder and Susan Dyer, which for him entailed conducting surveys and erecting monuments. EJD, Journal entry of January 21, 1910, container 1, folder: Diary 1910 Dorn Papers. "Members of Crew," 18; "Pretty Girls," 21; *Guam News Letter* 4, no. 5 (November 1912), 5. Governor Robert Coontz continued the tradition, holding two dances a month at Dorn Hall. Coontz, *From the Mississippi*, 4.

79. SHPD to Susie, July 1–20, 1904, 11, box 340.17.b, Dyer Papers.

80. "Address of Commodore George L. Dyer," 159, 163. An example of George Dyer's disapproval of a particular kind of "mix" and "mixing" is gleaned from his letter to Susan about interracial marriage, the kind in the autobiographical novel by the French naval officer Pierre Loti, on his romance with a Tahitian woman, Rarahu. GLD to SHPD, September 28, 1890, box 340.8.a, Dyer Papers.

81. EJD, Journal entry of September 12, 1910, container 2, folder: Diary 1910, Dorn Papers. Dorn's journal entry also furnishes an example of naval governors' anxieties about CHamoru women's mobilities and newfound freedoms, as in the case of Dolores Duarte, who he described as having "bad conduct with various men." No further information is provided except that Dorn's comment about the "incident" is in the context of his nephew, Edward "Teddy" Mayhew, and Teddy's marriage to Dolores's sister, Maria, in the Philippines.

82. SHPD to Susie, June 29, 1904, 7, box 340.17.b, Dyer Papers.

83. SHPD to Susie, March 18, 1905, 40, box 340.17.b.

84. SHPD to Susie, November 20, 1905, 67, box 340.17.b.

85. Beets, "Images of Maori Women"; Suaalii, "Deconstructing the 'Exotic' Female"; Schroeder, "Another View of Guam"; P. O'Brien, *Pacific Muse*.

86. Jolly, "From Point Venus"; Holland, *Erotic Life of Racism*.

87. SHPD to Susie, July 1–20, 1904, 11, box 340.17.b, Dyer Papers. Anita Elvidge's attempts to turn the civilian governor of Guam's residence into a "middle class dwelling in which a family can be raised in peace and serenity" is described in Anita Elvidge, "Government House," n.d., 3, folder: Government House, Anita Elvidge Papers, Richard Flores Taitano Micronesian Area Research Center, University of Guam, Mangilao, Guam.

88. Hoganson, *Consumers' Imperium*, 88.

89. Charles A. Pownall, Oral History 156, Naval Historical Collection Archives, U.S. Naval War College, Newport, RI.

90. "Transport Day," 7.

91. SHPD to Susie, July 1–20, 1904, 9–10, Dyer Papers.

92. SHPD to Susie, July 1–20, 1904, 9–10.

93. SHPD to Susie, August 19, 1904, 14, box 340.17.b.

94. Rafael, *White Love*, 53.

95. SHPD to Susie, June 19, 1904, 5, box 340.17.b, Dyer Papers.

96. Pascoe, *Relations of Rescue*; Jacobs, *White Mother*; Shah, *Contagious Divides*; Santiago-Valles, "'Higher' Womanhood."

97. Naval Government of Guam, *Annual Report of the Governor*, 1904; *Annual Report of the Governor*, 1905; "A Memory," 8. The Dyers envisioned these schools to help bring order

out of chaos and to preempt Native schoolchildren from "running wild in the streets." SHPD to Susie, December 12, 1904, 6, box 340.17.b, Dyer Papers.

98. SHPD to Susie, December 12, 1904, 6.

99. SHPD to Susie, December 12, 1904, 6.

100. SHPD to Susie, December 12, 1904, 6.

101. Ginzberg, *Women and the Work*, 68, 70.

102. SHPD to Susie, July 12, 1905, 55, box 340.17.b, Dyer Papers; SHPD to Susie, August 21, 1905, 59, box 340.17.b.

103. For specific references to Governor Dyer helping Susan, refer to SHPD to Susie, September 20, 1905, 62, box 340.17.b ; SHPD to Susie, November 20, 1905, 67, box 340.17.b.

104. "The Cry of the Little People" [from] "The American Women in Guam, Island of Guam," August 1, 1905 (Dångkolu na si yu'os ma'åse to Emelie Johnston for sharing a copy of this original circular); E. Johnston, "Medical Services."

105. SHPD to Susie, October 1904, 22, box 340.17.b, Dyer Papers.

106. Hattori, *Colonial Dis-Ease*, 126.

107. Joan W. Scot, "Experience"; Felski, *Gender of Modernity*; Ardis and Lewis, *Women's Experience of Modernity*.

108. SHPD to Susie, July 12, 1905, 55, box 340.17.b, Dyer Papers.

109. "Campaign to Eliminate," 53.

110. SHPD to Susie, July 12, 1905, 55, Dyer Papers.

111. SHPD to Susie, November 20, 1905, 67, box 340.17.b; "Address of Commodore George L. Dyer," 164.

112. "Number fifty-five: Deed of constitution of a Civil Society," October 20, 1905, box 340.25.a, Dyer Papers; EJD, Journal entry of February 27, 1909, container 1, folder: Diary 1909, Dorn Papers; EJD, Journal entries of January 21, January 24, March 24, and October 31, 1910, container 2, folder: Diary 1910, Dorn Papers; EJD to GLD, December 12, 1909, container 3, folder: 1907–1910, Dorn Papers.

113. Robert de Forest (hereafter RDF) to GLD, June 19, 1907, box 340.17.e, Dyer Papers; RDF to GLD, June 21, 1907, box 340.17.e; GLD to RDF, July 1, 1907, box 340.17.e (my emphasis).

114. Crocker, *Mrs. Russell Sage*, 150; Crocker, "His Absent Presence."

115. SHPD to Margaret Olivia Sage, May 2, 1915, box 94, folder 935, Russell Sage Foundation Papers, Rockefeller Archive Center, Sleepy Hollow, New York.

116. Williams, "Structures of Feeling."

117. SHPD to Susie, November 20, 1905, 68, box 340.17.b, Dyer Papers; Daisy to Edna, circa 1921, box 340.19.f.

118. Following Governor and Susan Dyer's departure and also their passing, others would commemorate Susan Dyer: *Guam News Letter* 1, no. 10, January 26, 1910, 1; "Am I My Brother's Keeper?," 26. For a special "tribute" to a "Great Woman" by an anonymous CHamoru of the Young Men's League, refer to "A Tribute," 7.

119. Rosa Perez to SHPD, November 20, 1905, box 340.17.d, Dyer Papers. I am grateful to Juanita Cabello for translating the original letter, written in Spanish.

120. Williams, "Structures of Feeling."

121. SHPD to Susie, August 21, 1905, 59, box 340.17.b, Dyer Papers.

234 Notes to Chapter Three

122. Jolly, "Colonizing Women."

123. Moreton-Robinson, *Talkin' Up*, 24. On how this history of white feminism resonates for Kānaka Maoli, refer to Trask, "Review," 474–75.

124. SHPD to Susie, July 12, 1905, 54, box 340.17.b, Dyer Papers.

125. Sallie Williams to SHPD, c. 1921, box 340.19.f, Dyer Papers; Weatherford, *Women in American Politics*, 25; Mould, "Did You Know?," 4. I am grateful to Kim Mould for sharing information about Susan Dyer and the Woman's Club of Winter Park (Florida).

126. Dorothy Dyer to SHPD, Between Guam and Manila, c. 1913, box 340.18.f, Dyer Papers.

127. Duarte to the Dyers, November 5, 1916, box 340.19.d, Dyer Papers.

128. Diaz, "Voyaging for Anti-Colonial Recovery."

Chapter Three

1. Agueda I. Johnston, "The Guam Flag," 1948, box 1, folder 32, Johnston Papers; Agueda Johnston, "History of the Guam Flag," folder: Flag and Seal of Guam, Nieves M. Flores Memorial Library, Guam Public Library

2. Stoler, *Carnal Knowledge*, 201.

3. Wexler, *Tender Violence*. On refusing the idea of the "innocent eye" for understanding the way colonial optics have shaped images of Māori women and have been deployed in the colonization of Aotearoa, refer to Erai, *Girl of New Zealand*.

4. Burnett and Marshall, *Foreign in a Domestic*; Sparrow, *Insular Cases*; Lanny Thompson, *Imperial Archipelago*.

5. Campbell, *Agitating Images*, xiii–xiv.

6. Rickard, "Sovereignty"; Raheja, *Reservation Reelism*. On "counter-archive" in the context of white women photographers and Indigenous communities, refer to Bernardin et al., *Trading Gazes*. Other discussions of visual sovereignty in the context of contemporary Native American art and photography are in Morris, *Shifting Grounds* and Bell, "Some Thoughts on 'Taking.'"

7. In addition to announcing the couple's marriage on March 25, 1911, the *Register* also shared the news that the couple was soon to relocate to their new home overseas in Cavite. "Personal Matters"; Allaback, *First American Women Architects*, 234; Christensen, "Helen Longyear Paul."

8. Simonsen, *Making Home Work*, 3–4.

9. "Guam" (April 1916), 8. American teachers like Paul were few and far between compared to the five hundred teachers who arrived on board the USS *Thomas* to the Philippines in 1901. For a discussion of the ship as a "vehicle of uplift" and the role of the Thomasites as missionaries, refer to Kramer, *Blood of Government*.

10. Naval Government of Guam, *Annual Report of the Governor*, 1918; "'Easiest Way,'" 20.

11. J. Griffith, "Do Some Work"; Caylor, "Promise Long Deferred."

12. "The Following Naval Station Orders"; "Guam Normal School" (August 1916).

13. Pye and Shea, *Navy Wife*. A similar code of conduct can be found in the history of British naval wives, as discussed in Lincoln, *Naval Wives and Mistresses*.

14. I am deliberately invoking the idea of the "telling object" and histories and museologies of Indigenous practices involving material culture, such as collecting, crafting, and curating.

Bal, "Telling Objects"; Racette, "My Grandmothers Loved"; Tone-Pah-Hote, *Crafting*; Robinson and Barnard, "'Thanks.'"

15. Mimeographed Copies Released to All Correspondence at CINCPAC, Guam, August (n.d.)—box 1, folder 32, The Guam Flag 1948, Johnston Papers.

16. DeLisle, "Civilizing the Guam Museum"; "Faninadahen Kosas Guåhan."

17. Farrell, *Liberation–1944*, 184.

18. T. Teaiwa, "Reading." Teaiwa attributes its initial coinage to the Native American scholar Louis Owens in "Reflections on Militourism." For an analysis of militourist constructions in Hawai'i and the Philippines, refer to V. Gonzales, *Securing Paradise*. For a decolonizing guide to militourist sites in Hawai'i, refer to Aikau and Gonzales, *DeTours*.

19. Braun, "Duty and Diversion," 650.

20. Braun, 650.

21. Dauser, "Tour of Duty," 949. Dauser, the first woman in the U.S. Navy to be promoted to captain, was the fifth superintendent (1939–45) of the U.S. Navy Nurse Corps.

22. Thomas, *Colonialism's Culture*.

23. Jolly, "From Point Venus," 100.

24. Clancy-Smith and Gouda, *Domesticating the Empire*, 5–6.

25. "Bulletin of the Massachusetts Institute of Technology," 17; John Case, personal communication, December 3, 2001, in *eye/land/people: Images of a Navy Wife in Guam, 1917–1990*, Isla Center for the Arts, Mangilåo, Guåhan, July 2003 (Humanities Guåhan).

26. Paul, *Landlooker*; Fountain, *Michigan Gold*; Berger, "Into the Wilderness."

27. "John Munro Longyear—Landlooker from Michigan."

28. Christensen, "Helen Longyear Paul." Helen Paul also helped establish a room at Dartmouth's Baker Library as a tribute to Carroll Paul (and father-son alumni of the Paul family). Hoefnagel, "Paul Room." On the emergence of twentieth century women's historic preservation work, refer to Dubrow and Goodman, *Restoring Women's History*.

29. Batchen, *Burning with Desire*, 56.

30. Batchen, 69.

31. Lydon, *Eye Contact*, 5.

32. Pratt, *Imperial Eyes*, 3.

33. Batchen, *Burning with Desire*, 72.

34. Sontag, *On Photography*, 108.

35. Miguel Salas, "Can the Guamanians Govern Themselves?," April 1919, folder: Original Compositions by Chamorro Students, Helen L. Paul Papers, Richard Flores Taitano Micronesian Area Research Center, University of Guam, Mangilåo Guam (hereafter Paul Papers).

36. Ana B. Charfauros to Margie Fraker, October 23, 1921, Letters from Agueda Johnston's Students, Margie Fraker Papers, Richard Flores Taitano Micronesian Area Research Center, University of Guam, Mangilåo Guam (hereafter Fraker Papers).

37. John Case, personal communication, December 3, 2001, in *eye/land/people: Images of a Navy Wife in Guam, 1917–1990*, Isla Center for the Arts, Mangilåo, Guåhan, July 2003 (Humanities Guåhan).

38. Beatrice Perez to Margie Fraker, January 9, 1922, Letters from Agueda Johnston's Students, Fraker Papers.

39. Beatrice Perez to Margie Fraker, March 2, 1923, Letters from Agueda Johnston's Students, Fraker Papers.

40. Thompson in Souder, *Daughters of the Island*, 49.

41. "Basketry, Embroidery and Lace-Making," 1; Naval Government of Guam, *Annual Report of the Governor*, 1918; "First Guam Industrial Fair," 1–2.

42. PSECC, *Hale'-ta: Hinasso'*, 28; PSECC, *Hale'-ta: I Ma Gobetna-ña Guam*, 75.

43. Wexler, *Tender Violence*, 133.

44. Wexler, 127.

45. Wexler, 7. One such photographer was Frances Benjamin Johnston. Johnston was commissioned in 1899 to photograph the *peaceful* assimilation of Native Americans and African Americans at the Hampton Normal and Agricultural Institute. Johnston also captured Admiral George Dewey and his crew aboard the flagship USS *Olympia* after the Battle of Manila Bay. On the deception and power of family photographs, refer to Hirsch, *Familial Gaze*. For another new woman's photography work among American Indian tribes, refer to Jensen and Patterson, *Travels with Frances Densmore*. An example of this gendered masking of violence in the Pacific is represented in U.S. nuclear testing in the Marshall Islands. The swimsuit itself, the bikini, created by a French designer in commemoration of the Allied victories, is another way that gender, sexualized and objectified in its "visibility," served to render "invisible" the atrocities in the lives of Bikini Islanders. Teaiwa, "Bikinis."

46. The drive for U.S. citizenship, which began in 1901, was first and foremost a CHamoru-led movement whose motives were critical of military governance under the U.S. Navy as discussed in Hofschneider, *Campaign*. For a history of the Guam Congress walkout of 1949, which led to the passage of the Organic Act of Guam, refer to Hattori, "Righting." An analysis of the citizenship movement as an expression of a local Indigenous elite desire to reconsolidate itself is in Stade, *Pacific Passages*.

47. Simon Sanchez, "Juan Kissed Carmen," n.d., folder: Original Compositions by Chamorro Students, Paul Papers.

48. Roediger, *Wages of Whiteness*, 99.

49. M. Miller, *Slaves to Fashion*, 11.

50. E. Crose, "A Navy Wife Remembers," 41, Edith Wilson Crose reminiscences (MSI 302) (1894–1923), box 17, folders 2–3, Naval Historical Collection Archives, U.S. Naval War College, Newport, Rhode Isand, Edith Wilson Crose Papers; Ngai, *Ugly Feelings*.

51. Naval Government of Guam, *Annual Report of the Governor*, 1932, 153; R. Underwood, "American Education," 135.

52. On the physicality of working-class men's labor and early twentieth-century fears of overcivilized head-over-hands work, refer to Chauncey, *Gay New York*, 112–13. On how U.S. capitalism under the navy reshaped CHamoru masculinity, including a discussion of the Catholic Church's fears of CHamoru expressions of manhood through organizations like the Young Men's League of Guam, refer to Viernes, *Negotiating Manhood*. My discussions of the dandy (and flaneur) are also informed by Benjamin, *Arcades Project*; Mrazek, *Engineers of Happy Land*; Landau and Kaspin, *Images and Empires*; and Parsons, *Streetwalking the Metropolis*. The links between dandyism and rowdyism and the manakhilo' and ilustrado class were informed by discussions with Vince Rafael during his visit with the Philippine Study Group in Ann Arbor, Michigan, in March 2002.

53. On anxieties of Native boys beating the military at its own game, in the context of Pacific Islander masculinities, refer to Diaz, "'Fight Boys.'" Elsewhere, Native Papuan men

were accused of becoming too "cheeky" when they beat white British men at cricket or came too close to emulating them in their display of fashion and intelligence. Inglis, *White Women's Protection Ordinance*.

54. Discussions of the 1931 Massie case in Honolulu involving the elite white American navy wife Thalia Massie are in Stannard, *Honor Killing*; Rosa, *Local Story*.

55. Similarly, American photographer Caroline Gurrey, in the early 1900s, focused on images of hybridized Polynesians in Hawai'i as a way of erasing Kānaka 'Ōiwi political struggles. Maxwell, *Colonial Photography and Exhibitions*, 219–20. On how racializing discourses of hybridity and whiteness justified settler colonial expropriation of Kānaka 'Ōiwi lands, refer to Arvin, *Possessing Polynesians*.

56. On the uneven balance between those who photographed and those who were photographed, and the nineteenth century scientific and aesthetic paradigms of what Americans were supposed to look like, refer to Smith, *American Archives*.

57. "Red Cross Vaudeville Show," 1–2. Refer also to "That Red Cross Vaudeville" and "Red Cross Vaudeville" (advertisement).

58. Punzalan, "Maria de los Santos y Castro"; Chapman, *Bonin Islanders*, 44–45; Cholmondeley, *History of the Bonin Islands*; Hawks, "Correspondence Touching the Bonin Islands," 305–6; "Who's Who in Guam: Mr. Henry Millinchamp." Maria de los Santos's first marriage was to the Genoese Matteo "Matthew" Mazarro (b. 1768), with whom she had two children.

59. Hezel, "Yankee Trader in Yap"; Hezel, *First Taint*; Hezel, *Strangers*; Madrid, *Beyond Distances*.

60. Allen, *Trans-Indigenous*. Just as one must analyze how colonial discourse might foreclose on Indigenous histories of travel and mobility, one must also examine the extent to which Indigenous mobilities become complicit with settler colonialism.

61. Pye and Shea, *Navy Wife*, 192. Lomawaima and McCarty, "Concluding Commentary."

62. Naval Government of Guam, Executive General Order No. 326, September 29, 1919, RG 80, box 484, 9351, General Records of the Department of the Navy, NARA. Gilmer's law prohibited whites—defined as "those not having Chamorro, Filipino, or Negro blood"—from marrying CHamorus or Filipinos.

63. "Executive General Order No. 243," 6.

64. Diaz, *Sacred Vessels*.

65. Rosaldo, "Imperialist Nostalgia"; Stewart, *On Longing*.

66. "First Guam Industrial Fair," 1–2.

67. "Address at Closing of Industrial Fair," July 7, 1918, box 7, folder 2, Roy Campbell Smith Papers, Naval Historical Collection Archives, U.S. Naval War College, Newport, R.I. (hereafter Smith Papers).

68. "Address at Closing of Industrial Fair."

69. Carmen Leon Guerrero, "What the Moon Has to Do with Chamorros," n.d., folder: Original Compositions by Chamorro Students, Paul Papers; Atanasio Perez, "Notes on Planting Rules," n.d., folder: CHamoru Customs, Paul Papers.

70. McKenna, *American Imperial Pastoral*.

71. Though the Guam Industrial Fair was established in 1917, it was not until 1919 that the first election for a Guam Fair Queen was held. The only other close-up in Paul's collection is a photograph of a woman (unnamed) stricken with gangosa. Out of respect for her family,

I have chosen not to include this photo. On the importance of naming and reclaiming a CHamoru past through photography in the context of the navy's policy and treatment of Hansen's disease on the island, refer to Hattori, "Remembering the Past."

72. "Guam Fair Queen," Photographs, Paul Papers; "Guam Industrial Fair 1919 [April 1919], 3"; "Guam Industrial Fair 1919 [June 1919]," 5.

73. Rosario E. Perez, untitled essay on the Guam Fair Queen, n.d., folder: Original Compositions by Chamorro Students, Paul Papers.

74. Carmen Leon Guerrero, "The Guam Fair and Its Queen," n.d., folder: Original Compositions by CHamoru Students, Paul Papers.

75. Baltazar Carbullido, "Election Contest for Queen of the Guam Industrial Fair," n.d., folder: Original Compositions by Chamorro Students, original essay, Paul Papers.

76. "Coronation of Josefina I.," 1.

77. Maria Ulloa, untitled essay on the Guam Fair Queen, n.d., folder: Original Compositions by Chamorro Students, original essay, Paul Papers.

78. Joaquin Torres, "Brief History," 185; PSECC, *Hale'-ta: I Manfåyi*. According to Torres, the Guam Militia evolved out of the Guam Cadets and, before that, the Rifle Club.

79. "Guam Cadets, Guam Militia," 16.

80. "Address at Closing of Industrial Fair."

81. Perez, "Guam Seal Means," folder: Guam Flag, Paul Carano Papers.

82. Perez, "Guam Seal Means."

83. "The Guam Flag," *The Tablero*.

84. A. Johnston, "History of the Guam Flag."

85. R. Smith, "Universal Military Training."

86. Bill No. 60, Fourteenth Guam Legislature. Mallo, "For Guam Seal, Flag," 6.

87. Mallo, "Flag Hearing Today," 3.

88. Mallo, "Residents Rally."

89. Mallo, "Residents Rally." Refer also to J. Miller, "The Flag," 3.

90. J. Miller, "The Flag," 3.

91. Lee, "Santos," 4.

92. Governor Bradley adopted the flag's seal as the "official" seal of the U.S. Naval Government of Guam. Order by Governor Willis W. Bradley, Jr., April 4, 1930, Willis Winter Bradley, Jr. Papers, Richard Flores Taitano Micronesian Area Research Center, University of Guam, Mangilao, Guam (hereafter Bradley Papers). In February 1992, Senator Gordon Mailloux of the twenty-first Guam Legislature introduced Bill No. 21 to adopt the flag as Guåhan's "official" flag and to establish protocols for it. "Mailloux Introduces New Flag," 7; Lee, "Mailloux Says," 4.

93. Lee, "Santos," 4.

94. J. Flores, "Francisco Feja"; Rindraty Celes, "Flags Figure in Identity Factor"; Resolution No. 308, Twenty-First Guam Legislature, March 13, 1992; Bernadita Camacho-Dungca, personal communication, June 15, 2001.

Chapter Four

1. "Guam Flag Raising Ceremonies," July 3, 1945, 2, folder 1943 (3 of 6), Correspondence Number 79, Johnston Papers.

2. "Guam Flag Raising Ceremonies," July 3, 1945, 3; Passos, "American Marianas" 54; Johnston and Cramlet, *Chamorrita as Gleaned*.

3. "Guam Flag Raising Ceremonies," July 3, 1945, 5–6; Sanchez, *Guahan Guam*, 288–89.

4. Lujan, "Sleeping Beauty"; R. Underwood, "Red, Whitewash and Blue"; Souder, "Psyche under Seige"; A. Santos, "United States Return Was Reoccupation"; Cecilia Perez, "Chamorro Re-Telling"; Diaz, "Deliberating Liberation Day"; K. Camacho, *Cultures of Commemoration*; Viernes, "Fanhasso"; Aguon, "The Fire"; Bevacqua, "These May"; Borja-Kicho'cho', "Re-Occupation Day." Refer also to Craig Perez's "malologue" entries, "from the legends of juan malo," in *from unincorporated territory [lukao]*. On the relationship between archives and collective memory in Guåhan, with specific attention to Manenggon, refer to Taitano, "Archives." Other scholarship challenging assimilationist narratives of Indigenous women includes: On Ella Deloria, Cotera, "All My Relatives," and Pexa, "Peoplehood Proclaimed" in *Translated Nation*, 183–220; and Ackley and Stanciu, *Laura Cornelius Kellogg*.

5. Johnston and Cramlet, *Chamorrita as Gleaned*, ii–iii. Johnston passed away in 1977 before her memoirs could be completed, and so they remain unpublished.

6. As a result of the 1975 covenant, which established the Northern Mariana Islands as a commonwealth of the United States, the Refaluwasch people (Carolinians), who migrated from Satawal (Yap, Federated States of Micronesia) to Saipan in the early nineteenth century, are now also considered Indigenous to the Marianas.

7. For a study of how CHamoru public memories of World War II developed in distinct and divergent ways in the Marianas, refer to Camacho, *Cultures of Commemoration*.

8. For a history of postwar militarization of Guåhan and the racialization and creation of a Filipino labor class, refer to A. Flores, "'No Walk in the Park.'"

9. Johnston and Cramlet, *Chamorrita as Gleaned*, 20.

10. Weinbaum et al., *Modern Girl*.

11. "Eulogy for Agueda Iglesias Johnston 1892–1977 from the Fourteenth Guam Legislature," January 6, 1978, box 1, Johnston Papers; Robert Underwood, personal communication, February 7, 2011.

12. "Eulogy."

13. Johnston and Cramlet, *Chamorrita as Gleaned*, 144.

14. Palomo and Borja, "Strength of Agueda." Reynolds, "These are Americans," 73; "Speaking of Pictures," 12; Phillips, "Queen Bee"; E. Johnston, *Saga of Agueda*; PSECC, *Hale'-ta I Manfåyi*; DeLisle, "Guamanian-Chamorro"; E. Flores, "Reclaiming the Suppressed."

15. For an analysis of the matlina as "othermother" in the context of the CHamoru story of Sirena, refer to Naholowa'a, "Beyond Matrifocality."

16. Johnston and Cramlet, *Chamorrita as Gleaned*, 134.

17. Johnston, "Governor E. J. Dorn," n.d., Chamorrita Notes, box 16, folder 38, Johnston Papers; Johnston and Cramlet, *Chamorrita as Gleaned*, 113. At the close of the Normal School's first term, the *Guam News Letter* posted final grades with Johnston (at 99.5 percent) at the top of her class of twenty-nine. "Guam Normal School," October 1916, 8.

18. Johnston, "To Speak English Like Tai," n.d., Chamorrita Notes, box 16, folder 82, Johnston Papers.

19. Governor Richard Leary's General Order No. 12 established compulsory education under the navy, thereby terminating religious instruction, and mandated that children attend schools, "unless excused . . . by competent authority for good reasons that interfere

with their attendance." Naval Government of Guam, General Order No. 12, January 22, 1900, RG 80, Box 383, 9351-10, General Records of the Department of the Navy, NARA. Later, Governor George Dyer issued General Order No. 80, changing the age limit to twelve. Naval Government of Guam, General Order No. 80, September 3, 1904, RG 80, Box 383, 9351-10, General Records of the Department of the Navy, NARA. Cramlet and Johnston, *Chamorrita as Gleaned*, 76, 78–79, 88–89.

20. Johnston and Cramlet, 39, 41. On life-changing and transformative possibilities of the låncho, refer to D. Sablan's autobiography, *Book of My Life*.

21. Hattori, "Colonialism, Capitalism and Nationalism"; R. Griffith, "From Island Colony," 93, 128.

22. Naval Government of Guam, General Order No. 4, August 25, 1899, RG 80, box 383, 9351-10, General Records of the Department of the Navy, NARA; General Order No. 19, May 14, 1900, RG 80, box 383, 9351-10, General Records of the Department of the Navy, NARA. As noted by William Safford, Leary's orders—in particular, his ban on the ringing of church bells four days after his prohibition of village fiestas—did not bode well with devout Catholics like the CHamoru matriarch Emilia Castro Anderson Millinchamp, who was married to the aforementioned Henry Millinchamp (refer to chapter 3). Si yu'os ma'åse to Larry Cunningham for sharing this story. Leon-Guerrero, *Year on the Island*, 242.

23. Johnston and Cramlet, *Chamorrita as Gleaned*, 109.

24. R. Underwood, "American Education"; Hezel, "Schools in Micronesia"; Del Priore, "Education on Guam," 17. For cautions against essentializing CHamoru experiences under Spanish colonialism, refer to Madrid, *Beyond Distances*.

25. Hezel, "Schools in Micronesia"; Del Priore, "Education on Guam."

26. Bassett, *Realms and Islands*, 137.

27. R. Underwood, "American Education," 145.

28. R. Underwood, 177.

29. Lomawaima and McCarty, *"To Remain an Indian,"* 168.

30. Hartman, *Scenes of Subjection*. Daily flag observances were codified in 1928 under Governor Lloyd Shapley as discussed in "Orders, Naval Government of Guam," 305.

31. Naval Government of Guam, *Annual Report of the Governor*, 1905, 15.

32. Naval Government of Guam, General Order No. 12.

33. Johnston and Cramlet, *Chamorrita as Gleaned*, 319–20.

34. Valedictory Address by Richard F. Taitano, March 31, 1937, box 1, folder 29, Johnston Papers; Naval Government of Guam, *Annual Report of the Governor*, 1907, 8.

35. R. Underwood, "American Education," 40, 151–53, 160–65. Among the other reasons American-style education did not take hold: prewar education often did not exceed primary schooling and was divided into half-days, with boys attending morning sessions and girls attending afternoon sessions; the school system involved a lockstep system of rote memory that required students to remember meaningless information often not retained; and CHamoru teachers had limited knowledge and understanding of American culture, especially since many of them were no more than ten years senior to their students. For a CHamoru short story about this harsh school system, focused on the rote memorizing of patriotic songs and verses, refer to M. Taitano, "Stars and Stripes," 68–69.

36. R. Underwood, "American Education," 374.

37. Schroeder, "Another View"; Naval Government of Guam, *Annual Report of the Governor of Guam*, 1904, 12; American naval governors of American Samoa—Captain William Crose (1910–1913) and his predecessor, Commander Edmund B. Underwood (1903–1905)—faced similar conundrums, as discussed in Fink, "United States Naval Policies," 123, 125.

38. Johnston and Cramlet, *Chamorrita as Gleaned*, 10, 102–3, 118, 134.

39. John Clifford, *History of the Pioneer*.

40. J. Palomo, *Recollections of Olden Days*, 39, 43. Palomo would later teach Romance languages at Ohio State University in the 1930s.

41. In 1907, 33 CHamorus (including Johnston, Carmen Leon Guerrero, and Ana M. Underwood) and roughly 10 Americans were employed as teachers. By 1919, there were 50 CHamorus and 9 Americans. By 1941, there were roughly 155 CHamoru teachers. Carano and Sanchez, *Complete History of Guam*, 411–12.

42. J. Sablan, *My Mental Odyssey*, 23–24, 30.

43. J. Sablan, 24.

44. Cramlet and Johnston, *Chamorrita as Gleaned*, 73.

45. Goeman, *Mark My Words*, 3. An earlier history that traces these tangible and intangible fences of Hagåtña can be found in the exhibit *I Kelat The Fence: Historical Perspectives on Guam's Changing Landscape*, presented by the T. Stell Newman Visitor Center, War in the Pacific National Historical Park, Sumay Hågat, Guåhan, March 29–May 10, 2012, Humanities Guåhan (curator: Christine DeLisle, co-curator: Monaeka Flores).

46. Johnston and Cramlet, *Chamorrita as Gleaned*, 72. In a similar feminist intellectual project, Denise Cruz argues that contrary to what assimilationist and colonial narratives on the Philippines convey, the modern Filipina was not simply a product of Spanish colonialism or U.S. benevolent assimilation but a subject-position deriving from political, economic, and cultural intersections among Filipino, Spanish, American, and Japanese subjects. D. Cruz, *Transpacific Femininities*.

47. Johnston, "The Agana River," n.d., Chamorrita Notes, box 16, folder 1, Johnston Papers.

48. Vizenor, *Survivance*.

49. Johnston and Cramlet, *Chamorrita as Gleaned*, 275–76.

50. "Mr. Jose Villagomez," n.d., 2, General, box 14, folder 14, Johnston Papers. Vicente Diaz argues that the Japanese occupation accomplished in two and a half years what the United States could not do in the preceding forty-one years—bind with religious zeal the CHamorus to the United States. Diaz, "Deliberating."

51. Johnston and Cramlet, *Chamorrita as Gleaned*, 102, 104–5.

52. "Who's Who in Guam: Rouston's School."

53. Johnston, "Teacher's Pay," n.d., box 16, folder 72, Johnston Papers; Johnston, "Teaching School," n.d., box 16, folder 73, Johnston Papers.

54. "That Red Cross Vaudeville," 1–2.

55. Johnston and Cramlet, *Chamorrita as Gleaned*, 102–3, 106, 118.

56. Though Garcia's account in Spanish has become something of a national treasure in Guam, it was Higgins's late-1930 English translations as they were serialized in *The Guam Recorder* that first provided CHamorus with a formal, coherent accounting of their past that differed from vernacular versions contained in legends, church rituals, and devotions like the nubena.

57. "Faninadahen Kosas Guåhan"; Sanchez *Guahan/Guam*, 144.

58. T. Palomo, *Island in Agony*.

59. Higgins to Johnston, October 5, 1944, box Johnston Correspondence, folder 1944, 1 of 2, Johnston Papers.

60. Reference to Johnston being on the list for a Quonset is found in "Quonset List," February 6, 1948, box 11, folder N-1(1), Records of the Naval Operating Forces, NARA, San Bruno, Calif.; "The Guam Teacher: Rear Admiral Charles A. Pownall, New Governor of Guam," n.d., box 1, folder P11: Education, Records of the Naval Operating Forces.

61. Johnston and Cramlet, *Chamorrita as Gleaned*, 177–78. Johnston, "First Permanent Waving in Guam," n.d., Chamorrita Notes, box 16, folder 36, Johnston Papers. On the making of American beauty shops, refer to Willett, *Permanent Waves*; Banks, *Hair Matters*; Peiss, *Hope in A Jar*.

62. A. Johnston, "First Permanent Waving in Guam," n.d., Chamorrita Notes, box 16, folder 36, Johnston Papers.

63. E. Johnston, *Saga of Agueda*.

64. Joseph Roach's work has been instrumental in illustrating the way that memories of a specific time and place become embodied in and through performances. Roach, *Cities of the Dead*. Refer also to Taylor, *Archive and the Repertoire*.

65. Johnston, "Shoe Gang," n.d., Chamorrita Notes, Johnston Papers; Johnston and Cramlet, *Chamorrita as Gleaned*, 89. Of these elite CHamoru women about the town (Hagåtña), Helen Paul wrote: "The ordinary native wears rawhide sandal or at best, a velvet-topped, heel-less chinele [sic]. When she becomes well-to-do, or when she marries an American, they put on shoes." "Shoe Gang," n.d., folder: CHamoru Customs, Paul Papers.

66. Johnston, "Teacher's Pay," n.d., Chamorrita Notes, Johnston Papers.

67. Johnston and Cramlet, *Chamorrita as Gleaned*, 89, 119.

68. Johnston and Cramlet, *Chamorrita as Gleaned*, 125; "Schmitt Herrero Wedding."

69. Johnston and Cramlet, *Chamorrita as Gleaned*, 325. Shirley P. Lehman to AJ, October 22, 1953, 7, box 1, folder 31, Johnston Papers; Dorothy Dyer to SHPD, Between Guam and Manila, c. 1913, box 340.18.f., Dyer Papers; "Wives' Wails," in *The Guam Recorder*. On the sexual economy of fur and its relationship to national identity and settler colonialism in Canada, refer to Nadeau, *Fur Nation*.

70. "Piti Swimming Parties," 8.

71. The "large and enthusiastic party" included Mr. and Mrs. R. C. Gibson, Mr. and Mrs. J. Schnabel, Master Arthur Raphael Schnabel, Mr. and Mrs. W. W. Rowley, Mr. and Mrs. H. W. Elliott, Mr. and Mrs. W. G. Johnston, Miss Antonia Martinez, the Misses Herrero, and the pay clerks Wilcox and Underwood. Most if not all of these couples consisted of American men married to CHamoru women, while the "misses" hailed from elite CHamoru families. *Guam News Letter* 2, no. 12 (June 1911): 2.

72. The reference here is to a picnic organized by the chief navy nurse Josephine Bowman at Dungca Beach in Apotgan. "The Nurse Corps Picnic," 3.

73. "School Children's Christmas," 2; Johnston and Cramlet, *Chamorrita as Gleaned*, 306. Some of these CHamoru women included Mrs. Duarte, Mrs. Underwood, Mrs. Elliott, Mrs. V. Herrero Jr., the "Misses" Magdalena Herrero, Ignacia Bordallo, and R. Eclavea. "Christmas Late on Guam."

74. Charles A. Pownall, Oral History 156, Naval Historical Collection Archives, U.S. Naval War College, Newport, R.I.

75. "Who's Who in Guam: Rouston's School," 13. Vivid accounts of CHamoru celebrations of Noche Buena (the good night) are in Agueda Johnston, "Christmas on Guam."

76. Johnston, "Entertainment for the Armed Forces," n.d., Chamorrita Notes, box 16, folder 34, Johnston Papers; Johnston and Cramlet, *Chamorrita as Gleaned*, 292–93.

77. Johnston, "The Show Kept Up ... ," n.d., Chamorrita Notes, box 16, folder, 34, Johnston Papers; Johnston, "Schools Reopened," n.d., Chamorrita Notes, box 16, folder 66, Johnston Papers.

78. Johnston, "Entertainment for the Armed Forces, U.S.," n.d., Chamorrita Notes, box 16, folder 34, Johnston Papers; Johnston, "Entertainment," n.d., Chamorrita Notes, box 16, folder 34, Johnston Papers; "Schools Reopened," n.d., Chamorrita Notes, box 16, folder 66, Johnston Papers; Johnston and Cramlet, *Chamorrita as Gleaned*, 292, 295.

79. Johnston, "Entertainment for the Armed Forces," n.d., Chamorrita Notes, box 16, folder 34, Johnston Papers.

80. On the appropriation and "whitening" of hula, refer to Desmond, *Staging Hula*; Trask, "'Lovely Hula Hands.'" I thank Hokulani Aikau for her suggestions on further readings of the appropriation of hula. On a semiotic read of the military in Hawaiʻi, refer to Turnbull and Ferguson, *Can You See?*

81. References to Native belles at the monthly Dorn Hall dance and Native belles performing during wartime are from Johnston and Cramlet, *Chamorrita as Gleaned*, 150, 293.

82. McManus, "When the Japs Held Guåhan," 8; Josephy, *Long and Short and Tall*.

83. McManus, "When the Japs Held Guåhan," 8.

84. W. Johnston, "There Were ... ."

85. In a similar study of gratitude within the context of U.S. empire, Mimi Thi Nguyen cautions that while the American "gift of freedom" grants genuine stories of love, hope, life, and happiness, it also renders the subjects of freedom, through the figure of the Vietnamese refugee, as incapable of escaping the colonial histories that deem Vietnamese "unfree" and thus remaining forever indebted to empire. Nguyen, *Gift of Freedom*.

86. Reynolds, "These Are Americans," 13. Johnston earned the title "first lady" because she was the principal of George Washington high school when the war broke out and returned to this post postwar. The linking of Guåhan's revered civic leader and maga'håga with President George Washington is especially troubling given his violent legacy of waging war and destruction on Haudenosaunee lands and peoples—a legacy that earned Washington the name, "town destroyer." Michelson, "'Hanödaga:yas.'"

87. Reynolds, 73. On CHamoru women's experiences during the Japanese occupation, refer to Howard, *Mariquita*; *Ai Hagå-hu* [Oh, My Daughter], full-length drama-tragedy by Peter R. Onedera, produced by the University Theater on March 6–8 and 12–15, 1997, at the University of Guam's Fine Arts Theater; and Higuchi, *Japanese Administration*.

88. "The Marianas."

89. "Glamour on Guam."

90. "Speaking of Pictures," 12.

91. "Speaking of Pictures," 12–13.

92. On the figure of the Mother-Goddess-Queen and Native women defined in terms of their relationship with white men, refer to R. Green, "Pocahontas Perplex." On Native women as intermediaries, refer to Jager, *Malinche, Pocahontas, and Sacagawea*.

93. C. Phillips, "Queen Bee"; T. O'Brien, "The Ghost of Guam."

94. For an analysis of the film, refer to Fojas, *Islands of Empire*.

95. Brawley and Dixon, *Hollywood's South Seas*.

96. Maxwell, *Colonial Photography and Exhibitions*; Beets, "Images of Maori Women"; Suaalii, "Deconstructing the 'Exotic' Female"; P. O'Brien, *Pacific Muse*.

97. Marubbio, *Killing the Indian Maiden*.

98. Imada, *Aloha Circuits*, 222, 63. Buszek, *Pin-up Grrrls*.

99. From 1946 to 1949, Captain Martin E. Carlson served as chief defense counsel for the Japanese during the U.S. Navy's war crimes trials held in Guåhan (between 1944 and 1949). For a study of the war crimes tribunal, refer to Camacho, *Sacred Men*.

100. "Eulogy for Agueda Iglesias Johnston 1892–1977 from the Fourteenth Guam Legislature," January 6, 1978, box 1, Johnston Papers.

101. Johnston and Cramlet, *Chamorrita as Gleaned*, 322, 329, 333.

102. Johnston and Cramlet, 335, 338; "The Guam Teacher: Rear Admiral Charles A. Pownall, New Governor of Guam," n.d., box 1, folder P11: Education, Records of the Naval Operating Forces.

103. Tun Kiko Suilo referred to Dorn as "Guam's Patriarch of Ex-Governors" when Dorn testified on behalf of a bill to confer U.S. citizenship to the CHamorus. United States. Congress. Senate. Committee on Territories and Insular Affairs. "Citizenship for Residents of Guam." The reference to the "pretty little teacher" is in Dorn's diary entry of January 27, 1910, container 1, folder: Diary 1910, Dorn Papers.

104. Johnston, "Governor EJ Dorn," n.d., Chamorrita Notes, box 16, folder 38, Johnston Papers.

105. Johnston, "Governor EJ Dorn."

106. Johnston, "Governor EJ Dorn."

107. Johnston, "Governor EJ Dorn."

108. Johnston and Cramlet, *Chamorrita as Gleaned*, 89, 111.

109. "Address by Mrs. Agueda Johnston to the People of Agaña during the 1939 Political Campaign" (appendix 2), in Laura Thompson, *Guam and Its People*, 284.

110. Higginbotham, *Righteous Discontent*.

111. "Address by Mrs. Agueda Johnston to the People of Agaña during the 1939 Political Campaign," in Laura Thompson, *Guam and Its People*.

112. Freire, *Pedagogy of the Oppressed*.

113. Gaonkar, *Alternative Modernities*.

114. Cogan, *We Fought the Navy*, 71.

115. *Guam Commonwealth Act: Hearing on H.R. 100, Before the Comm. on Resources*, 105th Cong., October 29, 1997.

116. Johnston and Cramlet, *Chamorrita as Gleaned*, 241. It is noteworthy that in her memoirs, this section is titled "Tweed," whereas in her Chamorrita Notes, this section is titled "Arrested for Tweed."

117. Johnston, "Mr. Jose Villagomez," n.d., General, box 14, folder 14, Johnston Papers; Johnston and Cramlet, *Chamorrita as Gleaned*, 241.

118. Tweed and Clark, *Robinson Crusoe*, 199, 287; W. Johnston, "There Were . . ."
119. Tweed and Clark, *Robinson Crusoe*, 199, 287.
120. Tweed and Clark, 199, 287.
121. Letter from J. C. to J., August 31, 1943, 1, box 14, folder 8, Johnston Papers.
122. W. Johnston, "No Flowers from My Camp."
123. Johnston, "Mr. Jose Villagomez," n.d., General, box 14, folder 14, Johnston Papers, Johnston and Cramlet, *Chamorrita as Gleaned*, 247.
124. Coulehan, *Portrait of Guam*.
125. Johnston, "Arrested for Tweed," n.d., Chamorrita Notes, box 16, folder 19, Johnston Papers.
126. Camacho, *Cultures of Commemoration*, 147, 153.
127. Coulehan, *Portrait of Guam*.
128. Coulehan.
129. Enstad, *Ladies of Labor*, 161.
130. Letter of August 10, 1944, to Admiral Chester W. Nimitz in Farrell, in *The Pictorial History of Guam*, 180–81. Nimitz, who later that year was promoted to fleet admiral, the highest rank in the U.S. Navy, was commander in chief, Pacific Fleet, and commander in chief, Pacific Ocean Areas. At a press conference, Admiral Nimitz read the letter before other military brass, including Admiral Raymond Spruance and U.S. Marine Corps general Alexander Vandegrift.
131. Farrell, 181.
132. Linda Taitano Reyes, personal communication, August 14, 2018; Mahone, "William G. Johnston."
133. Said, Culture and Imperialism.
134. Nimitz, "An Estimate of Enemy Intentions, 789.
135. Johnston and Cramlet, *Chamorrita as Gleaned*, 182; R. Taitano, interview by author, May 21, 1993.
136. M. Phillips, "Land," 7.
137. Johnston and Cramlet, *Chamorrita as Gleaned*, 319.
138. Johnston and Cramlet, 280–81, 284, 319.
139. Johnston and Cramlet, 282.
140. I was unable to locate anything from Johnston's Chamorrita Notes or other writings that suggested she would make this comparison between CHamorus and American Indians. I wonder then if it was Cramlet who made the comparison, especially given the prevalence of the romance/tragedy theme in non-Indian U.S. literature, as discussed in V. Deloria Jr., "Indians of the American Imagination," in *God is Red*. Comparing the legacies of colonialism between Pacific Islanders and American Indians can be problematic for several reasons, a discussion of which is beyond the scope of this book. Examples from the Pacific include Arvin, *Possessing Polynesians*, and Kauanui, *Paradoxes*. A discussion of the ways postcolonial writings relegate American Indians to a tragic, lamentable past in ways that foreclose on Indigenous futurities is in Byrd, *Transit*.
141. Johnston and Cramlet, *Chamorrita as Gleaned*, 310.
142. Johnston and Cramlet, 245, 39, 41.
143. Johnston and Cramlet, 39, 41.
144. Johnston and Cramlet, 141, 146. Santos-Bamba and Hattori, "The Mother's Tongue."

145. Johnston, "Governor E. J. Dorn," n.d., Chamorrita Notes, box 16, folder 38, Johnston Papers; Farewell Address of November 5, 1910, container 4, folder: Governor's Address & Farewell, Nov. 5, 1910," Dorn Papers.

146. Letter from AJ (Agueda Johnston) to Chamorro Studies Convention, January 3, 1977; Letter from Robert A. Underwood (hereafter RAU) to AJ, January 17, 1977; and Letter from RAU to AJ, February 1, 1977, all in Johnston, folder: Correspondence, 1977, Johnston Papers.

147. Coulehan, *Portrait of Guam*.

Conclusion

1. Clinton, "America's Pacific Century." As part of a bilateral agreement between the United States and Japan, the Department of Defense (DOD) in 2005 announced its plans to transfer roughly eight thousand American marines and their dependents from Okinawa (a prefecture of Japan) to Guåhan. This agreement of the post–9/11 era of global anti-terrorist militarization, which transpired largely because of mass Okinawan protests against U.S. bases, has sparked numerous CHamoru-led protests in Guåhan since DOD's announcement of the buildup and continues despite the scaledown to five thousand troops. On the military's plans to make the island a "power projection hub" and center for logistics and strategic planning, refer to Brook, "Looking for Friendly Overseas Base." On resistance to the buildup, refer to Aguon, *Fire This Time*; Aguon, *What We Bury at Night*; Natividad and Kirk, "Fortress Guam"; Natividad and Leon Guerrero, "Explosive Growth"; L. Camacho, "Resisting the Proposed Military Buildup"; Na'puti and Bevacqua, "Militarization and Resistance"; Frain, "Resisting Political," Kuper, "Living at the Tip of the Spear." For an analysis of the sexual economy of power and desire, which underpins militourism in Okinawa, refer to Ayano Ginoza, "R&R at the Intersection."

2. Statement of Ann Marie Arceo, Hearing of August 12, 2007, Tomhom, Guåhan; "Maga'haga: Part 1."

3. Refer also to Natividad, "The Question of Guåhan."

4. Testimony of Senator Judith T. Won Pat, August 13, 2007, in *The U.S. Military Buildup on Guam*; Testimony of Senator Hope Cristobal, August 13, 2007, in *The U.S. Military Buildup on Guam*. For an example of Indigenous feminist truthtelling in Dakota context, refer to Waziyatawin, *What Does Justice Look Like?*

5. Statement of Fanai Castro, Hearing of August 12, 2007, Tomhom, Guåhan, "Maga'haga Part 2." Refer also to Testimony of Senator Hope Cristobal, August 13, 2007, in *The U.S. Military Buildup on Guam*. On Fuetsan's demand for more accountability, refer to Cagurangan, "Women's Group."

6. Testimony of Admiral Bice, August 13, 2007, in *The U.S. Military Buildup on Guam*; Testimony of Governor Felix Camacho, May 1, 2008, in *The U.S. Military Buildup on Guam*. On the DOD and GovGuam "four pillars" partnership, as outlined by Under Secretary of the Navy Robert Work in collaboration with the administration of Governor Eddie Calvo (Governor Camacho's successor), refer to "Under SECNAV Releases Statement." On the "roadmap to realignment," refer to Chanlett-Avery, Mann, and Williams, "U.S. Military Presence." On the rhetoric of stewardship and conservation as a way of expanding the imperial footprint, refer to DeLisle, "Destination Chamorro Culture"; Perez, "Bluewashing." Other

groups that have protested the buildup include Our Islands are Sacred, Guam Coalition, We are Guåhan, and Nasion CHamoru.

7. Cachola and Bautista, "Women's Rights Groups." For Perez's inversion of "Isla de los Ladrones" (Ferdinand Magellan's misnomer for Guåhan) to "thieves of the island" and the continued colonial land grab under the United States following Spanish colonialization, refer to S. Perez, "Ladrones de la Isla." For a fuller treatment of competing discoures of security in Guåhan, refer to Kuper, "Kontra I Peligru."

8. Fojas, *Islands of Empire*.

9. Statement by Donna Christensen, August 13, 2007, in *The U.S. Military Buildup on Guam*. Congresswoman Donna Christensen was the first black woman and first black physician to be elected to Congress. Congresswoman Madeleine Bordallo, a longtime resident of Guåhan who moved to the island with her family from Minnesota in the late 1940s, gained prominence in the political arena as the wife (and former first lady) of the late CHamoru governor, Ricardo "Ricky" Bordallo.

10. Formal Transcripts of the Hearing, Guam Legislature, Maria Hernandez, Formal Testimony before the Guam Legislature, Public Hearing on Ritidian, Roundtable Guam—U.S. Military Buildup, Office of Senator Frank B. Aguon, Jr., October 5, 2017, as posted on Prutehi Litekyan—Save Ritidian, Facebook, October 6, 2017, https://www.facebook.com/saveritidian/videos/717973421732685/. The U.S. military's plans to use Tailålo' and lands around the CHamoru village of Litekyan came after an unsuccessful attempt to use the CHamoru village of Pågat, on the island's northeastern coast. On the struggle to protect Litekyan, refer to Na'puti, "Archipelagic Rhetoric." On the struggle and eventual lawsuit to save Pågat, refer to Na'puti and Bevacqua, "Militarization and Resistance."

11. Moreton-Robinson, *Talkin' Up*. 20. This incommensurability and disconnect is palpable when analyzing statements by descendants of Litekyan and those by Rear Admiral Shosana Chatfield. Statements by Lou Flores Bejado and Cathy Flores McCollum given in Terlaje, "Original Landowners." Roberto, "Rear admiral"; J. Borja, "Guam Chamber."

12. Delfin, "Chatfield Assumes Command."

13. McRrae, *Mothers of Massive Resistance*.

14. Taitano, "Ceremonies Performed." Refer also to Cristobal, "The Organization of Peoples for Indigenous Rights."

15. Terlaje, "Letter: Renew Commitment to the Inifresi."

16. T. Teaiwa, "Paul Gauguin's Noa Noa."

17. Antonio Babauta, personal communication, February 22, 2001.

Bibliography

Manuscript Collections

Ann Arbor, Mich.
  Clements Library
    Broadsides
Biddeford, Mass.
  Maine Women Writers Collection, University of New England
    Margaret Jane Mussey Sweat Papers
Greenville, N.C.
  East Carolina Manuscript Collection, J. Y. Joyner Library, East Carolina University
    George Leland Dyer Papers
Hagåtña, Guam
  Guam Museum
    Archivo de los Capuchinos de Navarra
  Nieves M. Flores Memorial Library, Guam Public Library
    Flag and Seal of Guam
Mangilao, Guam
  Richard Flores Taitano Micronesian Area Research Center, University of Guam
    Willis Winter Bradley Jr. Papers
    Paul Carano Papers
    Anita Elvidge Papers
    Margie Fraker Papers
    Agueda Iglesias Johnston Papers
    Frederick J. and Evelyn G. Nelson Papers
    Helen L. Paul Papers
Newport, R.I.
  Naval Historical Collection Archives, U.S. Naval War College
    Edith Wilson Crose Papers
    Admiral Chester W. Nimitz Papers
    Roy Campbell Smith Papers
San Bruno, Calif.
  National Archives and Records Administration
    Records of the Naval Operating Forces
Sleepy Hollow, N.Y.
  Rockefeller Archive Center
    Russell P. Sage Foundation Papers
Suitland, Md.
  National Anthropological Archives, Smithsonian Institution
    Laura Thompson Papers

Washington, D.C.
  Manuscripts Division, Library of Congress
    Edward John Dorn Papers
    John L. McCrea Papers
    Margaret Mead Papers
  National Archives and Records Administration
    Bureau of Medicine and Surgery
    General Records of the Department of the Navy

Oral History Collections

Newport, R.I.
  Naval Historical Collection Archives, U.S. Naval War College
    Charles A. Pownall, Oral History 156. Transcript of Interview by Etta-Belle Kitchen, April 11–12, 1970. U.S. Naval Institute, Oral History Program, Annapolis, Maryland.
    Wilma Leona Jackson, Oral History 210, Interview by Paul Stillwell, September 26, 1986, transcript 70. U.S. Naval Institute, Oral History Program, Annapolis, Maryland.

Oral History Interviews

Benavente, Elena Cruz. Interview by author. Dedidu, Guåhan, May 8, 1994.
Blas, Jose Ogo. Interview by author. Hågat, Guåhan, October 5, 1994.
Diego, Fred Paulino. Interview by Karen A. Cruz and author. Tomhom, Guåhan, June 1, 2000.
Duenas, Catalina Eustaquio. Interview with Karen A. Cruz and author, Tomhom, Guåhan, June 1, 2000.
Duenas, Emeteria Quichocho. Interview by author, Sinahåñña, Guåhan, June 13, 1994.
Guerrero, Olivia Siguenza. Interview by Karen A. Cruz and author, Tomhom, Guåhan, June 1, 2000.
Herrera, Joaquina Babauta. Interview by author. Hågat, Guåhan, April 2, 2001.
Herrera, Joaquina Babauta. Interview by author. Hågat, Guåhan, May 7, 1998.
Herrera, Joaquina Babauta. Interview by author. Hågat, Guåhan, June 12, 1998.
Herrera, Joaquina Babauta. Interview by Karen A. Cruz and author, Hågat, Guåhan, May 13, 2000.
Mesa, Rosalia Ulloa. Interview by author. Yigu, Guåhan, April 16, 1998.
Mesa, Rosalia Ulloa. Interview by author. Yigu, Guåhan, June 24, 1998.
Mesa, Rosalia Ulloa. Interview by Karen A. Cruz and author. Yigu, Guåhan, May 16, 2000.
Perez, Felix Taitano. Interview by Karen A. Cruz and author. Tomhom, Guåhan, June 1, 2000.
Rosario, Ana Mendiola. Interview by Karen A. Cruz and author. Barigåda, Guåhan, June 1, 2001.
Taitano, Richard Flores. Interview by author. Yigu, Guåhan, May 21, 1993.
Tenorio, Soledad Pablo. Interview by author. Sinahåñña, Guåhan, January 18, 1994.

Government Documents and Reports

Chanlett-Avery, Emma, Christopher T. Mann, and Joshua A. Williams. "U.S. Military Presence on Okinawa and Realignment to Guam." Congressional Research Service, April 9, 2017. https://www.bing.com/search?q=guam%20roadmap%20to%20 realignment&pc=cosp&ptag=G6C24AA37F7FBE93&form=CONBDF&conlogo =CT3210127.

Crose, Commander William M. *American Samoa: A General Report*. Washington, D.C.: Government Printing Office, 1927.

Guam Commonwealth Act: Hearing on H.R. 100, Before the Comm. on Resources, 105th Cong., October 29, 1997.

Guam Legislature. Bill No. 60, Fourteenth Guam Legislature. Introduced January 17, 1977.

———. Public Law 20-99 (Bill No. 249). Twentieth Guam Legislature, October 13, 1989.

———. Resolution No. 308. Twenty-First Guam Legislature, March 13, 1992.

Naval Government of Guam. *Annual Report of the Surgeon General*. United States Navy, Chief of the Bureau of Medicine and Surgery, Washington, D.C.: U.S. Government Printing Office, 1910.

———. *Annual Report of the Surgeon General*. United States Navy, Chief of the Bureau of Medicine and Surgery, Washington, D.C.: U.S. Government Printing Office, 1912.

———. *Annual Reports of the Naval Governor of Guam*. Washington, DC: U.S. Government Printing Office, 1901–1941.

Office of the Chief of Naval Operations. *U.S. Navy Report on Guam, 1898–1950*. Washington, D.C.: Department of the Navy, 1951.

Order to Adopt the Guam Seal as the Official Seal of the U.S. Naval Government of Guam, Governor Willis W. Bradley Jr., April 4, 1930, Willis Winter Bradley Jr. Papers, Richard Flores Taitano Micronesian Area Research Center, University of Guam.

United States Congress, Senate. Committee on Territories and Insular Affairs. *Citizenship for Residents of Guam: Hearings Before a Subcommittee of the Committee On Territories And Insular Affairs, United States Senate, First Session, On S. 1450, a Bill to Confer United States Citizenship Upon Certain Inhabitants of the Island of Guam And Extend the Naturalization Laws Thereto*. April 9, 10, 16, and June 9, 1937. Washington, D.C.: U.S Government Printing Office, 1937.

United States Navy Department. "Funeral Services: Dr. Norman T. McClean, (M.C), U.S.N. Retired" (press release). July 28, 1941, 1–2.

The U.S. Military Buildup on Guam and Challenges Facing the Community: Oversight Field Hearing before the Subcommittee on Insular Affairs of the Committee on Natural Resources, U.S. House of Representatives, 110th Congress, First Session, Monday, August 13, 2007, Mangilao, Guam. Washington, D.C.: U.S. Government Printing Office, 2008. https://www.govinfo.gov/content/pkg/CHRG-110hhrg37527/html/CHRG-110hhrg37527.htm.

Primary Sources

"Address of Commodore George L. Dyer." October 21, 1910. Report of the Twenty-Eighth Annual Meeting of the Lake Mohonk Conference of Friends of the Indian and Other

Dependent Peoples. Lake Mohonk, New York: Lake Mohonk Conference of Friends of the Indian and Other Dependent Peoples, 1910, 154–67.

"Albany Society Awakes." *New York Times*, January 13, 1895, 12.

"Albany Society Dines." *New York Times*, January 7, 1904, 9.

"Am I My Brother's Keeper?" *The Guam Recorder* 14, no. 6 (September 1937): 26.

Army and Navy Journal 45, no. 18, Whole Number 2315, August 15, 1908, 1384.

"Arrivals in Guam." *Guam News Letter* 5, no. 5 (November 1913): 14.

"Basketry, Embroidery and Lace-Making in the Public Schools." *Guam News Letter* 9, no. 5 (November 1917): 1.

Bennett, B. C. "The History and Development of the Navy Nurse Corps." *American Journal of Nursing* 25, no. 5 (May 1925): 356–60.

———. "History of Nursing in the Navy." *American Journal of Nursing* 28, no. 9 (September 1928): 883–89.

———. "The Nursing Service of Guam." *The Guam Recorder* 2 (October 1925): 198–99.

Bowman, J. Beatrice. "The Navy Nurse Corps and its Relations to the Advancement of Nursing Education." *U.S. Naval Medical Bulletin*, 20 (November 1924): 686–91.

Braun, Frederica. "Duty and Diversion in Guam." *American Journal of Nursing* 18, no. 8 (May 1918): 650–52.

Brooks, Elsie. "Maria Roberto: A Further Tribute." *U.S. Naval Medical Bulletin* 23, nos. 3/4 (September–October 1925): 283–84.

"Bulletin of the Massachusetts Institute of Technology." *President's Report* 49, no. 2 (1914): 69

"Business in the Susana Pharmacy." *Guam News Letter* 6, no. 12 (June 1915): 10.

"By the U.S.A. Thomas." *Guam News Letter* 2, no. 9 (March 1916): 4.

Celes, Rindraty. "Flags Figure in Identity Factor." *Pacific Daily News*, February 25, 1992, 3.

"The Charity Fair." *Guam News Letter* 6, no. 6 (December 1914): 10.

"Christmas Late on Guam." *New York Times*, January 3, 1911.

Clifford, John H. *History of the Pioneer Marine Battalion at Guam, L. I., 1899 and the Campaign in Samar, P. I., 1901*. Portsmouth, N.H.: Chronicle Job, 1914.

"Commandant Makes Report: Naval Governor of Guam Tells of Conditions on the Island." *Los Angeles Herald*, December 18, 1904.

"Conclusions Reached by Concession Holders: First Guam Industrial Fair, Red Cross Concession." *Guam News Letter* 9, no. 1 (July 1917): 21.

"Coronation of Josefina I., Queen of the Guam Industrial Fair." *Guam News Letter* 7, no. 1 (July 1919): 1–4.

Dauser, Sue S. "A Tour of Duty in Guam and the Philippines." *U.S. Naval Medical Bulletin* 26 (October 1928): 948–55.

"Department of Red Cross Nursing." *American Journal of Nursing* 29, no. 5 (May 1929): 595–99.

Dos Passos, John. "The American Marianas: Their Battle Scars Slowly Healing, Guam and Saipan Become Great Bases on the Tokyo Road." *Life*, May 21, 1945, 53–58.

"'The Easiest Way': 'Captain' Barlett Shows Civil Engineer That Grade-Less Route from Inarajan to Ordot." *Guam News Letter* 9, no. 2 (August 1917): 20.

"Executive General Order and Notices." *Guam News Letter* 11, no. 4 (August 1920): 10.

"Executive General Order No. 243, July 1, 1917." *Guam News Letter* 9, no. 1 (July 1917): 6.

"First Guam Industrial Fair—1917." *Guam News Letter* 9, no. 1 (July 1917): 1–2.
"The Following Naval Station Orders and Executive Special Orders Were Issued since the Last Issue of the News Letter (Insert), Executive Special Order No. 37, July 22, 1916." *Guam News Letter* 8, no. 2 (August 1916): 12d.
"Glamour on Guam." *Pacific Leatherneck*, June 1, 1945, 16–17.
"Go to the Susana Pharmacy for Ice Cream Soda and Sundries" (advertisment). *Guam News Letter* 5, no. 9 (March 1914): 12.
"Guam." *Guam News Letter* 8, no. 2 (April 1916): 8.
"Guam Cadets, Guam Militia." *Guam News Letter* 8, no. 8 (February 1917): 16.
"Guam Flag." *Guam News Letter* 9, no. 2 (August 1917): 4.
"The Guam Flag." *The Tablero* 1, no. 10 (March 13, 1968): 1.
"Guam Industrial Fair 1919." *Guam News Letter* 10, no. 10, April 1919: 3.
"Guam Industrial Fair 1919." *Guam News Letter* 10, no. 12, June 1919: 5.
Guam News Letter 1, no. 10 (January 26, 1910): 1.
Guam News Letter 2, no. 12 (June 1911): 1–6.
Guam News Letter 3, nos. 3 and 4 (September–October 1911): 2.
Guam News Letter 4, no. 5 (November 1912): 5.
Guam News Letter 7, no. 8 (February 1916): 4.
"Guam Normal School." *Guam News Letter* 8, no. 2 (August 1916): 3–4.
"Guam Normal School." *Guam News Letter* 8, no. 4 (October 1916): 8.
The Guam Recorder 11, no. 5 (October 1938): 1.
"Guam under the United States." *Guam News Letter* 3, no. 11 (August 1911): 6.
Hartwell, Laura. "Impressions of Samoa." *American Journal of Nursing* 23, no. 5 (February 1923): 397–400.
Hawks, Francis L. "Correspondence Touching the Bonin Islands." In *Narrative of the Expedition of an American Squadron to the China Seas and Japan, Performed in the Years 1852, 1853, and 1854 under the Command of Commodore M. C. Perry, United States Navy*. Washington, D. C.: Beverly Tucker, Senate Printer, 1856.
Higbee, Lenah S. "Letters from Navy Nurses." *American Journal of Nursing* 17, no. 3 (December 1916): 248–49.
Jackson, [Wilma] Leona. "I Was on Guam." *American Journal of Nursing* 42, no. 11 (November 1942): 124–26.
Johnson, L[ucius] W. "United States Naval Hospital on the Island of Guam." *The Modern Hospital* 8, no. 1 (January 1917): 16–20.
Johnson, Lucius W. "Guam—before December, 1941." *United States Naval Institute Proceedings* 68, no. 473 (July 1942): 991–98.
Johnston, Agueda Iglesias, and Clyde Myron Cramlet. "Chamorrita as Gleaned from Memorias de una Chamorrita of Agueda Iglesias Johnston." Unpublished Manuscript.
Johnston, William G. "'No Flowers from My Camp, No. 3 Yet.'" The Johnston Diaries (1941–43), Part 4 of 4, *Pacific Daily News*, July 21, 2005. http://content-static.guampdn.com/guampublishing/special-sections/liberation2005/diary4.htm.
———. "'There Were . . . No Fortifications on Guam.'" The Johnston Diaries (1941–43), Part 1 of 4, *Pacific Daily News*, July 21, 2005. http://content-static.guampdn.com/guampublishing/special-sections/liberation2005/diary1.htm.

Knight, Della V. "Maria Roberta: A Tribute." *U.S. Naval Medical Bulletin* 17 (September 1922): 515–18.
———. "Maria Roberto." *U.S. Naval Medical Bulletin* 23, nos. 3/4 (September–October 1925): 281–83.
Lee, Laura. "Mailloux Says Guam Needs Flag, Protocol Law." *The Tribune*, February 21, 1992, 4.
———. "Santos: Guam Needs Chamorro Designed Flag." *The Tribune*, February 20, 1992, 4.
L[eonhardt], E[lisabeth] M. "Letters from Navy Nurses." *American Journal of Nursing* 14, no. 2 (November 1913): 126–29.
———. "Letters from Navy Nurses." *American Journal of Nursing* 14, no. 4 (January 1914): 295–96.
———. "Letters from Navy Nurses." *American Journal of Nursing* 15, no. 2 (November 1914): 151–52.
———. "Letters from Navy Nurses." *American Journal of Nursing* 15, no. 7 (April 1915): 595–97.
———. "Letters from Navy Nurses III." *American Journal of Nursing* 14, no. 8 (May 1914): 655–56.
"A Little Civic Pride Please." *The Guam Recorder* 5, no. 5 (August 1928): 100.
"Mailloux Introduces New Flag Legislation." *The Tribune*, February 19, 1992, 7.
Mallo, Josephine. "Flag Hearing Today: He Wants to Find Guam's Betsy Ross." *Pacific Daily News*, March 14, 1977, 3.
———. "For Guam Seal, Flag: Senators Want New Design." *Pacific Daily News*, March 8, 1977, 6.
———. "Residents Rally around the Flag." *Pacific Daily News*, March 15, 1977, 4.
"The Marianas." *Yank, the Army Weekly* 4, no. 10 (August 24, 1945): 8–13.
McManus, Sergeant Larry. "Pacific Liberation: The People of Guam Found They No Longer Had to Bow to Anyone When the Americans Freed Their Island from Co-Prosperity." *Yank, the Army Weekly*, September 22, 1944, 8–9.
"Members of Crew of USS Saturn Give Vaudeville Show in Dorn Hall." *Guam News Letter* 10, no. 8 (February 1919): 18.
"A Memory." *The Guam Recorder* 1, no. 3 (May 1924): 8.
Miller, Judy J. "The Flag: Along with Sex and Religion, You Just Don't Talk about It." *Pacific Daily News*, April 19, 1977, 3.
N., J. L. "The Susana Hospital." *Guam News Letter* 6, no. 6 (December 1914): 1–3.
"The Native Nurse Corps," *The Guam Recorder* 14, no. 6 (September 1937): 27, 42.
"Naval Hospital Notes." *Guam News Letter* 7, no. 11 (January 1916): 15.
Nelson, Captain Frederick J. "Lieutenant William E. Safford, Guam's First Lieutenant Governor." *U.S. Naval Institute Proceedings* 78, no. 8 (August 1952): 594.
"The New Hospital Buildings for Guam." *Guam News Letter* 1, no. 11 (February 1910): 1.
"News and Comment," *Army and Navy Register*, December 28, 1907, 5.
"News of Guam." *Army and Navy Journal*, June 20, 1908, 1172.
Nimitz, Admiral Chester. "An Estimate of Enemy Intentions, Month of August—1942." Command Summary of Fleet Admiral Chester W. Nimitz, USN. *Nimitz "Graybook,"* December 7, 1941–August 31, 1945, Vol. 1 of 8. Newport, Rhode Island: United States Naval War College. American Naval Records Society. http://www.ibiblio.org/anrs/graybook.html.

"Notes of Guam." *Army and Navy Journal*, July 18, 1908, 1277.
"The Nurse Corps Picnic." *Guam News Letter* 7, no. 12 (June 1916): 3.
O'Brien, Tom. "The Ghost of Guam." *Yank, the Army Weekly* 3, no. 12 (September 8, 1944): 7–8.
"Opening Susana Diet Kitchen." *Guam News Letter* 9, no. 2 (August 1917): 21–23.
"Orders, Naval Government of Guam." *The Guam Recorder* 4, no. 12 (March 1928): 3.
Perry, Dorothy Tardy. "The Governor Calls on the Hospital." *The Guam Recorder* 16, no. 9 (December 1939): 364–66, 390–91.
"Personal Matters." *Army and Navy Register* 49, no. 1632 (April 1, 1911): 17.
Phillips, Coles. "The Queen Bee of Guam." *The Elks Magazine*, September 1945, 8–9, 40–41.
"Piti Swimming Parties." *Guam News Letter* 7, no. 5 (November 1915): 8.
Potter, Jane Grey. "A Lass Who Loved a Sailor." *Scribners Magazine* 67 (January–June 1920): 603–7.
"Pretty Girls, Jazz Music, Clever Skits Coming in Red Cross Vaudeville," *Guam News Letter* 10, no. 6 (December 1918): 21.
"Red Cross Nursing and the Navy." *American Journal of Nursing* 40, no. 9 (September 1940): 981–84.
"Red Cross Vaudeville" (advertisement). *Guam News Letter* 10, no. 6 (December 1918): 21.
"Red Cross Vaudeville Show at Dorn Hall." *Guam News Letter* 10, no. 7 (January 1919): 1–2.
"Red Cross Work." *Guam News Letter* 9, no. 1 (July 1917): 26.
"Red Cross Workers in Guam." *The Guam Recorder* 15, no. 8 (November 1938): 12.
Reed, E. U. "Health Notes." *The Guam Recorder* 1, no. 1 (March 1924): 9.
"Rehabilitation School Turns Out Gift Items." *Guam Daily News*, December 26, 1961, 8.
Reynolds, Quentin. "These Are Americans." *Collier's*, May 19, 1945, 13, 73–74.
Safford, Lieutenant William E. Address. "Addresses Delivered and Papers Read before the District of Columbia Society at the Monthly Meetings between February 22, 1911, and February 22, 1912." District of Columbia Society, Sons of the American Revolution, Washington, D.C., March 12, 1912, 56–57.
"Schmitt Herrero Wedding." *Guam News Letter* 7, no. 6 (December 1915): 4.
"The School Children's Christmas." *Guam News Letter* 4, no. 5 (November 1912): 2.
Schroeder, Seaton. "Another View of Guam." *Booklovers Magazine*, May 1905, 717–19.
Seaton, Oren Andrew, ed. *The Seaton Family, with Genealogy and Biographies*. Topeka, Kansas: Crane & Co., 1906.
Smith, Roy C. "Universal Military Training." *U.S. Naval Institute Proceedings* 44, no. 9 (September 1918): 1987–93.
"Speaking of Pictures . . . Marines Find Pin-ups and Glamour on Guam." *Life*, June 18, 1945, 12–14.
"Susana Hospital." *Guam News Letter* 8, no. 4 (October 1916): 2–3.
"The Susana Hospital Association." *The Guam Recorder* (May 1924): 7.
"Susana Hospital Needs Help." *The Guam Recorder* 3, no. 12, (December 1936): 4–5.
Sweat, Margaret Jane Mussey. "Annals of the Cobweb Club." Washington, D.C., 1890. https://dune.une.edu/mjms_cobweb/1.
"That Red Cross Vaudeville." *Guam News Letter* 9, no. 4 (October 1917): 1–2.
Torres, Joaquin. "Brief History of the Guam Militia." *The Guam Recorder* 9, no. 11 (February 1933): 185.

Torres, Jose C. "Following the Flag." *The Guam Recorder* 2, no. 16 (June 1925): 122.

"Transport Day." *Guam News Letter* 7, no. 6 (June 1915): 7.

"A Tribute: By a Young Men's Leaguer." *The Guam Recorder* 1, no. 3 (May 1924): 7.

Underwood, Gene. "Uncle Sam in Samoa—a Woman's Point of View." *Independent*, December 1, 1904, 1253.

"Uniform Requirements: Navy Nurse Corps 1925." *Navy Medicine*, January–February 2000, 12.

"Wanted: American Farmers for Guam." *The Guam Recorder* 5, no. 4 (July 1928): 88.

Wead, Carrie B. "The Lighting of the Seven Candles." *American Journal of Nursing* 26, no. 12 (December 1926): 933–34.

"Who's Who in Guam: Mr. Henry Millinchamp." *The Guam Recorder* 14, no. 5 (August 1937), 9.

"Who's Who in Guam: Routson's School." *The Guam Recorder* 14, no. 7 (October 1937): 13.

"Why Not Try a Dish of Our Delicious Ice Cream?" (advertisement). *Guam News Letter* 5, no. 12 (June 1914): 12.

Wilbur, George W. "Florence Nightingales of Mid-Pacific Attend School of Nursing on Guam." *Navy News*, October 19, 1947, 4.

"Wives' Wails." *The Guam Recorder* 17, no. 12 (March 1941), 505.

"Woman's Section." *The Guam Recorder* 1, no. 5 (July 1924): 23.

"Woman's Section." *The Guam Recorder* 1, no. 6 (August 1924): 34.

Workman, Hannah M. "Native Nurses in Guam." *U.S. Naval Medical Bulletin* 28, no. 1 (January 1930): 127–28.

Secondary Sources

Ackley, Kristina, and Cristina Stanciu, eds. *Laura Cornelius Kellogg: Our Democracy and the American Indian and Other Works*. Syracuse, NY: Syracuse University Press, 2015.

Aguon, Julian. *The Fire This Time: Essays on Life under U.S. Occupation*. Tokyo: Blue Ocean Press, 2006.

———. *What We Bury at Night: Disposable Humanity*. Tokyo: Blue Ocean Press, 2008.

Aikau, Hokulani K. *A Chosen People, a Promised Land: Mormonism and Race in Hawai'i*. Minneapolis: University of Minnesota Press, 2012.

Aikau, Hokulani K., and Vernadette Vicuña Gonzales, eds. *DeTours: A Decolonial Guide to Hawai'i*. Durham, N.C.: Duke University Press, 2019.

Allaback, Sarah. *The First American Women Architects*. Champaign: University of Illinois Press, 2008.

Allen, Chadwick. *Trans-indigenous: Methodologies for Global Native Literary Studies*. Minneapolis: University of Minnesota Press, 2012.

Alli, Alia. "Susan H. Dyer (1880–1922): Music Faculty." Olin Library Archives and Special Collections, Rollins College, Winter Park, Fla. Accessed March 3, 2018. https://lib.rollins.edu/olin/oldsite/archives/golden/Dyer.htm.

Althusser, Louis. "Ideology and Ideological State Apparatuses (Notes Toward an Investigation)." In *Media and Cultural Studies: Key Works*, edited by Meenakshi Gigi Durham and Douglas M. Kellner, 294–304. Malden, Mass.: Blackwell, 1998.

Amos, Valerie, and Pratibha Parmar. "Challenging Imperial Feminism." *Feminist Review* 17, no. 1 (1984): 3–19.
Anderson, Kim. *Life Stages and Native Women: Memory, Teachings and Story Medicine.* Winnipeg: University of Manitoba Press, 2011.
Anderson, Sue, Jaimee Hamilton, and Lorina L. Barker. "Yarning up Oral History: An Indigenous Feminist Analysis." In *Beyond Women's Words: The Personal, Political, and Ethical Challenges of Doing Feminist Oral History*, edited by Katrina Srigley, Stacey Zembrzycki, and Franca Iacovetta, 170–83. Oxford: Oxford University Press, 2018.
Anderson, Warwick. *Colonial Pathologies: American Tropical Medicine, Race, and Hygiene in the Philippines.* Durham, N.C.: Duke University Press, 2006.
Anzaldúa, Gloria. *Borderlands / La Frontera: The New Mestiza.* San Francisco: Spinsters / Aunt Lute, 1987.
Ardis, Ann L., and Leslie W. Lewis, eds. *Women's Experience of Modernity, 1875–1945.* Baltimore: Johns Hopkins University Press, 2003.
Arista, Noelani. *The Kingdom and the Republic: Sovereign Hawaiʻi and the Early United States.* Philadelphia: University of Pennsylvania Press, 2018.
Arvin, Maile. *Possessing Polynesians: The Science of Settler Colonial Whiteness in Hawaiʻi and Oceania.* Durham, N.C.: Duke University Press, 2019.
Arvin, Maile, Eve Tuck, and Angie Morrill. "Decolonizing Feminism: Challenging Connections between Settler Colonialism and Heteropatriarchy." *Feminist Formations* 25, no. 1 (Spring 2013): 8–34.
Atienza de Frutos, David, and Alexandre Coello de la Rosa. "Death Rituals and Identity in Contemporary Guam (Mariana Islands)." *Journal of Pacific History* 47, no. 4 (2012): 459–73.
Bal, Mieke. "Telling Objects: A Narrative Perspective on Collecting." In *The Cultures of Collecting*, edited by John Elsner and Roger Cardinal, 97–115. London: Reaktion Books, 1994.
Ballantyne, Tony, and Antoinette Burton, eds. *Moving Subjects: Gender, Mobility, and Intimacy in an Age of Global Empire.* Champaign: University of Illinois Press, 2009.
Banks, Ingrid. *Hair Matters: Beauty, Power, and Black Women's Consciousness.* New York: New York University Press, 2000.
Barclay, Lesley, Fulisia Aiavao, Jennifer Fenwick, and Kaisarina Tooloa Papua, eds., *Midwives' Tales: Stories of Traditional & Professional Birthing in Samoa.* Nashville: Vanderbilt University Press, 2005.
Bardwell-Jones, Celia T. "Placental Ethics: Addressing Colonial Legacies and Imagining Culturally Safe Responses to Health Care in Hawaiʻi." *The Pluralist* 13, no. 1 (Spring 2018): 97–114.
Barrett, W. Scott, and Walter S. Ferenz. "Peacetime Martial Law in Guam." *California Law Review* 48, no. 1 (March 1060): 1–30.
Bashford, Alison. "Domestic Scientists: Modernity, Gender, and the Negotiation of Science in Australian Nursing, 1880–1910." *Journal of Women's History* 12, no. 2 (2000): 127–46.
———. *Purity and Pollution: Gender, Embodiment and Victorian Medicine.* London: Palgrave McMillan, 1998.
Bassett, Marnie. *Realms and Islands: The World Voyage of Rose Freycinet, 1817–1820.* London: Oxford University Press, 1962.

Basso, Keith H. *Wisdom Sits in Places: Landscape and Language among the Western Apache.* Albuquerque: University of New Mexico Press, 1996.

Batchen, Geoffrey. *Burning with Desire: The Conception of Photography.* 2nd ed. Cambridge, Mass.: Massachusetts Institute of Technology Press, 1999.

Bederman, Gail. *Manliness and Civilization: A Cultural History of Gender and Race in the United States, 1880–1917.* Chicago: University of Chicago Press, 1995.

Beebe, Kathryne, Angela Davis, and Kathryn Gleadle. "Introduction: Space, Place and Gendered Identities Feminist History and the Spatial Turn." In *Space, Place and Gendered Identities*, edited by Kathryne Beebe and Angela Davis, 1–10. London: Routledge, 2015.

Beets, Jacqui Sutton. "Images of Maori Women in New Zealand Postcards after 1900." In *Bitter Sweet*, 17–32. Dunedin, New Zealand: University of Otago Press, 2000.

Bell, Morgan F. "Some Thoughts on 'Taking' Pictures: Imaging 'Indians' and the Counter-Narratives of Visual Sovereignty." *Great Plains Quarterly* 31, no. 2 (Spring 2011): 85–104.

Benjamin, Walter. *The Arcades Project.* Translated by Howard Eiland and Kevin McLaughlin. Cambridge, Mass.: Harvard University Press, 1999.

Berger, Adam. "Into the Wilderness with J. M. Longyear," *Mining Journal*, May 24, 2018. https://www.miningjournal.net/news/superior_history/2018/05/into-the-wilderness-with-j-m-longyear/.

Bernardin, Susan, Melody Graulich, Lisa MacFarlane, and Nicole Tonkovich. *Trading Gazes: Euro-American Women Photographers, 1880–1940.* New Brunswick, N.J.: Rutgers University Press, 2003.

Bevacqua, Michael Lujan. "Chamorros, Ghosts, Non-voting Delegates: GUAM! Where the Production of America's Sovereignty Begins." PhD diss., University of California, San Diego, 2010.

———. "The Exceptional Life and Death of a Chamorro Soldier: Tracing the Militarization of Desire in Guam." In *Militarized Currents: Toward a Decolonized Future in Asia and the Pacific*, edited by Setsu Shigematsu and Keith L. Camacho, 33–62. Minneapolis: University of Minnesota Press, 2010.

———. "My Island Is One Big American Footnote." In *Indigenous Literatures from Micronesia*, edited by Evelyn Flores and Emelihter Kihleng, 102–4. Honolulu: University of Hawai'i Press, 2019.

———. "These May or May Not Be Americans: The Patriotic Myth and the Hijacking of Chamorro History on Guam." MA thesis, University of Guam, 2005.

Bevacqua, Michael Lujan, and Isa Kelley Bowman. "Histories of Wonder, Futures of Wonder: Chamorro Activist Identity, Community, and Leadership in the 'Legend of Gadao' and 'The Women Who Saved Guåhan from a Giant Fish.'" *Marvels and Tales* 30, no. 1 (2016): 70–89.

Bhabha, Homi K. *The Location of Culture.* New York: Routledge, 1994.

Blair, Karen J. *The Clubwoman as Feminist: True Womanhood Redefined, 1868–1914.* New York: Holmes & Meier, 1980.

Bondi, Liz, and Joyce Davidson. "Situating Gender." In *A Companion to Feminist Geography*, edited by Lise Nelson and Joni Seager, 15–31. Oxford, Blackwell, 2005.

Bordallo, Audrey. "The Nurses." *Pacific Profile* 3, no. 4 (May 1965): 16–19.

Borja, John. "Guam Chamber of Commerce: Buildup Will Give Much-Needed Economic Boost." *Pacific Daily News*, October 6, 2017.

Borja-Kicho'cho', Kisha. "Re-Occupation Day (a.k.a. 'Liberation Day')." In *I Kareran I Palåbran Måmi: The Journey of Our Words*, by Anghet Hoppe-Cruz and Kisha Borja-Kicho'cho', 181. MA Portfolio Project, Center for Pacific Islands Studies, University of Hawai'i, August 2010. https://scholarspace.manoa.hawaii.edu/bitstream/10125/24267/Hoppe-Cruz_Borja_2010_r.pdf.

Brant, Jennifer. "Rebirth and Renewal: Finding Empowerment through Indigenous Women's Literature." In Lavell-Harvard and Anderson, *Mothers of the Nations*, 207–28.

Brawley, Sean, and Chris Dixon. *Hollywood's South Seas and the Pacific War: Searching for Dorothy Lamour*. New York: Palgrave McMillan, 2012.

Brewer, Carolyn. *Shamanism, Catholicism and Gender Relations in Colonial Philippines 1521–1685*. Aldershot, U.K.: Ashgate, 2004.

Briggs, Laura. *Reproducing Empire: Race, Sex, Science, and U.S. Imperialism in Puerto Rico*. Berkeley: University of California Press, 2002.

Brook, James. "Looking for Friendly Overseas Base, Pentagon Finds It Already Has One." *New York Times*, April 7, 2004.

Bruyneel, Kevin. *The Third Space of Sovereignty: The Postcolonial Politics of U.S.-Indigenous Relations*. Minneapolis: University of Minnesota Press, 2007.

Burnett, Christina Duffy, and Burke Marshall, eds. *Foreign in a Domestic Sense: Puerto Rico, American Expansion and the Constitution*. Durham, N.C.: Duke University Press, 2001.

Burton, Antoinette, ed. *Archive Stories: Facts, Fictions, and the Writing of History*. Durham, N.C.: Duke University Press, 2005.

———. *At the Heart of Empire: Indians and the Colonial Encounter in Late-Victorian Britain*. Berkeley: University of California Press, 1998.

———. *Burdens of History: British Feminists, Indian Women, and Imperial Culture, 1865–1915*. Chapel Hill: University of North Carolina Press, 1994.

Buszek, Maria Elena. *Pin-Up Grrrls: Feminism, Sexuality, Popular Culture*. Durham, N.C.: Duke University Press, 2006.

Byrd, Jodi A. *The Transit of Empire: Indigenous Critiques of Colonialism*. Minneapolis: University of Minnesota Press, 2011.

Cachola, Ellen-Rae, and Terry Bautista. "Women's Rights Groups Urge the Philippines to Rethink Guam Military Buildup Bid." *Women for Genuine Security*, March 1, 2010. http://www.genuinesecurity.org/actions/FilipinosNoBidGuam.html.

Cagurangan, Mar-Vic. "Women's Group Demands Impact Study on Troop Buildup." *Variety News*, August 15, 2007, as cited in "Fuetsan Famalao'an in Action," August 15, 2007, http://decolonizeguam.blogspot.com/2007/08/fuetsan-famalaoan-in-action.html.

Cahill, Cathleen D. *Federal Fathers and Mothers: A Social History of the United States Indian Service, 1869–1933*. Chapel Hill: University of North Carolina Press, 2011.

Camacho, Keith L. *Cultures of Commemoration: The Politics of War, Memory and History in the Mariana Islands*. Honolulu: University of Hawai'i Press, 2011.

———. "Fuetsan Famalao'an: Chamorro Women's Activism in the Wake of 9/11." UCLA Center for the Study of Women Newsletter. Los Angeles, June 2010, 1–12.

———. *Sacred Men: Law, Torture, and Retribution in Guam*. Durham, N.C.: Duke University Press, 2019.

Camacho, Leevin. "Resisting the Proposed Military Buildup on Guam." In *Under Occupation: Resistance and Struggle in a Militarised Asia-Pacific*, edited by Daniel Broudy,

Peter Simpson, and Makoto Arakaki, 183–90. Newcastle upon Tyne: Cambridge Scholars Publishing, 2013.

Campbell, Craig. *Agitating Images: Photography against History in Indigenous Siberia.* Minneapolis: University of Minnesota Press, 2014.

Carano, Paul, and Pedro C. Sanchez. *A Complete History of Guam.* Rutland, Vt.: Charles E. Tuttle, 1964.

Caronan, Faye. *Legitimizing Empire: Filipino American and U.S. Puerto Rican Cultural Critique.* Champaign: University of Illinois Press, 2015.

Case, Martin. *The Relentless Business of Treaties: How Indigenous Land Became U.S. Property.* St. Paul: Minnesota Historical Society Press, 2018.

Cassidy, Tina. *Birth: The Surprising History of How We Are Born.* New York: Grove Press, 2006.

Caylor, Ann. "A Promise Long Deferred: Federal Reclamation on the Colorado River Indian Reservation." *Pacific Historical Review* 69, no. 2 (May 2000): 193–215.

Césaire, Aimé. *Discourse on Colonialism.* New York: Monthly Review Press, 2000.

Chapman, David. *The Bonin Islanders, 1830 to the Present: Narrating Japanese Nationality.* Lanham, Md.: Lexington Books, 2016.

Charbonneau, Sinead, Robina Thomas, Caitlin Janzen, Jeannine Carriere, Susan Strega, and Leslie Brown. "Storying the Untold: Indigenous Motherhood and Street Sex Work." In Lavell-Harvard and Anderson, *Mothers of the Nations*, 163–78.

Chaudhuri, Nupur, and Margaret Strobel, eds. *Western Women and Imperialism: Complicity and Resistance.* Bloomington: Indiana University Press, 1992.

Chauncey, George. *Gay New York: Gender: Urban Culture, and the Making of the Gay Male World 1890–1940.* New York: Basic Books, 1994.

Child, Brenda. *Holding Our World Together: Ojibwe Women and the Survival of Community.* New York: Penguin Books, 2012.

Cholmondeley, Lionel Berners. *The History of the Bonin Islands from the Year 1827 to the Year 1876, and of Nathaniel Savory, One of the Original Settlers.* London: Archibald Constable, 1915.

Christensen, Pam. "Helen Longyear Paul: A Woman of Vision." *Marquette Monthly,* March 23, 2009. http://marquettemonthly.org/helen-longyear-paul-a-woman-of-vision/.

Clancy-Smith, Julia Ann, and Frances Gouda, eds. *Domesticating the Empire: Race, Gender, and Family Life in French and Dutch Colonialism.* Charlottesville: University Press of Virginia, 1998.

Clement, Michael R., Jr. "Kustumbre, Modernity and Resistance: The Subaltern Narrative in Chamorro Language Music." PhD diss., University of Hawai'i at Mānoa, 2011.

Clifford, James. "Indigenous Articulations." In "Native Pacific Cultural Studies on the Edge," edited by Vicente M. Diaz and J. Kehaulani Kauanui. Special issue, *Contemporary Pacific* 13, no. 2 (Fall 2001): 468–89.

———. *Routes: Travel and Translation in the Late Twentieth Century.* Cambridge, Mass.: Harvard University Press, 1997.

Clinton, Hillary. "America's Pacific Century." *Foreign Policy,* October 11, 2011, 56–63.

Coello de la Rosa, Alexandre. *Jesuits at the Margins: Missions and Missionaries in the Marianas.* New York: Routledge, 2016.

Cogan, *We Fought the Navy: Guam's Quest for Democracy.* Honolulu: University of Hawai'i Press, 2008.

Cole, Anna, Victoria Haskins, and Fiona Paisley, eds. *Uncommon Ground: White Women and Aboriginal History*. Canberra: Aboriginal Studies Press for the Australian Institute of Aboriginal and Torres Strait Islander Studies, 2005.

Connor, Helene. "Māori Mothering: Repression, Resistance and Renaissance." In Lavell-Harvard and Anderson, *Mothers of the Nations*, 231–50.

Cook, Kealani. *Return to Kahiki: Native Hawaiians in Oceania*. New York: Cambridge University Press, 2018.

Coontz, Robert E. *From the Mississippi to the Sea*. Philadelphia: Dorrance, 1930.

Cooper, Diane E. "Diplomat and Naval Intelligence Officer: The Duties of Lt. George L. Dyer, U.S. Naval Attaché to Spain." In *Crucible of Empire: The Spanish-American War and Its Aftermath*, edited by James C. Bradford, 1–22. Annapolis, Md.: Naval Institute Press, 1993.

Cotera, Maria Eugenia. "'All My Relatives Are Noble': Recovering the Feminine in Ella Cara Deloria's 'Waterlily.'" *American Indian Quarterly* 28, no. 1/2 (Winter–Spring 2004): 52–72.

Cott, Nancy. *The Bonds of Womanhood: Woman's Sphere in New England, 1780–1835*. New Haven, Conn.: Yale University Press, 1977.

Coulthard, Glen Sean. *Red Skin, White Masks: Rejecting the Colonial Politics of Recognition*. Minneapolis: University of Minnesota, 2014.

Cristobal, Hope Alvarez. "The Organization of Peoples for Indigenous Rights: A Commitment towards Self-Determination." *Pacific Ties* 13, no. 4 (1990): 10–11, 14–15, 17, 21.

Crocker, Ruth. "His Absent Presence: The Widowhood of Mrs. Russell Sage." In *Women on Their Own: Interdisciplinary Perspectives on Being Single*, edited by Rudolph M. Bell and Virginia Yans, 140–56. New Brunswick, N.J.: Rutgers University Press, 2010.

———. *Mrs. Russell Sage: Women's Activism and Philanthropy in Gilded Age and Progressive Era America*. Bloomington: Indiana University Press, 2006.

Cruz, Denise. *Transpacific Femininities: The Making of the Modern Filipina*. Durham, N.C.: Duke University Press, 2012.

Cruz, Karen A. *The Pattera of Guam: Their Story and Legacy*. Maite, Guam: Guam Humanities Council, 1997.

Cunningham, Lawrence J. *Ancient Chamorro Society*. Honolulu: Bess Press, 1992.

Daigle, Michelle. "Tracing the Terrain of Indigenous Food Sovereignties." *Journal of Peasant Studies* 46, no. 2 (2017): 297–315.

Daly, Mary. *Gynecology: The Metaethics of Radical Feminism*. 2nd ed. Boston: Beacon, 1990.

Dames, Vivian Loyola. "Chamorro Women, Self-Determination, and the Politics of Abortion in Guam." In *Asian/Pacific Islander American Women: A Historical Anthology*, edited by Shirley Hune and Gail M. Nomura, 365–84. New York: New York University Press, 2003.

D'Amico, Francine J., and Laurie Weinstein, eds. *Gender Camouflage: Women and the U.S. Military*. New York: New York University Press, 1999.

Davis-Floyd, Robbie, and Christine Barbara Johnson, eds. *Mainstreaming Midwives: The Politics of Change*. New York: Routledge, 2006.

Dawley, Katy. "The Campaign to Eliminate the Midwife." *American Journal of Nursing* 100, no. 10 (October 2000): 53.

Delfin, JoAnna. "Chatfield Assumes Command of Joint Region Marianas." Joint Region Marianas Public Affairs, January 27, 2017. https://www.cnic.navy.mil/regions/jrm/news/News_Releases/chatfield-assumes-command-of-joint-region-marianas.html.

DeLisle, Christine Taitano. "Civilizing the Guam Museum." University of Michigan Working Papers in Museum Studies. On-line Publication of the University of Michigan, No. 4, 2010. http://hdl.handle.net/2027.42/77460.

———. "Delivering the Body: Narratives of Family, Childbirth and Prewar Pattera." MA thesis, University of Guam, 2001.

———. "Destination Chamorro Culture: Notes on Realignment, Rebranding, and Post-9/11 Militourism in Guam." In "Tours of Duty and Tours of Leisure," edited by Vernadette Vicuña Gonzales, Jana K. Lipman, and Teresia Teaiwa. Special issue, *American Quarterly* 68, no. 3 (September 2016): 563–72.

———. "'Guamanian-Chamorro by Birth but American Patriotic by Choice': Subjectivity and Performance in the Life of Agueda Iglesias Johnston." In "Transoceanic Flows: Pacific Islander Interventions across the American Empire," edited by Keith L. Camacho and Russell Leong. Special issue, *Amerasia Journal* 37, no. 3 (2011): 61–75.

———. "A History of Chamorro Nurse-Midwives in Guam and a 'Placental Politics' for Indigenous Feminism." *Intersections*, no. 37 (March 2015). http://intersections.anu.edu.au/issue37/delisle.htm.

———. Segment in "Indigenizing Environmental Thinking." *Open Rivers: Rethinking Water, Place, and Community* 17 (Fall 2020). https://editions.lib.umn.edu/openrivers/article/indigenizing-environmental-thinking/.

———. "Tumuge' Påpa' (Writing It Down): Chamorro Midwives and the Delivery of Native History." In "Women Writing Oceania: Weaving the Sails of Waka," edited by Caroline Sinavaiana and J. Kehaulani Kauanui. Special issue, *Pacific Studies* 30, no. 1/2 (March/June 2007): 20–32.

DeLisle, Christine Taitano, and Vicente M. Diaz. "Itinerant Indigeneities: How to Navigate Modern Guåhan's Treacherous Roads." In *Allotment Stories: Indigenous Responses to Settler Land Privatization*, edited by Daniel Heath Justice and Jean M. O'Brien. Minneapolis: University of Minnesota Press, Forthcoming.

Deloria, Philip Joseph. *Indians in Unexpected Places*. Lawrence: University Press of Kansas, 2004.

———. *Playing Indian*. New Haven, Conn.: Yale University Press, 1998.

Deloria, Vine, Jr. *God Is Red: A Native View of Religion*. Golden, Colo.: Fulcrum, 2003.

DeLoughrey, Elizabeth M. *Roots and Routes: Navigating Caribbean and Pacific Island Literatures*. Honolulu: University of Hawai'i Press, 2007.

Del Priore, Maritza R. "Education on Guam during the Spanish Administration from 1668 to 1899." EdD diss., University of Southern California, 1986.

Denetdale, Jennifer. *Reclaiming Diné History: The Legacies of Navajo Chief Manuelito and Juanita*. Tucson: University of Arizona Press, 2007.

Dening, Greg. *Beach Crossings: Voyaging across Times, Cultures, and Self*. Philadelphia: University of Pennsylvania Press, 2004.

Dennison, Jean. *Colonial Entanglements*. Chapel Hill: University of North Carolina Press, 2012.

Desmond, Jane. *Staging Hula: Bodies on Display from Waikiki to Sea World*. Chicago: University of Chicago Press, 2001.

De Vera, Reverend P. Roman Maria. *Diccionario Chamorro-Castellano*. Manila: Imprenta y Litografía Germania, Cacho Hermanos, 1932.

Diaz, Vicente M. "Deliberating Liberation Day: Identity, History, Memory, and War in Guam." In *Perilous Memories: The Asia-Pacific War(s)*, edited by Tak Fujitani, Geoffrey White, and Lisa Yoneyama, 155–80. Durham, N.C.: Duke University Press, 2001.

———. "'Fight Boys, til the Last . . .': Islandstyle Football and the Remasculinization of Indigeneity in the Militarized American Pacific Islands." In *Pacific Diasporas: Island Peoples in the United States and across the Pacific*, edited by Paul Spickard, Joanne Rondilla, and Deborah Hippolite Wright, 169–94. Honolulu: University of Hawai'i Press, 2002.

———."In the Wake of Matå'pang's Canoe: The Cultural and Political Possibilities of Indigenous Discursive Flourish." In *Critical Indigenous Studies*, edited by Aileen Moreton-Robinson, 119–37. Tucson: University of Arizona Press, 2016.

———. "Oceania in the Plains: The Politics and Analytics of Trans-Indigenous Resurgence in Chuukese Voyaging of Dakota Lands, Waters, and Skies in Miní Sóta Makhóčhe." *Pacific Studies* 42, no. 1/2 (April/August 2019): 1–44.

———. *Repositioning the Missionary: Rewriting the Histories of Colonialism, Native Catholicism, and Indigeneity in Guam*. Honolulu: University of Hawai'i Press, 2010.

———. "Simply Chamorro: Telling Tales of Demise and Survival in Guam." *Contemporary Pacific* 6, no. 1 (Spring 1994): 29–57.

———. "Sniffing Oceania's Behind." *Contemporary Pacific* 24, no. 2 (2012): 324–44.

———. "Stepping in It: How to Smell the Fullness of Indigenous Histories." In *Sources and Methods in Indigenous Studies*, edited by Chris Andersen and Jean M. O'Brien, 86–92, New York: Routledge, 2017.

———. "Tackling Pacific Hegemonic Formations on the Gridiron." In "Transoceanic Flows: Pacific Islander Interventions across the American Empire," edited by Keith L. Camacho and Russell Leong. Special issue, *Amerasia Journal* 37, no. 3 (2011): 90–113.

———. "Voyaging for Anti-Colonial Recovery: Austronesian Seafaring, Archipelagic Rethinking, and the Re-mapping of Indigeneity." *Pacific Asia Inquiry* 2, no. 1 (Fall 2011): 21–32.

Diaz, Vicente M., and J. Kehaulani Kauanui, eds. "Native Pacific Cultural Studies on the Edge." Special issue, *Contemporary Pacific* 13, no. 2, (Fall 2001): 315–41.

Domosh, Mona, and Joni Seager. *Putting Women in Place: Feminist Geographers Make Sense of the World*. New York: Guilford Publications, 2001.

Drew, Benjamin. "Lenah Sutcliffe Higbee: Navy Nurse Corps Pioneer." *Naval History Magazine* 31, no. 2 (April 2017). https://www.usni.org/magazines/naval-history-magazine/2017/april/lenah-sutcliffe-higbee-navy-nurse-corps-pioneer.

Driver, Marjorie G. "The Account of a Discalced Friar's Stay in the Islands of the Ladrones." *The Guam Recorder* 7, no. 1 (1977): 19–21.

———. "Fray Juan Pobre de Zamora and His Account of the Mariana Islands." *Journal of Pacific History* 18, no. 3 (1983): 198–216.

Dubrow, Gail Lee, and Jennifer B. Goodman, eds. *Restoring Women's History through Historic Preservation*. Baltimore: Johns Hopkins University Press, 2003.

Dvorak, Greg. *Coral and Concrete: Remembering Kwajalein Atoll between Japan, America, and the Marshall Islands*. Honolulu: University of Hawai'i Press, 2018.

Ehrenreich, Barbara, and Deirdre English. *Witches, Midwives, and Nurses: A History of Women Healers*. New York: Feminist Press, 2010.

Emberson-Bain, 'Atu, ed. *Sustainable Development or Malignant Growth? Perspectives of Pacific Island Women*. Suva, Fiji: Marama Publications, 1994.

Enloe, Cynthia. *Bananas, Beaches and Bases: Making Feminist Sense of International Politics*. Berkeley: University of California Press, 1990.

———. *The Curious Feminist: Searching for Women in a New Age of Empire*. Berkeley: University of California Press, 2004.

Enstad, Nan. *Ladies of Labor, Girls of Adventure*. New York: Columbia University Press, 1999.

Erai, Michelle. *Girl of New Zealand: Colonial Optics in Aotearoa*. Tucson: University of Arizona Press, 2020.

Ettinger, Laura E. *Nurse-Midwifery: The Birth of a New American Profession*. Columbus: Ohio State University Press, 2006.

"Eulogy for Agueda Iglesias Johnston 1892–1977, Fourteenth Guam Legislature," January 6, 1978.

"Faninadahen Kosas Guåhan—Guam Museum." Multi-Year Report. January 1999. Unpublished. Prepared by Antonio M. Palomo, Executive Director, with assistance by Priscilla C. Villagomez. Hagåtña, Guam.

Farrell, Don A. *The Pictorial History of Guam: Liberation–1944*. Tamuning, Guam: Micronesian, 1984.

Felski, Rita. *The Gender of Modernity*. Cambridge, Mass.: Harvard University Press, 1995.

Findlay, Eileen J. Suárez. *Imposing Decency: The Politics of Sexuality and Race in Puerto Rico, 1870–1920*. Durham, N.C.: Duke University Press, 1999.

Fink, T. Ross. "United States Naval Policies in the Dependent Areas." PhD diss., University of North Carolina, 1948.

Fitzgerald, Stephanie. *Native Women and Land: Narratives of Dispossession and Resurgence*. Albuquerque: University of New Mexico Press, 2015.

Flinn, Juliana. *Mary, the Devil, and Taro: Catholicism and Women's Work in a Micronesian Society*. Honolulu: University of Hawai'i Press, 2010.

Flores, Alfred. "'No Walk in the Park': U.S. Empire and Racialization of Civilian Military Labor." *American Quarterly* 67, no. 3 (September 2015): 813–35.

Flores, Evelyn Rose. "Reclaiming the Suppressed through Testimonio: The Role of Oral Histories in Excavating Crucial Roles of Women in Subversive Acts of War and Political Struggle." Paper presented at the Pacific History Association Conference, University of Auckland, Wellington, New Zealand, December 6, 2012.

Flores, Judith S. "Dress of the Chamorro." In *Berg Encyclopedia of World Dress and Fashion*. Vol. 7, *Australia, New Zealand, and the Pacific Islands*, edited by Margaret Maynard, 508–11. New York: Berg, 2010.

Flores, Judy. "Francisco Feja Feja—the Artist behind the Guam Flag Design." Interview with Delfine Feja Arciga. Unpublished essay for the Guam Council on the Arts and Humanities, July 10, 1998.

Foerstel, Lenora, and Angela Gilliam, eds. *Margaret Mead Legacy: Scholarship, Empire, and the South Pacific*. Philadelphia: Temple University Press, 1992.

Fojas, Camilla. *Islands of Empire: Pop Culture and U.S. Power*. Austin: University of Texas Press, 2014.

Fontaine, Lorena, Lisa Forbes, Wendy McNab, Lisa Murdock, and Roberta Stout. "Nimâmâsak: The Legacy of First Nations Women Honouring Mothers and Motherhood." In Lavell-Harvard and Anderson, *Mothers of the Nations*, 251–66.
Forbes, Eric. "Chamorro Expressions: *Ma Håfot i Toayå-Ho!*" *Paleric* (blog), November 11, 2011. https://paleric.blogspot.com/2011/11/chamorro-expressions-ma-hafot-i-toaya.html.
Foucault, Michel. *The Birth of Biopolitics: Lectures at the College de France, 1978–79*. Edited by Michelle Senellart. New York: Palgrave McMillan, 2008.
Fountain, Daniel. *Michigan Gold: Mining in the Upper Peninsula*. Duluth, Minn.: Lake Superior Port Cities, 1992.
Frain, Sylvia. "Resisting Political Colonization and American Militarization in the Marianas Archipelago." *AlterNative* 12, no. 3 (September 2016): 298–315.
Frankenberg, Ruth. *White Women, Race Matters: The Social Construction of Whiteness*. Minneapolis: University of Minnesota Press, 1993.
Fraser, Gertrude Jacinta. *African American Midwifery in the South: Dialogues of Birth, Race, and Memory*. Cambridge, Mass.: Harvard University Press, 1998.
Freire, Paulo. *Pedagogy of the Oppressed*. Translated by Myra Bergman Ramos. New York: Continuum, 2000.
Ganter, Regina, and Patricia Grimshaw. "Introduction: Reading the Lives of White Mission Women." *Journal of Australian Studies* 39, no. 1 (2015): 1–6.
Gaonkar, Dilip Parameshwar, ed. *Alternative Modernities*. 2nd ed. Durham, N.C.: Duke University Press, 2001.
Garcia, Francisco. *The Life and Martyrdom of the Venerable Father Diego Luis de San Vitores of the Society of Jesis, First Apostle of the Mariana Islands, and Events of These Islands from the Year Sixteen Hundred and Sixty-Eight through the Year Sixteen Hundred and Eighty-One*. Translated by Margaret M. Higgins, Felicia Plaza, and Juan M. H. Ledesma. Edited by James A. McDonough. Mangilao: Richard Flores Taitano Micronesia Area Research Center, 2004.
Ginoza, Ayano. "R&R at the Intersection of U.S. and Japanese Dual Empire: Okinawan Women and Decolonizing Militarized Heterosexuality." In "Tours of Duty and Tours of Leisure," edited by Vernadette Vicuña Gonzales, Jana K. Lipman, and Teresia Teaiwa, Special issue, *American Quarterly* 68, no. 3 (2016): 583–91.
Ginsburg, Faye D., and Rayna Rapp, eds. *Conceiving the New World Order: The Global Politics of Reproduction*. Berkeley: University of California Press, 1995.
Ginzberg, Lori D. *Women and the Work of Benevolence: Morality, Politics, and Class in the 19th-Century United States*. New Haven, Conn.: Yale University Press, 1990.
Glakas, Barbara. "Remembering Herndon's History: Elisabeth Leonhardt and the Navy's 'Sacred Twenty.'" Patch.com, posted by Greg Hambrick, November 5, 2016. https://patch.com/virginia/herndon/remembering-herndons-history-elisabeth-leonhardt-navy-s-sacred-twenty.
Godson, Susan H. *Serving Proudly: A History of Women in the U.S. Navy*. Annapolis: Naval Institute Press, 2002.
Goeman, Mishuana. "Disrupting a Settler-Colonial Grammar of Place: The Visual Memoir of Hulleah Tsinhnahjinnie." In *Theorizing Native Studies*, edited by Audra Simpson and Andrea Smith, 235–65. Durham, N.C.: Duke University Press, 2014.

———. "From Place to Territories and Back Again: Centering Storied Land in the discussion of Indigenous Nation-building." *International Journal of Critical Indigenous Studies* 1, no. 1 (2008): 23–34.

———. "Indigenous Interventions and Feminist Methods." In *Sources and Methods in Indigenous Studies*, edited by Chris Andersen and Jean M. O'Brien, 185–94. New York: Routledge, 2017.

———. *Mark My Words: Native Women Mapping Our Nations*. Minneapolis: University of Minnesota Press, 2013.

Goetzfridt, Nicholas J. *Guåhan: A Bibliographic History*. Honolulu: University of Hawai'i Press, 2011.

Goldsmith, Elizabeth C., and Dena Goodman, eds. *Going Public: Women and Publishing in Early Modern France*. Ithaca, N.Y.: Cornell University Press, 1995.

Gonzales, Patrisia. *Red Medicine: Traditional Indigenous Rites of Birthing and Healing*. Tucson: University of Arizona Press, 2012.

Gonzales, Vernadette. *Securing Paradise: Tourism and Militarism in Hawai'i and the Philippines*. Durham, N.C.: Duke University Press, 2013.

Goodyear-Ka'opua. *The Seeds We Planted: Portraits of a Native Hawaiian Charter School*. Minneapolis: University of Minnesota Press, 2013.

Grafton, Anthony. *The Footnote: A Curious History*. Cambridge, Mass.: Harvard University Press, 1997.

Grande, Sandy, Natalie Avalos, Jason Mancini, Christopher Newell, and Endawnis Spears. "Red Praxis: Lessons from Mashantucket to Standing Rock." In *Standing with Standing Rock*, edited by Jaskiran Dhillon and Nick Estes, 245–60. Minneapolis: University of Minnesota Press, 2019.

Green, Harvey. *Fit for America: Health, Fitness, Sport and American Society*. Baltimore: Johns Hopkins University Press, 1986.

Green, Rayna. "The Pocahontas Perplex: The Image of Indian Women in American Culture." *Massachusetts Review* 16, no. 4 (Autumn 1975): 698–714.

———. "The Tribe Called Wannabee: Playing Indian in America and Europe." *Folklore* 99, no. 1 (1988): 30–55.

Greenberg, Amy S. *Manifest Manhood and the Antebellum American Empire*. New York: Cambridge University Press, 2005.

Griffith, Jane. "Do Some Work for Me: Professional Communication, and Representations of Indigenous Water." *Decolonization: Indigeneity, Education and Society* 7, no. 1 (2018): 132–57.

Griffith, Richard Roy. "From Island Colony to Strategic Territory: The Development of American Administration on the Island of Guam, 1898–1950." PhD diss., University of Denver, 1978.

Grimshaw, Patricia. *Paths of Duty: American Missionary Wives in Nineteenth-Century Hawaii*. Honolulu: University of Hawai'i Press, 1989.

Guerrero, Olivia. "Growth of Nursing on Guam." *Pacific Profile* 3, no. 4 (May 1965): 14–15, 41, 43–44.

Guevara, Claudia. "I Pattera." *Glimpses of Guam* 15, no. 3, (1975): 60–63.

Hadley, Alice E. "A Brief History of the U.S. Naval Hospital, Guam, 1899–2001." 1996. Accessed January 3, 2017. https://www.guam.net/home/ahadley/images/hyusnhgu.html.

Haggis, Jane. "Gendering Colonialism and Colonising Gender: Recent Women's Studies Approaches to White Women and the History of British Colonialism." *Women's Studies International Forum* 13, nos. 1–2 (1990): 105–15.

———. "White Women and Colonialism: Towards a Non-Recuperative History." In *Gender and Imperialism*, edited by Clare Midgley, 45–78. Manchester: Manchester University Press, 1998.

Hall, Lisa Kahaleole. "Navigating Our Own 'Sea of Islands': Remappping a Theoretical Space for Hawaiian Women and Indigenous Feminism." *Wicazo Sa Review* 24, no. 24 (Fall 2009): 15–38.

Hall, Stuart. "The Rediscovery of Ideology." In *Literary Theory: An Anthology*, edited by Julie Rivkin and Michael Ryan, 1050–87. Malden, Mass.: Blackwell, 1998.

———. "Signification, Representation, Ideology: Althusser and the Post-Structuralist Debates." *Critical Studies in Mass Communication* 2, no. 2 (June 1985): 91–114.

Hanlon, David. *Making Micronesia: A Political Biography of Tosiwo Nakayama*. Honolulu: University of Hawaiʻi Press, 2014.

Hanna, Monica, Jennifer Harford Vargas, and José David Saldívar, eds. *Junot Díaz and the Decolonial Imagination*. Durham, N.C.: Duke University Press, 2016.

Haraway, Donna Jeanne. *Primate Visions: Gender, Race, and Nature in the World of Modern Science*. London: Routledge, 1989.

Harris, Aroha. "History with Nana: Family, Life, and the Spoken Word." In *Sources and Methods in Indigenous Studies*, edited by Chris Andersen and Jean M. O'Brien, 15–22. New York: Routledge, 2017.

———. "'I Wouldn't Say I Was a Midwife': Interviews with Violet Otene Harris." *Health and History* 3, no. 1 (2001): 109–23.

Harris, Aroha, and Mary Jane McCallum. "Assaulting the Ears of Government." In *Indigenous Women and Work: From Labor to Activism*, edited by C. Williams, 225–39. Urbana Champaign: University of Illinois Press, 2012.

Hartman, Saidiya V. *Scenes of Subjection: Terror, Slavery, and Self-Making in Nineteenth-Century America*. New York: Oxford University Press, 1997.

Hattori, Anne Perez. *Colonial Dis-Ease: U.S. Navy Health Policies and the CHamorus of Guam, 1898–1941*. Pacific Islands Monograph Series. Honolulu: University of Hawaiʻi Press, 2004.

———. "Colonialism, Capitalism and Nationalism in the U.S. Navy's Expulsion of Guam's Spanish Catholic Priests, 1898–1900."

———. "'The Cry of the Little People of Guam': American Colonialism, Medical Philanthropy, and the Susana Hospital for CHamoru Women, 1898–1941." *Health and History* 8, no. 1 (2006): 4–26, 11.

———. "Remembering the Past: Photography, Leprosy and the Chamorros of Guam, 1898–1924." *Journal of Pacific History* 46, no. 32 (2011): 293–318.

———. "Righting Civil Wrongs: Guam Congress Walkout of 1949." In PSECC, *Haleʼ-ta: Kinalamten Pulitikåt: Siñenten I Chamorro / Issues in Guam's Political Development; The Chamorro Perspective*, 57–69 Agana, Guam: Political Status Education Coordinating Commission, 1996.

———. "Textbook Tells: Gender, Race, and Decolonizing Guam History." *AlterNative* 14, no. 2 (2018): 173–84.

Hau'ofa, Epeli. "Our Sea of Islands." In *A New Oceania: Rediscovering Our Sea of Islands*, edited by Eric Waddell, Vijay Naidu, and Epeli Hau'ofa, 2–16. Suva, Fiji: University of the South Pacific, 1993.

———. "Pasts to Remember" (Epilogue). In *Remembrance of Pacific Pasts: An Invitation to Remake History*, edited by Robert Borofsky, 453–72. Honolulu: University of Hawai'i Press. 2000.

Hezel, Francis X. *The First Taint of Civilization: A History of the Caroline and Marshall Islands in Pre-colonial Days, 1521–1885*. Honolulu: University of Hawai'i Press, 1983.

———. "Schools in Micronesia Prior to American Administration." *Pacific Studies* 8, no. 1 (Fall 1984): 95–111.

———. *Strangers in Their Own Land: A Century of Colonial Rule in the Caroline and Marshall Islands*. Honolulu: University of Hawai'i Press, 1995.

———. "A Yankee Trader in Yap: Crayton Philo Holcomb." *Journal of Pacific History* 10, no. 1 (1975): 3–19.

Higginbotham, Evelyn Brooks. *Righteous Discontent: The Women's Movement in the Black Baptist Church, 1880–1920*. Cambridge. Mass.: Harvard University Press, 1993.

Higuchi, Wakako. *The Japanese Administration of Guam, 1941–1944: A Study of Occupation and Integration Policies, with Japanese Oral Histories*. Jefferson, N.C.: McFarland, 2013.

Hill, Patricia R. *Their World Their Household: The American Women's Foreign Mission Movement and Cultural Transformation, 1870–1920*. Ann Arbor: University of Michigan Press, 1985.

Hill, Susan M. *The Clay We Are Made of: Haudenosaunee Land Tenure on the Grand River*. Winnipeg: University of Manitoba Press, 2017.

Hirsch, Marianne. *The Familial Gaze*. Hanover, N.H.: University Press of New England, 1999.

"The History of the Seal of Guam." *Guam Daily News*, July 21, 1965, 7.

Hoefnagel, Dick. "The Paul Room at Baker Library." *Dartmouth College Library Bulletin*. Accessed January 6, 2017. https://www.dartmouth.edu/library/Library_Bulletin/Nov1992/LB-N92-Hoefnagel.html.

Hofschneider, Penelope Bordallo. *A Campaign for Political Rights in Guam, 1899–1950*. Saipan, Northern Mariana Islands: NMI Division of Historic Preservation, 2001.

Hoganson, Kristin L. *Consumers' Imperium: The Global Production of American Domesticity, 1865–1920*. Chapel Hill: University of North Carolina Press, 2007.

———. *Fighting for American Manhood: How Gender Politics Provoked the Spanish-American and Philippine-American Wars*. New Haven, Conn.: Yale University Press, 1998.

Holland, Sharon Patricia. *The Erotic Life of Racism*. Durham, N.C.: Duke University Press, 2012.

Howard, Chris Perez. *Mariquita: A Tragedy of Guam*. Suva, Fiji: University of the South Pacific, 1986.

Howe, K. R. *The Quest for Origins: Who First Discovered and Settled New Zealand and the Pacific Islands*. Honolulu: University of Hawai'i Press, 2003.

Huhndorf, Shari M., and Cheryl Suzack. "Indigenous Feminism: Theorizing the Issues." In *Indigenous Women and Feminism: Politics, Activism, Culture*, edited by Cheryl Suzack, Shari M. Huhndorf, Jeanne Perreault, and Jean Barman, 1–17. Toronto: UBC Press, 2010.

Ibanez y Garcia, Luis. *The History of the Marianas, with Navigational Data, and of the Caroline, and Palau Islands from the Time of Their Discovery by Magellan to the Present*

(1887). Translated and annotated by Marjorie G. Driver. Mangilao, Guam: Richard Flores Taitano Micronesian Area Research Center, 1992.

Ikeya, Chie. *Refiguring Women, Colonialism, and Modernity in Burma*. Honolulu: University of Hawai'i Press, 2017.

Imada, Adria L. *Aloha Circuits: Hula Circuits through the U.S. Empire*. Durham, N.C.: Duke University Press, 2012.

Inglis, Amirah. *The White Women's Protection Ordinance: Sexual Anxiety and Politics in Papua*. London: Sussex University Press, 1975.

Isaac, Allan Punzalan. *American Tropics*. Minneapolis: University of Minnesota Press, 2006.

Jackson, Moana. "James Cook and Our Monuments to Colonization." *E-Tangata*. June 3, 2019. https://e-tangata.co.nz/comment-and-analysis/james-cook-and-our-monuments-to-colonisation/.

Jacobs, Margaret D. *White Mother to a Dark Race: Settler Colonialism, Maternalism, and the Removal of Indigenous Children in the American West and Australia, 1880–1940*. Lincoln: University of Nebraska, 2011.

Jager, Rebecca Kay. *Malinche, Pocahontas, and Sacagawea: Indian Women as Cultural Intermediaries and National Symbols*. Oklahoma City: University of Oklahoma Press, 2015.

Jensen, Joan M., and Michelle Wick Patterson, eds. *Travels with Frances Densmore: Her Life, Work, and Legacy in Native American Studies*. Lincoln: University of Nebraska Press, 2015.

"John Munro Longyear—Landlooker from Michigan." *Quarterly News: Mary Baker Eddy Museum and Historic Sites* 11, no. 3 (Autumn 1974): 169–72.

Johnson, Joan Marie. *Funding Feminism: Monied Women, Philanthropy, and the Women's Movement, 1870–1967*. Chapel Hill: University of North Carolina Press, 2017.

Johnston, Agueda I. "Christmas on Guam." *The Guam Recorder* 2, no. 4 (October–December 1972): 3–6.

Johnston, Anita. "The Ethnic Identity Experience of Chamorro Women." PhD diss. The California School of Professional Psychology, 1980.

Johnston, Emilie G. "Medical Services for the Island of Guam until World War Two." *The Guam Recorder* 1, no. 1 (October–December 1971): 40.

———, ed. *A Saga of Agueda*. 2nd ed. Agana, Guam: Johnston Enterprises, 1974.

Jolly, Margaret. "Colonizing Women: The Maternal Body and Empire." In *Feminism and the Politics of Difference*, edited by Sneja Gunew and Anna Yeatman, 103–27. Sydney: Allen and Unwin, 1993.

———. "From Point Venus to Bali Hai: Eroticism and Exoticism in Representations of the Pacific." In *Sites of Desire/Economies of Pleasure: Sexualities in Asia and the Pacific*, edited by Lenore Manderson and Margaret Jolly, 99–122. Chicago: University of Chicago Press, 1996.

———. "Introduction." In *Maternities and Modernities: Colonial and Postcolonial Experiences in Asia and the Pacific*, edited by Kalpana Ram and Margaret Jolly, 1–25. Cambridge: Cambridge University Press, 1998.

———. "White Shadows in the Darkness: Representations of Polynesian Women in Early Cinema." In "Representation and Photography of the Pacific Islands," edited by Max Quanchi. Special issue, *Pacific Studies* 20, no. 4 (1997): 125–50.

Jolly, Margaret, and Martha Macintyre, eds. *Family and Gender in the Pacific: Domestic Contradictions and the Colonial Impact*. Cambridge: Cambridge University Press, 2010.

Jorgensen, Marilyn A. *Guam's Patroness: Santa Marian Kamalen.* Austin: University of Texas Press, 1984.

Josephy, Alvin M. *The Long and the Short and the Tall: Marines in Combat on Guam and Iwo Jima.* Washington, D.C.: Zenger, 1946.

Kadetz, Paul. "Risk and Resistance: Creating Maternal Risk through Imposed Biomedical 'Safety' in the Post-colonial Indigenous Philippines." In Lavell-Harvard and Anderson, *Mothers of the Nations,* 47–70.

Kahn, Miriam. *Tahiti beyond the Postcard: Power, Place, and Everyday Life.* Seattle: University of Washington Press, 2011.

Kale, Steven. *French Salons: High Society and Political Sociability from the Old Regime to the Revolution of 1848.* Baltimore: Johns Hopkins University Press, 2004.

Kameʻeleihiwa, Lilikalā. *Native Land and Foreign Desires: Pehea La E Pono Ai? How Shall We Live in Harmony?* Honolulu: University of Hawaiʻi Press, 1992.

Kaplan, Amy. *The Anarchy of Empire in the Making of U.S. Culture.* Cambridge, Mass.: Harvard University Press, 2002.

———. "Black and Blue on San Juan Hill." In *Cultures of U.S. Imperialism,* edited by Amy Kaplan and Donald Pease, 219–36. Durham, N.C.: Duke University Press, 1993.

Kauanui, J. Kehaulani. *Paradoxes of Hawaiian Sovereignty: Land, Sex, and the Colonial Politics of State Nationalism.* Durham, N.C.: Duke University Press, 2018.

———. "A Structure, Not an Event: Settler Colonialism and Enduring Indigeneity." In *Lateral* 5, no. 1 (Spring 2016). https://doi.org/10.25158/l5.1.7.

Kelley, Mary. *Learning to Stand and Speak: Women, Education, and Public Life in America's Republic.* Chapel Hill: University of North Carolina Press, 2006.

Kerber, Linda. "The Republican Mother: Women and the Enlightenment-An American Perspective." *American Quarterly* 28, no. 2 (Summer 1976): 187–205.

Kim, Myjolynne Marie. "Nesor Annim, Niteikapar (Good Morning, Cardinal Honeyeater): Indigenous Reflections on Micronesian Women and the Environment." *Contemporary Pacific* 32, no. 1 (2020): 147–63.

Knapman, Claudia. *White Women in Fiji 1835–1930: The Ruin of Empire.* London: Allen and Unwin, 1986.

Koopman, Colin, Bonnie Sheehey, Patrick Jones, Laura Smithers, Sarah Hamid, and Claire Pickard. "Standard Forms of Power: Biopower and Sovereign Power in the Technology of the U.S. Birth Certificate, 1903–1935." *Constellations,* July 25, 2018, 1–16. https://doi.org/10.1111/1467-8675.12372.

Kramer, Paul A. *The Blood of Government: Race, Empire, the United States, and the Philippines.* Chapel Hill: University of North Carolina Press, 2006.

Kraus, Natasha Kirsten. *A New Type of Womanhood: Discursive Politics and Social Change in Antebellum America.* Durham, N.C.: Duke University Press, 2008.

Kuper, Kenneth Gofigan. "Kontra I Peligru, Naʼfansåfo Ham: The Production of Military (In)Security in Guåhan." PhD diss., University of Hawaiʻi–Manoa, May 2019.

———. "Living at the Tip of the Spear: Guam and Restraint." *Responsible Statecraft,* July 20, 2020. https://responsiblestatecraft.org/2020/07/20/living-at-the-tip-of-the-spear-guam-and-restraint/.

Kushima, Kayoko "Historiographies of Guam and Discourses of Isolation: Canonical and Alternative Historical Narratives. MA thesis, University of Guam, 2001.

Landau, Paul S., and Deborah D. Kaspin, eds. *Images and Empires: Visuality in Colonial and Postcolonial Africa*. Berkeley: University of California Press, 2002.
Langmore, Diane. *Missionary Lives, Papua 1874–1919*. Honolulu: University Press of Hawai'i, 1989.
LaRocque, Emma. "Long Way from Home." In *Making Space for Indigenous Feminism*, edited by Joyce Green, 321–25. Halifax: Fernwood, 2017.
Lauer, Nancy Cook. "Hawaiian Law Now Permits Parents to Keep Placentas." *We News*, July 28, 2006. http://womensenews.org/story/parenting/060728/hawaiian-law-now-permits-parents-keep-placentas#.UegooVMVxXE.
Lavell-Harvard, D. Memee, and Kim Anderson, eds. *Mothers of the Nations: Indigenous Mothering as Global Resistance, Reclaiming and Recovery*. Bradford, Ontario: Demeter Press, 2014.
Lavell-Harvard, D. Memee, and Jeanette Corbiere-Lavell. *Until Our Hearts Are on the Ground: Aboriginal Mothering, Oppression, Resistance and Rebirth*. Bradford, Ontario: Demeter Press, 2006.
Lawcock, Larry A. "Guam Women: A Hasty History." In *Women of Guam*, edited by Cecilia Bamba, Laura Souder and Judy Tompkins, 7–11. Agana, Guam: The Guam Women's Conference, 1977.
Leckie, Shirley A., and Nancy J. Parezo. *Their Own Frontier: Women Intellectuals Revisioning the American West*. Lincoln: University of Nebraska Press, 2008.
Lee, Valerie. *Granny Midwives and Black Women Writers: Double-Dutched Readings*. New York: Routledge, 1996.
Le Gobien, Charles. *History of the Mariana Islands*. Translated by Father Paul Daly. Agana: Nieves Flores Library, 1949.
Leon-Guerrero, Jillette. *A Year on the Island of Guåhan, 1899–1900: Extracts from the Notebook of Naturalist William Edwin Safford*. Agana Heights: Guamology, 2016.
Lévesque, Rodrique, ed. *History of Micronesia: A Collection of Source Documents*. Vol. 8, *Last Chamorro Revolt, 1683–1687*. Gatineau, Quebec: Levesque Publications, 1996.
Lévesque, Rodrigue, ed. *History of Micronesia: A Collection of Source Documents*. Vol. 19, *The Freycinet Expedition, 1818–1819, Plus Reference Tables*. Quebec: Levesque Publications, 2002.
Levine, Philippa. ed. *Gender and Empire*. New York: Oxford University Press, 2004.
Lewis, Reina. *Gendering Orientalism: Race, Femininity and Representation*. London: Routledge, 1995.
Lincoln, Margaret. *Naval Wives and Mistresses*. London: National Maritime Museum, 2007.
Lizama, Tricia. "Yo'åmte: A Deeper Type of Healing Exploring; The State of Indigenous Chamorro Healing Practices." *Pacific Asia Inquiry* 5, no. 1 (Fall 2014): 97–106.
Lomawaima, K. Tsianina, and Teresa McCarty. "Concluding Commentary: Revisiting and Clarifying the Safety Zone." *Journal of American Indian Education* 53, no. 3 (2014): 63–67.
———. *"To Remain an Indian": Lessons in Democracy from a Century of Native American Education*. New York: Teachers College, Columbia University, 2006.
Lovett, Laura L. *Conceiving the Future: Pronatalism, Reproduction, and the Family in the United States, 1890–1938*. Chapel Hill: University of North Carolina Press, 2007.

Lujan, Frank C. "Sleeping Beauty: Time Passes by." In *Hale'-ta Hinasso': Tinige' Put Chamorro* [Insights: The Chamorro Identity], 86–88. Hagåtña, Guam: Political Status Education Coordinating Commission, 1993.

Lukere, Vicky. "Conclusion: Wider Reflections and a Survey of Literature." In *Birthing in the Pacific: Beyond Tradition and Modernity?*, edited by Vicki Lukere and Margaret Jolly, 178–202. Honolulu: University of Hawai'i Press, 2001.

Lydon, Jane. *Eye Contact: Photographing Indigenous Australians*. Durham, N.C.: Duke University Press, 2005.

Madrid, Carlos. *Beyond Distances: Governance, Politics and Deportation in the Mariana Islands from 1870 to 1877*. Saipan, Northern Mariana Islands: Northern Mariana Islands Council for Humanities, 2006.

Mahone, Rene C. "William G. Johnston: 1880–1943 (a Bibliography)." *The Guam Recorder* 5, no. 2 (1975): 11–15.

Mahuika, Nēpia. *Rethinking Oral History and Tradition: An Indigenous Perspective*. New York: Oxford University Press, 2019.

Mallon, Sean. "Against Tradition." *Contemporary Pacific* 22, no. 2 (2010): 362–81.

Manderson, Lenore. "Shaping Reproduction: Maternity in Early Twentieth-Century Malaya." In *Maternities and Modernities: Colonial and Postcolonial Experiences in Asia and the Pacific*, edited by Kalpana Ram and Margaret Jolly, 26–49. Cambridge: Cambridge University Press, 1998.

Mani, Lata. *Contentious Traditions: The Debate on Sati in Colonial India*. Berkeley: University of California Press, 1998.

Mar, Tracey Banivanua. *Decolonisation and the Pacific: Indigenous Globalisation and the Ends of Empire*. Cambridge: Cambridge University Press, 2016.

Marcus, George E., and Michael M. J. Fischer. *Anthropology as Cultural Critique: An Experimental Moment in the Human Sciences*. Chicago: University of Chicago Press, 1999.

"Marquette Suffragist: Abby Beecher Longyear Roberts." *Mining Journal*, January 29, 2020. https://www.miningjournal.net/news/superior_history/2020/01/marquette-suffragist%E2%80%88abby-beecher-longyear-roberts/.

Marubbio, M. Elise. *Killing the Indian Maiden: Images of Native American Women in Film*. Lexington: University Press of Kentucky, 2009.

Massey, Doreen B. *For Space*. London: Sage, 2005.

Maxwell, Anne. *Colonial Photography and Exhibitions: Representations of the "Native" and the Making of European Identities*. London: Leicester, 1999.

McCallum, Mary Jane Logan. *Indigenous Women, Work, and History, 1940–1980*. Winnipeg: University of Manitoba Press, 2014.

McClintock, Anne. *Imperial Leather: Race, Gender and Sexuality in the Colonial Context*. New York: Routledge, 1995.

McGrath, Thomas B. "The Capuchins in the Marianas: A Note on Events and Sources." *Journal of Pacific History* 20, no. 1 (January 1985), 57–64.

———. "Records in Spain of the Augustinian Recollects in the Marianas." *Journal of Pacific History* 24, no. 1 (April 1989): 106–9.

McKenna, Rebecca Tinio. *American Imperial Pastoral: The Architecture of U.S. Colonialism in the Philippines*. Chicago: University of Chicago Press, 2017.

McRae, Elizabeth Gillespie. *Mothers of Massive Resistance: White Women and the Politics of White Supremacy.* New York: Oxford University Press, 2018.
Merrett-Balkas, Leanne. "Just Add Water: Remaking Women through Childbirth, Anganen, Southern Highlands, Papua New Guinea." In *Maternities and Modernities: Colonial and Postcolonial Experiences in Asia and the Pacific,* edited by Kalpana Ram and Margaret Jolly, 213–38. Cambridge: Cambridge University Press, 1998.
Michelson, Alan. "Hanödaga:yas (Town Destroyer) and Mantle." *Third Text* 32, nos. 5–6 (February 2019): 1–4.
Miculka, Cameron. "Changes to Seal Sought." *Pacific Daily News,* June 28, 2015.
Miller, Monica L. *Slaves to Fashion: Black Dandyism and the Styling of Black Diasporic Identity.* Durham, N.C.: Duke University Press. 2009.
Miller, Stuart Creighton. *"Benevolent Assimilation": The American Conquest of the Philippines, 1899–1903.* New Haven, Conn.: Yale University Press, 1982.
Million, Dian. "Felt Theory: An Indigenous Feminist Approach to Affect and Theory." *Wicazo Sa Review* 24, no. 2 (Fall 2009): 53–76.
Monahan, Evelyn. *All This Hell: U.S. Nurses Imprisoned by the Japanese.* Lexington: University Press of Kentucky, 2000.
Monnig, Laurel. "Proving Chamorro." PhD diss., University of Illinois, Urbana-Champaign, 2007.
Moraga, Cherríe. "From a Long Line of Vendidas: Chicanas and Feminism." In *Feminist Studies / Critical Studies,* edited by Teresa de Lauretis, 173–90. Bloomington: Indiana University Press, 1986.
Moreton-Robinson, Aileen. *Talkin' Up to the White Woman: Aboriginal Women and Feminism.* St. Lucia, Australia: University of Queensland Press, 2000.
———. "Towards an Australian Indigenous Women's Standpoint Theory: A Methodological Tool." *Australian Feminist Studies* 28, no. 78 (2013): 331–47.
———. *The White Possessive: Property, Power, and Indigenous Sovereignty.* Minneapolis: University of Minnesota Press, 2015.
Morris, Kate. *Shifting Grounds: Landscape in Contemporary Native American Art.* Seattle: University of Washington Press, 2019.
Mould, Kim. "Did You Know?" *Newsletter of the Woman's Club of Winter Park,* January 2017, 5.
Mrazek, Rudolph. *Engineers of Happy Land: Technology and Nationalism in a Colony.* Princeton, N.J.: Princeton University Press, 2002.
Murphy, Patricia. *Time Is of the Essence: Temporality, Gender, and the New Woman.* Albany: State University of New York Press, 2001.
Naber, Nadine. "Arab American Femininities: Beyond Arab Virgin / American(ized) Whore." *Journal of Feminist Studies* 32, no. 1 (2006): 87–111.
Nadeau, Chantal. *Fur Nation: From the Beaver to Brigitte Bardot.* New York: Routledge, 2001.
Naholowa'a, Leiana San Agustin. "Beyond Matrifocality: A Literary Analysis of Mothering in Chamorro Narratives in Guam." PhD diss., University of Guam, 2018.
Na'puti, Tiara R. "Archipelagic Rhetoric: Remapping the Marianas and Challenging Militarization from a 'Stirring Place.'" *Communication and Critical/Cultural Studies* 16, no. 1 (2019): 4–25.
Na'puti, Tiara R., and Michael Lujan Bevacqua, "Militarization and Resistance from Guåhan: Protecting and Defending Pågat," *American Quarterly* 67, no. 3 (2015): 837–58.

Natividad, LisaLinda. "CHamoru Values Guiding Nonviolence." In *Conflict Transformation: Essays on Methods of NonViolence*, edited by Rhea DuMont, Tom Hastings, and Emiko Noma, 134–40. Jefferson, N.C.: McFarland, 2013.

———. "The Question of Guåhan: Statement of the Guahan Coalition for Peace and Justice." United Nations Special Committee on the Situation with Regard to the Implementation of the Granting of Independence to Colonial Countries and Peoples (C-24), June 21, 2011.

Natividad, LisaLinda, and Gwyn Kirk. "Fortress Guam: Resistance to U.S. Military Mega-Buildup" *Asia-Pacific Journal* 8, no. 1 (May 10, 2010): 1–17.

Natividad, LisaLinda, and Victoria-Lola Leon Guerrero. "The Explosive Growth of U.S. Military Power on Guam Confronts People Power: Experience of an Island People under Spanish, Japanese, and American Colonial Rule." *Asia-Pacific Journal* 8, no. 3 (December 6, 2010): 1–16.

Naval Historical Foundation. *U.S. Navy: A Complete History*. Washington: Naval Historical Foundation, 2002.

Nelson, Frederick, and Evelyn Nelson. *The Island of Guam: Description and History from a 1934 Perspective*. Washington, D.C.: Ana Publications, 1992.

Newman, Louise Michele. *White Women's Rights: The Racial Origins of Feminism in the United States*. New York: Oxford University Press, 1999.

Ngai, Sianne. *Ugly Feelings*. Cambridge, Mass.: Harvard University Press, 2005.

Nguyen, Mimi. *The Gift of Freedom: War, Debt, and Other Refugee Passages*. Durham, N.C.: Duke University Press, 2012.

Nickel, Sarah A. "'I Am Not a Women's Libber Although Sometimes I Sound Like One': Indigenous Feminism and Politicized Motherhood." *American Indian Quarterly* 41, no. 4 (Fall 2017): 299–335.

O'Brien, Jean M. *Firsting and Lasting: Writing Indians Out of Existence in New England*. Minneapolis: University of Minnesota Press, 2010.

———. "Historical Sources and Methods in Indigenous Studies: Touching on the Past, Looking to the Future." In *Sources and Methods in Indigenous Studies*, edited by Chris Andersen and Jean M. O'Brien, 15–22. New York: Routledge, 2017.

O'Brien, Patty. *The Pacific Muse: Exotic Femininity and the Colonial Pacific*. Seattle: University of Washington Press, 2006.

O'Connell, Robert L. *Sacred Vessels: The Cult of the Battleship and the Rise of the U.S. Navy*. New York: Oxford University Press, 1991.

Olive y Garcia, Francisco. *The Mariana Islands, 1884–1887: Random Notes of Governor Francisco Olive y Garcia*. Translated and annotated by Marjorie G. Driver. Mangilao, Guam: Richard Flores Taitano Micronesian Area Research Center, 1984.

Onedera, Peter R., ed. *Nå'an Lugåt Siha gi ya Guåhan* [Guam Place Names]. Agaña, Guam: Chamorro Language Commission, n.d.

Oparah, Julia Chinyere, and Alicia D. Bonaparte, eds. *Birthing Justice: Black Women, Pregnancy, and Childbirth*. New York: Routledge, 2015.

Oriard, Michael. *Reading Football: How the Popular Press Created an American Spectacle*. Chapel Hill: University of North Carolina Press, 1998.

Ortiz, Felina Mychelle. "History of Midwifery in New Mexico: Partnership between Curandero-parteras and the New Mexico Department of Health." *Journal of Midwifery and Women's Health* 50, no. 5 (September–October 2005): 411–17.

Palomo, Jose R. *Recollections of Olden Days*. Mangilao, Guam: Micronesian Area Research Center, University of Guam, 1992.

Palomo, Tony. *An Island in Agony*. Agana: T. Palomo, 1984.

Palomo, Tony, and Paul J. Borja, eds. "The Strength of Agueda." In *Liberation—Guam Remembers: A Golden Salute for the 50th anniversary of the Liberation of Guam*. Accessed January 7, 2010. https://www.nps.gov/parkhistory/online_books/npswapa/extContent/Lib/contents.htm.

Parmenter, Jon. *The Edge of the Woods: Iroquoia, 1534–1701*. Ithaca, N.Y.: Cornell University, 2010.

Parsons, Deborah L. *Streetwalking the Metropolis: Women, the City and Modernity*. New York: Oxford University Press, 2000.

Pascoe, Peggy. *Relations of Rescue: The Search for Female Moral Authority in the American West, 1874–1939*. New York: Oxford University Press, 1990.

Pateman, Carol. *The Sexual Contract*. Palo Alto, Calif.: Stanford University Press, 1988.

Patterson, Martha H. *Beyond the Gibson Girl: Reimagining the American New Woman, 1895–1915*. Urbana-Champaign: University of Illinois Press, 2005.

Paul, John Munro. *Landlooker in the Upper Peninsula of Michigan—from the Reminiscences of John Munro Longyear*. Compiled by Helen Longyear Paul. Marquette, Mich.: John M. Longyear Research Library, 1983.

Peiss, Kathy. *Hope in a Jar: The Making of America's Beauty Culture*. New York: Holt, 1999.

Perez, Cecilia C. T. "A Chamorro Re-Telling of 'Liberation.'" In *Hale'-ta: Kinalamten Pulitikåt: Siñenten I Chamorro / Issues in Guam's Political Development; The Chamorro Perspective*, 70–77. Hagåtña, Guam: Political Status Education Coordinating Commission, 1996.

Perez, Craig. "Bluewashing the Colonization and Militarization of Our Ocean: How U.S. Marine National Monuments Protect Environmentally Harmful U.S. Military Bases throughout the Pacific and the World." *Hawaii Independent*, June 26, 2014.

———. *from unincorporated territory [hukao]*. Oakland, Calif.: Omnidawn, 2017.

———. "Guam and Archipelagic American Studies." In *Archipelagic American* Studies, edited by Brian Russell Roberts and Michelle Ann Stephens, 97–112. Durham, N.C.: Duke University Press, 2017.

Perez, Jesse R. A. "American Colonialism on Guam and Its Challenges." MA thesis, Dartmouth College, 2018.

Perez, Michael P. "Chamorro Resistance and Prospects for Sovereignty in Guam." In *Sovereignty Matters: Locations of Contestation and Possibility in Indigenous Struggles for Self-Determination*, edited by Joanne Barker, 169–90. Lincoln: University of Nebraska Press, 2005.

———."Contested Sites: Pacific Resistance in Guam to U.S. Empire." *Amerasia* 27, no. 1 (January 2001): 97–114.

Perez, Sabina. "Ladrones de la Isla / Thieves of the Island." *(Re)Collection: A WGS Quarterly Publication, Women for Genuine Security*, June 2008. http://www.genuinesecurity.org/Newsletter/countryhighlightjune2008.htm.

Petersen, Glenn. "Politics in Postwar Micronesia." In *American Anthropology in Micronesia*, edited by Robert C. Kiste and Mac Marshall, 145–95. Honolulu: University of Hawai'i Press, 1999.

Pexa, Christopher. *Translated Nation: Rewriting the Dakhóta Oyáte*. Minneapolis: University of Minnesota Press, 2019.

Phillips, Michael F. "Land." In *Hale'-ta: Kinalamten Pulitikåt; Siñenten I Chamorro / Issues in Guam's Political Development; The Chamorro Perspective*, 2–16. Agana, Guam: Political Status Education Coordinating Commission, 1996.

Piatote, Beth H. *Domestic Subjects: Gender, Citizenship, and Law in Native American Literature.* New Haven, Conn.: Yale University Press, 2013.

Pihama, Leonie E. "Tihei Mauri Ora: Honouring Our Voices: Mana Wahine as a Kaupapa Māori Theoretical Framework." PhD diss., University of Auckland, 2001.

Pineda-Tinio, Ma. Teresa. "Review of *Bearers of Benevolence*: The Thomasites and Public Education in the Philippines." *Philippine Studies* 50, no. 4 (Fourth Quarter 2002): 581–83.

Poehlman, Sister Joanne. "Culture Change and Identity among Chamorro Women of Guam." PhD diss., University of Minnesota, 1979.

Poovey, Mary. "Scenes of an Indelicate Character." In *The Making of the Modern Body: Sexuality and Society in the Nineteenth Century*, edited by Catherine Gallagher and Thomas Laqueur, 137–68. Berkeley: University of California Press, 1987.

Pratt, Mary Louise. *Imperial Eyes: Travel Writing and Transculturation.* New York: Routledge, 1992.

PSECC (Political Status Education Coordinating Commission). *Hale'-ta: Hestorian Taotao Tano: The History of Our People.* Agana, Guam: Political Status Education Coordinating Commission, 1993.

———. *Hale'-ta: Hinasso'; Tinige' Put Chamorro / Insights; The Chamorro Identity.* Agana, Guam: Political Status Education Coordinating Commission, 1993.

———. *Hale'-ta: I Ma Gubetna-ña Guam / Governing Guam before and after the Wars.* Agana, Guam: Political Status Education Coordinating Commission, 1994.

———. *Hale'-ta: I Manfåyi: Who's Who in Chamorro History, Volume I.* Agana, Guam: Political Status Education Coordinating Commission, 1995.

———. *Hale'-ta: Inafa'maolek: Chamorro Traditional Values.* Agana, Guam: Political Status Education Coordinating Commission, 1996.

———. *Hale'-ta: Kinalamten Pulitikåt; Siñenten I Chamorro / Issues in Guam's Political Development; The Chamorro Perspective.* Agana, Guam: Political Status Education Coordinating Commission, 1996.

Punzalan, Bernard. "Maria de los Santos y Castro (1828–1890): Matriarch of the Savory and Mazarro Families Bonin Islands/Chichijima." Håle' Taotao Håya Genealogy Project. Chamorroroots.com, November 17, 2012. https://www.chamorroroots.com/v7/index.php/pubs-projects/49-taotao-tano/history/429-maria-de-los-santos-y-castro-1828-1890-matriarch-of-the-savory-and-mazarro-families-bonin-islandschichijima.

Pye, Anne Briscoe, and Nancy Shea. *The Navy Wife.* New York: Harper & Brothers, 1942.

Racette, Sherry Farrell. "My Grandmothers Loved to Trade: The Indigenization of European Trade Goods in Historic and Contemporary Canada." *Journal of the Museum Ethnography* 20 (March 2008): 69–81.

Rafael, Vicente L. *White Love and Other Events in Filipino History.* Durham, N.C.: Duke University Press, 2000.

Raheja, Michelle H. *Reservation Reelism: Redfacing, Visual Sovereignty, and Representations of Native Americans in Film.* Lincoln: University of Nebraska Press, 2010.

Ram, Kalpana, and Margaret Jolly, eds. *Maternities and Modernities: Colonial and Postcolonial Experiences in Asia and the Pacific.* Cambridge: Cambridge University Press, 1998.

Ramirez, Malia Angelica Leon Guerrero. *Los Ehemplus CHamoritus: Chamorro Proverbs*. Hagåtña, Guam: Malia Ramirez, 2016.

Ramirez, Reyna. *Native Hubs: Culture, Community, and Belonging in Silicon Valley and Beyond*. Durham, N.C.: Duke University Press, 2007.

Rand, Jacki Thompson. "Primary Sources: Indian Goods and the History of American Colonialism and the 19th-Century Reservation." In *Clearing a Path: Theorizing the Past in Native American Studies*, edited by Nancy Shoemaker, 137–57. New York: Routledge, 2002.

———. "Status, Sustainability, and American Indian Women in Twentieth Century." In *Sources and Methods in Indigenous Studies*, edited by Chris Andersen and Jean M. O'Brien, 171–77. New York: Routledge, 2017.

Reilly, Brandon. "Reproductive Anticolonialism: Placental Politics, Weaponised Wombs and the Power of Abjection in the Early Spanish Mariana Islands." *Intersections*, no. 44 (April 2020). http://intersections.anu.edu.au/issue44_contents.html.

Revilla, Noʻu and Jamaica Heolimeleikalani Osorio. "Aloha Is Deoccupied Love." In *Detours: A Decolonial Guide to Hawaiʻi*, edited by Hokulani K. Aikau and Vernadette Vicuña Gonzalez, 125–31. Durham, N.C.: Duke University Press, 2019.

Rich, Adrienne. *Of Woman Born: Motherhood as Experience and Institution*. 2nd ed. New York: Norton, 1986.

Rickard, Jolene. "Sovereignty: A Line in the Sand." *Aperture* 139 (Summer 1995): 50–59.

Rivera, Ron F. "Organization of People for Indigenous Rights." Statement to the Special Committee on Decolonization, July 28, 1992. Papua New Guinea.

Roach, Joseph. *Cities of the Dead: Circum-Atlantic Performance*. New York: Columbia University Press, 1996.

Robert, Dana L. *American Women in Mission: A Social History of Their Thought and Practice*. Macon, Ga.: Mercer University Press, 1996.

Roberto, Andrew. "Rear Admiral: Buildup Important for Regional Security." *Guam Daily Post*, September 29, 2017.

Robinson, Olivia, and Trish Barnard. "'Thanks, but We'll Take It from Here': Australian Aboriginal and Torres Strait Islander Women Influencing the Collection of Tangible and Intangible Heritage." *Museum International* 59, no. 4 (2007): 34–45.

Roediger, David R. *The Wages of Whiteness: Race and the Making of the American Working Class*. Rev. ed. London: Verso, 2001.

Rogers, Robert F. *Destiny's Landfall: A History of Guam*. Honolulu: University of Hawaiʻi Press, 1995.

Rohde, Joy Elizabeth. "It Was No 'Pink Tea': Gender and American Anthropology, 1885–1903." In *Significant Others: Interpersonal and Professional Commitments in Anthropology*, edited by Richard Hander, 261–90. Madison: University of Wisconsin Press, 2004.

Rojas, Gena. "Navigating Contested Terrain: A Critical Case Study of Guam's Chamorro Land Trust Residential Land Lease Program." PhD diss., Union Institute and University, June 2018.

Rosa, John. *Local Story: The Massie-Kahahawai Case and the Culture of History*. Honolulu: University of Hawaiʻi Press, 2014.

Rosaldo, Renato. "Imperialist Nostalgia." *Representations* 26 (Spring 1989): 107–22.

Ross, Loretta J., and Rickie Solinger. *Reproductive Justice: An Introduction (Reproductive Justice: A New Vision for the 21st Century)*. Oakland: University of California Press, 2017.

Ross, Luana. "From the 'F' Word to Indigenous/Feminisms." *Wicazo Sa Review* 24, no. 2 (Fall 2009): 39–52.

Rubinstein, Donald. "Culture in Court: Notes and Reflections on Abortion in Guam." *Journal de la Societe des Oceanistes* 1, no. 1 (1992): 35–44.

Russell, Scott. *Tiempon I Manmofo'na: Ancient Chamorro Culture and History of the Northern Mariana Islands*. Saipan, Commonwealth of the Northern Mariana Islands: Division of Historic Preservation, 1998.

Rutherdale, Myra, ed. *Caregiving on the Periphery: Historical Perspectives on Midwifery and Canada*. Montreal: McGill-Queen's University Press, 2010.

Sablan, David Lujan. *The Book of My Life*. Hagåtña, Guam: Guam Publications, 1983.

Sablan, Jaye. "åpuya." *As Us Literary Journal: Decolonial Love Issue*, 2014. https://asusjournal.org/issue-4/jaye-sablan-poetry/.

Sablan, Joaquin F. *My Mental Odyssey: Memoirs of the First Guamanian Protestant Minister*. Poplar Bluff, Mo.: Stinson, 1990.

Said, Edward W. *Beginnings: Intention and Method*. New York: Columbia University Press, 1975.

———. *Culture and Imperialism*. New York: Vintage Books, 1993.

———. *Orientalism*. New York: Pantheon Books, 1978.

Salesa, Damon I. *Mixing Races: An Early Victorian Imperial Problem*. Oxford: Oxford University Press.

Salman, Michael. *The Embarrassment of Slavery: Controversies over Bondage and Nationalism in the American Colonial Philippines*. Berkeley: University of California Press, 2001.

Sanchez, Pedro C. *Guahan Guam: The History of our Island*. Hagåtña, Guam: Sanchez Publishing House, 1989.

Santiago-Valles, Kelvin. "'Higher Womanhood' among the 'Lower Races': Julia McNair Henry in Puerto Rico and the 'Burdens' of 1898." *Radical History Review*, no. 73 (Winter 1999): 47–73.

Santos, Angel. "United States Return Was Re-occupation, Not Liberation." *Pacific Daily News*, July 21, 1991, 21–22.

Santos, Carmen Iglesias. "Guam's Folklore." In *Umatac by the Sea: A Village in Transition*, Micronesian Area Research Center Educational Series no. 3, edited by Rebecca Stephenson and Hiro Kurashina, 87–110. Mangilao, Guam: Micronesian Area Research Center, University of Guam, 1989.

Santos-Bamba, Sharleen. "The Literate Lives of Chamorro Women in Modern Guam." PhD diss., Indiana University of Pennsylvania, 2010.

Santos-Bamba, Sharleen, and Anne Perez Hattori. "The Mother's Tongue: Language, Women, and the Chamorros of Guam." In *Our Voices, Our Histories: Asian American and Pacific Islander Women*, edited by Shirley Hune and Gail M. Nomura, 287–303. New York: New York University Press, 2020.

Scharff, Virginia. *Twenty Thousand Roads: Women, Movement, and the West*. Berkeley: University of California Press, 2003.

Schreiner, Olive. *The Story of an African Farm*. London: Penguin Classics, 1982.

Schroeder, Seaton. "Another View of Guam." *Booklovers Magazine*, May 1905, 717–19.

———. *A Half Century of Naval Service.* New York: D. Appleton, 1922.
Schuller, Kyla. *The Biopolitics of Feelings: Race, Sex, and Science in the Nineteenth Century.* Durham, N.C.: Duke University Press, 2018.
Scott, Joan Wallach. "'Experience.'" In *Feminists Theorize the Political*, edited by Joan W. Scott and Judith Butler, 22–40, New York: Routledge, 1992.
Seth, Suman. *Difference and Disease: Medicine, Race, and the Eighteenth-Century British Empire.* Cambridge: Cambridge University Press, 2018.
Shah, Nyan. *Contagious Divides: Epidemics and Race in San Francisco's Chinatown.* Berkeley: University of California Press, 2001.
Sianturi, Dinah Roma. "'Pedagogic Invasion': The Thomasites in Occupied Philippines." *Kritika Kultura* 12 (2009): 5–26.
Silva, Noenoe K. *The Power of the Steel-Tipped Pen: Reconstructing Native Hawaiian Intellectual History.* Durham: N.C.: Duke University Press, 2017.
Simmonds, Naomi. "Honouring Our Ancestors: Reclaiming the Power of Maori Maternities." In *Indigenous Experiences of Pregnancy and Birth*, edited by Hannah Tait Neufeld and Jaime Cidro, 111–28. Bradford, Ontario: Demeter Press, 2017.
———. "Mana Wahine: Decolonising Politics." *Women's Studies Journal* 25, no. 2 (December 2011): 11–25.
Simonsen, Jane E. *Making Home Work: Domesticity and Native American Assimilation in the American West, 1860–1919.* Chapel Hill: University of North Carolina Press, 2006.
Simpson, Audra. *Mohawk Interruptus: Political Life across the Borders of Settler States.* Durham, N.C.: Duke University Press, 2014.
Simpson, Audra, and Andrea Smith, eds. *Theorizing Native Studies.* Durham, N.C.: Duke University Press, 2014.
Simpson, Leanne Betasamosake. *As We Have Always Done: Indigenous Freedom Through Radical Resistance.* Minneapolis: University of Minnesota Press, 2017.
———. "Birthing an Indigenous Resurgence: Decolonizing Our Pregnancy and Birthing Ceremonies." In *Until Our Hearts Are on the Ground: Aboriginal Mothering, Oppression, Resistance and Rebirth*, edited by D. Memee Lavelle-Harvard and Jeanette Corbiere-Lavell, 25–33. Bradford, Ontario: Demeter Press, 2006.
———. *Islands of Decolonial Love.* Winnipeg, Manitoba: Arbeiter Ring Publishing, 2013.
Smith, Linda Tuhiwai. *Decolonizing Methodologies: Research and Indigenous Peoples.* London: Zed Books, 1999.
Smith, Shawn Michelle. *American Archives: Gender, Race, and Class in Visual Culture.* Princeton, N.J.: Princeton University Press, 1999.
Smith, Susan L. *Japanese American Midwives: Culture, Community, and Health Politics, 1880–1950.* Urbana-Champaign: University of Illinois Press, 2005.
Smith-Rosenberg, Carroll. *Disorderly Conduct: Visions of Gender in Victorian America.* New York: Oxford University Press, 1985.
———. "The Female World of Love and Ritual: Relations between Women in Nineteenth-Century America." *Signs* 1, no. 1 (Autumn 1975): 1–29.
Sobocinski, André B. "The 'Sacred Twenty': The Navy's First Nurses." *Navy Medicine Live* (blog). Accessed 21 July 2018. http://navymedicine.navylive.dodlive.mil/archives/2834.
Sontag, Susan. *On Photography.* New York: Picador, 1977.

Souder, Laura M. T., and Robert A. Underwood, eds. *Chamorro Self-Determination / I Direchon y Taotao*. Agana, Guam: Chamorro Studies Association and Micronesian Area Research Center, University of Guam, 1987.
Souder, Laura Marie Torres. *Daughters of the Island: Contemporary Chamorro Women Organizers on Guam*. 2nd ed. Lanham, Md.: University Press of America, 1992.
——. "Feminism and Women's Studies on Guam." *National Women's Studies Association Journal* 3, no. 3 (Autumn 1991): 442–46.
——. "A Not So Perfect Union." In *Chamorro Self-Determination*, edited by Laura Torres Souder and Robert A. Underwood, 5–22. Mangilao, Guåhan: CHamoru Studies Association and Micronesian Area Research Center, University of Guam, 1987.
——. "Psyche under Siege: Uncle Sam, Look What You've Done to Us." In *Sustainable Development or Malignant Growth? Perspectives of Pacific Island Women*, edited by 'Atu Emberson-Bain, 193–98. Suva, Fiji: Marama Publications, 1994.
——. "Unveiling Herstory: Chamorro Women in Historical Perspective." In *Pacific History: Papers from the 8th Pacific History Association Conference*, edited by Donald Rubinstein, 143–61. Mangilao, Guam: University of Guam Press and Micronesian Area Research Center, 1992.
Sparrow, Bartholomew H. *The Insular Cases and the Emergence of American Empire*. Lawrence: University Press of Kansas, 2006.
Stade, Ronald. *Pacific Passages: World Culture and Local Politics in Guam*. Stockholm: Sweden University, 1998.
Stannard, David E. *Honor Killing: How the Infamous "Massie Affair" Transformed Hawai'i*. New York: Viking, 2005.
Sterner, Doris M. *In and out of Harm's Way: A History of the Navy Nurse Corps*. Seattle: Peanut Butter Publications, 1996.
Stewart, Susan. *On Longing: Narratives of the Miniature, the Gigantic, the Souvenir, the Collection*. Durham, N.C.: Duke University Press, 1993.
Stivens, Maila. "Modernizing the Malay Mother." In *Maternities and Modernities: Colonial and Postcolonial Experiences in Asia and the Pacific*, edited by Kalpana Ram and Margaret Jolly, 50–80. Cambridge: Cambridge University Press, 1998.
Stoler, Ann Laura. *Carnal Knowledge and Imperial Power: Race and the Intimate in Colonial Rule*. Berkeley: University of California Press, 2002.
Suaalii, Tamasaailau. "Deconstructing the 'Exotic' Female Beauty of the Pacific Islands." In *Bitter Sweet*, 93–109. Dunedin, New Zealand: University of Otago Press, 2000.
Summers, Annette. "Sairey Gamp: Generating Fact from Fiction." *Nursing Inquiry* 4, no. (1997): 14–18.
Tadiar, Neferti. *Things Fall Away: Philippine Historical Experience and the Makings of Globalization*. Durham, N.C.: Duke University Press, 2009.
Taitano, Melissa G. "Archives and Collective Memory: A Case Study of Guam and the Internment of Chamorros in Manenggon during World War II." PhD diss., University of California, Los Angeles, 2007.
——. "Stars and Stripes and Boñelos Aga' Forever." *Latte*, May 1995, 68–69.
Tallbear, Kim. "Making Love and Relations beyond Settler Sexualities." YouTube, February 24, 2016, 55:39. https://www.youtube.com/watch?v=zfdo2ujRUv8.

Tamaz, Margo Garcia. "Our Way of Life Is Our Resistance: Indigenous Women and Anti-Imperialist Challenges to Militarization along the U.S.-Mexico Border." In "Invisible Battle Grounds: Feminist Resistance in the Global Age of War and Imperialism," edited by Susan Comfort, 281–318. Special issue, *Work and Days* 20, nos. 57/58 (2011): 281–318.

Taylor, Diana. *The Archive and the Repertoire: Performing Cultural Memory in the Americas.* Durham, N.C.: Duke University Press, 2003.

Teaiwa, Katerina Martina. *Consuming Ocean Island: Stories of People and Phosphate from Banaba.* Bloomington: Indiana University Press, 2015.

Teaiwa, Teresia K. "Articulated Cultures: Militarism and Masculinities in Fiji during the Mid 1990s." In *Fijian Studies* 3, no. 2 (2005): 201–22.

———. "Bikinis and Other S/Pacific N/Oceans." In *Voyaging through the Contemporary Pacific*, edited by David Hanlon and Geoffrey M. White, 91–112. Lanham, Md.: Rowman and Littlefield, 2000.

———. "Lo(o)sing the Edge." In "Native Pacific Cultural Studies on the Edge," edited by Vicente M. Diaz and J. Kehaulani Kauanui. Special issue, *Contemporary Pacific* 13, no. 2 (Fall 2001): 343–57.

———. "Microwomen: U.S. Colonialism and Micronesian Women Activists." In *Pacific History: Papers from the 8th Pacific History Association Conference*, edited by Donald H. Rubinstein, 125–41. Mangilao, Guam: University of Guam and Micronesian Area Research Center, 1992.

———. "Militarism, Tourism and the Native: Articulations in Oceania." PhD diss., University of California, Santa Cruz, 2001.

———. "On Analogies: Rethinking the Pacific in a Global Context." *Contemporary Pacific* 18, no. 1 (2006): 71–87.

———. "Reading Paul Gauguin's Noa Noa with Epeli Hauʻofa's Kisses in the Nederends: Militourism, Feminism, and the 'Polynesian' Body." In *Inside Out: Literature, Cultural Politics, and Identity in the New Pacific*, edited by Vilsoni Hereniko and Rob Wilson, 249–64. Lanham, Md.: Rowman and Littlefield, 1999.

———. "Reflections on Militourism, U.S. Imperialism, and American Studies." In "Tours of Duty and Tours of Leisure," edited by Vernadette Vicuña Gonzales, Jana K. Lipman, and Teresia Teaiwa. Special issue, *American Quarterly* 68, no. 3 (September 2016): 847–53.

———. "Review of *Speaking to Power: Gender and Politics in the Western Pacific*." *Contemporary Pacific* 9, no. 1 (1997): 290–94.

———. "Yaqona/Yagona: Roots and Routes of a Displaced Native." *UTS Review* 4, no. 2 (1998): 92–106.

Te Awekotuku, Ngahuia. *Mana Wahine Maori: Selected Writings on Maori Women's Art, Culture, and Politics.* Auckland: New Women's Press, 1991.

Tengan, Ty P. Kawika, Tevita O. Kaʻili, and Rochelle Tuitagavaʻa Fonoti, eds. "Genealogies: Articulating Indigenous Anthropology in/of Oceania." Special Issue, *Pacific Studies* 33, no. 2/3 (August/December 2010).

Te Punga Somerville, Alice. *Once Were Pacific: Maori Connections to Oceania.* Minneapolis: University of Minnesota Press, 2012.

Te Punga Somerville, Alice, and Daniel Heath Justice, eds. "Introduction: Indigenous Conversations about Biography." In "Indigenous Conversations about Biography," edited by Alice Te Punga Somerville, Daniel Heath Justice, and Noelani Arista. Special issue, *Biography* 39, no. 3 (Summer 2016): 239–47.

Terlaje, Speaker Therese M. "Original Landowners and Agencies Voice Concerns about Live-Fire at Ritidian" (press release). September 8, 2017. https://senatorterlaje.com/original-landowners-and-agencies-voice-concerns-about-live-fire-at-ritidian/.

———. "Renew Commitment to the Inifresi." *Pacific Daily News*, February 17, 2018.

Tetrault, Lisa. *The Myth of Seneca Falls: Memory and the Women's Suffrage Movement, 1848–1898*. Chapel Hill: University of North Carolina Press, 2014.

Teves, Stephanie Nohelani. *Defiant Indigeneity. The Politics of Hawaiian Performance*. Chapel Hill: University of North Carolina Press, 2018.

Theobald, Brianna. *Reproduction on the Reservation: Pregnancy, Childbirth, and Colonialism in the Long Twentieth Century*. Chapel Hill: University of North Carolina Press, 2019.

Thigpen, Jennifer. *Island Queens and Mission Wives: How Gender and Empire Remade Hawai'i's Pacific World*. Chapel Hill: University of North Carolina Press, 2014.

Thomas, Nicholas. *Colonialism's Culture: Anthropology, Travel, and Government*. Cambridge: Polity, 1994.

Thompson, Lanny. *Imperial Archipelago: Representation and Rule in the Insular Territories under U.S. Dominion after 1898*. Honolulu: University of Hawai'i Press, 2010.

Thompson, Laura. *Archaeology of the Marianas Islands*. Honolulu: Bishop Museum, 1932.

———. *Guam and Its People: A Study of Culture Change and Colonial Education*. San Francisco: American Council Institute of Pacific Relations, 1941.

———. "The Women of Guam." *Asia and the Americas* 45, no. 9 (September 1944): 412–15.

Todd, Elley Wiley. *The "New Woman" Revised*. Berkeley: University of California Press, 1993.

Tone-Pah-Hote, Jenny. *Crafting an Indigenous Nation: Kiowa Expressive Culture in the Progressive Era*. Chapel Hill: University of North Carolina Press, 2019.

Tonkovich, Nicole. *The Allotment Plot: Alice C. Fletcher, E. Jane Gay, and Nez Perce Survivance*. Lincoln: University of Nebraska Press, 2012.

Topping, Donald M., Pedro M. Ogo, and Bernadita C. Dungca. *Chamorro-English Dictionary*. Honolulu: University of Hawai'i Press, 1975.

Trask, Haunani-Kay. "Feminism and Indigenous Hawaiian Nationalism." *Signs* 21, no. 4 (Summer 1996): 906–16.

———. "'Lovely Hula Hands': Corporate Tourism and the Prostitution of Hawaiian Culture." In *From a Native Daughter*, 136–47. Honolulu: University of Hawai'i, 1999.

———. "Review of *Talkin' Up to the White Woman: Indigenous Women and Feminism*." *Contemporary Pacific* 15, no. 2 (Fall 2003) 474–75.

Trouillot, Michel-Rolph. *Silencing the Past: Power and the Production of History*. Boston: Beacon Press, 1995.

Tuck, Eve, and K. Wayne Yang. "Decolonization Is Not a Metaphor." *Decolonization* 1, no. 1 (2012): 1–40.

Turnbull, Phyllis, and Kathy E. Ferguson. *Oh, Say, Can You See? The Semiotics of the Military in Hawai'i*. Minneapolis: University of Minnesota Press, 1998.

Tweed, George R., and Blake Clark. *Robinson Crusoe, USN: The Adventures of George R. Tweed RM1c on Japanese-Held Guam*. New York: Whittlesey House, 1945.

"Under SECNAV Releases Statement Following Visit to Guam." *Navy News Services*, January 20, 2011. Story Number: NNS110120-15. https://www.globalsecurity.org /military/library/news/2011/01/mil-110120-nns07.htm.

Underwood, Robert Anacletus. "Afterword: Guam in the 20th Century. In *A Campaign for Political Rights in Guam, 1899–1950* by Penelope Bordallo Hofschneider, 201–13 (Saipan, Northern Mariana Islands: NMI Division of Historic Preservation, 2001).

———. "American Education and the Acculturation of the Chamorros of Guam." PhD diss., University of Southern California, 1987.

———. "Chamorro History: Is the Forward the Conclusion?" Conference keynote address at the 22nd Pacific History Association Biennial Conference, Mangilao, Guam, May 19, 2016.

———. "The Colonial Era: Manning the Helm of the U.S.S. Guam." *Pacific Daily News*, May 22, 1977, 4.

———. "Red, Whitewash and Blue . . . Painting Over the Chamorro Experience." *Pacific Daily News*, July 17, 1977, 6–8.

———. "Teaching Guam History in Guam High Schools." In *Guam History: Perspectives*, edited by Lee D. Carter, William L. Wuerch, and Rosa Roberto Carter, Vol. 1, 1–10. Mangilao, Guam: Richard F. Taitano Micronesian Area Research Center, 1997.

Valentine, Gill. "The Geography of Women's Fear." *Area* 21, no. 4 (1989): 385–90.

Ventura, Desiree Taimanglo. "Maria Anderson Roberto." In *Famalao'an Guåhan: Women in Guam History*, 32–33. Mangilao, Guam: Guampedia, 2019.

Vick, Brian E. *The Congress of Vienna: Power and Politics after Napolean*. Cambridge, Mass.: Harvard University Press, 2014.

Viernes, James Perez. "Chamorro Men in the Making: Capitalism and Indigenous Masculinities under U.S. Naval Colonialism in Guam." *eJournal of the Australian Association for the Advancement of Pacific Studies*, 1.2 and 2.1 (April 2010). http:// intersections.anu.edu.au/pacificurrents/viernes.htm.

———. "Fanhasso i Taotao Sumay: Displacement, Dispossession and Survival in Guam." MA thesis, University of Hawai'i at Mānoa, 2008.

———. "Negotiating Manhood: Chamorro Masculinities and U.S. Military Colonialism in Guam, 1898–1941." PhD diss., University of Hawai'i at Mānoa, 2015.

Vizenor, Gerald, ed. *Survivance: Narratives of Native Presence*. Lincoln: University of Nebraska Press, 2008.

Warrior, Robert. *Tribal Secrets: Recovering American Indian Intellectual Traditions*. Minneapolis: University of Minnesota Press, 1995.

Waziyatawin. *What Does Justice Look Like? The Struggle for Liberation in Dakota Homeland*. St. Paul, Minn.: Living Justice Press, 2008.

Weatherford, Doris. *Women in American Politics: History and Milestones*. Vol. 2. Los Angeles: Sage, 2012.

Webber, C. W. *Tales of the Southern Border*. Philadelphia: J. B. Lippincott, 1887.

Weinbaum, Alys Eve, Lynn M. Thomas, Friti Ramamurthy, Uta G. Poiger, Madeleine Yue Dong, and Tani E. Barlow. *Modern Girl around the World*. Durham, N.C.: Duke University Press, 2008.

Welter, Barbara. "The Cult of True Womanhood: 1820–1860." *American Quarterly* 18, no. 2, pt. 1 (Summer 1966): 151–74.

Wendt, Albert. "Towards a New Oceania." *Mana Review* 1, no. 1 (January 1976): 49–60.

Wexler, Laura. *Tender Violence: Domestic Visions in an Age of U.S. Imperialism*. Chapel Hill: University of North Carolina Press, 2000.

Whimp, Graeme. "Interdisciplinarity and Pacific Studies: Roots and Routes." *Contemporary Pacific* 20, no. 2 (2008): 397–421.

Wilkins, David E., and K. Tsianina Lomawaima. *Uneven Ground: American Indian Sovereignty and Federal Law*. Norman: University of Oklahoma Press, 2001.

Willett, Julie A. *Permanent Waves: The Making of the American Beauty Shop*. New York: New York University Press, 2000.

Williams, Raymond. "Structures of Feeling." In *Marxism and Literature*, 128–35. Oxford: Oxford University Press, 1977.

Wolfe, Patrick. "Settler Colonialism and the Elimination of the Native." *Journal of Genocide Research* 8, no. 4 (December 2006): 387–409.

Workman, Ann M., Linda Cruz-Ortiz, and Debbie Kaminga-Quinata. "Use of Traditional Medicine and Healers on Guam." In *Science of Pacific Island Peoples: Fauna, Flora, Food and Medicine*, edited by John Morrison, Paul Geraghty, and Linda Crowl, 201–33 Suva, Fiji: University of the South Pacific, 1994.

Workman, Ann Pobutsky, Linda Cruz Ortiz, and Debbie Kaminga Quinata. "I Che'cho Suruhåna Yan Suruhånu: The Use of Traditional Medicine and Healers on Guam." A project funded by the Guam Council on the Arts and Humanities, Office for Women's Research, University of Hawai'i–Manoa, and the Guam Humanities Council, n.d.

Yazzie, Melanie K., and Cutcha Risling Baldy. "Introduction: Indigenous Peoples and the Politics of Water." *Decolonization* 7, no. 1 (2018): 1–18.

Young, Robert J. C. *Colonial Desire: Hybridity in Theory, Culture and Race*. London: Routledge, 1995.

Films, Videos, CDs

Aguero, Francisco. "Forum on Guam's Pattera: Their Story and Legacy." Videotaped recordings by KGTF TV-Channel 12. Sponsored by the Guam Humanities Council. Government House, Hagåtña, Guåhan, April 11, 1997.

Coulehan, Kathy. *Portrait of Guam: Agueda Johnston, a Biography*. Guam Council on the Arts and Humanities, KGTF TV-Channel 12, 1990. VHS, 28 min.

Cruz, Karen A. *Pattera: Midwives of Guam*. Barigåda, Guam, Pattera Video Project, 2001. VHS, 25 min.

Diaz, Vicente M. *Sacred Vessels: Navigating Tradition and Identity in Micronesia*. Hagåtña, Guam: Moving Islands Production, 1997.

"Maga'haga: Part 1." YouTube, February 8, 2008, 8:39. Tomhom, Guåhan. https://www.youtube.com/watch?v=SW5aFuw5MDM.

"Maga'haga: Part 2." YouTube, February 8, 2008, 7:33. Tomhom, Guåhan. https://www.youtube.com/watch?v=n3e1jMofKrE.

Monks, John, and Richard Goldstone, *No Man Is an Island*. Universal City: Gold Coast Productions, 1962.

Teaiwa, Teresia. "For Salome." *Terenesia: Amplified Poetry and Songs by Teresia Teaiwa and Sia Figel*. Produced by Richard Hamasaki and Doug H. Matsuoka, compact disc. Honolulu: Hawai'i Dub Machine: Elepaio Press, 2000.

Index

abortion, 34–35; abortion laws, 227n94
achafñak. *See* familia
Ada, Joseph F., 227n94
Aguero, Francisco Taitano (Tun Frank), 2–4, 22
Aguero, Maria Taitano (Tan Marian Dogi'), 3, 25–26, 43, 66–67, 70; as "midnight wife," 2, 4–5
Aguon, Katherine, 156
Americanization: of CHamorus, 17–18, 41, 158–59; of Guåhan, 143, 155; modernization and, 40–43, 143, 166; of pattera, 40–41; professionalization and, 43–47. *See also* Johnston, Agueda; modernization
åmot CHamoru, 23, 42, 66, 107; atmagosu, 71
åmot palai, 42, 68
Angeles, Antonio de los, 28, 46, 224n25
Anthony, Susan B., 86, 100
anticolonialism: feminism and, 5, 27; of Hale'-ta project, xiv; placental politics and, 30
apuya', 60, 72; burial of ga'chong i patgon and, xi–xii, 28, 30, 33, 35–36, 39, 49, 203
Arceo, Ann Marie, 199, 228n110
Artero, Antonio, 188–90
Arvin, Maile, 11
assimilation: American schools and, 159; as benevolent, 8–9, 13, 241n46; of CHamorus, 1, 25, 40–41, 47, 131; of CHamoru women, 1, 5–6, 25, 40–41, 47, 153, 156, 179; of Guåhan, 8; of pattera, 156; photography and, 236n45; white women and, 112, 131
Atienza, David, 33, 35, 221n103

Babauta, Antonio "Min" Cruz, 203
Babauta, Felix, 52–54

Baldy, Cutcha Risling, 220n93
Bashford, Alison, 42
Basso, Keith H., 213n1
Batchen, Geoffrey, 123–24, 126
beauty culture, 13, 169–77
Bederman, Gail, 10, 217n32
Beecher, Catharine, 81
Bejado, Lou, 201
Better Babies campaign, 14, 49
birth control, 66
Blas, Dominga Ogo (Tan Inga'), 75–76
Bolivar, Babette "Bette," 201
Bordallo, Baltazar Jerome (B. J.), 184, 189–90
Bordallo, Madeleine, 200
Bowman, Josephine Beatrice, 47–48, 50, 242n72
Bradley, Willis W., 149, 238n92
Braun, Frederica, 121–22
Brunton, Maria Gutierrez, 168–69
Burton, Antoinette, 8, 80

Cadigan, Mary Elaine, 148
Camacho, Keith L., 190
Camacho, Vicente P., 191
Camacho-Dungca, Bernadita "Benit," 149, 202
Campbell, Craig, 117
canoes: Guåhan flag and, 114, 143, 146–47; Indigenous mobilities and, 113; metaphor for decolonization, 113; presence and absence of, 139
Carbullido, Baltazar, 142
Carbullido, Rosa, 76
Carlson, Martin E., 178, 244n99
Catholicism, CHamoru, 18–25; gender and, 38; indigenization of, 9–10; as watchdog of female virtue, 66; women's religiosity and, 138, 186, 190, 240n22. *See also* kostumbren CHamoru

CHamoru language, 195–96; decolonization and, 213n1; loss of, 154, 159–60; proscription of, 138. *See also* fino' CHamoru (fino' håya)

CHamorus: Americanization of, 17–18, 41, 158–59; American patriotism of, 152, 155, 157, 160, 166, 169–81 passim, 185, 190, 194; assimilation of, 25, 40–41, 47, 131; citizenship movement of, 128, 155–56, 184–85, 186, 189, 236n46; citizenship of, 77, 135, 140, 143, 152, 153, 236n46; class hierarchy of, 95–96, 163–65, 196; compared to Filipinos, 88–89, 133, 134; dispossession of, 11–13, 119, 217n37; education of, 105–6, 119, 129–31, 134, 140, 146, 157–64, 185–86, 194, 232n97, 239n19; history and, xii–xiii; infantilizing of, 41, 121–22, 185; kinship with U.S. military, 69–70, 191–92, 201 mobility of, 138, 156, 162, 167–69, 183; modernity and, 145, 155, 156, 183, 196–97; navy modernization program, 17–18, 74–75, 124, 127, 155, 158–59, 166, 216n15; of Northern Marianas, 153–54; nostalgia of, 139, 155; racialization of, 43–49; self-determination of, xii, 135, 140, 143, 186–87, 202; self-identification of, 153; sexualization of, 122, 134, 142–43, 154–55, 174–75; sovereignty of, xii–xiii, 202; surveillance of, 25; use of term, 178–79, 196, 213n1. *Also* CHamoru women; mestisas/mestizas (mixed-race CHamorus); pattera (ná'fafañågu)

CHamoru studies, 40

CHamoru women: activism of, 198–203; adaptability of, 47, 54, 65, 156; in American magazines, 173–75; assimilation of, 1, 6, 25, 40–41, 47, 153, 156, 179; "civilizing" of, 51; domesticity and, 105, 134; entry into American spaces, 94; exoticization of, 101, 103, 174–76; gender roles, 21; inadahi and inayuda duties of, 4, 26, 37, 55, 199; inagångi of, 201; labor of, xii, 5, 36, 38, 76, 219n66; matrilineality and, 21, 27, 34, 157; as ma ulitao, 24; minesngon and minetgot of, 26–27, 54, 157, 195, 199; mobility of, 167–68, 232n81; modernity and, 108, 129, 145; modernization and, 19–23, 51; pinilan and pineksai duties of, 27, 32, 36–38, 50, 57, 157, 181, 186, 203; racialization of, 43, 45, 49, 65, 105, 122, 134, 142–43, 177, 185; resistance of, 33–35, 65–66; sexualization of, 122, 134, 142–43, 154–55, 174–75; surveillance of, 41; truth telling of, 199; U.S. colonialism and, xii, 1–2, 5; virgin/whore dichotomy, 21–22. *See also* CHamorus; pattera (ná'fafañågu)

Chandler, Harriett O., 175–76

Charfauros, Ana B., 128

Chatfield, Shoshana, 200

chenchule', 9–10, 76, 77, 82, 203

childbirth, 36, 77; inafa'maolek and, 38; traditional practices, 71–73, 76, 228n108. *See also* pattera (ná'fafañågu)

Christensen, Donna, 199, 200

citizenship: CHamoru movement for, 77, 135, 140, 143, 152–53, 184, 236n46

Clancy-Smith, Julia, 96, 122–23

class: CHamoru hierarchy of, 95–96, 163–65, 196; CHamoru motherhood and, 13–14; CHamoru nurses, recruitment of, 40, 47–48; education and, 162–63; manakhilo' class, 55, 96, 102, 159, 162, 164–65; mestiso/a people and, 99–103, 105

cleanliness, 40, 161; as CHamoru value, 46; pattera and, 46–47, 223n24

Clinton, Hillary, 198

Cobweb Club, 85–86

Coello de la Rosa, Alexandre, 24, 33, 35, 221n103

Cogan, Doloris Coulter, 186

colonial gaze, 234n3; of Helen Paul, 115–19, 123, 126, 146; of new women, 115–23

colonialism: feminist critiques of, 7; gender and, 18, 226n70; leisure and, 121–22; modernity and, 117, 186; photography and, 124–25; the picturesque and, 138; sexualization and, 122; violence of, 1;

white feminism and, 7; white womanhood and, 8, 90, 112. *See also* settler colonialism
colonialism, Spanish, 127–28, 214n1, 241n46; education under, 159; gender and, 23–24, 226n70; kostumbren CHamoru and, 19–20, 21; patriarchy and, 164; reducciones under, 23; via sacra of, 26
colonialism, U.S: as "benevolent," 8–10, 14, 40, 84, 88, 107–8, 127, 222n10, 241n46; CHamoru women and, xii, 1–2, 5; domesticity and, 105, 134; education under, 129–31, 134, 140, 146, 152, 159–60, 194; gender and, 14, 24–25, 81, 226n70; gendered labor of, 81; gendered violence of, 24–25; Indigenous bodies and, 115; "long road to rehabilitation," 5, 127; paternalism of, 185; in Philippines, 9; photography and, 237n55
comfort women, 169, 175
Concepcion, Juan de la, 34
Coontz, Robert, 149, 232n78
cordage: directionality and, 72–73; land and, xi–xiii; pattera and, 31–32; Polynesian concepts of, 35–36
Coulthard, Glen, 226n65
Cramlet, Clyde Myron, 152, 155, 245n140
Cristobal, Hope Alvarez, 202
Crose, Edith, 133
Cruz, Adrian, 221n103
Cruz, Denise, 241n46
Cruz, Joaquina de la, 137–38
Cruz, Karen, 31–32
Curzon, George Nathaniel, 91

dandyism, 131–34, 138, 236n52; racialization of, 133–34
Darr, Frances, 169
Daughters of Mary Society, 22
Dauser, Sue, 122, 235n18
decolonization, 113; canoe as metaphor for, 113; feminism and, 5–6, 28; of Guåhan, 117, 148–49, 157, 196, 228n124; Guåhan flag and, 148–49; historiography and,

xii–xv; imperialism and, 215n11; Indigenous feminism and, 5–6; language and, 213n1; research and, xiv; resurgence and, 157, 196
defiant indigeneity, 20–21, 218n60
de Forest, Robert, 109
DeLeon, Julia, 164
Delgado, Joannis Joseph, 34
Deloria, Philip, 81
Deloria, Vine, Jr., 245n140
diasporic studies, 215n3
Diaz, Vicente M., 139, 241n50; on "Following the Flag," 17–18
Diego, Concepcion Paulino, 75
Diego, Fred, 75
directionality, 30, 33, 76, 203, 228n110; cordage and, 72–73
dispossession: of CHamoru land, 10–13, 27, 217n37; of CHamoru people, 119; gender and, 84; of Indian land, 193; modernization and, 119; race and, 84
Doctrine of Territorial Incorporation, 116–17
domesticity: CHamoru women and, 180; colonialism and, 105; empire and, 118; kostumbren CHamoru and, 21, 25–26, 57; pattera and, 61–65; U.S. colonialism and, 104–5, 134; U.S. imperialism and, 39, 80–81; violence of, 41; white women and, 15–16, 39, 89
Dorn, Edward John, 100, 102, 157, 167, 195, 232n78, 232n81, 244n103; banning of mestisa dress, 159; defense of Agueda Johnston, 181–82
Dorn, Syble, 100
Dorn Hall, 100–101, 136, 166, 232n78
Doss, Darrell, 187
Duarte, Dolores, 232n81
Duarte, Maria, 102, 232n81
Duarte, Pedro, 102, 108, 113
Duenas, Catalina Eustaquio, 75
Duenas, Emeteria Quichocho (Tan Emeteria), 55, 59, 69
Duenas, Eugenia, 164
Dyer, Dorothy, 79, 89–90, 95, 113; homeschooling of, 98

Dyer, George, 50, 80, 83–93 passim, 99–100, 104–6, 161, 229n15; creation of "special laborer" category, 99, 163; educational initiatives of, 105–6, 232n97; on mestisa women, 101; on race-mixing, 232n80

Dyer, Susan, 13–15, 47, 78–79, 83–85, 229n15; anti-imperialism of, 79–80, 87, 100; class and, 95, 99, 106; Cobweb Club membership, 85–86, 106; duties of, 12, 93–95; flexibility of, 97–98; governor's ball, 95–97; imperialism, defense of, 87–88; impressions of Guåhan, 91–93; inagradesi and, 82; labor and leisure of, 36, 78–79, 81–82, 92–93, 97, 103–6, 118–19; letters to George, 86–87; maternal patriarchy of, 98; mestisa women, relationship with, 99–105, 110–12; new womanhood of, 36, 79–80, 82, 85–87, 98–99, 112; palace (palåsyo) socials of, 70–80, 94–96, 99–102, 169; patriotism of, 87–88; philanthropic work of, 50–51, 79–80, 93–94, 106, 229n21; "small matters" of, 36, 79–82; Susana Hospital founding, 96–97, 106–10, 141, 168, 232n78; tour-of-duty feminism of, 80–81, 96, 109–10, 119; vaudeville performances and, 122, 135–36; work ethic of, 81–82

Dyer, Susan "Daisy" (daughter), 79, 89–90, 95, 96, 110; homeschooling of, 98; as new woman, 97

education: of Agueda Johnston, 157–58, 162–63, 167; of CHamorus, 105–6, 119, 129–31, 134, 140, 146, 157–64, 185–86, 194, 232n97, 239n19; class and, 162–63; in Guåhan, 105–6, 115, 129–31, 134, 157–64, 232n97, 234n9, 239n19, 240n35, 241n41; in Philippines, 162; race and, 162–64; racialization of, 163–64; Spanish colonial, 21, 159; U.S. colonial, 129–31, 134, 140, 146, 152, 159–60, 194

Elvidge, Anita, 232n87

Elvidge, Ford, 25, 181–82

empire, 198; domesticity and, 118; gender and, 6, 93; gendered violence of, 6; modernity and, 7; navy wives and, 12, 16, 38; navy women and, 38; photography and, 116; sentimentalism and, 8, 118, 131

enfetmera (nurses), 3–4, 55–56, 59, 110. See also pattera (ná'fafañågu)

España, Damian de, 34

ethnography, 19–22; ethnographic refusal, 43; synchronic bias, 19–20

eugenics, 14, 141

Eustaquio, Antonia Blas, 55

Eustaquio, Natividad Iriarte (Tan Da'), 75

fafa'na'gue (CHamoru teachers), 141, 161–63, 167–70, 181, 240n35, 241n41; Agueda Johnston, 151, 156, 162, 203; pattera and, xiii, 5; as new women, 21

famalao'an CHamoru. See CHamoru women

familia, 3, 4, 14, 39, 68; of Agueda Johnston, 188; American patriarchy and, 42; kostumbren CHamoru and, 57; system of, 42, 57, 63–64

fa'taotao, 74

Feja, Francisco (Tun Kiko), 149

feminism: anticolonialism and, 5, 27; CHamoru, 37; colonialism, critiques of, 7; decolonization and, 5–6, 28; history and culture, Indigenous critiques of, 5–7, 27–28, 220n87; of navy wives and nurses, 5; oral histories and, 29, 73, 220n89, 215n10; tour-of-duty feminism, 80–81, 96, 109–10, 119; white feminism, 7, 98, 110; women of color critiques, 21, 26, 219n77, 223n19. See also Indigenous feminism

feminist studies, 28; "new woman" in, 8

fino' CHamoru (fino' håya), 4–5; Agueda Johnston and, 195–96; decolonization and, 213n1; English-only policy, 52, 131, 161; Helen Paul and, 138; loss of, 154, 159–60; pattera insistence on, 52; prohibition of, 52–53, 131, 161; proscription of, 52–53, 131, 138, 161; resurgence of, 196; revitalization of, 199, 205. See also CHamoru language

Index 289

flag of Guåhan, 37, 113–16, 143–50, 180, 238n92; CHamoru nationalism and, 139, 148; decolonization movement and, 117, 148–49; designing of, 37, 113, 139, 146–50; kostumbren CHamoru and, 148; nostalgia for, 148; the picturesque and, 114–15, 164; protocol, 117; redesign of, 147–48
Flores, Felixberto, 148
Flores, Guillerma Chargualaf, 55
Fojas, Camilla, 200
Fo'na and Pontan, story of, 29, 31
Fonoti, Rochelle, 35–36
Forbes, Eric, xi–xii
Fraker, Margie, 128–29
Fraser, Gertrude, 76
Freycinet, Louis de, 16
Freycinet, Rose de, 16, 159
Fuetsan Famalao'an, 198–99

ga'chong i patgon: burial of, xi–xii, 28–39 passim, 49, 73, 77, 203, 228n110, 228n124; care for, 161, 228n110
galaide. *See* canoes
Ganter, Regina, 216n20
Garcia, Francisco, 168, 241n56
Garrido, Bartola, 136, 137–38
Garrido, Maria T., 148, 165
gender: Catholicism and, 138; CHamoru men's bodies, regulation of, 36; CHamoru motherhood and, 13–14; colonialism and, 18, 226n70; dispossession and, 84; empire and, 93; feminization of Guåhan, 10–11; health and, 107; heteronormativity, 49, 58; history and, xiii–xv; inafa'maolek and, 32–33; indigeneity and, 26; Indigenous subjectivities and, 5; kostumbren CHamoru and, 21–22; labor and, 81, 105; masculinity, 10, 24, 45, 93, 217n32; mobility, 4, 16, 21–22, 57, 89, 138, 156, 162, 167–69, 183; modernity and, 6–7; patriarchy, 42, 49, 64, 98, 164; the picturesque and, 129; roles, 21, 164; settler colonialism and, 6; Spanish colonialism and, 23–24, 226n70; travel and, 16; U.S. colonialism and, 14, 18, 24–25, 226n70; U.S. Navy regulation of, 10; violence and, 6, 24–25, 236n45
genocide, cultural, 6
Gilmer, William, 95, 142–43; antimiscegenation law, 101, 138
Glass, Henry, 84
Goeman, Mishuana, 165, 213n1
Gokña, 201–2
Goodyear-Ka'ōpua, Noelani, xiii
Gouda, Frances, 96, 123
Gould, Helen, 106
Gould, Jay, 106
Grande, Sandy, 220n85
Grimshaw, Patricia, 216n20
Guåhan (Guam): Americanization of, 155; "benevolent" assimilation of, 8; decolonization movement in, 117, 148–49, 157, 196, 228n124; education in, 105–6, 115, 129–31, 134, 157–64, 232n97, 234n9, 239n19, 240n35, 241n41; environmental destruction in, 192–93, 199; feminization of, 10–11; independence movement, 128, 135, 140, 143; Japanese occupation of, 54, 120–21, 151, 154–56, 173, 187, 191, 193, 226n84, 241n50; liberation from Japan, 152; militarization of, 6, 29, 154, 197, 198–203, 246n1, 247n10; modernization of, 77, 119–20, 143, 154, 155, 202; post–World War II, 152, 192–93; race-mixing in, 97–98; settler colonialism and, 198, 202, 217n35; sovereignty of, 27; tourism in, 199–200; unincorporated status of, 116–17, 153, 186–87, 199, 222n10; usage of term, 213n1; U.S. colonization of, 84; U.S. occupation of, 5
Guamanians: use of term, 153–54, 178–79, 195–96. *See also* CHamorus
Guam Chamber of Commerce, 11–12
Guam Dramatic Club, 94–95
Guam Industrial Fair, 140–43; Fair Queen of, 141–43, 237n71
Guam Militia, 143–44, 238n78; militia flag, 143, 146

Guam Museum, 120, 168–9
Guam Normal School, 36–37, 115, 119, 123, 127–138, 157, 162
Guam Organic Act of 1950, 5, 77, 116–17, 153, 186
Guerrero, Olivia, 55, 74
guma' ulitao, 24
Guzman, Sylvia, 148

Haggis, Jane, 7–8
Hale'-ta public history project, xii–xiv
Hall, Stuart, 26, 38
Hannah, Ana Siguenza, 59
Harris, Aroha, 27
Hartman, Saidiya, 160–61
Hattori, Anne Perez, xiii, 10, 108
Hawley, Edith H., 85, 106
Hayes, William "Bully," 137
Hearst, Phoebe, 106
Hernandez, Maria, 200–201
Herrera, Jesus Santos (Tun CHu'), 64, 199
Herrera, Joaquina Baubata (Tan Kina'), xiv–xv, 22–23, 29, 43, 65, 197, 199, 203; domestic tensions of, 58, 61–64; on pattera practice, 32, 49, 61–65, 199, 203; on pattera training, 52–56; on Tan Marian Dogi', 43; on traditional birthing practices, 72–73
Herrero, Dolores, 170
heteronormativity, 49, 58
Higbee, Lenah, 51
Higginbotham, Evelyn Brooks, 185
Higgins, Margaret, 168, 241n56
Higgins, Spencer, 168
Hīroa, Te Rangi (Sir Peter Henry Buck), 104
history: decolonial habit of, xii–xiii; footnotes and, 1–2, 4, 215n4; gender and, xiii–xv; historiography and, xiii, 1–7, 37–40, 151, 216n18; new imperial, 7, 216n17; Pacific history, 7, 40, 216n17; the picturesque and, 126; public history, xii–xiv
Holcomb, Crayton Philo, 137
"Humalom Enfetmera" (kåntan CHamorita), 56–57, 225n64

Imada, Adria, 177
imperialism, U.S., 83, 87–88; anti-imperialism, 79–80, 87, 100; decolonization and, 215n11; domesticity and, 80–81; gender and, 88; in Hawai'i, 84; Susan Dyer and, 79–80, 87, 100. See also colonialism, U.S.
inafa'maolek, 4, 9, 82, 141, 192; activism and, 202; Agueda Johnston and, 180, 190, 192, 195–96, 199; balance and, 68, 192; chenchule' and, 82; childbirth and, 38; disease and, 226n77; gender and, 6, 32–33; Gokña and, 202; kostumbren CHamoru and, 9, 195–96; labor of, 26–27, 180, 190, 199; pattera practice and, 32–33, 36, 38–39, 58, 68, 76–78, 107; as radical relationality, 30; as tåddong practice, 9–10, 30, 138; values of, 32, 39
indigeneity: as analytic, xiv–xv, 5, 113, 157; articulation and, 64, 155; defiant, 20–21, 218n60; gender and, 26, 115, 190; land back and, 149; modernity and, 6–7, 71, 76–77, 82, 105, 179, 181, 194–98; roots and routes of, 26–27, 38–39
Indigenous feminism, 27–29, 33; decolonization and anticolonialism, 5–7; placental politics, 6, 28–33, 39; theory and practice, xiv, 6–8, 28, 37, 187, 194, 198–99
"Inifresi" (pledge), 202
Insular Cases, 116–17, 222n10

Jackson, Wilma Leona, 48, 51, 68–70
Johnson, Lucius, 49
Johnston, Agueda Iglesias, 5, 27, 37, 94, 120–21, 199, 215n10; American patriotism of, 152, 155, 157, 160, 166, 169–81 passim, 185, 190, 194; as assimilated, 153, 179; "Chamorrita Notes," 152, 154–55, 157, 165–67, 239n5, 245n140; CHamoru womanhood of, 195; civic engagement of, 168–69, 172, 180, 185; education of, 157–58, 162–63, 167; familia of, 158, 162, 165–66, 188, 195; fino' håya and, 195–96; as "First Lady of Guam," 156, 176, 192, 243n86; George Tweed, relationship

with, 151–52, 167, 176–77, 186, 187–90, 193–94; on Guåhan flag, 114, 116, 146, 147; kostumbren CHamoru of, 195; Liberation Day creation, 190; as maga'håga, 156–57, 173, 191, 197; as matlina, 156–57, 169, 173, 186, 190–91, 194, 196; modernity of, 152, 156, 194; new womanhood of, 150, 156; as pin-up girl, 172, 173–74; radio show, 178; self-identification of, 152–53, 154–55; Servicio Para I Manåmko', 196; show productions of, 169, 172–73; smear campaign against, 181–82; social mobility of, 164–71, 182–83; tåddong practice and, 191–92; teaching career of, 119, 128, 151, 152, 161–64, 197, 241n41; traditional knowledge of, 194; "Victory Tour" of, 179–80
Johnston, Frances Benjamin, 236n45
Johnston, Margaret, 169
Johnston, Marian, 169, 173–74
Johnston, William Gautier, 168–69, 179, 181, 183, 195; death of, 174; imprisonment of, 167, 175, 187–88, 189
Jolly, Margaret, 112, 122
Jorgensen, Marilyn, 23

Kahn, Miriam, 35
Ka'ili, Tevita, 35–36
Kalakaua (king of Hawai'i), 84
Kame'eleihiwa, Lilikala, 35
kåntan Chamorita, 56–57
Kaplan, Amy, 80–81
kinship, 220n93; CHamoru, 28–32; between CHamorus and U.S. military, 69–70, 191–92, 201; Indigenous, 11; of manåmko', 42–43; between Native and navy nurses, 69–70; placental care and, 35
Knight, Della, 47, 50, 60
knowledge, Indigenous, 13, 33–36, 60, 66–67, 107, 138, 198; ecological, 194; ontology and, xiii, 6, 33; of pattera, xi; politics of, 36
kompaire system, 10, 75–76

kostumbren CHamoru, 9, 18–26; of Agueda Johnston, 195; Catholicism and, 128; decline of, 178; domesticity and, 21, 25–26; familia and, 47; gender and, 21–22; Guåhan flag and, 148; inafa'maolek and, 196; matlina and, 186, 190–91; modernity and, 22–23, 33; sexuality and, 22–23, 26, 56–58, 128–29, 183; Spanish colonialism and, 19–20, 21

labor: Aboriginal, 7; of CHamoru women, xii, 5, 36, 38, 76, 219n66; gender and, 105; of inafa'maolek, 27; land and, xi; of leisure, 36, 78–82, 92–93, 97, 103–6, 118–19; modernity and, 7; pattera, post-World War II, 76; reproductive, 9; "special laborer" category, 99, 163, 167
Lamour, Dorothy, 176–77
land (tåno'): CHamorus and, xi; cordage and, xi–xiii; dispossession of, 11–13, 28, 30, 32, 157, 166, 192–94, 201–2, 217n37; labor and, xi; oral tradition and, 29–30; relations with, 157, 166, 192–94, 201; Spanish Crown lands, 217n37; stewardship of, 29, 220n85; as storied sites, 213n1
Leary, Richard, 8–9, 158–59, 163, 217n37, 239n19, 240n22
Le Gobien, Charles, 34
Lehman, Shirley, 170–71
leisure: colonialism and, 121–22; labor of, 36, 78–82, 92–93, 97, 103–6, 118–19; of navy wives, 118–22; white womanhood and, 97, 103–4
Leon Guerrero, Ana, 175
Leon Guerrero, Carmen, 141, 142, 241n41
Leon Guerrero, Concepcion (Tan Chong Arugon), 73
Leon Guerrero, Eugenia Aflague, 55
Leon Guerrero, Francisco Baza (Tun Kiko Suilo), 184, 189, 191, 244n103
Leon Guerrero, Ignacia, 175–76
Leon Guerrero, Lourdes "Lou," 55
Leon Guerrero, Maria, 164
Leonhardt, Elisabeth, 40, 42, 48; on pattera, 49–50

Lili'uokalani (queen of Hawai'i), 100
Litekyan (Ritidian), 114, 147, 198, 200–201, 247nn10–11
Lomawaima, K. Tsianina, 160
Longyear, John Munro, 123
Longyear, Mary Beecher, 123
Lopez de Legazpi, Miguel, 214n1
lotus flowers, 81–82, 104, 229n9
Lukere, Vicki, 35
Lydon, Jane, 124–25

maga'håga, 28–29, 37, 196–97, 199, 201–3, 220n90; Agueda Johnston as, 156–57, 173, 191, 197
Mailloux, Gordon, 238n92
makåhna/kakåhna, 107, 221n107
mamåhlao (gai/tai mamahlao), 9, 141; Agueda Johnston and, 196; pattera and, 32, 66–67, 74
mañaina, 32, 58, 60, 67, 73, 158, 202, 228n110; healers, 71; pattera, 49; language and, 195
manåmko', 42–43, 49, 71, 141–42, 155, 196
Manderson, Lenore, 65
Mani, Lata, 8
Manibusan, Jose C., 191
manmofo'na, 3, 202, 228n110
mannginge', 9
Mar, Tracey Banivanua, 215n11
Mariana Islands, 153, 213n1; matrilineal society of, 34; Northern Mariana Islands, 8, 153–54, 187, 213n1, 239n6
Maria Schroeder Hospital, 50, 107, 226n74
Marshall Islands, 35; nuclear testing on, 236n45
Martinez, Pedro P., 191
masculinity, 217n32; CHamoru, 24; paternalism and, 45; U.S. crisis of, 10, 93; white, 45
Masongsong, mother-in-law of, 34
matlina, 37, 42–43, 58; Agueda Johnston as, 156–57, 169, 173, 186, 190–91, 194, 196; matlina politics, 186; as pattera compensation, 75–76
McCallum, Mary Jane, 7
McCarty, Teresa, 160

McClintock, Anne, 82
McKenna, Rebecca, 141
McKinley, William, 8
McLean, Bertha Cheney, 50–51, 109
McLean, Norman T., 50
McMillan, George, 179, 180
Mead, Margaret, 12–13
Mesa, Rosalia Aquiningoc Ulloa (Tan Liang), 5, 51–52, 55, 58–59, 65, 71–73, 197, 203; birthing practices of, 72–73
mestisa/mestiza (dress), 48, 134, 170; banning of, 159; as picturesque, 51
mestisas/mestizas (mixed-race CHamorus), 79, 134; class and, 99–100, 101–3, 105; education and, 106; manakhilo' class, 55, 96, 102, 159, 162, 164–65; relationship with Susan Dyer, 99–105, 110–12; as "sought after wives," 135–38; Susana Hospital and, 109
midwives, 40; African American, 76; Filipina, 223n12; Japanese, 227n89; midwifery problem, 40–45; phasing out of, 76. See also pattera (ná'fafañågu)
militarization, 6, 29, 154, 197–203, 246n1, 247n10; modernization and, 143
militourism, 199–200, 235n18; photography and, 121
Miller, Monica, 133
Millinchamp, Emilia Anderson, 240n22
Millinchamp, Henry, 135–36, 240n22
Million, Dian, 5
modernity: of Agueda Johnston, 152, 156, 194; authenticity and, 71; CHamorus and, 145, 155, 156, 183, 196–97; CHamoru women and, 37, 108, 129, 145; colonialism and, 117, 186; empire and, 7; gender and, 6–7; health care and, 107; indigeneity and, 6–7, 71; Indigenous women and, 7; kostumbren CHamoru and, 22–23, 33; labor and, 7; logic of elimination, 43; pattera and, 23, 70; tradition and, 71
modernization: Americanization and, 40–41, 143; CHamoru women and, 19–23, 51; cultural costs of, 166; dispossession and, 119; of Guåhan, 77,

119–20, 143, 154, 155, 202; militarization and, 143; professionalization and, 43–47; progress and, 40; U.S. Navy program of, 17–18, 74–75, 124, 127, 155, 158–59, 166, 216n15; wage economy and, 74–75. *See also* Americanization

mo'na, 1, 5, 214n2

Moraga, Cherríe, 26

Moreton-Robinson, Aileen, 10, 112, 203

Morrill, Angie, 11

motherhood, CHamoru, 13–14; nåna, 2–4, 22, 41, 54–58, 60, 75, 158, 165–66, 195; nånan biha, 14, 42, 58, 77

ná'fafañågu xi, xiii, 21, 77. *See also* pattera (ná'fafañågu)

Nagel, Lillian A., 114

Native Pacific cultural studies, 26, 38

Native studies, 28

navy wives, 6, 8, 80, 167–68, 203; adjustment to tropics, 170–71; duties of, 12, 93–95, 121; empire and, 12, 16, 38; feminism of, 5; flexibility of, 96; leisure of, 118–22; "navy wife" as analytic, 8, 134. *See also* Dyer, Susan

navy women, 6, 13, 14. *See also* Dyer, Susan; Paul, Helen

Nelson, Evelyn: "Following the Ship" essay, 15, 18

Nelson, Frederick, 15

new womanhood, 8, 86–87; of Agueda Johnston, 150, 156; "new woman" as analytic, 8; of Susan Dyer, 36, 79–80, 82, 85–87, 98–99, 112

new women, 97; colonial gaze of, 115–23; "diversion of," 115; photographers, 131. *See also* Paul, Helen

Nguyen, Mimi Thi, 243n85

Nimitz, Chester, 191–92, 245n130

Nixon, Richard, 200

No Man Is an Island (film), 176–77

Northern Mariana Islands, 8, 187, 213n1, 239n6; CHamorus of, 153–54

nostalgia, 115; CHamoru, 139, 155; CHamoru nationalism and, 139; colonial, 143,

147; for Guåhan flag, 148; of Helen Paul, 139, 143; the picturesque and, 139, 143; sakman and, 143

nurse-midwives, CHamoru, 118; adaptability of, 47; enfetmera and, 3; interpellation and, 5; heteronormativity and, 49; heteropatriarchy and, 49, as lay pattera replacements, 41–44; racial progress of, 47; recruitment of, 40, 42, 47–51, 58–60; training of, 51–56. *See also* pattera (ná'fafañågu)

nurses, Navy: empire and, 38; feminism of, 5; kinship with Native nurses, 69–70; as mediators, 68–70; philanthropy of, 38; Sacred Twenty, 50; training under, 118

nurses, Samoan, 48–49, 224n35

O'Brien, Jean, 43

Pacific Islanders: sexualization of, 101, 103, 122, 177; stereotypes of, 103, 177

Pågat, 247n10

palao'an (famalao'an) chålan, 25–26, 76, 219n75

Palmer, Oliver Hazard, 84–85, 87

Palmer, Susan Augusta Hart, 85

Palomo, Jose (Påle' Engko'), 108, 113

Palomo, Jose R., 163, 241n40

Pangelinan, Josefina, 141, 142

patriarchy, 42, 49, 98; gender roles under, 64; Spanish colonialism and, 164

patriotism, American: of Agueda Johnston, 152, 155, 157, 160, 166, 169–81 passim, 185, 190, 194; of CHamorus, 155, 173–74, 181; of Susan Dyer, 87–88

pattera (ná'fafañågu), 2; Americanization of, 40–41; birthing practices of, 71–73, 76, 228n108; burial of ga'chong i patgon and apuya', xi–xii, 28, 33, 36, 39, 49, 73, 77, 203, 228n110, 228n124; cleanliness and, 46–47, 223n24; compensation of, 73–76, 203; cordage and, 31–32; decline of, 76–77; domestic tensions of, 61–65; as gatekeepers, 65; inafa'maolek and, 39, 76–77, 107; inagradesi of, 75, 77;

pattera (ná'fafañågu) (continued)
   independence of, 70; Indigenous
   feminist practice of, 32–33; labor of,
   32–35, 36, 76; lasa and, 23, 42, 68;
   mamåhlao and, 74; mobilities of, 38–39,
   57–58, 60, 63–65, 70; modernity and, 23,
   70; motivations of, 55; as palao'an
   chålan, 26; post–World War II, 76;
   practices of, xi–xii, 38–39, 49, 60–61,
   71–72, 76–77, 79, 177; professionalization
   of, 45–47; recruitment of, 47–51, 58–60;
   romanticizing of, xiii; stigmatizing of,
   55–56; support systems of, 58–59;
   surveillance of, 43, 45, 60, 70; tåddong
   practice and, 23, 105; tinifok and, 32;
   training of, 51–56; trust building, 65–67;
   use of term, 222n1
Paul, Carroll E., 114, 118, 119, 144, 234n7,
   235n28
Paul, Helen, 16, 36–37, 234n7, 235n1, 235n28;
   Agueda Johnston, teaching of, 157, 168;
   captions of, 126–27, 129, 131, 132–37,
   144–45, 146; colonial gaze of, 115–19, 123,
   126, 146; Guåhan flag, design of, 37, 113,
   139, 146–50; nostalgia of, 139, 143;
   painting of, 119–21; photography of,
   123–27, 129–37, 139, 144–46, 150, 164,
   237n71; the picturesque and, 119, 124–27,
   129, 131–33, 144–45; on the Shoe Gang,
   242n65; teaching career, 115, 119, 138, 139,
   141–42, 162, 163, 166, 234n9. See also new
   womanhood
Peck, Eva Belle, 37, 157, 162–63, 167, 169, 180;
   white womanhood of, 168
Peck, Leo, 162–63
peonage, 9
Perez, Atanacio, 141
Perez, Beatrice, 128–29
Perez, Felix, 75
Perez, Maria, 131
Perez, Remedios (née Leon Guerrero), 136,
   146, 161, 171
Perez, Rosa (lay matron), 110–12
Perez, Rosario, 142
Perez, Rosa Taitano ("Na' Nai," pattera), 75

Perez, Sabina Flores, 200
Perez, Teresita, 151
Philippine-American War, 88–89, 133
Phillips, Coles, 176
photography, 115; assimilation and, 236n45;
   captions, 126, CHamoru bodies in,
   117–18; colonialism and, 124–25, 237n55;
   empire and, 116; imperial gaze and, 125;
   militourism and, 121; new women and,
   131; the picturesque and, 123–27, 144–46;
   settler colonialism and, 237n55. See also
   Paul, Helen
Piatote, Beth, 41
picturesque, the, 37; colonialism and, 138;
   gender and, 129; in Helen Paul's work,
   119, 124–27, 129, 131–33; history and, 126;
   mestisa dress as, 51; nostalgia and, 139,
   143; photography and, 123–27, 144–46;
   violence of, 137
pin-up girls, 172, 173–74, 177
placenta: burial of, xi–xii, 28–39 passim, 49,
   73, 77, 203, 228n110, 228n124; Indigenous
   Pacific care for, 35–36, 161, 228n109
placental politics, 6–7, 28–36, 39, 197,
   202–3; anticolonial potential of, 30; as
   decolonial history, 5; Indigenous/
   CHamoru practice of, 8, 28–30; orality
   and, 30; resurgence and, 28; as tåddong
   and takhilo' practice, 28, 203. See also
   Indigenous feminism
Political Status Education Coordinating
   Commission (PSECC), xii–xiv
Potter, David, 16
Potter, Jane Grey, 16
Pownall, Charles, 104, 117, 179
Pownall, Mary Ellen Chenoweth, 104, 179
Pratt, Mary Louise, 125
Prutehi Litekyan, 200, 247n10
Pule, John, 35

Quintanilla, Ignacia, 175

race: authenticity and, 48; dandyism and,
   133; health and, 107; interracial marriage,
   101; mixed-race bodies, 101–4; palace

socials and, 95–97, 99–103; the picturesque and, 143; Polynesians and, 48; race-mixing in Guåhan, 97–98
racialization: of CHamorus, 94–95, 100, 103, 105, 107, 134, 185; of CHamoru women, 43, 45, 49, 65, 105, 122, 134, 142–43, 177, 185; dandyism and, 133–34; dispossession and, 84; of education, 163–64; of landscape, 4; of Native women, 45; of the tropics, 45, 82, 121, 177
radical relationality, 30, 220n93
Rafael, Vicente, 8, 104–5, 236n52
reproductive health, 66–67, 107; birth work, xiv
respetu (gai/tai), 9, 42, 49, 54, 63, 74, 77, 181, 196
resurgence, Indigenous, 28, 157, 196, 228n124
Reittemberger, Francisco Javier, 24
Rickard, Jolene, 118
Rios, Jose L. G., 119
Roberto, Jose, 191
Roberto, Maria Anderson, 60, 226n77
Roediger, David, 133
Roosevelt, Franklin Delano, 25
Roosevelt, Theodore, 50, 217n32
Root, Edmund, 133
roots and routes, Indigenous, 1, 18, 26–28, 39, 64, 214n3, 219n79
Rosaldo, Renato, 139
Rosario, Ana Mendiola (Tan Ånan Siboyas), 5, 55, 57–58, 60–61, 63, 71, 197, 199, 203; compensation of, 73–75; traditional birthing practices of, 72–73, 76
rowdyism, 133–34, 236n52

Sablan, David L., 148–49
Sablan, Dolores Mesa, 73
Sablan, Jaye: "åpuya" poem, 30–31
Sablan, Joaquin F., 64, 164, 165, 190–91
Såddok Hagåtña, 148–49, 166, 179
Safford, William, 9, 165, 180, 240n22
Sage, Margaret "Olivia," 107, 109–10, 168

Sairy Gamps (Sairey Gamps), 40, 42, 49, 225n43
sakman. *See* canoes
Salas, Miguel, 128
Salesa, Damon, 95
Sanchez, Pedro ("Doc"), 148
Sanchez, Simon A., 119, 131, 161–62, 164, 192
San Nicolas, Rain Flores, 198
Sånta Marian Kåmalen, 23, 190
Santos, Angel, 148–49
Santos, Carmen Iglesias, 56–57
Santos, Maria de los, 137–39
Santos, Tomas R., 148
San Vitores, Diego Luis de, 159, 213n1, 214n1
Savory, Nathaniel, 136
Scharff, Virginia, 16
Schreiner, Olive, 87
Schroeder, Maria, 13, 45, 107, 232n78; Maria Schroeder Hospital, 50
Schroeder, Seaton, 13, 43, 45, 47
seal of Guåhan, 139, 147, 149, 164, 238n92
self-determination, xii, 135, 140, 143, 186–87, 202
sentimentalism, 86; empire and, 8, 118
settler colonialism: gendered violence of, 6; in Guåhan, 198, 202, 217n35; in Hawai'i, 218n60; Indigenous mobility and, 237n60; photography and, 237n55; social networks and, 94; white feminism and, 7; white women's complicity in, 216n20. *See also* colonialism; colonialism, U.S.
Sewell, William, 47
sexuality, CHamoru: Agueda Johnston and, 183; as analytic, xiv; CHamoru men and, 134; CHamoru women, policing of, 10–11, 41, 56–58, 60, 129; kostumbren CHamoru and, 22, 57; pattera and, 66; settler colonialism and, 11, South Seas narrative, 175–77
sexualization: of CHamoru women, 122, 134, 142–43, 154–55, 174–75; colonialism and, 122; of Native Americans, 177; of Pacific Islanders, 177
Shapley, Lloyd, 41

Shelton, Amanda Guzman (Tan Amånda), 52, 226n76; Tan Marian Dogi' and, 59
Shoe Gang, 95–96, 101–3, 108, 184, 242n65; social mobility of, 168, 170
Siguenza, Joaquina Taitingfong, 59, 69–70
Simmonds, Naomi, 35
Simonsen, Jane, 118
slingstones, 24, 147, 149, 183
Smith, John, 193
Smith, Linda Tuhiwai, xiv
Smith, Roy Campbell, 52, 129, 138, 140–42, 143; on Guåhan flag, 143–44, 146
Smith-Rosenberg, Carroll, 97, 216n21
Sodality of Mary, 23
Sontag, Susan, 126
Souder, Laura Torres, 21, 226n70
sovereignty: over body, 68; CHamoru, xii–xiii, 202; of Guåhan, 27; Indigenous feminism and, 6, 28; intellectual xiii; land and, 220n85; radical relationality and, 31; sovereign pedagogies, xiii; visual, 118
Spanish-American War, 5, 41, 90, 106, 116, 153, 217n32; Treaty of Paris and, 8
stewardship, Indigenous, 9, 29, 33, 193, 199, 201–2, 220n85; appropriation of, 246n6; Indigenous feminism and, 27–29
Stewart, Susan, 139
subjectivity: of Indigenous women, 5, 33, 126, 156–57, 196; white womanhood and, 80, 89, 216n21
suruhåna/u (CHamoru traditional healers), 34, 41–43, 46, 55, 71, 221n107; inafa'maolek and, 107; practices of, 68, 76–77
Susana Hospital, 45, 50–51, 78; CHamoru underclass and, 105; fundraising for, 14; Indigenous ownership of, 82; mestisos and, 109; naming of, 82, 111
Susan Hospital Aid Association (Susana Hospital Association), 109
Sweat, Margaret Jane Mussey, 85–86

Tadiar, Neferti, 2
Taitano, Richard "Dick" Flores, 25, 161, 191, 192

Tanaka, Thomas, V. C., 147–48
tåno'. See land (tåno')
teachers, American, 80, 88–89, 93, 99, 230n38, 234n9, 241n41; as "special laborer," 98, 162–63, 167, 185; Thomasites, 162, 230n38, 234n9. See also Paul, Helen
teachers, CHamoru, 141, 161–63, 167–70, 181, 240n35, 241n41; Agueda Johnston, 151, 156, 162, 203; as new women, 21; pattera and, xiii, 5
Teaiwa, Teresia, xiv, 121, 198, 203, 235n18
temporality, Indigenous, xi, 27, 104
Tengan, Ty Kāwika, 35–36
Tenorio, Kitty, 173
Tenorio, Soledad Pablo, 55
Terlaje, Therese, 202
Terlaje, Toni, 175, 176
Teves, Stephanie Nohelani, 21, 218n60
Thompson, Laura, 13, 34, 66–67, 218n60; on CHamoru women's labor, 219n66; on kostumbren CHamoru, 18–20, 22–23; on traditional birthing practices, 71–73, 228n108
Tibbitts, Mabel, 119–20
Torres, Cynthia Johnston, 196
Torres, Jose, C.: "Following the Flag" poem, 15, 17–18, 29
Torres, Rosa, 47
tour-of-duty feminism, 36, 79–81, 96, 109, 119
traditional healers, 34, 74, 221n107. See also makåhna/kakåhna; pattera (ná'fafañågu); suruhåna/u (CHamoru traditional healers)
trans-Indigenous scholarship, 215n3
Trapp, Howard, 147–48
tropical medicine, 41
tropics: gendered discourse of, 13, 45, 88–90, 93, 118, 121–22, 124, 170; lotus as a marker of, 81–82, 104, 229n9; primitivism, 122; racial progress in, 47; tour-of-duty feminism and, 80–82, 95–96, 107–10
true womanhood, 85, 99, 112, 229n19
Tuck, Eve, 11

Tull, Lawrence E., 179
Tweed, George, 151–52, 167, 176–77, 186, 187–90, 193–94; threatening of Agueda Johnston, 188–89

Ulloa, Maria A., 119, 143
Underwood, Ana M., 241n41
Underwood, James Holland, 95
Underwood, Robert A., xii–xiii, 156, 159–60, 161–62, 194, 215n10
U.S. Navy: "civilizing" mission of, 5, 10, 40–41, 45–51, 124, 138; English-only policy, 52; modernizing mission of, 17–18, 74–75, 124, 127, 155, 158–59, 166, 216n15; public health policies, 40–41

Viernes, James, 24
Vizenor, Gerald, 167
Votaw, Homer, 179

Warrior, Robert Allen, xiii
Washington, George, 243n86
Webb, James, 201
Wexler, Laura, 116, 131
Williams, Raymond, 111
Williams, Sallie, 112
Wolfe, Patrick, 11

womanhood, CHamoru: minesngon of, 21, 38, 77, 156–57, 195; modernity and, 37; new forms of, 20–21, 150–52, 168, 218n60; safeguarding of inafa'maolek relations. *See also* CHamoru women; new womanhood
womanhood, Native, 7
womanhood, white, 6–7, 230n37; colonialism and, 8, 90, 112; domesticity and, 39, 89; of Eva Peck, 168; imperialism and, 39; labor of leisure and, 97, 103–4; matriarchy, 98–99; mobility and, 16, 89; moral authority and, 105, 119, 168; Native womanhood and, 7; philanthropy and, 5, 38, 45, 50, 79, 106, 110, 119; prescribed roles of, 89–90; racism and sexism, implication in, 112; tour-of-duty feminism, 80–81, 109–10, 119; true womanhood, 85, 99, 112, 229n19. *See also* new womanhood

Yazzie, Melanie, 220n93
yo'åmte. *See* suruhåna/u (CHamoru traditional healers); traditional healers

Zamora, Ana Salas Rios (Tan Ånan Rios), 58, 59

www.ingramcontent.com/pod-product-compliance
Lightning Source LLC
Chambersburg PA
CBHW032032300426
44117CB00009B/1027